Upton Sinclair Presents William Fox

UPTON SINCLAIR

PRESENTS

WILLIAM FOX

BOOKS BY
Upton Sinclair

THE JOURNAL OF ARTHUR STIRLING

MANASSAS, A NOVEL OF THE CIVIL WAR

THE JUNGLE

THE OVERMAN

THE MILLENNIUM

THE METROPOLIS

THE MONEYCHANGERS

SAMUEL, THE SEEKER

THE FASTING CURE

LOVE'S PILGRIMAGE

SYLVIA

SYLVIA'S MARRIAGE

DAMAGED GOODS

THE CRY FOR JUSTICE

THE PROFITS OF RELIGION

KING COAL, A NOVEL OF THE COLORADO STRIKE

JIMMIE HIGGINS

THE BRASS CHECK

100%—THE STORY OF A PATRIOT

THEY CALL ME CARPENTER

THE BOOK OF LIFE

THE GOOSE-STEP—A STUDY OF AMERICAN EDUCATION

THE GOSLINGS—A STUDY OF THE AMERICAN SCHOOLS

MAMMONART

LETTERS TO JUDD

THE SPOKESMAN'S SECRETARY

OIL!

MONEY WRITES!

BOSTON

MOUNTAIN CITY

MENTAL RADIO

ROMAN HOLIDAY

THE WET PARADE

AMERICAN OUTPOST

PLAYS

PRINCE HAGEN

THE NATUREWOMAN

THE SECOND STORY MAN

THE MACHINE

THE POT-BOILER

HELL

SINGING JAILBIRDS

BILL PORTER

OIL (DRAMATIZATION)

WILLIAM FOX

UPTON SINCLAIR

PRESENTS

WILLIAM FOX

PUBLISHED BY THE AUTHOR

LOS ANGELES (WEST BRANCH), CALIFORNIA

UPTON SINCLAIR
PRESENTS
WILLIAM FOX

A FEATURE PICTURE OF WALL STREET AND HIGH FINANCE

In Twenty-nine Reels with Prologue and Epilogue

A Melodrama of Fortune, Conflict and Triumph. Packed with Thrills and Heart Throbs. East Side Boy Conquers Fame and Power. The Masters of Millions Envy His Triumph and Plot His Downfall. The Octopus Battles the Fox. The Duel of a Century! The Sensation of a Lifetime!

Never in Screen History has there been a Feature so Stupendous as this. An Inside Story, a First-Hand Revelation of Politics and Finance, with a Ten Billion Dollar Cast of Statesmen and Financiers.

At the same time a Story for the Family, tense and moving, with Love, Loyalty and a Woman's Soul. A Romance so fine, so true, so loaded with Laughter and Tears, that none can resist it.

AMERICA WAITS FOR THIS DRAMA!
PUT IT AT THE HEAD OF YOUR PROGRAM!
IT WILL PACK THEM IN!!

FLOYD DELL REPORTS TO A NEW YORK PUBLISHER:

I think this is a very important book.

First, because it tells what a man important to his times thinks about himself.

Second, because of the importance of the war between the financiers and the organizers in this motion picture field.

Third, because of the immense human interest and enthralling excitement of the story. There has never been a book on this subject so completely readable by ordinary people. I myself am bored with statistics, I don't like business stories, and I started this book with no hope of ever being able to read it through. It kept me awake all night—I could not stop reading it. The story has terrific interest and suspense.

Also it hits the public interest of the times right in the center. It will be in every middle class home this winter, and millions of people will be talking about it. It is going to be one of the great literary sensations in the history of American publishing.

Upton Sinclair's reputation has survived every exposé he has handled, and no one has ever sued him for libel. He has the goods on people and they know it. There can be no question but that the facts are substantially as the book states them, for these are all matters of court record. The interpretations alone can be questioned.

I should say that the only reason for not taking advantage of the greatest opportunity of our times in publishing would be a belief in the actuality of this alleged criminal conspiracy, and the fear that the conspiracy would extend to the point of a criminal attempt to punish and wreck the publisher who put Fox's case before the public. Or have the bankers burned their fingers enough in this Fox business without attempting illegitimate interference? In the end it would be useless, for the book will be published and they can't stop it.

This is the most exciting book I have read for years. It adds a new and significant figure to American industrial biography. It is destined to an immense popularity, and it will make Upton Sinclair the most widely read author in America. It will be in front page headlines, and a Congressional inquiry may keep it there for weeks or months. The films are dear to the heart of America.

CONTENTS

CONTENTS

PROLOGUE

FOR thirty years I have been "presenting" to the public the princes, dukes and barons of our industrial feudalism. As a rule I have "presented" them under the guise of fiction. Sometimes my critics have said "Good melodrama" and sometimes "Bad melodrama," but always they have agreed that "Sinclair exaggerates." Learned book reviewers in Siam and Tasmania declare: "Such things are impossible." Living as far away as it is possible to get on this earth, they still feel safe in asserting: "America cannot be like that."

So this time I am presenting a living man. This time I am telling a story which happened in New York City less than three years ago. This time there are names, places, recent dates and an appendix full of documents and court records. This time even Siam and Tasmania will have to admit that "America is like that"; for no melodrama that I have been able to invent in my thirty years of inventing has been more packed with crimes and betrayals, perils and escapes, than the story of William Fox. No thriller among the 750 feature pictures which Fox himself produced during twenty-five years as a producer was ever so perfectly constructed, with its humble hero battling his way to power, its polished villains, conspirators of high estate, each with a carnation in his buttonhole; its complications of intrigue, its mysteries, some of them never solved to this day, its cruel suffering and its grand climax—the hero escaping with the greater part of his fortune, and the villains dragged down to ruin by the judgment of an implacable Providence.

A couple of months ago I had the honor of being invited to the home of a Hollywood author; one of those new-style authors of the screen-world who could not think of writing for less than $2,000 a week, and who live in Moorish palaces on hilltops, and have Negro servants in swallow-tail coats to serve you calavo salad and caviar sandwiches and liquids enough to float a battleship. The company fell to discussing the state of America, and I explained that when I started muckraking thirty years ago, the significant phenomenon had been the eliminating of the little

business man by the big business man; but now the situation had
changed, and the feature was the replacing of the big business
man by the investment banker. I mentioned a case in Boston,
the story of a manufacturer who had his business taken away
from him by a conspiracy of bankers. He had brought suit, and
after a trial lasting more than a year, the jury had given him a
verdict of $10,000,000.

My friend, the Hollywood author, broke in: "Sinclair, why
do you fool with pikers like that, little $10,000,000 men? Why
don't you tell us about the $1,000,000,000 men, or the $100,000,000
ones at least?"

I answered that I had never met any $1,000,000,000 men, nor
even $100,000,000 ones, and I feared that my imagination would
not be equal to the task. Said my host: "Why don't you write
the story of William Fox? There's one made to order for you:
a plain hold-up in broad daylight—and by our most eminent and
respectable financiers!"

The company talked for a while about William Fox. He
had been the biggest man in the industry, the one real business
man of them all, the one who could have saved them in this
slump. And not because he was in trouble, but because he was
so successful, because he was making too much money, the Wall
Street crowd had surrounded him, blocked him off, and taken
his profit-making machine away from him. And the strangest
thing—when they had got it, they didn't know what to do with
it, all they were able to do was to loot the properties, and now
they were a shell, ready to collapse. They had bought Fox's
business, but not his brain.

My mind was on other things, and I gave no thought to my
friend's suggestion. But a couple of days later my telephone
rang, and a woman's voice said: "This is Mr. William Fox's
secretary. Mr. Fox wants to know if he may call to see you."

I have learned to be shy over the telephone. "What does
he want?" I asked.

"He didn't tell me," said the voice; "but he told me to say
he had nothing to sell you."

"Well, tell him I have nothing to buy with," I answered.

Next morning a limousine rolled up to my humble door, and
William Fox descended, accompanied by a little gentleman, who,

I learned, was his lawyer. It turned out that he had come to sell me something after all; in the slang of our commercial era, he wanted to "sell" me himself. Ever since his battle had begun, he had thought of me as the person to be its historian. His wife had read some of my books and believed in me. A year ago his brother-in-law had sent me a telegram, asking if I had any plans to come east. As I had no such plans, he had waited until he came west.

He showed me some "rushes" of the story. He brought the stars of the production, one after another, before the foot-lights, some of them persons whom I knew, all of them persons whom the world knows, or wants to know: Herbert Hoover, Henry Ford, John D. Rockefeller, jr., Charles Evans Hughes, Samuel Untermyer, Will H. Hays, Bernard M. Baruch, Adolph Zukor, Louis B. Mayer, Clarence M. Dillon, Albert H. Wiggin, Harry L. Stuart, Harley L. Clarke—a score of leading statesmen and financiers. He pulled the strings and made these figures rehearse their parts. Every now and then Mr. Reass, the lawyer, would think of some detail which had been omitted; they would take turns, or sometimes it would be a duet.

What William Fox was offering me was a theme for a novel. But I have written six novels of Wall Street and high finance, and the critics of the last one, "Mountain City," said I was repeating myself. I saw at once that this, if I wrote it, would be a fact story, told in detail and documented.

I asked for time to think it over, and the limousine rolled away. In the end I said I would go in with William Fox on two conditions: he would leave the matter of the form and style of the book to me, and he would pledge me two weeks of his time, with a stenographer sitting by.

He accepted, and we set to work. His story stretched out, and the two weeks became three weeks, four weeks, five weeks. Every day for thirty-six days he came to my home, and from 10 in the morning until 1 or 2 he talked and I questioned. The stenographer fell behind and we had to have two. When we got through, there were 758 typewritten pages, enough for two volumes. In addition, there is a suitcase and two drawers full of correspondence, pamphlets, court records and corporation reports; also there are the New York newspapers, both the news and financial pages, telling the day by day story of the year long battle. If you who read this book do not know the story of William Fox, it will be my fault, not his.

William Fox started in the motion picture business in the year 1904, he being then twenty-six years of age, and putting in a capital of $1,600. He worked with demoniac energy for twenty-five years, at the end of which time he controlled from four to five hundred millions of dollars. Only a small part of it, perhaps 10 per cent, belonged to him personally; the rest was the property of stockholders and investors who trusted him. He never took a penny of salary for his labors as president of the Fox Theatres Corporation, and in 1926 he voluntarily stopped his salary of $200,000 yearly as president of Fox Film Corporation. He owned the majority of voting shares, which gave him the power to name the boards of directors. These shares drew dividends on equal terms with all the other shares, and William Fox was content to take his chances with the rest of the stockholders. Practically all the money had come out of profits, and anyone might receive these profits, provided that Fox was master of the machine and allowed to direct its activities.

Just what was it that happened to William Fox? It is no new thing, but an old story, which I have told several times before. In the year 1908, I wrote a novel called "The Money-changers," which was considered at the time to be a very desperate and daring thing. I have told in "The Brass Check" how I got the information for this novel. Suffice it here to say, I charged that the elder Pierpont Morgan deliberately brought on the panic of 1907, in order to wreck and take over three independent trust companies in New York which were interfering with his domination. Trust companies were new things in those days, and these three were taking in too much money, and Morgan considered that Oakleigh Thorne and F. Augustus Heinze and Charles T. Barney were improper persons to have the handling of so much money. It is quite true that Thorne and Heinze were irresponsible persons, gamblers and hard drinkers; but the main thing wrong with them was the fact that they did not take Morgan's orders.

The method used was to lend them money and lead them to "extend themselves"; to "string them along" with promises which were not kept; to start a stock market raid and beat down the price of the securities in which they were known to have invested; to start rumors that they were in financial trouble, and have all the hired financial writers of Wall Street publish these reports; then to call all their loans at once, start a "run" of their depositors, and use the power of the banking world to see that they got no credit.

That is the way the job is done. You pass the word to certain key bankers that Oakleigh Thorne and F. Augustus Heinze and Charles T. Barney are marked for destruction, and that assistance given to them will constitute an unfriendly action towards J. P. Morgan & Co. So they will get no credit, and the three trust companies will close their doors, and interests friendly to J. P. Morgan & Co. will take them over. F. Augustus Heinze and Oakleigh Thorne will retire into obscurity, and Charles T. Barney will shoot his head off, and if the panic gets out of hand and threatens the entire financial structure of the country, J. P. Morgan will summon his banker colleagues to his office and tell them how much cash is needed to stop the runs on banks, and what proportion each of them will put up.

I heard a story of that conference. Said one banker: "Mr. Morgan, I have kept my institution safe and sound, and I do not feel responsible for the troubles of those institutions which have allowed their funds to be used for stock market manipulation. I propose to stay inside my bank and let the others look out for themselves."

Old Morgan's purple nose turned several shades darker, and he hit the table a bang and answered: "You stay in your bank, and I'll build a wall around it and you'll never come out of it until you are dead!"

Twenty years later, I told of another such hold-up in my novel, "Boston." The gentleman who in that novel is called "Jerry Walker" was a manufacturer of felt; a business man who must have worked with the same intensity as William Fox, for he had taken over most of the felt plants in New England, and was reaching out for allied enterprises. Here was a treasure chest, and the bankers decided that it would be safer in their hands than in his. They promised him new financing and encouraged him to spread out, then they began stalling, and presently they had him surrounded and walled off, and in the end he was forced to sign his properties over to them.

I got a peculiar line on this story through an old friend in Boston, who owns one of the largest paper manufacturing industries in America. This gentleman thought that on points of law the jury had been mistaken in awarding $10,000,000 damages to "Jerry Walker," and that the Supreme Court justices of Massachusetts had been justified in overthrowing this verdict for the benefit of their intimate friends and fellow club members, the great Boston bankers. But my friend said that there could be no question that there had been a bankers' conspiracy, it was a regular practice and becoming more common all the time. Said he: "It is so dangerous that I have not dared to let my business expand as it normally should, because I am afraid to owe money to the Boston banks."

I smiled, and told him of something that had happened twenty-two years back. I had been in the office of "Everybody's Magazine," talking with E. J. Ridgway, the publisher. These were the old muckraking days, and the magazine was publishing Tom Lawson and my attacks upon the Beef Trust, and its circulation was growing a hundred thousand a month. Ridgway was needing new carloads of paper, and was bitterly criticizing the concern which furnished him paper, because it would not contract to supply the larger quantity required. "One of those moss-backs up in Boston," he said. "He inherited his business, and hasn't got the nerve to let it grow." To give you the full significance of that incident I must add that my friend the paper manufacturer is still head of his concern; while "Everybody's Magazine" was soon swallowed by the bankers, and Erman J. Ridgway retired into private life.

So you see that what happened to William Fox was no accident and no sporadic episode. It is a stage in the evolution of American industrial affairs. There is no longer any room in our competitive world for the little $10,000,000 business man, nor even for the little $100,000,000 business man. It is the day of the $1,000,000,000 giants. To sit in at this poker game, it is not enough to have hundreds of millions in capital, you must have hundreds of millions in surplus. You must have enormous cash deposits in the great Wall Street banks, to use in "rigging the market." You must be able to beat down the securities of your rivals. You must be able to manipulate your own stocks, driving them up and selling them, then driving them down and buying them back.

If you are an honest executive or director, you are doing these things for the benefit of your corporation, using the profits to increase the corporation's surplus; while if you are an ordinary executive or director, you are doing these things for your own profit. Have your corporation lend you money upon shaky collateral or none at all, and then use those funds with your inside knowledge to make a fortune for yourself.

If you are a great Wall Street banker today, you have formed a securities corporation allied with your bank, which will enable you to borrow money from your bank, and to speculate in all the securities which the banking laws of the state and nation do not allow the bank to own. If you are one of the really big and active insiders, you have forced yourself into a position of power where you are able to intimidate other bankers, and forbid them to lend money to a certain victim whom you have marked for your own. If, for example, you come upon a Fox who owns a treasure chest—something which a Fox has no business whatever to be in possession of—you can take that Fox and put a brand or label on him: "Property of the Telephone Company and the Chase National Bank. Hands Off."

If you studied economics in college, you were taught the classic defense of capitalism. You were given the touching picture of the man who worked and saved his money and gradually built up a business. You were told that he was the "entrepreneur," the one who undertook or adventured, and ran the business risks, and therefore was entitled to the profits of his great service. American civilization has been built whole out of respect for these great adventurers. The public saw business in the hands of men who had started as office boys, or laborers in the plant, and had built up the concern and proved their ability to run it better than anybody else; so the public believed that the system was sound and the claims of the capitalist justified.

But now America has come to a new stage. Business is no longer to be left in the hands of the men who built it up. It has become too big, its financial requirements are too great, and the business man is subject to the financier. In the moving picture industry, for example, it became necessary four or five years ago to make an enormous expansion. The "movies" gave place to the "talkies," and new sound-proof studios had to be built by the hundred, with enormously expensive new equipment. It became necessary for 20,000 theatres in America to install sound apparatus costing $20,000 per theatre. For all this, new financing was needed, and the ex-clothing merchants and proprietors of nickelodeons who had built up the moving picture industry were obliged to seek allies among the great masters of finance who have the securities and the gold in their vaults, and who are able to create hundreds of millions of new dollars by writing a memorandum on a pad.

And what more natural than that these great men, knowing their power, should look covetously upon a chain of moving picture theatres with millions of patrons? What more natural than that they should think themselves better able to handle such a business than the ex-clothing merchants and proprietors of nickelodeons? The financial men have formed chains of banks, they have taken over railroad systems and strings of power companies, coal mines and steel mills; the securities of these far-flung enterprises are in their vaults, deep beneath the sidewalks of Wall Street, protected by twenty layers of steel and twenty feet of concrete, and various devices in the form of electrically charged surfaces, water chambers, poison gas chambers, and corridors in which guards are locked up all night with arrangements of mirrors whereby they can see all around the vault, and electric buttons which they are required to push every five minutes throughout the night.

In the old days it used to be the business which got into trouble which fell into the hands of the bankers   But nowadays the bankers want all the successful businesses. They know how to run all business—or can hire experts to do it for them. All through the Middle West they are taking over the farms and reorganizing them as corporations. Their directors have the financial say in most of the railroads of the country, in most of the power companies, and in the great key industries. So far as the motion picture industry is concerned, they have their directors on the boards of every one of the big concerns, and not one of these concerns would be running today, were it not for money furnished by Wall Street banks and investment houses. This is the new stage to which America has come; and the story of how the change has been brought about, how the wires are pulled and the snares set—you will never see it more plainly and in greater detail than in this "inside" story of Fox Film and Fox Theatres.

One final word as to my part in this narrative. There are scores of interviews and scenes here narrated, at none of which I was present, and concerning which I can give no testimony. This is William Fox's story as he told it to me, and my job has been to put it into literary form: to order it, select the vital parts, cut out the repetition, and clear up the obscurities by questioning my subject. Wherever there are letters, affidavits, court records, financial statements, etc., I have mentioned these sources, and am of course responsible for quoting these correctly. Also, I have here and there stated my own opinions, always making clear that they are mine. But for all the statements in the book which rest upon the authority of William Fox, he stands responsible. The manuscript has been submitted to him and the story is his. The letter which I wrote to him, embodying our understanding, declares: "It is agreed that all statements of fact which have been read and verified by you shall be made upon your authority, and that you agree to be responsible for them." The letter furthermore states: "It is understood that your interest in the work is the vindication of your good name and the education of the public in the matter of present-day practices in high finance; and I am pledging myself to co-operate with you to these ends and to produce a work which will serve them."

At the request of William Fox, I state that he has no share in the royalties from this book. He does not wish anyone to think that he is telling his story for money. Not wishing to lag behind him in altruism, I am making the book over to the Sinclair Foundation, and the royalties derived from its sale will be used for the purpose of putting a set of twelve volumes of my books into public libraries throughout the world.

REEL ONE

CLOSE-UP

I BEGIN by "presenting" William Fox as he sat in my study presenting himself to me.

The study is a long high room—like a church, with a row of windows along the north, and open doors through which the Southern California sunshine streams in—or if it happens to be a day of Southern California "high fog," then there are logs burning in a fireplace. William Fox sits in an old-fashioned walnut rocking-chair, the kind known as a "cradle-rocker." He has beside him a little stand for his ash tray, and his glass of water, and his orange juice or lemonade when it arrives. The stenographer sits at one side, and her fingers fly busily. Benjamin Reass, the family lawyer, listens attentively, for the most part quiet as a mouse. I sit in another rocking-chair, ten feet from my subject, and watch his every aspect and gesture, study his moods, and now and then jot down a question. I never had so long a story told to me, and there are few human beings I have watched for so many hours. If I cannot make him real to you, I will prove myself ill equipped for a novelist.

He is a man of my size, which is medium. He used to be stout, but the long battle wore him down, and now he is medium again. Years ago he wore a black mustache, but now he is smooth shaven. He has a good Jewish nose, and a rather round face with a round dome above it. Time and hard work and worry have taken the hair off the dome, and our Southern California sunshine has made it like that of a bronze Buddha.

He is going to play golf in the afternoon, and wears a light blue coat, or sometimes a brown one, and trousers of white flannel or striped. Under his coat is a white sweater; and in an article published in "Fortune," the magazine which caters to bankers and magnates, I read that William Fox was accustomed to appear

1

at directors' meetings of his companies wearing a sweater, also
white socks; whereas Mr. Harold Leonard Stuart of Halsey,
Stuart & Co., the investment banker who helped to oust Fox,
invariably appears at directors' meetings wearing a carnation in
his buttonhole.

Perhaps I should mention that the sweater is of soft and fine
material, and that it is always clean. Mr. Fox explains that he
wears it because his doctor has told him to keep his shoulders
warm. As to the white socks, he points out that they are free
from dye and naturally more healthful, and that they offer less
danger of infection.

Since this is not a treatise on hygiene, I content myself with
remarking that when the directors of a corporation are selected
for the color of their socks and the flowers in their buttonholes,
it is certainly time for the stockholders of that corporation to
look out for their own interests; which proved to be the case with
Fox Film and Fox Theatres.

In the breast pocket of the blue coat, or the brown one, there
is a row of long brown cigars, each wrapped in cellophane. At
the outset of our session, my subject draws out one of these
cigars, tears off the wrapper and rolls it into a little ball and
deposits it carefully in the ash tray; if it rolls off, he picks it up
from the floor—from which you may conclude that he has been
well drilled by thirty-two years of domestic life. He lights the
cigar and puffs it meditatively for a while, then he starts to talk.
After a few minutes, the cigar goes out, and he strikes a match,
lights it again, gives a few more puffs, and then forgets it again.
This continues all through our session of three or four hours, and
at the end the cigars are gone from the pocket and the stubs are
in the ash tray.

Our subject has many funny stories, and enjoys telling them.
One records how he was temporarily cured of the tobacco habit
by no less a personage than Carry Nation. It appears that at the
height of her hatchet-wielding career, the old lady from Kansas
visited New York, and William Fox engaged her for a three-a-
day vaudeville performance at a salary of $3,000 a week. She
was a great hit, and everything was lovely, until she came into
the office of the theatre magnate. Says the magnate:

"When I was introduced, I took the cigar out of my mouth,

and four huge cigars which were in my pocket were visible to the eyes of Mrs. Nation. I said I was pleased to meet her. She said: 'I'm not pleased to meet you at all. I will not appear on that stage again. I will not work for a man who is an habitual tobacco fiend.' Of course, I was shocked at the idea of losing our stage performer, so I said that I would quit smoking. She said I couldn't ever stop smoking. I said: 'I give you my word I will never light another cigar for twelve months.' I threw the rest of my cigars away, and Mrs. Nation resumed her lecturing. I ate more candy in the first three of those twelve months than ever before, and it was not until November 17, 1910, that I again had a cigar in my mouth; but I have had one there ever since."

Little Will Fox grew up, as you shall presently hear, in a rear tenement on the East Side of New York. He left school and went to work to help support his brothers and sisters at the age of eleven. Therefore, you will not be surprised if I tell you that he is not always impeccable in his use of the English language. Sometimes when he is not on his guard, he will say, "I seen it," or, "I done it," and frequently he will mix a tense or a declension. A person who spends a good part of his life in the study of words notices these things; but I take them as part of the local color of an East Side boy. It may, however, have seemed different to the elegant and cultured New York bankers with the carnations in their buttonholes: children of Fifth Avenue in its old fashionable days, or of Madison Avenue with its dignity and reserve; boys who had been to Groton and St. Mark's, and then to Harvard or Princeton or Yale. They would invite this grown-up East Side Jewish boy to luncheon at the Bankers' Club or to dinner at the Metropolitan Club for business conferences, but their wives would not appreciate him, and he would never belong to their inner circle of fashionable culture. I have been in those circles on a few occasions, and can hear the matrons whispering over their teacups, and the old dowagers tittering while the cards are being dealt at bridge. "My dear, can you imagine—he says insipid when he means insignificant. 'The amount is too insipid to be discussed!'"

I came to New York at the age of eight or nine and went to a public school on the East Side, and played with a swarm of boys just like little Will Fox, so I know every tone of his voice and every peculiarity of his accent. We New York boys said "becauss"; we said "seccatary," if we had occasion to use such a long word. Wishing to convey to you our manner of swallowing our consonants, I pick one phrase: "a thousan' 'ollas." You must say that phrase rapidly, with your mind upon the supreme importance of the "thousan' 'ollas," the things you could do with it if you could get it. There were no movies in those days, but they came before long, and we called them "fill-ums." To me this word is touched with the hues of romance, the emotional tone which attaches itself to events of our lives as they recede into the mists of the distance. It may be that I met little Will Fox in those far-off golden days. He used to sell candy in Central Park, and I used to play all over that park, and many times bought candy in little packages wrapped in pink and blue and green papers at one cent a package. "Lozengers," we called them, and one of them, of course, was a "lozenger." If there was such a thing as a "passenger" and a "soljer," why shouldn't there be such a thing as a "lozenger"? Of course!

Maybe I paid him a penny, and maybe he took it home and dropped it into his little tin bank; presently, after a month or two, there was a dollar or more, and he took it and put it in a savings bank at 3 per cent. Presently there was $100, and he was a capitalist, ready to engage in business ventures. Some of these ventures were funny and some of them were tragic, but all of them are full of the spirit of New York, of the desperate urgency to get ahead, to climb out on top.

William Fox never played and he seldom rested. He learned to work all day and most of the night, and to sleep in snatches when he could, and he came out of it with a strong constitution and the energy of a great dynamo.

"Mr. Sinclair, he was a slave," said Mrs. Fox; "and the only way I could ever have a husband was to go and be a slave with him. We hardly ever got home from the studio before 3 o'clock in the morning, and the canary bird in our home adjusted its hours and sang for us at whatever hour we returned."

He knew every detail of his business, no matter how vast it became. He knows it, no matter how far back into the distance it recedes. He can tell you how much money he made in the "lozenger" business, and how much he stood to lose when his sandwich business was ruined by a wind storm on the day of Admiral Dewey's welcome to New York. He knows the price he paid for every theatre in the Fox Theatres chain, and how much Mrs. Fox spent for the decorations. He knows these things as I know the contents of each of my forty volumes, and how many copies they sold. I quote his own statement:

"My business career—I was as devoted to it as you are to your literary career. For more than thirty years I avoided carrying a watch. I never wanted to know what time it was. My day ended when my day's work was completed. Again and again, I didn't go to bed at all during the twenty-four hours. There was work to do. I was working not only for myself but to help others. I had an ambition to build this monumental institution. From a humble beginning, from a scholar at school who hated geography, I had developed a business so that the flag of the company was flying in every civilized and uncivilized country in the world. My affairs were so organized that at the end of the day, whenever the time arrived, there was never a piece of paper on my desk for the following day.

"I was acquainted with every story that was selected by my companies. I read every story they ever produced. I made suggestions in the majority of the stories produced by our companies. In the early years I wrote most of the scenarios. No picture ever produced by the Fox Film Corporation was permitted to be viewed by the general public, until every title it contained had been approved and passed by me, and I don't remember a single picture ever made by the company that the titles contained therein were not corrected, edited and rewritten by me. I always bragged of the fact that no second of those contained in the twenty-four hours ever passed but that the name of William Fox was on the screen, being exhibited in some theatre in some part of the world.

"I knew the condition of every nation we traded with. I knew the value of every currency of every nation we traded with. I thought I knew the politics of every nation we traded with. No question could arise that by a push of a button could not be answered from the extensive files that I had adjoining my office. I had it completely systematized, so that I knew every move that was made throughout the organization.

"The number of theatres controlled by the companies that I was at the head of in the United States alone was more than 800. Early each morning I knew the exact number of people that attended the performances the day before. I knew the number that entered that building every hour, and just as soon as one of these buildings showed the slightest inclination towards the falling off of receipts, I was able to send for the executive of that theatre and rearrange the policy to prevent it from making a loss.

"It was always a charge that the Fox organization was a one-man organization. That was never said as a compliment to me, but as a criticism. They were right when they said that. It is a fact that if all the executives of the organization gathered to continue the business in case I died or became disabled, they would have had a problem on their hands. If they had produced the knowledge that each had and pieced it all together, they wouldn't have understood that which was continuously being generated in my brain. That is best illustrated in the fact that after I had sold out, and the bankers captured all the executives of the corporations, the business crumbled, disappeared and melted away. They provided these companies with millions, but the millions were of no avail."

This is, you perceive, an autocrat speaking. We live under an industrial autocracy, and get our work done that way. William Fox was called egotistical; but my feeling is that if a man can do something, he generally knows that he can do it, and it is sensible for him to say so, and hypocrisy not to say so. If you had asked Napoleon if he knew how to command an army, he would have answered just as William Fox answered. If you should ask Bernard Shaw if he knows how to write a play, you would get the same sort of response.

Worry and strain have made William Fox impatient, and delay and obstructions are intolerable to him. Mr. Benjamin Reass, his fidus Achates, is the kindest and sweetest little gentleman who ever practiced corporation law in New York, but his mind is not geared to the terrific tempos of the Fox dynamo. Sometimes he is asked for a name or a date; or perhaps he is required to produce a copy of Fox Theatres balance sheet for 1928, and he is sure it is down at the hotel, while his employer thinks it is in the suitcase on the table. When these two get into

an argument, it is exactly as if they were married. "Ben, *dear!*"
Mr. Fox exclaims, and the amount of emphasis on the "dear" is
proportioned to the intensity of his irritation.

He has a keen sense of humor, and a quick mind which gets
instantly whatever you say. Now and then in his narrative I
interpose some remark, perhaps a bit of sarcasm born of my
inside knowledge of the big business game; he favors me with a
glance, a twinkle of the eye—and then repeats my words so that
they will go into the record. His face is mobile and expressive,
and I get a good part of his story there. He begins quietly, speaking in measured tones for the benefit of the stenographer. Sometimes he goes on like that for an hour, recording figures and
facts; but then comes some part of his story which appeals to his
sense of humor, and his face wears a schoolboy grin; or he is
exposing some rascality, and his lips curl with scorn. Warming
up to his job, he gets up and begins to pace back and forth. We
have to arrange the furniture so that he has a stamping ground,
and will not upset the little stand with the cigar ashes and the
glass of water.

His voice rises. He is in the presence of his enemies, and he
clenches his hands, and you think of him as a creature more
dangerous than a fox. He talks more rapidly—until suddenly
he stops and glances at the stenographer and says, "Too fast,
young lady?"—but soon he is going on as fast as ever. When his
fighting mood is roused, he orates to our little company of three
as if we were the 16,000 stockholders of Fox Film and Fox Theatres—or perhaps the hundreds of millions of Fox patrons all
over the world.

I pointed out to him that if I was to make a real job of this
book, he must think of me as a family lawyer, about to defend
him in a libel suit which involved his whole career, and in which
his enemies would have the right to put him on the stand. I
asked him every question I could think of, and he answered
without hesitation. He took me into the intimacies of his family
life and told me his griefs and agonies. He invited me to meet
his wife, and I questioned her for six hours, everything about her
husband from their first meeting when she was ten. Six hours
was too long for politeness, but I forgot the time, being something
like her husband when I have a job to do.

He is a man of intense feeling, and it was an ordeal to him to live over again that series of agonies. Many times his voice trembled, and once he broke down completely. He was telling me about the sufferings of his wife at the height of his trouble. She had been grievously ill out at their home on Long Island, and he was kept in the city day and night for many weeks, getting only a couple of hours' sleep out of twenty-four. It was at one of the most desperate moments of his struggle, he thought he was ruined, and was all but overwhelmed by the mass of slanders which had been poured out upon him. He was ill, and so came the anniversary of his wedding, which happens to be also his birthday and the birthday of the new year. He went home, and when he told me of his wife, and how she appeared, and what happened between them, his voice began to break, and he began sobbing, and had to walk up and down for a long time to get himself together.

Afterwards he was ashamed of this, and apologized; but I told him that I also had had troubles, some of which I would not care to rehearse. As a matter of fact, although I am of Anglo-Saxon descent, I am more like the Jews in my willingness to tell my troubles. I have put them into books, and the reserved and aloof Anglo-Saxon critics have rebuked me sternly. But it seems to me that we don't stay so long in this mysterious world, and possibly are not of such importance as we think. If we can help one another, and inform and guide one another, by telling our blunders and the penalties we have paid for them—that is far better than locking ourselves up in an ivory tower, and contemplating the image of our own dignity.

When William Fox is in repose, the lines of his face drop down, and you see that he is a tired and stricken man. The memory of his long ordeal haunts him and goads him. He has lost the one thing in his life which stood first to him, and try as he will, he cannot make anything else take its place. He tells me that he found his first happiness in telling his story to me. He takes me not merely as a father confessor, but as a judge who will set him right to the world. I told him that he overestimated my power; he answered that he had come to me because he knows me to be an honest writer. It is not merely that he wants his name cleared, but that his sense of justice is outraged; he cannot understand how such a monstrous evil as a credit conspiracy could be carried through in America. This, of course, is what appeals to me, and not the individual misfortunes and sufferings of William Fox.

"Mr. Sinclair," said my subject at our first meeting, "I want you to understand that this is not a hard-luck story; I have more money than I know what to do with." And that was not boasting, but a statement of significance, in its bearing upon the mind of my subject, and also upon the mind of America, of which he is a part. This wary and hard-fighting "Fox"—he likes to play with his own name—got away with $20,000,000 of his enemies' money; they had to pay that in cash to get him loose from his properties. In addition, he has valuable real estate in many cities, and talking picture patents which may some day make him the richest man in the world. And money is convenient; with large sums, a man can provide for his loved ones a beautiful home in the country, and one in the city, a private railroad car and a fleet of automobiles. But still William Fox is not happy. I had some photographs taken of him by my friend Odiorne, a sleight-of-hand artist who keeps you entertained and busy, and changes his plates and squeezes his bulb so fast that he gets your moods before you know you have them. I picked one of these portrait studies, because it gives you the sadness in its subject's face, and lets you see the marks of the conflict.

When William Fox is in the bosom of his family, he can forget for a while; but when he is at his desk, he is miserable, and when he lies down to sleep, he broods over the thing he has lost, and to which he gave his lifetime and name. He learned to make moving pictures; he learned to manage theatres in which these pictures could be shown; he had strings of these theatres all over the United States. He had distributing agencies in every country in the world. He was turning out a motion picture every week to keep these theatres busy and perhaps a hundred million people every week were seeing his products, and paying him money to be used in making more pictures, and in buying more theatres, and in building up this tremendous entertainment machine.

This was his life. It was his work and his play, the expression of his personality. Presently I shall show you Bernard M.

Baruch, a man who had the spending of some $17,000,000,000 for the allies during the World War, looking over the financial statements of this entertainment machine and exclaiming: "Why, this is a pot of gold!" It was too rich a pot to be left in the hands of one man, a Jewish boy who had been born in a village in Hungary and raised in a slum tenement of the East Side of New York. There gathered around him the elegant and cultured gentlemen of Wall Street, with the carnations in their buttonholes, and they put a whole battery of machine guns against his head, and held him up and took away from him the control of that business. When they took it over, it represented a book value of two or three hundred million dollars. They looted it of more than a hundred million in two years, and have brought it to a condition where, as I write, its value is about $10,000,000, and bankruptcy is just around the corner.

William Fox sits with the recent financial statements of the Fox Film Corporation and the Fox Theatres Corporation in his hands, and on his face is that look of grief. He finds no malicious pleasure in the fact that his enemies have been unable to run his machine. On the contrary, his voice trembles, and there is a trace of tears in his eyes. "Look, Mr. Sinclair! Just look!"—and he shows me how the surpluses have disappeared, and lays bare the tricks by which rascalities have been hidden.

There is another aspect of William Fox which must not be overlooked, and that is his religion. He comes back to it again and again. He is not an orthodox Jew, but has "sublime faith in God," and believes in the direct guidance of Providence. He told me how, when he was a child, and when the Fox family was hungry, an old butcher trusted little Will for meat, and how little Will promised to repay him by taking care of him in his old age, and carried out that promise. After telling me this story, the grown-up Will added: "Do you mean to tell me that God didn't give the butcher the idea to give me that meat because He knew that he was going to be taken care of? That was God's way."

The present-day William Fox, of course, understands that this point of view is considered out of date among the intelligentsia. He suspected that I would not share his theolo , and persisted in impressing it upon me. Said he:

"During any calamity that befell me, it always was made clear to me that it wasn't any ability that I possessed that straightened me out again, but it was God Himself who came to my rescue. At the time when my enemies had me down, I read the Bible, and by the passages I came upon it was clearly indicated to me that He who wrote this Bible foresaw what was going to happen to me, and saw how it was going to come out; that there was nothing new in this bankers' crusade to take my business away from me. Perhaps there was not a description of my particular case, but a general description. I think the Bible shows you clearly what you ought to do and how to save yourself. I intend to show you passages that gave me a clear vision that my difficulties would come straight in the end. Of course, I presume God knows which side is right."

Setting aside questions of external fact, and considering merely those of psychology, it is obvious that a man who goes out to do battle in the world, convinced that he has God behind him, guiding his destiny—such a man will be a more formidable foe than one who relies upon his own powers alone. It will be less easy to discourage him; and the New York bankers who undertook to plunder William Fox may be interested to know why he proved so tough and tenacious. Oddly enough, Mr. Harley L. Clarke, the Chicago utilities magnate who took over his properties, considers himself a devout Christian Scientist, and so one branch of theology was pitted against another.

I would hesitate to deprive any warrior of his shield and buckler, so the questions I asked William Fox were intended not to weaken his faith in a personal Providence, but merely to make him plain to you. He explained:

"The mere fact that a man prays to accomplish a thing that is wrong—he is just wasting his time to expect God to help him in that. That is fair to assume, isn't it? Well, as I have been taught, He likes the idea of your believing in Him and praying to Him and praising Him. He never can hear too much of that."

I asked whether this idea of God did not seem to involve a certain human weakness in His personality, a desire to have the attention of human beings. The answer was:

"Well, I don't think praise in that sense, as you have just described it, is the praise God expects. The praise that a human expects is vanity. I don't think God is vain, and I don't think that is the reason He likes to have you praise Him. Two men are in a business deal, the one perfectly honest and the other a thief. I consider the prayers of the thief in vain. I would like to give you proof that there is a Supreme God, and that when you pray to Him to give you the right thing, He helps you. I have had very conclusive proof of it in my life."

I pointed out that controversies in men's affairs are sometimes complicated. There is right and wrong on each side, and it might be a little difficult for even God to make a choice. But William Fox would not have it so.

"One man in the deal almost always knows he is wrong. Where we all get confused in this religious subject is that sometimes you are right, and you pray to God to help you get out of difficulties, and He doesn't, and you think your prayer hasn't been answered. I prayed the Lord not to let these men take my business away from me. I felt at that time that God had not answered my prayer. But I wait, and a year or two later I find that it was answered. The average fellow that sits down and prays, says: 'Well, I prayed this morning, but I didn't get any answer this morning'—he may get it later. If Harley L. Clarke and I both prayed at the same time, the day he bought me out of business he said, 'Thank you, dear God, You have answered my prayer'; and I probably said, 'Dear God, I have prayed hard, and here You have destroyed me. You have taken this thing I have built up, and given it to Harley L. Clarke.' But two years later we find Fox in comfort, while Clarke is entirely ruined, having started out with the wrong idea in his mind. When we look back now, we see God answered the right prayer."

For myself, I cannot claim to know enough about this universe to make assertions about its moral purposes and ultimate causes. But William Fox has his opinions, which are of great importance to him, and therefore are part of his story.

So you see him, a serious man, who will produce serious and moral pictures, such as "A Fool There Was," "Thou Shalt Not Steal," "The Walls of Jericho," and "The Honor System"; also sentimental pictures such as "My Mamie Rose," and "Mother Machree" and "Mother Knows Best," and "Over the Hill" to touch the people's hearts and moral feelings. He will make it a rule of his company that any rabbi, priest, or clergyman may have any Fox film free of charge at any time for showing in any synagogue, church or Sunday school, any hospital, orphan asylum, or home for the aged. He will dream a wonderful dream of having the twelve greatest preachers preach their greatest sermons before a sound apparatus, and having these reproduced in a hundred thousand churches all over the world. He will not often please the highbrows and the art-for-art's sakers; neither will his name ever be whispered in connection with any of the numerous female stars he employs. On the contrary, he will be a family man and a good citizen, a Republican in national affairs and a Democrat in New York City affairs, and he will raise millions for the Red Cross in war time, and give away millions of his own money in peace time—he will assert that throughout his whole life he has given 20 per cent of his working time and not less than 20 per cent of his earnings to the service of others.

REEL TWO

SHOE-BLACKING AND LOZENGERS

WILLIAM FOX was born in the village of Tulchva in Hungary. His parents were of German descent. His father ran a general merchandising store, and as a side line he extracted teeth. He advertised that he was a painless dentist, guaranteeing that no one would feel the pain of tooth extraction. The patient would sit in a chair and strip himself to the waist, and at the crucial moment someone would touch him with a hot iron on the back, and this would be so painful that the extraction of the tooth would not be noticed. When he came to America, he was not permitted to practice this form of dentistry, but he kept the extracting instruments, and his son often saw them.

Little Will never saw the village in which he was born, because his mother brought him to America at the age of nine months. He has never revisited the place, but years ago he sent a cameraman to take moving pictures of it, and invited his family and friends to a showing. It was forty-eight years after the elder Fox had left the village, but he said that it looked exactly the same, there had not been a new house built.

The elder Fox came to America to look for his brother, who had come over ten years previously, and had suddenly stopped writing. The father searched for him in America for many years, but never found him, and never learned what had happened to him. The father found it possible to earn a living in America, so the mother sold the merchandising business and brought her baby to this new world. There she gave birth to twelve other children, of whom two boys and three girls are now living. The father learned the trade of machinist, and worked at it until William Fox arrived at manhood. During all this period, his earnings were never more than a thousand dollars a year.

The first home that little Will remembers is a place on Stanton

14

Street between Columbia and Sheriff, adjoining the Sheriff Street public school. Little Will attended that school from the age of six. The home was in a rear tenement, an extra building stuck on the back part of the lot, excluding almost all the light and air. What little yard was left had a tall pole in the center of it, and to this pole there were pulleys attached, and from the windows of each tenement ran clotheslines, and from these clotheslines dangled the sheets and bedding of the Fox family and the shirts and underclothing of little Will. The toilet was downstairs and so was the pump, and the family's water had to be carried up in buckets. I can recall visiting such tenements in my boyhood, because we had our washing done there and our clothes dried by this device of pulleys and ropes, and sometimes we would go there to seek a new washerwoman.

I arrived in this world 103 days ahead of William Fox, and if I seem to take charge of him in this book, you may attribute it to this advantage of seniority. We exchanged reminiscences of old days in New York, and one of them was the blizzard of 1888. I remember the snow drifted up to the second story windows, and romping in these drifts with my father and being thrown in head first. What little Will remembers is that at that time his father was out of a job, and had conceived the idea of supporting his family by manufacturing stove blacking in the home. It was Will's job to trudge up and down the stairs of tenements, tapping on doors and selling stove blacking to his customers at 5 cents per can. To have the stove well blacked was important to the family dignity, because the kitchen served as the dining room, and also as a reception room for guests. As a rule, there was an inside bedroom or possibly two of such. For a year and a half little Will had been selling stove blacking, and now at the age of nine the blizzard put an end to his business, because it was a week or more before a little boy could travel about the streets.

So then came the business of selling "lozengers," 1 cent a package, or six for 5, with a riddle inside each package. A good place to sell them was at the foot of the Third Street dock, where the excursion boats used to leave. Afterwards, when you had built up the business, you could afford ten cents car-fare to take you up to Central Park and back. The child is father to

3

the man, and you will see little Will at the age of ten fore-
shadowing the great captain of industry. He has enlisted the aid
of boys in the neighborhood in the lozenger business. These boys
have no capital to buy lozengers, but Will furnishes the capital
and pays them a commission on their sales. So now he is a contractor, with a string of boys under his orders.

The business was a nuisance in the parks, because the people
would throw away the pink and green and blue wrappers of the
lozengers; so the Park Department decided to do away with the
peddling. But somehow they failed to convey notice of this
decision to the kid contractor on Stanton Street. What they did
was to send policemen one day and arrest all the peddlers. This
included the troop of Will Fox, and because they had no money
for bail, they were kept all night in the station house, and next
day made their appearance in the 57th Street Magistrate's Court.
The parents of the other boys had obtained attorneys to represent them, but the elder Fox did not know what to do, since no
member of his family had ever been arrested before; so he
brought his family physician with him.

One by one the parents were summoned before the magistrate, and one by one they stated that they hadn't known what
their boys were doing. It had been the contractor who employed
the boys and was responsible. "The contractor," always "the contractor." So finally the magistrate said, "Let's have this contractor here." The answer was, the contractor was before him. The
magistrate's desk was high, and he had to rise up and peer over
the top to see the tiny figure of Will Fox gazing up at him. He
took one glance, and then said: "Case dismissed. Go home and
keep out of the parks." Little Will went home, and after that
he kept out of the parks—when the police were looking. The
business was an important one, for during the summertime he
would earn as much as $10 or $12 a week.

At the age of eleven, little Will quit school and took a job
with a clothing firm. He continued at night school until he was
fourteen. But there were some kinds of education which he had
decided did not interest him. He could not see, for example, any
use in geography—having no idea that some day he would have
a selling agency in every country in the world, and would need
to know the seating capacity of the theatres in Bangkok, and how

many milreis, rupees, pesos or piastres it took to make a dollar. He decided that what he needed above everything else was arithmetic. He would have to do that in his head and do it quickly. He became so expert that he would trade answers to questions in geography for answers in arithmetic.

The elder Fox was orthodox, and sent his sons to the "cheder" to learn Hebrew and religious doctrine. It was taught by a little old man, sturdily built, about sixty years of age, with a white beard; he was severe and brutal, and if a boy missed an answer, he would rap him with a walking cane. He was supposed to be representing God, but little Will did not consider this a Godlike method. Class was conducted in the German language, and Hebrew texts were learned by heart and translated into German and explained. The school was in a tenement-house basement, the teacher's home, and there were twenty or more boys in the class. The mature William Fox, looking back upon this teacher, says: "I should classify him as a very stupid, ignorant man. The only thing he knew was what he was trying to teach his scholars."

On his thirteenth birthday, the orthodox Jewish boy is confirmed, and takes his sins upon his own conscience, relieving his father of this burden. On his thirteenth birthday, little Will had a responsible position. He was working for the clothing firm of D. Cohen & Sons, and had charge of cutting the linings. There were twelve men and boys working under him—in short, he was foreman of the lining-cutters. He was tall for his age, and he managed to get by by saying he was sixteen years old and acting the part. But now here was a problem. He had to be excused from work for a day, and if he stated why, all Jewish people would know that he was only thirteen years old. So he decided that it was necessary for him to become ill, and two days ahead he began to develop a sore throat. Mr. Cohen, a tall, stoop-shouldered old gentleman with a grey beard, was very kind, and took an interest in his youthful foreman, and insisted on going out and buying him a bottle of medicine, and seeing that he gargled his throat with it. It was terrible medicine, and little Will did not enjoy the ordeal—nor did it help his throat. The next day he was much worse, and so the boss told him to stay at home and rest up.

Quite recently the grown-up Will met in New York a man

who reminded him of having been let in on this grave secret: the tailor who cut the little grey frock coat which the thirteen year old culprit wore in the synagogue while taking his sins upon his own shoulders. Presumably the sin of deceiving his kind boss was not included in the accounting, because this deception had been practiced two days previously, and would, therefore, rest upon the conscience of little Will's father, who did not know about it. No doubt the old teacher at the cheder could have found somewhere in the Talmud a text covering that detail of casuistry.

I asked for a description of Cohen's place of business and was told: "It was a three-story building. There was no elevator, and only a hatchway for the goods. We were obliged to pull them up by rope and that was not an easy task either. Of course there was no telephone. Orders had to be placed in person or by mail. There was no stenographer or typewriter. All letters and bills were written by pen and ink. The first floor was the sales room, the second floor the stock room, and the third floor the cutting room. From here the contractors would take the work out to their shops to be made into garments. I started working there when about eleven, and worked until I was fifteen. The highest wage was about $8."

This was his life: he walked to work, an hour's walk, leaving his house at 6 in the morning; he worked from 7 to 12, took thirty minutes for lunch, then worked from 12:30 to 6:30, and then marched home, having his dinner at 7:30. After dinner he went to the night school about a block from his home. Concerning all this he says: "I was reaching for a goal, and I enjoyed every moment of it."

The reason he worked so hard was because he watched his father, and was dissatisfied with the progress his father was making. The father had remained a workingman, and was content to remain a workingman all his life. Says the son:

"My father was perfectly happy. He was just as happy when he worked as when he didn't work. He never worried. He was very proud of my success. But long before I had reached the point of success, he was perfectly happy and contented. I never heard the man complaining about anything in my life. When I came home and told him that the butcher and baker had refused to trust us any more during the period he was out of work, he was sure that tomorrow would be all right, or that the butcher and baker would most likely change their minds."

It was the mother who did the worrying for the family; you can imagine that, bearing thirteen children and losing seven of them, she had plenty of worrying to do. During the out of work periods, she helped to support the family. Her occupation was sewing slippers for a manufacturer who sent them to the home. It was because of her and through her teaching that the oldest son learned to carry responsibility. From the age of ten, when he began to earn money, he helped to keep the family in comfort, and has done that now for forty-three years, though I could not get him to tell me much about it.

As a boy, Will was not interested in religion; he was interested in making money and getting ahead. But his father was stern, and insisted that he should pray, and so he learned to pray. On his thirteenth birthday, he was greatly impressed by the confirmation ceremony, and the fact that he was taking his sins onto his own conscience. From that time on, he did his own praying, and he watched the results, and made note of the fact that when he asked God for anything, God always gave it to him—if it was a good thing for him to have. If God didn't give it to him, he knew it was because it was *not* a good thing for him to have, and so he stopped praying for it. God gave him a devoted wife, who has been his helpmate and guide for more than thirty years. God gave him two lovely daughters, and, in due course, gave each of them a lovely son. God gave him continuous and expanding prosperity, and both he and his wife proved their gratitude by being generous to their relatives and friends, and charitable to the poor.

A vital part in the life story of William Fox is the story of little Eve Leo. It was an odd coincidence that a Fox should have married a Lioness; they both of them make puns upon this coincidence. I shall tell you much about Mrs. Fox as we go on. I have to tell now the story of the first meeting of Will and Eve when she was ten and he was fourteen. It seems that Will's mother gave a party for her children on Thanksgiving. They had moved now to a better neighborhood and had six rooms in a tenement on Rivington Street, and Will no longer had to carry the water up from the basement.

Little Eve's father was a clothing manufacturer, and somewhat higher in social station than the German-speaking machinist named Fox. But she came to the party, and when she entered the room, she was introduced to a number of splendid young gentlemen dressed in the costumes of knights and courtiers and Spanish grandees, hired from a costumer's in the neighborhood. It was tremendously impressive to a child, and she seated herself shyly in a corner and gazed with wide-open eyes at the fairy-story scene; when suddenly there entered a ragamuffin with torn clothing and dirty face and a bootblack's kit over his shoulder. This was just as real to Eve as the knights and courtiers and grandees, and, of course, she was displeased with the little ragamuffin. When he presumed to come up to her and start shining her shoes, her dignity was offended. She was about to order him away, when someone whispered into her ear that this was the son of the host, and that he was not really a bootblack, but a foreman of lining-cutters. As for this foreman, he looked over the girls in their pretty dresses, and decided that there was only one for him, and he has not changed that opinion in forty years.

When he was fifteen, Will took on another occupation. He purchased a stock of umbrellas and kept them in the house, and on rainy evenings he would rush to the theatres, and sell his umbrellas to the ladies who were coming out and did not want their bonnets and clothing ruined.

Also he found a form of play—at least an occupation which was at once play and work. He met a boy somewhat older than himself, who suggested the idea of embarking upon a theatrical career. Will had become a devotee of the drama; he had made the discovery that storekeepers who put announcements of shows in their windows got a couple of tickets in exchange, and if they did not care for the theatre, would sell the tickets for five or ten cents. So after Will quit night school, he would go to the theatre, and he and Cliff Gordon watched Weber and Fields, the burlesque comedians, then at the London Theatre on the Bowery, and they conceived an act in imitation of this pair.

Cliff was taller than Will, and a little cross-eyed, but a very charming boy. He played Fields, and Will played Weber, and I asked the grown-up Will if he could tell me any of the jokes that they gave in those performances. Here are two samples, which you may judge for yourself:

Said Will: Someone wanted to buy my blind horse.

Said Cliff: No one would buy that.

Said Will: Why do you say that? Ikey offered me $200 for him yesterday.

Said Cliff: Why, he hasn't got two cents.

Said Will: I know, but wasn't it a good offer?

The other joke was as follows:

Said Cliff: I am having a lot of trouble with my wife. Every morning when I open my eyes she asks me for money. One morning it was $1, then $2, until this morning she asked me for $10.

Said Will: What does she do with the money?

Said Cliff: I don't know—I never give her any.

They gave this act on a number of occasions in connection with dances, and they got anywhere from $5 to $10 a night, and divided it. Two of these occasions stand out in the mind of the grown-up Will. One was at Bayonne, New Jersey, and after completing the performance—which was as bad as usual, or possibly worse—they took off their grease-paint, and Cliff became engaged in dancing, and when the dance was over, they awoke to the discovery that the man in charge had disappeared with the money. It was midnight and they had not a cent in their pockets. They walked from Bayonne to Jersey City, quite a distance, and at 6 o'clock in the morning there was a stretch of water between them and their jobs. How to get across was the question; and you will note the ready wits which served to make Will Fox a many times over millionaire. He managed to get hold of a piece of cardboard and a piece of string, and to borrow a pencil. He wrote the word "Blind" on the cardboard, and tied it around Cliff's neck, and the two of them took up their seats at the ferry entrance. The fare was two cents at that time, and before many ferry-boats had arrived and departed, they had four cents and were on their way to New York.

The other notable engagement took place at Arlington Hall on the East Side, and was an entertainment and dance for the benefit of "Spike" Hennessey, a well-known prize-fighter who had developed consumption. When the two actors arrived in front of the hall, they noticed a big three page picture of "Spike" in his prime, and Will turned to Cliff in alarm and said: "If that bird is in here, we are going to get a licking." (That is how the grown-up Will tells the story, but I am not sure if we used the word "bird" in those days; we said "bloke.")

Anyway, Will decided that if he was going to take a licking from "Spike" Hennessey, he would have to be paid first. Cliff said it couldn't be done, but after Will insisted, Cliff finally produced $5 which he had received that afternoon, his week's wages as messenger boy for the telegraph company.

They did their act, and there was very little applause, and a few hisses. Will left the building with all his grease-paint and everything on, and walked home just as fast as he could. Apparently the report that "Spike's" lungs were bad was incorrect, for he had plenty of energy for Cliff. Said "Spike," "You ruined the whole show," and punched him in one of his eyes and blacked it. When Cliff arrived home with one eye and no money, and told his father what had happened, his father punched the other eye and blacked that. It is characteristic of Will Fox that, having driven a shrewd bargain and got his money, his heart was touched by his friend's plight, and he gave him back his $5.

That ended the career of Will Fox as a professional actor. Cliff Gordon afterwards became what is called a "classic." He was the foremost German-speaking comedian in this country, and began producing shows and made quite a success. The acting had been his idea, and he had tried his best to pass on his talents to Will, but in vain.

REEL THREE

PRETZELS AND BUFFALO PANS

AT this stage in the life of little Will Fox, he shared the fate of many an East Side Jewish boy and found out about Socialism. I will let him tell this adventure in his own words.

"Between the ages of thirteen and sixteen, I was a Socialist. The leader of the Socialist party in New York at that time was a man by the name of DeLeon. I knew him very well and was his follower, and during the elections of those three years I stood on the soap-boxes and made speeches. In my mind I was satisfied that the system then in operation was wrong, and that the proper social system of the world should be socialistic. I despised both capital and capitalists. Of course, this was during the period when I had as yet not been able to save a single dollar, and my earnings were just sufficient from hand to mouth. Then came the beginning of my savings, and finally in my penny bank I found myself one day the possessor of $10 in change, with which I opened my bank account.

"Among my friends and acquaintances, who were likewise struggling and just earning enough from hand to mouth, I had failed to mention that I was opening a bank account. I knew that if I had $10, the proper thing for me to do was not to hide it in the bank but to divide it with my friends. Instead I kept adding to this account, until I had $100 in the bank—and to me that $100 looked like a large percentage of the capital of the world. After that I couldn't make as fine an address on a soap-box. The things that I used to say from this soap-box were contrary to what I was practicing, and the larger my savings grew, the further was I getting away from my socialistic principles.

"Then I observed this—that my friends and comrades with whom I was associating socially, and who were earning about

23

the same wage as I, and whose responsibilities were no fewer than mine, were freely spending that which they were earning, while I was denying myself many things. Therefore, I had a surplus each week and was putting it in the bank. Then it occurred to me that we were not equal; that they could also have saved some money, and I began to see the distinction between these different people. As my fund grew larger, one day I found myself the possessor of $500. Of course, up to this time I hadn't cast a vote—I was a talking Socialist, not a voting one. When my time came to cast my first vote, I was a capitalist. My views had been changed entirely. I then found my political views as follows: for local politics, I was a Democrat, which is the usual thing in the City of New York, and for national politics, I was a Republican."

The grown-up Will Fox told me this story with a twinkle in his eye. He had an idea somehow that he was teasing me. Yet at the same time I know that he respects me because of my convictions which I have held to. And, oddly enough, he is anxious that I should not consider him a hide-bound conservative. Later on I shall tell you about his ideas on social reconstruction. Several times while he was telling them to me, he remarked: "You see, Mr. Sinclair, I have not forgotten entirely what I learned from Daniel DeLeon." The truth is that, like most Americans, he has water-tight compartments in his brain. He can admire and ardently defend Herbert Hoover, and at the same time hold quite sincerely some enlightened ideas on social planning.

At the age of fifteen, Will began working for a concern called G. Lippman & Sons, and here is his story about it:

"Old man Lippman had the reputation for forty years or longer of having always been on time to open the factory and always the last man out at night. He opened the door in the morning and locked it at night. He had a large clock in the center of this loft which was about 100 by 200 feet. He had a shrieky voice. He would wait until it was 7 o'clock and then he would yell the word 'Time!' That was the signal to begin work. One morning we were ready to go upstairs, but Lippman had not arrived yet. Everybody was perfectly happy about it and having a regular picnic. We all went upstairs, adjusted ourselves, and Lippman appeared and moved the hands of the clock back to seven, and when he got it there he yelled his usual 'Time!'—so we were 35 minutes late all around that day."

In the Rivington Street tenement it was the rule that each occupant had to clean and scrub the stairs and hallway of the floor he lived on. The property belonged to a man by the name of Michael, who had a butter and egg store downstairs, and here is a story of the struggle for existence in the ghetto of New York:

"Michael had a very fine cat, the largest cat I ever saw. I knew Michael's cat lived on cheese—cheese and milk was all this cat would eat. When the week-end came, I would like to go on picnics, so I would go down to borrow the cat and say we had mice, which we did not. Later I would go downstairs and say that I had offered the cat some chicken, and that he wouldn't eat it, and I wanted some cheese for the cat. Michael would thereupon cut some nice Swiss cheese for the cat, and I would leave with the cheese, but the cat never saw it, because I would take the cheese on my picnic. Then on Monday morning, I would bring Michael's cat back. Necessity is the mother of invention. I liked Swiss cheese in those days and that was the only way I had of getting it."

In connection with these struggles and temptations, the grown-up Will reports:

"I can recall going out with boys when I was sixteen, seventeen, or eighteen, and though I wanted to do the things they did, on checking up the cost I usually did without. I knew when the soles of my shoes had holes in them that that was the time to have them repaired, but I delayed it by putting pasteboard in them to save the half-soling. It would have been so easy to have spent all that I saved in those years. Every penny was something that I denied myself, with the thought in mind that if I was going forward, I had to have money. I saw that capital was what I needed. Either I had to be content to work for someone else all my life, or fight for independence. The latter course made it necessary to deny myself everything I could possibly contrive to do without until I had accomplished my aim and could afford to permit myself the things I missed.

"My father described his lack of progress by saying he had never had an opportunity to save. He was married when he came here and could never earn any more than it took to·keep his family. It must have been so because he didn't drink or gamble, and he always worked hard when he could, but could never save a dollar. My mother encouraged me to save, and I can recall many occasions when she thanked me for offering her an extra dollar or two that I'd earned, but said that she would much rather I put it in the bank. I still have the original account in the Drydock Savings Bank. That book is one of my proud possessions to this day."

Will Fox continued to work for different firms in the cutting trade and his wages increased until he was earning $17 a week; and his pennies, nickels and dimes mounted until at the age of twenty he had $580 in the bank. Then he saw his first opportunity. Admiral Dewey had captured Manila, and came back to New York to receive the welcome of a conquering hero. There was to be a parade starting at Grant's tomb, and going down to Washington Square. Will figured out what that enormous crowd would wish to purchase. He drew $500 from the bank, and with one-fourth of this money he bought bottled soda water—"pop," as it was called. With a second fourth he purchased soap-boxes; for another fourth, cheese and ham sandwiches; and for the last fourth, pretzels. This is what happened:

Wagons were engaged to move the supplies uptown to the neighborhood of 100th Street and Riverside Drive. During the night it turned cold after a hot spell, and in the morning there sprang up a terrific windstorm. It was impossible to sell the soda pop, because what people wanted was hot coffee. You couldn't sell the soap-boxes because if you tried to stand on one, the wind would blow you off. And as for the cheese and ham sandwiches, the amateur caterer had neglected to have them wrapped up, and the wind was blowing so hard across the dirt road that the sandwiches were rendered uneatable.

So all that was left was the pretzels—or "bretzels," as we called them in those days. You may think this a funny story, but don't forget that to the twenty-year old business man it was a serious matter, and might have meant his commercial life or death. He was about to lose the savings of ten years.

"I could picture my ruination. The maximum amount that I could get out of the pretzels would be the $125 plus about 50 per cent profit. Of course I had a dozen or more salesmen with me. I decided there was only one way out, and that was to bring back the $500 in pretzels. We soon learned that we had many competitors, who were not only selling at cost, but below cost. I conceived the idea of walking ahead of these dozen salesmen of mine, and delivering a talk on the qualities of my pretzels, and that there was a souvenir of Admiral Dewey on the inside of each one. Of course when the purchaser got the pretzels, he broke them apart or bit into them and looked for Admiral Dewey inside, but by that time the procession of salesmen had marched on. We sold those pretzels, and when we calculated the money, we had back our $500 with a slight profit."

For seven years now Will Fox had had his eye upon Eve Leo. As he described it to me, he wooed Eve's father first. The son of an ordinary workingman, he had to make good on his own; he had to convince him that he was a serious boy, with brains in his head and destined to rise in the world. He had a responsible position now, and was earning $17 a week, which was enough to keep a family modestly in those days. Having obtained her father's permission, he invited Eve, now a young lady of sixteen, to go to a show with him.

I must explain that Eve's mother had died when she was nine years old, leaving six children. As Eve was next to the oldest— the oldest being a boy—the burden of being a mother to her little sisters and brothers fell upon her shoulders. And now she was a very sedate and responsible person; also, I am told by the grown-up Will, the most beautiful girl he had ever seen. The second time they went to a show, they attended a performance of "The Liars," with John Drew as the star. Coming home on the street-car on a bitterly cold winter night, the street-car for some reason became stalled, and there they had to sit for two hours in the cold unheated car. Will Fox seemed to think that this was a suitable occasion on which to explain the state of his heart to Eve.

He told her that his hands were very cold. She had a fur muff, and it was his hope that she might offer to warm one of those cold hands. Maybe she missed the point, or maybe it was the too great kindness of her heart—anyway, she gave him the whole muff, and told him to put his two hands into it.

But even so, he managed to become engaged to her, and there was a fine public wedding which Eve's father provided. This wedding took place on the 31st of December, and the next day happened to be Will's twenty-first birthday. It happens also to be New Year's Day, which proved a very convenient arrangement, for throughout the rest of their life, the Fox family has been able to combine three celebrations in one. I don't know whether this economy was deliberate, but Mr. Fox tells me in this story how carefully he watched all his opportunities.

"Of course, my co-workers must be invited, and they felt their presence to be incomplete unless they contributed to a wedding gift. About forty or fifty had contributed enough apiece to make a fund of $100. They asked me what I wanted and I suggested some furniture. They gave me the money and told me to pick it out myself. I put the $100 in the bank, and bought the furniture on the installment plan."

So now our hero is no longer "Little Will," but has become a dignified married man, and we shall have to try to find a new way to address him. His wife and intimate friends call him "Bill," but neither you nor I know him that well. On the other hand, "Mister" is a somewhat formal and stilted mode of address. I notice that his lawyer and other associates address him as "W. F.," and that seems to denote about the right degree of intimacy; so that shall be his name throughout the rest of our narrative.

He had decided now to go into business for himself, and the line he had selected was the cloth examining and shrinking business. It appears that when cloth comes from the mills, the manufacturer must do two things before it can be used for garments. He must make sure that it is free of imperfections and of correct measurement, and it must be shrunk. This special work required little capital and little space to work in, and so W. F., with one of his fellow employees, established what they called "The Knickerbocker Cloth Examining and Shrinking Company." The partner was to do the examining and employ people to do the shrinking, while W. F. went out to solicit trade. The salary of the partner had been $25 a week, and that of W. F. had been $17, and for the first year they were hardly able to make this much.

That wasn't enough for the restless William Fox. He was casting about for ways to make money more quickly, and in his efforts he very nearly brought himself to ruin again. He had not learned his lesson from the Admiral Dewey celebration; there was another great public event on the way—the Buffalo Pan-American Exposition. This, you may recall, was the occasion on which President McKinley was shot, and chance brought it about that W. F. was walking down Main Street in Buffalo and was within 100 feet of the spot where Czolgosz drew his revolver and fired. He saw McKinley fall, and remained in Buffalo until Roosevelt came down from the Adirondacks and was made President of the United States. The trip to Buffalo was caused in the following way:

"A chap came to me one day and said that he had invented something that could make millions of dollars for himself and the person who backed him financially. He exhibited a patent paper that he had just received from Washington. It was a patent on a small miniature pan about one or two inches in diameter, and the length of the pan, including the handle, was about four or five inches. In the middle of the pan was an American flag with a buffalo printed on it; therefore, it was 'Buffalo' 'Pan' 'American'—all he needed was 'Exposition,' and the date of it. He estimated that there would be about 10,000,000 people in Buffalo to see the exposition, and it was fair to assume that every one of these people would buy at least ten of these pans for souvenirs. The price was $1, so the estimated gross return was $100,000,000.

"Whatever money I had at that time I invested in this enterprise. This was about a year and half or two years after I was married. I thought this was my big chance and proceeded to manufacture these pans. I think the total investment was about $600. Then I was assigned to go to Buffalo and market these pans, and of course the factory could manufacture them as quickly as we wanted them. I remember shipping the pans in cases to Buffalo.

"On my arrival there, I had but $3, as I was confident that my pans would sell promptly. From the railroad station to the fair grounds was about five miles, and on either side of the avenue the city had issued licenses to permit the erection of wooden stands on which wares could be displayed to the visitors to this exposition. And lo and behold, all that was displayed on these stands were pans with buffalos and American flags stamped on them! There were enough pans there to supply everybody with 100 pans. I had wired for reservations at the Iroquois Hotel, one of the nicest in town, but when I beheld those buffalo pans, I decided to change my residence to a boarding house on a side street, where I paid $1 a day, so I would have enough to last at least three days."

So here again was William Fox fighting for his savings. He walked the streets of Buffalo, and his attention was caught by a five-and-ten-cent store, then something new, owned by a man named Woolworth. This store sold novelties, but it did not have any buffalo pans, so the idea occurred to the pan salesman to get hold of Mr. Woolworth and persuade him to enter the pan business. He wired that he had a very important piece of business to talk over with him, and gave the address at the Iroquois Hotel, and waited there until the answer came making an appointment. Then he told frankly his hard-luck story; out of his last dollar, he had spent 25 cents for breakfast and 25 cents for a telegram to Mr. Woolworth. He had a wife and baby in New York and a business that was not very prosperous.

The great Mr. Woolworth was "a bit rough" at first. He didn't like the idea of having given an interview, supposedly for his own profit, and discovering that it was an amateur pan salesman in trouble. W. F. humbly proposed to leave the pans with him on a gamble, and be content with his railroad fare back to New York; but Woolworth finally paid him the cost of the pans —about $600—and so once more William Fox was saved for a great career. After the exposition was over, he inquired of Woolworth whether the transaction had proved profitable, and was relieved to learn that it had.

So our hero went back to the cloth examining and shrinking business, and during the second year the business grew and they made a profit of $10,000. Their partnership arrangement consisted of a piece of brown paper on which they had written their contract. Says W. F.:

"About the only provision was that checks had to be countersigned. Our partnership ended when on one Saturday the checks were tendered to me for countersigning, and I refused because there was no money in the bank. My partner insisted that on Monday I could go out and collect enough money to cover the checks and deposit it in the bank before the checks went through, but I said that was no way of doing business."

W. F. decided that he would buy out his partner and run the business according to his own ideas. It became necessary for him to raise the funds, and he went to the bank to borrow $1,000 that was needed, and here is his first experience with a banker:

"I bought myself a whole new outfit of clothing in order to make a good impression so the bank would lend me the money— I had no collateral. The bank was the German Exchange Bank and the president was Mr. Adrian. I can remember his words now; he said: 'You are broke. Now what made you go out and buy those clothes? What was your purpose? You have done nothing but spend money. When the bank lends money it wants to feel that it is lending it to someone who will save money and be able to pay it back some day.' However, I got the money, paid my partner off, and as times got better, business grew, and shortly thereafter I found myself with a capital of close to $50,000 made in that business."

4

REEL FOUR

NICKELODEONS AND COMMON SHOWS

IN 1894 Thomas Edison had invented a device which he called a "kinetoscope." Out at his place in East Orange he had spent the enormous sum of $25,000 upon experiments, and had built a shanty covered with tar paper and known to his friends as "the Black Maria." Inside this Black Maria was a huge device weighing more than a ton, a camera with a rapidly moving shutter by which you could take a series of pictures of something in motion—provided that its motion didn't carry it away from the front of the camera. To this place came pugilists and acrobats and dancers, and they performed in front of the camera, and so there began to spring up in the cities places called nickelodeons, a sort of arcade with a row of machines having eye-pieces. You dropped a nickel into the slot and gazed into the eye-pieces, and you saw as real as life the pugilists boxing and the acrobats turning somersaults and the dancers kicking up their skirts.

Then several years later appeared another device generally called the "vitagraph" or the "bioscope," which threw these same images upon a screen. The camera weighed somewhat less than a ton now, and it could be taken on a truck and placed, say by a railroad track, and so you could see the Twentieth Century Limited emerging from a tunnel and rushing down upon you. I well remember seeing the first pictures in a place called the Eden Musee on Twenty-third Street in New York. There were waxworks and all sorts of horrors—President Garfield being shot, and the Chicago anarchists making bombs, and a policeman who looked so lifelike that you went up and asked him the way to the labyrinth of mirrors or whatever delightful thrill you were seeking. Then you went into a little court with palm and rubber trees, and sat in rows of chairs, and there was the image of the Twentieth Century Limited. It trembled and jumped so that it

32

almost put your eyes out, but nevertheless it was so real that you could hardly keep from ducking out of the way as it bore down upon you. A tremendous adventure!

It happened that on Fourteenth Street there was a place called the "Automat," with phonographs, punching bags, weighing machines, chewing-gum machines and, of course, kinetoscopes. The Automat was one of the sights of the town, because no employees were needed, only a watchman. You dropped your nickels into the machines, and down in the basement there was a track running under the machines and a little car running on the track, and as it passed, the machines spilled their nickels into it, and then the car ran around to th ᴄ ʰ ᵉr side of the room and dumped the nickels into a funnel, from uᴄ other end of which they emerged, all counted and wrᴧpped and ready for deposit in the bank. It was almost as marvei ᐧ ᐧ s ᐧ ᐧ ᴄ Chicago stock-yards, where a hog was dropped into the machine at one end, and sausages and buttons and hair-combs came out at the other end.

The Automat pleased W. F., and he made it known that he was in the market to buy an establishment of that sort. Soon there came an agent suggesting that there was one at 700 Broadway, Brooklyn, owned by a man named J. Stewart Blackton, then president of the Vitagraph Company of America, and destined to become one of the big moving picture millionaires. W. F. made an appointment to inspect the property, and he tells this story:

"When I went there, by appointment, there was a large crowd. When I went again a little later in the week, also by appointment, there was an even larger crowd. I thought it was a good thing, and after certain negotiations, I bought the establishment. I took charge of it on the following Monday, and only about two persons dropped in all day. I realized that someone had supplied the crowd on the two former occasions when I had gone to see the place. This was somewhere around in May, and I was told that business was always bad in summer."

I asked W. F. to describe the agent who had sold him that "salted" gold-mine. The answer was: "He was the handsomest man you ever saw; well built, well dressed and always immaculate." Sometime afterwards, it appears, he came to W. F. and said he was broke, and borrowed $50 to go out West. Twenty years later, in a brokers' board-room, he recognized his old-time victim, and came up and introduced himself, and repaid the $50. The story he told was that he had discovered land containing sulphur, and had come back and sold it to New York capitalists, and was now worth $7,000,000. He offered his old-time victim a tip, to buy the stock of the Texas Gulf and Sulphur Company; in a year or two the buyer would make millions. W. F., having bought a "salted" gold-mine from this man, declined to buy a "salted" sulphur-mine. The joke of the story is that the tip was a real one, for the stock went from $40 a share to $240.

But let us return to No. 700 Broadway, Brooklyn, in the year 1903. It was another crisis like that of the sandwiches and pretzels, or that of the Buffalo pans. How was the crowd to be induced to enter the Fox Automat? Quite recently he had attended a showing of the new "moving pictures"; he had seen a picture of a tree, and the leaves of the tree had moved, and the man behind him had said that it was a trick, someone was shaking the curtain. But W. F., with his inquiring mind, had talked to the operator after the performance was over, and asked to have the trick explained. No, the screen had not been shaken; the pictures actually did move of themselves. The operator showed the film, which was nearly three times as wide as it is now, and did not run on sprockets, but merely through a groove. The length of the film was then 100 feet.

W. F. investigated further. He saw the pictures of the Twentieth Century Limited, and a still more marvelous production, a little story told in front of the camera, called "The Life of an American Fireman"; then another one, still more thrilling, "The Great Train Robbery." He saw the public pouring in to witness these spectacles, and he examined the premises he had rented and noted that there were rooms upstairs used as a dwelling. It occurred to him that he might rent these premises also, and put out the tenants and turn it into a showroom for the new picture stories. If he took the people up by the front stairway, and after the show sent them down by the rear stairway, they would enter the nickelodeon at the rear and have to walk past all the machines, and very probably they would drop some nickels on the way.

With W. F. a thing is done almost as soon as he thinks of it.

There was a show room with a screen, and 146 chairs, and some display posters outside informing the public that moving pictures were to be seen. But alas, the Brooklyn public didn't know what moving pictures were, and nobody went upstairs. W. F. stood outside for a whole day, gazing anxiously at the public, and regretting that he had no personal charms to lure them into his establishment.

But then came a man who had the necessary charms. W. F. describes him as a fellow with a great big Western hat. He said: "What are you worrying about?" and W. F. told his troubles. He had the greater part of his fortune in the place, and it wasn't so much the fortune as that he hated to fail. The fellow offered to take charge of it and run it, and told him to shut up the place that day and come back the next.

The next day he came, and had with him a coin-manipulator, a sword-swallower and a fire-eater—which did W. F. prefer? W. F. carried no fire insurance, so fire-eaters were ruled out; also swallowing swords might possibly be dangerous—there might be employers' liability laws. But there could be no harm in a coin-manipulator. He was a little fellow, dressed in black satin breeches and a black satin coat, wearing a black mustache and a little black goatee, neither of which belonged to him. All this was in imitation of "Hermann the Great." He set up his table and started to work in the doorway of the establishment; and when the crowd gathered, he told them that he would finish the performance upstairs, and show them yet more wonderful tricks, and that admission was free for the present. The crowd came trooping up, and there they found out what moving pictures were, and in a week there was such a crowd that the police had to be called in to control them.

So at last W. F. had found a real gold mine! Here was the way of fortune plain before him, and his one task was to get there ahead of the others. He got two friends to join him, and began renting stores on the crowded avenues of Brooklyn, and in each one of them they set up a screen and a projection machine and rows of chairs—of which the total must not exceed 299. Up to that limit you could have a "common show" license; but if you had 300 chairs or more, you were a theatre, and the fire laws took strict charge of you.

So presently here was William Fox with fifteen show places in Brooklyn and New York. I made him search his memory for all the details about those old-time pictures. There was one called "The Automobile Thieves." Automobiles were then just coming into fashion, and some producer had conceived the idea of a new way of stealing. Soon after this someone did actually steal an automobile, and was arrested, and there was a great clamor in the newspapers—this new device of moving pictures was corrupting public morals and stimulating crime! The New York "World," which built up its circulation by carrying on crusades, started a crusade against moving pictures.

Also there was one called "The Runaway Wagon." This was a trick picture. It wasn't an automobile, merely a wagon, yet it went running up and down hill all by itself. The trick was that the photographer had blotted out the horse. A still trickier one was a man putting on a pair of shoes and the shoes lacing themselves.

The names of the companies that made the pictures were Vitagraph, Biograph, Lubin, Pathe, and Essanay.

The clamor against these pictures continued in the newspapers. In court the lawyer would say: "Your Honor, this child never stole before. He saw stealing in a moving picture and that suggested it to him." This clamor disturbed the associates of W. F., whose wives thought they were in a disreputable business. So W. F. bought them out, and added more places until he had twenty-five. He had his own ideas about the moral effect of pictures, for he noticed that wherever the shows were going well, the business of saloons began to dwindle.

"My conclusion was that the workingman's wage was not large enough to buy tickets to the theatre for himself and family, so he found his recreation in drinking his glass of beer against the bar. But when the motion picture theatre came, he could buy a ticket for 10 cents, and for his wife the same, and if he had a child he could buy a ticket for 5 cents. They could be entertained anywhere from two and a half to three hours, and the man found he was getting a much bigger kick holding his kid's hand, or the hand of his wife, than he would be getting from his drink at the bar. I have always contended that if we had never had prohibition, the motion pictures would have wiped out the saloon. We then opened a theatre at 110th and Broadway. On the corner of this property was a saloon and we tried to buy the lease of the owner but he wouldn't sell. Within a year after that theatre opened, he could not get enough business to pay his rent."

W. F. went on to tell me of a later experience when he leased the Star Theatre, on Lexington Avenue near 107th Street, which had been used for melodrama. They were then called "ten-twenty-thirts." On the four corners of 107th Street there were four saloons, frequently called "gin-mills," but after this theatre was converted into a moving picture theatre, one after another the gin-mills closed up, and within two or three months were occupied by other tenants.

Not since the days of the forty-niners had there been such a way for the little fellow to get rich as in this new business. Everything depended upon a location where the crowds were passing. W. F. found that in order to get the right location, it would often pay him to lease the whole building—even though the fire laws required that the upstairs tenants be turned out before moving pictures were shown in the building.

He conceived the idea of combining motion pictures and vaudeville, with the admission price of 10 cents to any seat in the house. He tried in each case to find a manager who had a good voice, and this manager would sing what were called illustrated songs. It was easy to get new songs, because the song writers wanted them popularized before the sheet music was offered to the public. The manager would sing the song and there would be lantern slides with pictures illustrating the songs. The audience would be invited to join the singing—the more the merrier. There was always a line of people waiting to get into these shows. The problem was to rent new places ahead of the other fellow. Here is the story of the first Fox theatre:

"It was located at 194 Grand Street, Brooklyn, and had been devoted to burlesque. When I went to visit the premises, it was winter and the agent told me to bring along rubber boots. I did, and we walked in snow and water up to the knees; the roof was practically gone and it was the most dilapidated structure I ever saw. When I inquired as to how the building came to be in such a deplorable condition, the agent explained that the building was fifty years old and had been unoccupied for two years. He told me that the man who owned the mortgage had it now. It was known as the Bum Theatre and I changed the name to Comedy. I think I paid about $20,000 for the land and building.

"While making extensive repairs, there arose the necessity of a campaign to acquaint the people of the neighborhood that this was to be a theatre for nice people. We made a list of 10,000 names of people living in that vicinity, and for ten weeks we sent them a weekly letter, telling them how this building was progressing. The tenth letter quoted someone as saying that the theatre had been called the 'Bum' because the people around there were bums. I suggested that perhaps those who resented this reference would like to form a parade in the main street of town the night my theatre opened. That night there were 10,000 people in that parade. The theatre did a terrific business, and in a short-space of time we paid off the mortgage and declared hundreds of thousands of dollars in dividends."

The next theatre was the Folly, a place which had been showing melodramas and not doing so well. W. F. went to see a member of the firm, Richard Hyde, who offered the theatre on a ten-year lease for $35.000 a year, and required a deposit of half a year's rent to apply to the last half year. He said he would give W. F. twenty-four hours in which to make a decision. He offered to put this option into writing, but W. F. said he would take his word. The option was to expire at noon, and W. F. was on hand at 10 o'clock with a certified check in his pocket. But meanwhile, it happened some other motion picture concern had got wind of the matter, and had made Hyde an offer of $10,000 more for the lease. Apparently it was Hyde's idea that if he could keep Fox pre-occupied until after 12 o'clock, the deal would be off. So he started telling stories, and he told one after another without stopping until 11:15. Then W. F. broke in:

"Just a minute. I wish to give you an answer. I accept your terms and here is the check."

Hyde seemed troubled, and became solicitous concerning the welfare of his would-be tenant. "You had better not be hasty," he said, "but listen to a man who has been in the business for half a century."

Hyde called his bookkeeper and ordered him to tell W. F. the exact truth about the property. Said the bookkeeper: "Last year we took a loss of $7,500."

Said W. F.: "I am not interested in all that, because the policy I am going to use in the theatre is not the same as yours, and I think I can make a go of it."

Said Hyde: "Darn your soul, I dislike you! You are the first man who has taken my word in the last twenty-five years. I am known as a man who never keeps his word." So Hyde told him about the offer of $10,000 more. In closing the deal, he made only one request: "Wherever you get a chance to talk, be sure to tell people I kept my word with you."

This theatre held about 2,000 chairs, and the performance lasted two hours, with five performances a day. It was a tremendous success, and during the first ten years of the lease, it earned from five to six hundred thousand dollars in profit. At the expiration of this lease, Hyde was dead, and the sons renewed the lease to W. F., because they said: "If father were alive, he would want you to have that theatre."

W. F. realized that the people who were leasing the films to him were making more money than he was. So he began to buy films, and became president of a concern called "The Greater New York Film Rental Company." Two years later the manufacturers decided to form a trust, and set up a company known as "The Motion Picture Patents Company," and claimed that they owned all the patents used in motion pictures. All the manufacturers had to have licenses, and nobody could get films anywhere but from them. It was like the old days of the Beef Trust and the butcher stores. They set out to get possession of the business from top to bottom. They would offer to buy you out, and if you refused to sell, they would cancel your license. They had 120 licensees in America, and in a short time, 119 of them had been either bought out or forced out. The only one left was William Fox, by this time thirty years of age.

This was the greatest battle of his life so far, and he is proud of the service he rendered to the motion picture industry. At that time it was completely throttled. The trust fixed all the prices everywhere. The highest price paid for a scenario was $62.50. No writer's name ever appeared upon the screen, because they did not want anyone to become popular, and so have a chance to raise his price. Of course no writer of talent was going to work on that basis. The salaries of the actors were correspondingly low, and no actor's name ever appeared upon the screen. So long as these conditions continued, motion pictures could make no progress whatever.

The representatives of the trust sent for W. F., and I will let him tell the story of what happened:

"They said: 'We have been very kind to you. We have allowed you to make a large profit for the last two years by leaving you to the last. Now we have to get you out of the way—how much do you want for your plant?' I told them I wanted $750,000. They asked me if I thought that that was what I was going to get, and I told them yes. They told me to think it over and come back later. I came back the next day and still quoted $750,000. Then they told me they had decided to cancel my license. The next day there came a cancellation of my license in the mail."

They had a charge against W. F., whereby they justified their decision to cancel his license. They charged that he had permitted their motion pictures to be shown in a house of prostitution in Hoboken. W. F. tells a curious story about this which illustrates the method of monopolies, not merely in the moving picture industry, but in all others that I have investigated. It appears that W. F.'s concern was supplying pictures to an exhibitor in Paterson, New Jersey, and after the show the operator would bring the films back to New York and get the material for the next day's show. It appeared that the trust had bribed this operator to take the films each night after the show to a house of prostitution in Hoboken, and the trust had caused a projection machine to be set up in this place and had run the films.

Under the terms of his contract with the trust, they had been obliged to give him fourteen days' notice before stopping the supplies of films, and he used that period to play a shrewd trick upon them. He says:

"I went back and suggested that they tell me how much they would give me for my establishment. They said $75,000. I sold it. Then I said, 'Now you have cancelled my license. I think you ought to reinstate the license, so that you have an active business when you take it over and not a pile of junk.' They thought that was a good idea, and the next day I got a letter reinstating the license. A couple days after that I said I did not want to sell out, and I got another cancellation. I then had grounds, and began a legal action under the Sherman Anti-trust Act."

This controversy began in 1908 and was carried to the Court of Appeals of New York State, and was not settled until 1912.

"If successful, we were to get triple damages. We were suing for $600,000 dollars and if successful, it meant $1,800,000. One evening about 8 o'clock a man called and said that the other people were offering to settle out of court. While the decision was due soon, my lawyer thought we should settle out of court, as there was no assurance that the decision would be in our favor. We drew the settlement papers that night, working until 6 o'clock the next morning, and they paid me $350,000. The next day it was announced that the case had been settled. The judge told my lawyer that we should have waited, because they were in unanimous agreement that the judgment was to be in my favor."

This was a suit for damages, not selling. W. F. got his money, and he still had his company and the right to do business. The manufacturers were not permitted to cancel the license, and were compelled to market their films to William Fox at the same prices as to their own company.

The result of this campaign was to put the film trust out of business. Anyone could make pictures, and many began to do so. Under competitive conditions, writers and actors could ask higher prices for their work, and could demand that their names be advertised; so reputations could be built up and talent developed. An odd circumstance is that the men who had organized the trust were unable to meet this new competition, and within five years none of those who had fought William Fox were any longer in the business.

All these four years W. F. had been going ahead with the leasing, buying and building of theatres, and turning them into motion picture "palaces." When you were running a regular theatrical production, you had as a rule only one company, and drew your audience from all over the city. But for these 10-cent theatres, you drew the people of the neighborhood, and since you could make hundreds of prints of the film, you could have a theatre in every neighborhood; you could have a chain of theatres all over New York and Brooklyn and the suburbs—it was a series of gold mines, and the deeper you dug into these mines, the richer became the vein. The quality of the films became better, and a better class of people would come to see them. It became possible to have real "palaces"; to spend money on theatre decorations, and charge 15 cents, 25 cents, even 50 cents admission.

In the case of the City Theatre, Fourteenth Street between Third and Fourth avenues, W. F. put in one-fourth of the money; two-fourths of the remaining interest were taken by the two Timothy Sullivans, prominent leaders of Tammany Hall, known as "Big Tim" and "Little Tim." The total amount invested was $100,000, and the building was to cost $300,000. Big Tim produced a contractor who offered to do the rest of the financing, taking 50 per cent of his money in cash each month, and taking a six months' note for the other 50 per cent, agreeing to renew these notes for an additional six months. In this way the theatre would be making money before the first of the notes became due.

The work proceeded, and at the end of the first six months there was a note for $10,000 falling due at the Colonial Bank. W. F. received a notice from the bank, and set out to find Mahoney, the contractor, and take him to the bank to renew the note. For days W. F. hunted for Mahoney but Mahoney could not be found. Then W. F. went to Big Tim, who saw no reason to worry, it was Mahoney's problem, not Tim's. W. F. couldn't understand this attitude, but realized after a while that Big Tim was accustomed to signing notes quite freely; it meant no more to him than slapping somebody on the back; it was part of his stock in trade as a politician. Nobody who wanted to go on doing business in New York City would ever dream of suing Big Tim Sullivan on a note.

But it was different with a little fellow like William Fox. He had never had a note go to protest, and it seemed to him the most terrible thing in his whole life. For a week before the note was due, he worried Big Tim, but in vain. Then he went to the Colonial Bank and presented himself to the president,

Mr. Walker. W. F. laid $2,500 upon the banker's desk and asked the banker to release him from his share of the obligation. But Walker couldn't see it that way. Under the law, each of the signers was responsible for the full amount. As for W. F.'s statement that Mahoney had agreed to renew the note, Walker said he didn't want to know anything about that. Probably he thought it was just a bluff. Anyhow, he refused to take the $2,500, and when W. F. insisted, he brushed it onto the floor, and when W. F. went on insisting, he pressed a button, and a man in a gray uniform appeared and gently escorted the protestor to the door.

W. F. had until 3 o'clock that afternoon to save his good name, and he was in a terrible state. He called Walker on the telephone and heard him hang up the receiver. Then he waited outside the building, hoping that Walker would come out to lunch, but 1 o'clock came, and W. F. saw a tray carried in, and, peering through a window of the bank, he saw Walker seated at his desk eating his lunch.

"Then I noticed him light his pipe. I have always known that a man with a full stomach is in a better humor than with an empty. Back to Walker's office I went, and my presence caused the man to go into a convulsion. He yelled, 'Get out!' and this time two men came in and just threw me out. Mr. Walker could see me from the window standing outside, because from time to time I would rap on the window to let him know I was there. Finally I saw the clock hands turn to three. I had endorsed this note in good faith and it was to be protested. I knew of no humiliation in my whole career greater than at 3 o'clock that day."

But it turned out all right, as Mahoney appeared the next day, and the note was renewed, and the City Theatre was completed, and opened with the "Zeigfeld Follies of 1910." It was a loss from the beginning, and presently the theatre was closed, and W. F. leased it from his associates for $75,000 a year, and put moving pictures into it, and it has been making a profit of $45,000 a year ever since.

There is another story having to do with this president of the Colonial Bank; and W. F. laid stress upon this story, saying: "I want you to see that there is a difference in bankers."

W. F. thinks that a banker is all right when he is really a banker, and the trouble only begins when he ceases to be a banker, and becomes a speculator and promoter, or a conspirator and bandit. Throughout this period of his career, W. F. dealt with bankers, who looked into his business affairs, judged his character, and loaned him money with which to buy and rent new theatres, or to put up new buildings. If the buildings cost a little more than was expected, or if it took a little longer to finish them, they cheerfully renewed his notes, and in due course he opened his theatres, and the public came pouring into them, and he paid off his notes at the banks with the agreed amount of interest. That is W. F.'s conception of what banking should be, and if all the bankers had been like that, he would never have come to Upton Sinclair to write the story of his career.

Late in 1912 and early in 1913, W. F. conceived the idea of larger and more beautiful houses for the new motion picture art. One was to be the Audubon, on Broadway near 165th Street, and the other was to be on Tremont Avenue in the Bronx. He had at this time half a million dollars in cash, and this was to be the largest venture of his career. There were to be stores in connection with the theatres, and when the construction was half completed, it was found that the cost would be nearly twice as much as had been expected. Money was very tight at this time, and W. F. found himself chasing about the city trying to borrow some. It was the story of the sandwiches and pretzels and buffalo pans all over again—if he couldn't find the money, he would lose the buildings. Let him tell the story himself:

"One day while I was in this quandary, trying to see or find a way out, the man who had the plaster contract of these buildings called on me. He told me he was in trouble and that I could help him out. You can imagine my feelings as I realized that he must have come for his money. He said: 'I know I haven't any right to ask you to pay me in advance, but if you could give me a note for four months instead of paying me on the fifteenth, I would be very grateful.' What a load fell from my shoulders at his words! Of course I gave him the note and he gave me the receipted bill. It seemed that he must have spread the word around because one by one the contractors called and asked for notes. The same thing occurred every month until the buildings were completed and opened, which was inside of four months, and before the first payment came due on these notes.

"One day one of the contractors asked if I knew Mr. Walker, the president of the Colonial Bank, and if I had ever done any business with him. I told him I was sorry to admit I had not been successful in my attempt to do business with him. He suggested that I go around to the bank and see him, and he would say no more. I was mystified. I called on Mr. Walker. He remembered me and asked how I was getting along. I told him the whole story. He said, 'Then you have no worries.' I said, 'Yes, I have, as the first notes are soon due, and I am no better off now than the day I gave them as the theatres are only just opened.' He rang the bell (not the same bell he rang on the previous occasion to have me thrown out) and a young man brought in an envelope. He said: 'Here are $250,000 worth of those notes. The other $150,000 worth are with the Nassau Bank. I knew you were in trouble and sent those contractors to you.' When I asked him why he had done that, he replied: 'I became interested in you that day three years ago when you put up such a battle to keep your name from going to protest. Now it happens that I live across the street from the Audubon Theatre and early every morning during its construction I could see you from my window watching the work in progress, and it made me dizzy to see you climbing around on the scaffolding. And many nights I saw your white roadster circling the property. I felt that a man so zealous of his good name and so untiring and conscientious in his endeavors was a good risk and a good investment. Take your time and pay it back when convenient.'

"Within a year after that I had paid that debt all off. One of those places opened Thanksgiving Eve and the other a few days before Christmas in 1913."

REEL FIVE

THE ROAD TO FORTUNE

WE find William Fox now with a chain of moving picture "palaces" of all sizes in and about New York, and with hundreds of thousands of people coming every night to see what he has to show them. He has organized a concern called "The Box Office Attractions Film Rental Company" to buy and lease films for the Fox and other theatres; and his main trouble is to find suitable films. He has come to feel that he has a personal relationship with each of these patrons who pay him a dime or perhaps a quarter. If the patron likes the product he will come again, and perhaps bring his family; but some of the pictures are "off color," and the patron who sees these pictures may refuse to bring his family. Says W. F.: "I knew how little diversion or entertainment it was my good fortune to receive from the time I was twenty-two. All these years I craved something more than just eating, sleeping and working, but I had missed it. And now the thing that attracted me to this picture business was that I was able to give the pleasure to someone else. I was rather inspired. I had a feeling that I was doing something just a little bit more than making money. I was putting entertainment and relaxation within the reach of all."

The Box Office Attractions Film Rental Company began to manufacture pictures. The first one was called "Life's Shop Window," and its cost was six thousand dollars, a liberal sum in those days. It was made from a popular novel, supposed to be a naughty book. But for film purposes it was made moral, and then, unfortunately, there was nothing left of it.

The second picture was "St. Elmo," by Augusta J. Evans. The heroine is a humble village girl, the blacksmith's granddaughter, and she quotes long passages of Latin to the villain; also she swoons frequently. The Box Office Attractions Film

Rental Company kept the swoons, but omitted the Latin. By this time movie heroines had five reels in which to do their swooning, brought on by tight lacing to acquire the wasp-waist line.

In the meantime the public was manifesting such interest in this new art of motion pictures that illustrated songs and vaudeville were passing. The nickelodeons and penny arcades had been long since forgotten, likewise the fire-eaters, sword-swallowers and coin-manipulators. The movies were advancing to their place among the half dozen biggest industries of America.

At this point we must stop and go back to renew our acquaintance with Eve Leo. We left her on the day of her wedding. She and her bridegroom set up in a five-room flat on Myrtle Avenue in Brooklyn, at a rental of $11 per month. It was one of the old-fashioned "railroad type" of flat and W. F. describes it as a veritable doll's house.

"From the beginning Mrs. Fox made our home, no matter how simple, a heaven for me; her artistic fingers made everything she touched beautiful. I can see it now with those dainty swiss curtains and cretonne hangings at the windows, with cushions here and there to match, and beautiful panels, reproductions of great masterpieces given away with coupons of Babbit's soap, which she had framed to adorn our walls. We still have our old "Le Brun and Child" in our bedroom, from our first home during those days. It has been a sort of mascot all these years."

When prosperity began coming to W. F., someone offered him a real estate bargain in the form of a tenement house. It was only $12,000, and $11,000 of that was mortgage, so he took it, and got a marvelous thrill out of being a landlord at the age of twenty-three. But the thrill soon vanished, as he had no time to collect the rents, and turned the job over to his wife. Then he made the sad discovery that there weren't many rents, for the tenants found out that a hard luck story would touch the kind heart of their landlady. W. F. decided that the business of being a landlord was not as glorious as he imagined, and he sold the tenement at a still greater bargain.

Some time later the Fox motion picture company required a scenario department, and so we find Eve trying to be that department. In the early days of the industry there were no "executives," such as you now read about. At that time all the pictures

5

were made in New York, and when W. F. wanted a story, he would have to find one himself. One can readily imagine that through all his struggles he had very little time to read. But there was his wife who had read incessantly. She would tell him a story which she had been reading, and the next day, when he went to the studio, he would talk it off to a stenographer, or maybe tell it to the director, and between them they would put it into continuity, and after they had selected the actors, they would tell it to the actors. All day directors and actors would work, and in the evening there would be the "rushes," and W. F. would inspect them; before long his wife took to coming down and watching these "rushes," and helping him to judge whether their dramatic quality had been fully developed. If there was anything wrong, never did she say it in the presence of any other person, but took her husband aside and made her suggestion. That is the way to be a tactful wife! Says W. F.:

"For five years no one knew the work she was doing, for when the scenarios were submitted, I would pack them up every evening and bring them home to my wife. I remember one story being rejected by her, and the writer of the story then wrote me a letter, saying that his story had just been returned marked 'rejected,' but this was the greatest story he had ever written, and proved that my scenario department was in the hands of incompetents, and he would recommend that I immediately dismiss the party who rejected the story."

When the picture was finished and cut, the titles had to be written, and Mrs. Fox would help with that. So began the regime, under which the canary bird at home had to learn to wake up in the small hours of the morning. Says W. F.:

"It was not a rare occasion that we both left the building at five-thirty or six in the morning. When we were leaving, it was just about time for the job to open again. Even if we took a brief vacation at Atlantic City, the rushes would be brought down to me every night, and in the morning we would sit in some theatre and view them. I earned what I got; in fact I earned more than I got, because the first year under contract my salary was $1,000, and for the next four years I was to get $10,000"

When you marry a young man who is going into the cloth examining and shrinking business, you are presumably not expecting a very romantic or exciting life; it must have been a startling thing to Eve Leo when in the course of two or three years this prosaic source of livelihood was exchanged for a nickelodeon, and then for a "common show," and then for a string of 125 shows, and then for vaudeville theatres and whole chains of motion picture "palaces"—all of them like hungry birds in a nest, lifting their big heads and opening wide their beaks and clamoring for food. The Box Office Attractions Film Rental Company had to have more pictures, and pictures meant stories; so Eve Leo must hasten to read novels, or she must rack her memory for the novels she had read years ago—little dreaming how she would coin this reading into a fortune!

This went on for many years. They lived uptown, in the suburbs, and each night or early in the morning while they were driving home, Mrs. Fox would tell another story, and they would discuss changes in it, and perhaps make it all over. A few stories they bought from authors, but most of them they took out of the "common domain," as the copyright decisions phrase it, meaning works upon which the copyright had expired. They made Ouida's "Under Two Flags" and Dickens' "A Tale of Two Cities." Also that well-known classic "Les Miserables." I remember when I was a boy, one of my schoolmates read it and told me that he couldn't see why they were called "Less Miserables," because it seemed to him they were more miserable when they finishd than when they began.

The time came when the scenario department became too big for one woman and as others were engaged for the various departments, Mrs. Fox lost her job. She lost several jobs in the course of her life, she told me. Her first had been the tying of her husband's necktie each morning. It seems that when W. F. was a boy, he fell off a truck and broke his left arm, and an unskilled surgeon took out the elbow joint, and so this arm is crippled and his wife had to tie his ties. But after a while, it occurred to him that this was an imposition and he began to practice and soon learned to do it with one hand. So Eve lost her first job. Her second job was brushing his hair artistically, in an effort to cover his growing bald spot; but as the years passed, this effort became hopeless. The third was the scenario department; the fourth was the job of decorating the Fox theatres, which was lost when the enemies of William Fox took the Fox Theatres Corporation from him, and ran it into bankruptcy, as we shall see.

The quality of moving pictures produced by the Box Office Attractions Film Rental Company, and later by the Fox Film Corporation, was a matter of importance to the public, and it is a matter of importance to this narrative. Altogether there were produced, under the initiative and direction of William Fox, a total of 750 pictures. In discussing the matter with me, he made the statement, "Some of them were good and some of them, I suppose, were very bad." It seems to me that this statement may be accepted by all parties; the rest would be a question of percentages. Certainly, no one who saw "Sunrise," "What Price Glory," "Four Sons," and "A Yankee at the Court of King Arthur," will deny that William Fox produced some good pictures. On the other hand, when I read titles such as "Her One Mistake," "Flames of the Flesh," "The She Tiger," "The Splendid Sin," "The Sin-Sister," "Love Makes 'Em Wild," "Ankles Preferred," and "Girls Gone Wild," I feel quite certain that he produced a number of bad ones.

Little Will Fox left school at the age of eleven, and began working in a clothing factory to help support his parents, and to save half his young brothers and sisters from the death which took the other half. He peddled stove-blacking, "lozengers," umbrellas, sandwiches and pretzels, buffalo pans, and Weber & Fields jokes, and in none of these occupations was there any opportunity to acquire familiarity with "the best that has been thought and felt in the world." If you had wanted true culture in moving pictures, you would have had to get them from men with a different sort of training. But you believed in the sacred principle of American individualism—which meant that Edison's new invention was flung out into the market-place, to be scrambled for by those who had the quickest wit and the highest skill in the picking up of nickels and dimes. So presently you had "The Life of an American Fireman," and "The Great American Train Robbery," and "The Runaway Wagon," and "The Automobile Thieves"; then presently you had "Life's Shop Window," and "St. Elmo," and "Bertha the Sewing Machine Girl," and "No Mother to Guide Her," and "The Face on the Barroom Floor," and "Silk

Legs," and "Plastered in Paris." You had a swarm of men rushing to rent stores and install projection machines—the clothing merchant, Laemmle, and the band-musician, Lasky, and the shoemaker, Warner, and the fur-dealer, Zukor, and the jack-of-all-trading, William Fox, who spent most of his time reading contracts and inspecting the weekly reports of theatre earnings.

I questioned him closely about the sources of his culture, because he passed it on, not merely to a hundred million Americans, but to other hundreds of millions in Borneo and Iceland and Patagonia. My wife and I went one day to a picture show, and it was a Fox show—there was a time in our home city when you couldn't attend anything but a Fox show, because W. F. bought the West Coast Theatres Corporation, which included all the theatres in Pasadena, and all the leading theatres in eleven states west of the Rocky mountains. We saw a newsreel of some men climbing a tremendously high mountain covered with snow. It might have been Rainier in Washington, or Popocatepetl in Mexico, or Kinchinjunga in the Himalayas—anyhow, there they were, toiling up through endless snow and ice, and when they got to the top, they accomplished their purpose, which was to unfurl to the wind a banner reading: *"Fox Film."*

There were such banners in every country you could name, and W. F. thinks that in all these places there will be people curious to read this book; his prediction concerning its future sales reads like Colonel Sellers calculating the market for spectacles among the natives of Africa. Regarding his purpose and attitude from the beginning, he says:

"The first theatre had 146 chairs. It was strictly a commercial proposition. I was looking for an outlet for my business acumen which hadn't found sufficient expression in the cloth examining and shrinking business. I gradually acquired a chain of 125 theatres and during this period the commercial element was still uppermost. But as I became established and expanded my business, and life was no longer merely a battle to survive, my thoughts changed. I reached the period in 1912 or 1913 where I found myself with $500,000 in cash that I wanted to invest and I realized that there was a great deal more in life than just making money. What concerned me far more was to make a name that would stand for the finest in entertainment the world over.

I strove to provide more luxurious theatres than before and to refine the entertainment that we presented. I would not allow anything on the stage or screen I was unwilling to have my wife and daughters see. Many a picture that I had contracted for and would have to pay for whether I used it or not, was shelved on this account. You see, popular entertainment at this time was little above the crude burlesque stage, which had been all right for men, but now our audiences were made up of men and women too."

An important part of W. F.'s training he seemingly had forgotten, until I dug it out of his memory. In the year 1910, he leased the old Academy of Music, a large and famous show-place on Fourteenth Street and Waverly Place, the opera house of New York and the center of its social life in the days of our grandfathers. It was the home of Denman Thompson, who played "The Old Homestead" when I was a child, and gave me the keenest delight which I can remember in the theatre. It is just as vivid in my mind as if I had seen it yesterday—the famous scene representing Grace Church with the chimes, and the old countryman who comes to town and wants to mail a letter to his family, and is told to drop it into the post-box. He does so, and then stands and gazes in awe, and says: "I wonder if it's got there yet." Then comes the postman, collecting the letters, and the old farmer jumps upon him, shouting "Stop, thief!" Also I remember a production called "The Black Crook," which shocked everybody in New York because the leading lady danced in black tights.

Well, W. F. leased this theatre, and here was a grave social and artistic responsibility. He had to pay $100,000 a year rent, and at the same time, he had to produce dramas worthy of the traditions of the ancient institution. Never would it do to put moving pictures into the old Academy of Music where King Edward VII had been entertained at a grand state ball!

He tried a stock company, producing fifty-two plays a year, the admission 10, 20 and 30 cents. He carried out this program for three years, and attended rehearsals and watched the plays. He had his office right across the street, which made it possible to devote a great deal of time to this branch of production, and it was here that he got most of his schooling and experience in the drama.

At the end of the year 1912, he had lost $380,000 in attempting to conform to the traditions of the Academy of Music. He then went up to Boston to see the owners of the property, and told them that he was through. He would rather forfeit the $100,000 he had paid as rental for the last year of the ten-year lease than continue a losing proposition. As he started to walk away, one of the owners called him back. "What do you expect us to do with this theatre if you who are in the business couldn't make a go of it—what do you expect us to do?"

W. F. told them that he had a plan in his mind, but hadn't wanted to give it to them until they asked for it. There were two things to be done: the rental must be reduced by one-third; and the $100,000 which W. F. had just turned over to the owners must be used to tear down the blank walls of the building which fronted all the way on Fourteenth Street, and the grass plot in front of the wall must be turned into a row of stores. This was agreed to, and another ten-year lease was made, and W. F. went back to try another experiment with the Academy of Music.

He was just then making his decision to go into the business of manufacturing pictures. He was going to use his stock company for that purpose, and sent his director, J. Gordon Edwards, to Europe, where they were making good pictures, to learn how it was done. In the meantime, the Academy was dark, and one day W. F. was sitting in a restaurant across the way, when a man came over and persuaded him that he had a musical comedy that would be a big hit at $1.00. The Academy stage was big enough for a large production. Says W. F.:

"Before long he had sold me the idea. On the opening night the house was sold out. After the first act, the applause seemed unending. There were a half a dozen curtain calls. In the rear foyer my friends were congratulating me and telling me it was the greatest show they ever saw. I noticed one man standing in the corner, with a big cigar in his mouth and a black hat pulled down over his eyes. He nodded his head for me to come over and asked: 'What are they telling you?' I told him.

"Then he asked me if I believed them, and I replied, 'Yes. The applause indicated that.' He then told me it was the worst thing he had ever sat through. He said, 'Come back tomorrow and listen to the remarks of strangers if you want to know the truth. Don't listen to your friends.' The next afternoon I took his advice, and what I heard coincided with his criticism. Before the show was over there were only a few people left; the rest had walked out. At the end of the week we rang the curtain down on about $75,000."

That was the last effort to save the traditions of the old Academy of Music. It was turned into a picture house, and after that, like all the other Fox theatres, it made money.

There is one more story of the old Academy days: W. F.'s introduction to the Prince of Wales. This celebrity visited the United States in 1921, and W. F., the best of showmen, recalled the tradition that the grandfather of the Prince had been entertained at the Academy of Music. Wouldn't the grandson like to come to the theatre and occupy the same chair in which his forefather sat? The committee in charge of arrangements accepted the invitation and this is what happened to W F.:

"Several days before the Prince of Wales arrived, a member of his committee visited my office and told me what I should wear on this great occasion, and rehearsed the manner in which I was to receive the Prince, saying that if he offered to shake hands with me, I was to put no pressure in the handclasp but let my hand rest lightly in his. And having escorted the royal visitor to his box, I was to make a graceful exit.

"Finally the day came when the Prince of Wales arrived. Fox News cameras had followed him on his travels from the time he left England until his arrival at the Academy. We rushed these reels through and were ready in time for the show. Invitations had been sent to the old-time New Yorkers who had attended the reception to the former Prince, later King Edward. There were fifty or more and they were delighted to attend. The Prince was received in the grand foyer of the theatre by twenty-four debutantes, the blue blood of New York. They wore period costumes, crinoline and white wigs, and made a beautiful picture.

"When I met the Prince of Wales, he seemed a very genial and democratic sort of person and I liked him. I liked the pressure of his handclasp and I returned it. He was so natural, I forgot my instructions to address him as "Your Highness" and found myself saying, "Prince, I am happy to meet you, and I wish to express my thanks for accepting the invitation." When we reached the box, I said, 'This ends my part of the performance, as I have been instructed by your committee that I am to to leave you here.' He said, 'You will do nothing of the kind. Come and sit with me. Never mind what you have been instructed to do.'

"I walked into the box with him. Suddenly he turned to me and said, 'What is that gold chair doing there?' I told him it was supposed to be the royal chair his grandfather had sat in. He asked to have it taken out as he preferred to sit in one of our regular chairs. After the porter had removed the gold chair, we sat down together. The time alloted on the royal itinerary for the entertainment was to be just fifteen minutes. We had a funny dog comedy called 'The Yellow Dog Catcher.' All the parts were played by dogs; there must have been fifty of them. The Prince laughed until his sides ached and wanted to know the breeds of the different dogs. After looking at some of the mongrels I admitted it was beyond me.

"When his fifteen minutes were over, I told him his time was up. He said, 'Now don't drive me out. Isn't it the oddest things that they pick out for you to do on a visit like this? I have visited every dead man's grave in New York and placed flowers on them. This is the first bit of relief I have had since I arrived. Now let me stay.' He stayed about an hour, and impressed me as being just as human as any ordinary boy that came from one of our American families."

REEL SIX

OVER THE HILL

I ASKED W. F. about the authors he had dealt with in those early days, but he couldn't remember that he had ever met one; he rarely met them at any time. The purchases were made through agents. For "Life's Shop Window" $100 was paid. Later on prices rose. After some effort W. F. remembered an author—"Oh, yes, I met Zane Grey. We bought half a dozen of his stories. I don't remember that he made any impression on me. He seemed to be a nice sort of a man."

You can see how little the author was needed by one curious tale which W. F. tells me. "Some other film concern made a motion picture, using a musical comedy star by the name of Josie Collins. When the picture was completed, it was terrible, and there was no possible market for it. It so happened that just at this time Fox Film was behind on its schedule and in great need of a picture. Here was a chance to buy one at a bargain, so they bought it and cut it to pieces, and reconstructed it, making an entirely different story without an additional scene being shot. The aunts became grandmothers, the grandmothers became friends, and if anything was missing, we filled in the gaps with titles. It was previewed, and the trade papers all agreed that it was a fine picture. It was a success."

I asked about the movie stars and how they were made, which brought a very interesting story to mind:

"Before making 'A Fool There Was,' I consulted Robert Hilliard, who had produced it on the stage and played the leading role for years. He said, 'In my experience, I have had to change my leading lady six times. As soon as one scored a tremendous hit in the part, she believed herself to be a Sarah Bernhardt and became unmanageable, and I had to let her go. My advice would be to put the girl you choose under contract, as the part will make her.' We made a test of a girl called Theodosia Goodman, who had no theatrical experience, and decided she would do. She was the daughter of a tailor in Cincinnati. Miss Goodman gave a very remarkable performance in this picture; and then came our problem. If we were going to continue her services, the name didn't have quite the theatrical feeling, and we must find a stage name for her.

"One day it was conceived in our publicity department that we had had every type of woman on the screen except an Arabian; our publicity director felt that the public would like an Arabian. He conceived the story that this Miss Goodman was born in Arabia—her father was an Arab and her mother a French woman who had played the theatres in Paris. So we took 'Arab,' and spelling it backwards, made it 'Bara,' and shortened the first name 'Theodosia' to 'Theda' and thus the name 'Theda Bara.' Then the director said, 'Now let's not settle on this until we see if it will go over. Let me invite the newspapers to an interview and see if they will swallow this.'

"He dressed her in the regular Arabian costume, and surrounded her with the proper atmosphere, and then the newspaper boys all came in. He said, 'I want you to meet Miss Bara,' and gave them her history. He said she didn't speak a word of English. The newspaper men left that day and said that the Fox Film Corporation had discovered the greatest living actress in the world. At first when we would want to attract the attention of Miss Goodman, we would call her 'Miss Bara,' and she would not pay any attention. But after a short time she became used to it, and took to the name perfectly, and she still retains it. Miss Bara got $75 a week for her first picture, and when her contract expired, we were paying her $4,000 a week"

And here is a story of genius and temperament. There was a Broadway favorite by the name of Valeska Suratt. She had the reputation that whenever she got angry, she walked out and wouldn't appear at the studio to finish her picture; so W. F., as a precaution, took the last part of the picture first. There was a scene in a gambling house, and then a scene in which the leading lady fell downstairs. Next she was required to go up to Sing Sing and there encounter a prisoner who had once stabbed her. (They lived a varied and exciting career, the movie

stars of that early decade.)   Miss Suratt was supposed to be
happy at the idea that the prisoner in Sing Sing prison was
chopping stones into small pieces. She was supposed to sneer
at him, but she said to the director, "I can do anything but sneer
at a prisoner. I will laugh at him, but I will not sneer." There
was an argument, and in the end Miss Suratt said that she would
go home from Sing Sing, and home she went.

They heard no more from her, so W. F. decided that they
would put out the picture as it was, and it was so announced.
Then Miss Suratt came to his office.

"What is this rubbish about this picture being released?"

W. F. assured her that it was a very good picture indeed.

"But there is no ending to the picture!"

"Oh, yes," said W. F., "don't you remember where you rolled
down the flight of stairs from the gambling house? The camera
photographed you as you lay on the ground, and we have now
put in the title, 'And poor Suratt died from this fall.'"

Then W. F. told her that the director had written in some
more scenes. The next scene showed a hearse in front of an
old house. There were four dirty bums carrying a coffin, and
the hearse proceeded down Broadway with the director running
ahead with a megaphone yelling, "In this hearse lies Miss Suratt."
He went on to describe a scene in the cemetery, whereupon the
actress burst out laughing and gave up. She came back, and
from that time on never failed to appear on time at the studio.

In the early days the studio was out on Staten Island, and
the "rushes" were brought in every day. Later the studio was
moved into New York, and in 1916 the production part of the
enterprise was moved to Hollywood. On W. F.'s first visit to
the studio at the coast, he noticed a man leaning up against a
lamp post in front of the door, wearing a very loud cowboy
costume.

He says: "Every morning for a week this same figure was
waiting, always in a different costume, each one louder than the
last, until my curiosity was aroused. One day he approached
me and said: 'My name is Tom Mix. I made up my mind I
wouldn't work for any other company until I saw you, Mr. Fox.'

"He was a very picturesque figure and I interviewed him and
decided to engage him. When the subject of salary was broached,

he said that the thing he was interested in was the provision for the care and feeding of his horses. We agreed on $350 a week, including feed and stables for his horses. When his last contract expired, we were paying him $7,500 a week. His first pictures were two-reelers and the audience liked them. And though Tom became the hero to the youth of the nation, the interesting thing about him is that he never changed. He was with our company for ten years or more, and to me he was no different when he got $7,500 a week than when he was getting $350."

I think the production of which W. F. is proudest is the picture called "Over the Hill," produced about 1920. This picture had no stars. It cost $100,000 to make, and netted over $3,000,000—which is very high praise for a picture. The story was W. F.'s own idea, and started when he heard a young man recite Will Carleton's poem "Over the Hill to the Poor House." The poem made a sensation, and W. F. was led to read this volume. He was always on the lookout for plots, and this poem brought to mind all the old people left in institutions through the neglect of thoughtless and selfish children.

A short time after Mrs. Fox asked him to do her a favor. An old man had appealed to her to get him into a home. He was seventy-five years old, in broken health and great need and without a friend or relative in the world. W. F. went to see Jacob Schiff about it, and told him the sad story. A few days later Schiff sent for W. F. and, to the latter's great embarrassment, reported the result of an investigation: the old man had six children, several of them well-to-do. W. F. brought the report back to his wife, and naturally was much annoyed.

A month passed, and Mrs. Fox told her husband the sequel to the story. She had written to each of those six sons and daughters, inviting them to her home on a certain evening. They all came. There were six brothers and sisters meeting one another after long separation, and naturally they wondered what it was about. Said Mrs. Fox:

"I am confronted with a grave problem concerning a worthy old man seventy-five years of age, who appealed to me for help and begged that I provide a home for him, as he hadn't a soul to turn to. In my efforts to have him admitted to a home, I

find he has four sons and two daughters." At this point one
of the girls was crying with embarrassment and said she knew
Mrs. Fox was referring to their father. This daughter had
lost her husband and the others agreed to contribute money so
that the old man could live with her. They all agreed to send
their remittances to Mrs. Fox, so that she could be sure the plan
would be carried out.

So the story started in the mind of W. F. He worked it out
himself. He says:

"We used no script for this picture. The director came to
me every morning and I recited the scenes that he would photograph that day. Many times while the story was in progress,
he insisted that the material he had finished could not possibly
make a motion picture."

When it was finished, it was very sad and sentimental. It
was in ten reels, and nobody liked it as it "preached a sermon."
W. F. determined at least to give it a trial. It so happened that
he had a lease on the Astor Theatre in New York; the lease was
to expire in five days, and the picture that was showing there
was not very good. W. F. decided that since he had to pay for
the theatre anyway, he would put in "Over the Hill" for that
five days and see what happened. He continues:

"The next night this picture went in, and we gave free passes
to fill the theatre. I remember standing in the lobby after the
show, asking this one and that one how they liked the picture.
One of the last persons to come out was a man whom I wouldn't
want to meet on a dark night alone; he had the hardest face
of any man I had ever seen. He was smoking his pipe, and
I asked him for a light. While we smoked, I asked him how
he liked the picture. He spoke with a Scotch accent and said:
'I liked it very much, lad, but it's had a terrible effect on me.
You see, I'm a seaman—I am only fifty, but I have been out to
sea forty out of those fifty years. I ran away from home when
I was a lad and never returned or wrote me mither a line. Ah,
but tomorrow I buy me a ticket to go home to Scotland—I am
going to see me mither again.' I suggested he had better cable
first, because he had been away a long time and his mother might
be dead. He said, 'I will go home to Scotland, and if she be dead,
I am going to kneel at her grave and ask her to forgive me.' "

Says W. F.: "When I realized that this man was so affected that he would travel 3,500 miles to kneel at his mother's grave, I knew I had created a story that would do much good. Men and women by the millions poured into the theatres all over the world and came out thinking about their old parents and whether they were doing their duty. My publicity people communicated with homes for the aged to find out whether there were any old people being reclaimed from these homes; they found that in the eighteen months following the production of "Over the Hill," more than 5,000 old men and women had been taken back to live with their children! When the picture was sent to England, the government revised its regulations, and for the first time permitted a moving picture to be shown in the prisons."

Such is the power of the "movies," and that of the "talkies" is even greater. W. F. had a full realization of this power; and in common with every other producer, he used it to uphold the established social order. The "talkies" will tell all children to be kind to their parents, and all parents to be kind to their children; but they will never tell anyone that there is anything fundamentally wrong with our social system.

I shall have more to say about this later. For the moment we have come to the war time and W. F.'s attitude to that. He tells:

"I left instructions here in California that we must do all things that would help our cause, regardless of profit and gain; that sequences should be written into our pictures that would arouse patriotism . . . We sold Liberty bonds from the stage of every theatre we had, many times much to the annoyance of our patrons, who came there to be entertained, and not to be reminded that there was a war. They came to forget there was a war, which we never allowed them to do."

Also he gave the greater part of his time to the raising of Red Cross funds. He was "captain" of several teams which raised millions, and would have come out ahead of all the other teams with their millionaire captains—except that courtesy required him to permit John D. Rockefeller, Jr.'s team to come out No. 1. There is an interesting story connected with this, which I shall tell later, when we find W. F. having business dealings with young Rockefeller, and not getting a return of his courtesy. Also there was a curious experience with Henry Ford, which I shall save until we come to the Henry Ford part of our story.

All through the war the Fox Film Corporation prospered; it prospered even in the panic year of 1920. It broke all records in that year, and never had a loss so long as its founder was in charge. In 1925 it became a public corporation, and then it purchased the West Coast chain of theatres. Also the Fox Theatres Corporation was established, to take over all the theatres in which William Fox was interested. Ultimately he had 800 as an outlet for his productions, and his profits were growing at a rate which astounded Wall Street.

The radio had come in 1921, and had brought sharp competition to the moving picture business. W. F. first noticed it on rainy nights. "Prior to this, on a rainy night our business would be larger than it would be on a clear night. When the radio came in, I made a careful observation and found that on rainy nights we were doing little or no business." So he began to watch the experiments being tried with talking pictures The first efforts in America were made by means of a synchronization of a moving picture film with a phonograph disc. The film was run through a projection machine, and the disc was played by a phonograph, and the enlarged sound thrown into the theatre. But W. F. insisted from the beginning that this method was hopeless; real success would begin only when the sound track was put on the film with the pictures. He tells the basis of this conviction:

"I went to the Warner Theatre one day, to hear a man sing the introductory number of "Pagliacci." Of course, I went expecting to be thrilled. This was the first person from grand opera who consented to sing for talkies. The picture started, and he was making all the gestures he used on the stage, and the sound I heard was a banjo playing, accompanied by a colored man singing 'I Wish I Was in Dixie.' Of course the operator had put on the wrong record! And later they ran into this difficulty— they had the problem of shipping the reels to the exhibitor, and if one record was broken, no show could be given. When film gets old you must cut out the brittle part; and of course when this was done, the record and the film did not synchronize. At one time I wrote a paper with 101 definite reasons why it was not possible to have the industry adopt records and film and make them synchronize."

W. F. stood out for "sound on film," and tells the very interesting story of how he got it:

"In the winter of 1925 I was in California, and in the spring I returned to New York. The first day I arrived at my office I was greeted by my brother-in-law, Jack Leo, who said he would like to show me something in the projection room. I went to the room, and to my amazement, in this projection room that I had visited for many years and that had always been silent, the machine went into operation, and there was a little canary bird in a cage and it was singing. It sang beautifully from the lowest to the highest note it was possible to sing. It sang for several minutes, and then following that came a Chinaman who had a ukelele and he sang an English song. He sang terribly and played none too well, but to me it was a marvel. At the conclusion of that the lights went up, and they said, 'What do you think of it?' I said it was marvelous. Leo said, 'It is all right if you think it is marvelous, because I have incurred an expense of about $12,000 without your consent while you were away. Upstairs I have built a temporary sound-proof stage and we have been photographing sound-proof pictures. If you didn't like it, I was prepared to pay the $12,000 out of my own pocket.' I said, 'Like it? This is revolutionary!' This bird sang just as though it were in a tree, and I found that the sound had been recorded on film and that it was reproduced by light from the film to the screen. All mechanical sound was eliminated.

"I went up on this temporary stage floor and saw the temporary sound-proof room, where everything had to be done. I said that couldn't be right. If the photographing had to be done in a sound-proof room, then you are going to rob this camera of seeing nature. They said there was only one way to record sound, and that was in sound-proof rooms. I said, 'That can't be so—you must be in error.' But they were sure of their position, and it was necessary to build a perfected sound-proof room. We let a contract to build our first sound-proof stages on 54th Street and Tenth Avenue. The contractors said it would take four months to build this studio.

6

"I called for the inventor, Mr. Case, and said, 'I am going to give you a million dollars, and you can spend this million dollars in the next four months, any way you like, in experimenting how to make this camera photograph on the outside without a sound-proof room.' Shortly thereafter they brought the various things they had photographed outside. One was a rooster crowing and it sounded exactly like a pig squealing. Another was a dog barking which sounded like a cow. They recognized that they didn't have it, because of the confusion of sound. About thirty or forty days later they said, 'Here, this time we have it.' On the screen there came rushing before me a train photographed on the Jersey Central tracks, and I heard the whistles blowing and the wheels turning just as though the train were with me in that room. I said, 'Now you have it.'"

We shall deal later on with the complicated question of the patent rights to "sound on film," and the enormous financial interests involved. For the moment I am dealing with the cultural aspects of W. F.'s activities, and the benefits which the public got from his work. One of these was the Fox Movietone News. For the first time it was possible for the public not merely to see the crowned heads and generals of Europe marching in parades and reviewing their soldiers, but to hear the cheers of the crowds and the playing of the bands. The dwellers in remote cattle and lumber towns of the West could now leap magically over the world, and they came every week for this thrilling ten or fifteen minutes. Sound newsreels became the rage.

Also there was W. F.'s dream of educational, religious, and scientific pictures. He had been making silent pictures for schools, and was proud of them. The American Telephone and Telegraph Company claimed all the patent rights for sound pictures, and W. F. made a tie-up with them, and took Walter S. Gifford, president of the Telephone Company, to see some of his pictures in a school somewhere on the East Side of New York.

"We showed some of our silent educational pictures we had made to a classroom of boys and girls, and Mr. Gifford came and brought his little son with him. Of course, Gifford was delighted with it and thought it was wonderful. I said, 'If you think this is wonderful, wait until you see them when we make them in sound,' and he concurred." We shall hear later of a dispute with the Telephone Company over this issue, and the rights to the making of newsreels and educational pictures. There were mountains of treasure dumped out for those to seize who had the power, and W. F. made the mistake of trying to take his share.

He had been caught napping by the radio, which had taken away his audiences on rainy nights, and in 1928 he saw television on the way, and didn't want to be caught napping again. "I reached a conclusion that the one thing that would make it possible to compete with television was to use a screen ten times larger than the present screen, a camera whose eye could see ten times as much as at present. For example, Roxy's picture screen is eighteen feet wide, and the screen I proposed was about ninety feet. I believed this 'Grandeur' would come closer to the third dimension we hear scientists talking about."

W. F. proceeded to form the Fox Grandeur Corporation, and ordered the making of a 'Grandeur' projecting machine at his own expense. "This was an experiment William Fox was making—it was not an experiment of the Fox companies, because there was a great hazard about it, and I always took the hazards myself."

The other motion picture producers were greatly disturbed by the development of "Fox Grandeur." Zukor, president of Paramount, and Sarnoff, representing RKO, the all-powerful Radio Corporation of America, came to call on W. F. "They said I was about to make a great mistake: the industry had just changed from silent to sound; a great inventory had to be wiped down, and we were just about catching our breath, and here I was trying to upset it again. I was calling it progress, and they called it destruction. They said that enlarging the pictures could be done at another time, when all the companies would agree on a uniform size. Each company was claiming they had a much finer development at that time, and their purpose was to persuade me not to give the premiere performance. I described to them the necessity of it, that we could not see television destroy us. Of course, I was firm in my position, that my duty was to further the motion picture business—I hoped it would hurt no one. I was going to give my premiere, and if the public decided it was no good, that would be the end of it. Shortly thereafter, we gave the premiere of 'Sunny Side Up,' and it was hailed as a great success. I ordered more pictures made."

So here again we see William Fox, the stubborn and egotistical person, making powerful enemies. We shall see him thus making one enemy after another; playing a lone hand, insisting on having his own way, regardless of how much trouble he makes for his competitors, and for the great monopolies of manufacturing and finance. We shall see exactly how they stopped him. For the moment suffice it to say that with his "ousting," the "Grandeur" movement died, and has never been heard of since. A second picture, "The Big Trail," which he had in production, was the last the public ever saw.

And the same thing has happened to the elaborate schemes for the making of sound pictures for churches, schools, scientific institutions and homes. W. F. had this all figured out, and had begun production. He had plans for the making of school and church equipment, at very low prices. He is still cherishing this dream.

REEL SEVEN

THE MIDAS TOUCH

WE come now to the point where we must understand the finances of the Fox companies. I assume that my readers will be of two classes, a small number who are familiar with high finance, and a large number who are not. I write for the latter group, and the few more fortunate ones will have to endure a little boredom.

The Box Office Attractions Film Rental Company, started in 1912, was continually expanding, and in 1915 its assets were taken over by a new concern, the Fox Film Corporation. This was a closed corporation; its shares were never offered for sale. William Fox took one-half the common stock, and his associates in New Jersey took the other half. There was half a million dollars in preferred stock, which was paid off in a couple of years, so we don't have to bother with it. The point is that the men from New Jersey who invested $400,000 in the Fox Film Corporation got their money back in two years, and in the course of the next fourteen years they got $10,000,000 in dividends, and at the end of that period, their stock had a market value of $10,000,000.

W. F.'s arrangement with these associates was that he should select four directors of the corporation and they should select four. It was understood that this arrangement would never be changed. Now comes a curious story:

"Within a month after the company was formed, a man appeared in my office one day. He was a relation of one of the group who had put up the $400,000, and he had in his hand a certificate of stock for ten shares. He wanted to know how much I would give him for it. I asked him where he had gotten it, and he said Mr. Kuser had given it to him. He said Mr. Kuser had allowed him to buy some of the preferred stock and

67

had given him these shares   I said, 'You ought not to offer that to me. These ten shares would give me a majority.' He said he knew it and that was what he wanted. He said that he had had a row with them and he wanted to get even. He said, 'This will upset the thing Kuser has so carefully planned. If you don't buy them, I am going to give them to you.' I didn't want him to give them to me, so I asked him if $1,000 would do. I gave him the thousand dollars, took the certificate, and put it in my vault. From 1915 to 1925, no man in the Jersey contingent ever knew that I had the majority in that company. For the ten years that I had the majority of stock in my vault, at no time did I permit a single resolution to be passed by the board of directors that was not unanimous."

In 1925, the "Jersey contingent" suggested that they would like to have the company listed, so that they could sell the shares on the market if they wanted to; therefore, by agreement, it was recapitalized for a million shares of stock, of which only half a million were issued at the beginning. The administration of W. F. having been satisfactory, the associates were willing that he should keep control, and the million shares were divided into two groups: 900,000 A shares which had no votes, and 100,000 B shares which carried the voting control of the company.

This is a new wrinkle in high finance which has come into fashion in the last ten years. It seems to me to be wholly against public policy, and should be forbidden by law; but many of our biggest corporations have adopted it, and of course W. F. had a right to join the procession. It is amusing to note that his enemies were righteously indignant at the arrangement, and when they finally succeeded in ousting him and taking over his voting shares, they put them into a corporation which was controlled by *three* shares of stock!

The device of voting shares has one purpose—to deprive the people who put up the money of any say as to how their money shall be handled. It means the removal from our industrial system of every trace of democracy and self-government. It makes the corporation an absolute monarchy; and you will find what you may have noticed through all history, that absolutism may work not so badly when you have a benevolent monarch, but trouble begins when you get a bad one. So long as William Fox ran the Fox enterprises, the stockholders made money; but when his enemies took control, the stockholders lost everything. In neither case had they done anything to deserve what they got.

At the outset there were 235,000 shares of A stock issued to the old stockholders, and 165,000 were sold to the bankers at $40 a share, netting the company $6,600,000. The bankers sold these shares to the public for $43. Later on, to make possible the purchase of the West Coast Theatres, the bankers sold to the public new shares, until the total issue was 920,660. All shares paid a dividend of $4 a share per year as long as W. F. was in charge. I will give here a table showing the gross rentals and net earnings of the corporation:

Year	Gross Rentals	Net Earnings
1914	$ 272,401	$.......
1915	3,208,201	523,000
1916	4,244,658	365,000
1917	7,118,172	593,000
1918	7,300,301	270,000
1919	9,380,883	......
1920	12,605,725	1,413,542
1921	13,715,000	1,605,889
1922	12,327,957	2,660,158
1923	11,242,629	1,808,166
1924	9,926,025	2,009,043
1925	11,750,515	2,606,271
1926	14,274,234	3,030,926
1927	17,012,875	3,120,557
1928	22,626,747	5,957,218
1929	30,803,974	9,469,051

Up to 1926, Fox Film owned only two theatres. That year it bought a third interest in West Coast, and the next year it bought the balance of this concern. At this time, the West Coast owned something over 150 theatres. Under the management of W. F., it increased the number to over 500. It obtained another hundred in purchasing a company called the Midwest. It is clear enough that when you are turning out a feature picture every week, it is to your advantage to own theatres in every city and town in order to be sure of getting adequate releases for your product. It is what the Chicago packers tried to do when they started buying up butcher shops for the selling of their product. The Government stopped the packers, but it permitted the moving picture concerns to carry out this same program.

The figures for 1929 were prepared and issued after W. F. was ousted from the company, and it appears that more than $4,000,000 was taken from the 1929 earnings and held over to be reported in the 1930 earnings, so as to save the prestige of the new regime. The real earnings of Fox Film in 1929 were over $13,500,000; and in addition there was a "non-recurring" profit of $8,000,000, to be explained later.

Fox Theatres Corporation was formed to take over the many theatres in which W. F. had investments along with various associates. It became a public corporation with 3,900,000 shares of Class A stock, non-voting, and 100,000 shares of Class B stock, voting. W. F. took the 100,000 shares of voting stock and also 300,000 shares of non-voting stock—this in return for his theatres at their value of $8,800,000, certified to by accountants on the basis of their earnings. The price of the stock was $22 per share, and the bankers took a half million shares at this price and sold them to the public at $25. This netted the company $11,000,000 and made Fox Theatres a $20,000,000 corporation.

Here is a table of the earnings of Fox Theatres during the four years that W. F. was in charge.

1926	$ 454,101
1927	823,659
1928	1,522,079
1929	2,660,261

Get the picture of these two concerns. At the rate at which Wall Street capitalizes its enterprises, Fox Film is worth about $200,000,000, and Fox Theatres is worth about $50,000,000. In the ordinary course of high finance, each of these companies would have issued a vast quantity of bonds and debentures, and the money thus raised would have gone into the pockets of the promoters and financiers—not to mention a handsome rake-off for the bankers, ten or fifteen millions. You will see, when W. F. is ousted, that very thing happening. Bonds and stock to the amount of $103,000,000 are issued, and by various devices of refinancing the bankers get nearly half of this money. Who gets the rest is a mystery of this book; all I can show you is that the amount disappeared in the course of a couple of years.

The fact that W. F. worked day and night for his stockholders and that he paid them their dividends as they were earned—this news spread throughout the United States. It was helped, of course, by the public nature of the Fox business. Everybody saw the Fox Movietone newsreels; everybody went to the Fox theatres. So when William Fox wanted to buy more theatres or chains of theatres, and to make more pictures and newsreels, he had no difficulty in raising the money. The public hastened to take the Fox securities whenever they were put upon the market. In four years Fox was able to raise a total of $135,000,000. There was no preferred stock and no "stale" stock. The companies were owned entirely by their common shareholders and were controlled entirely by the voting shares which William Fox kept in his strong-box. In the case of Fox Theatres there was only one certificate for 100,000 shares of B stock. In the case of Fox Film there was one certificate for a majority of the voting shares. These two pieces of paper were highly precious, being the key of the treasure chest, and whoever owned them was the master of more than a quarter of a billion dollars. Many men dreamed of getting them, and the final battle over their possession is our theme.

W. F. tells how it feels to be the owner of two such pieces of paper:

"When you create a company and own part of its shares, if all shares vote alike, your responsibility is not very much. These shares have a right to elect the board of directors, and if they haven't exerted their rights, it is their own fault. But when you own the voting shares, exactly the opposite is the case. The stockholders have no power, they have no rights—their rights only come on a dishonest act. So the creator acts in a fiduciary capacity; the whole burden rests on his shoulders. That was my life during the time I owned these voting shares. I felt the responsibility keenly, and at no time in the Film company did I ever permit a resolution to be passed without a unanimous vote. The majority of the board would pass on the things that would be submitted to it. Ultimately I passed all the things I wanted, but I did it by persuasion and not by a mere vote.

"That is enough to make a young man old, to control the voting shares; but the man shoulders a double burden when he foolishly lends his name to the corporation. He then has a responsibility that he can never escape; his whole career is wound up in this enterprise. Of course, if he knows the business and likes it, he can enjoy this situation. With me, it was a new adventure every day."

What use does W. F. make of his monarchy? He will make his own statement about that:

"I was the president of the Fox Theatres Corporation and at no time from the time it was created in November, 1925, up to this moment did I ever receive a penny of salary. I was giving my services to Fox Theatres without compensation. I was getting no percentage of the profits. At no time since the creation of Fox Theatres in 1925 until the day I sold out did I ever present that company with a voucher for any personal expenses I had incurred in its behalf. Sometime in 1926 when I realized the corporation had assumed the task of paying $2,000,000 a year in dividends, $4 a share, the earnings were approximately $3,000,000 a year, and I felt that was a close margin between earnings and dividends. Up to this time I was receiving a salary of $200,000 a year from Fox Film and I voluntarily withdrew my name from the payroll. I had no agreement under which I was to receive any percentage of its profits. I was paying for the privilege of being president of these two companies. I had spent of my own funds between 1926 and the day I sold out several hundreds of thousands of dollars, for which I was never reimbursed and for which I never presented a voucher.

"I felt that I was a most unusual president of a corporation. I was receiving dividends on the stocks that I owned on the same basis as any other stockholder. Every other stockholder was receiving his dividends, but was not asked to devote any of his time. No other stockholder was asked to extend any part of his dividends for promoting the companies; no other stockholder was asked to render services to the companies without compensation. Fox was spending his own money and was not asking for the reimbursement of it."

The story has now come to the beginning of 1929. All the way through you will note that W. F. is expanding, taking in new enterprises; always running risks and never learning fear. He thinks he has learned how to make moving pictures which will appeal to the public, and he thinks he knows how to manage theatres and collect the public's money. He thinks he knows this better than other men, and so he expands. At the same time, when his rivals attempt to expand, he blocks them and thwarts their deals. He is somewhat naive, in that he fails to realize how this makes them hate him. He forgets their hatred quickly, because he is busy with new enterprises. But they do not forget, and wait their turn to pay him back.

The greatest mistake he made was that he sometimes failed to pay the bankers the "rake-off" to which they consider themselves entitled. Fox Theatres issued more than 700,000 shares which netted the company an average of $25 per share; and under the rules of the Wall Street game, some one of the big banking houses should have underwritten these shares, and charged about $3 per share for the service, which would have been over $2,000,000. For William Fox to have deprived the bankers of this money and saved it for his stockholders—that was the greatest crime he could have committed in Wall Street, and proved him wholly unfitted to carry on a big financial enterprise. When the time came that his enemies were ready to surround him and block him off, they did not have much trouble in persuading the other banks and investment houses to keep hands off. They could say: "You know this man; he is an interloper, and does not obey the rules; he is setting precedents which would put us out of business It is as much to your interest as to ours that he be punished. So lay off and let us do it."

In the managing of theatres W. F. admitted only one peer to himself, and that was Marcus A. Loew, who was dead. I am sure that he planned to get all the moving picture theatres in the United States under his control sooner or later. He was prepared to pay the price for them. When the others got into trouble, the price became cheaper. I think also that he planned to have the making of moving pictures entirely in his own hands.

He had had the wit to see that recording discs were useless, and that the future lay with sound on film. He had bought the really vital patents covering the photoelectric process. Also he

had conceived the wide screen and made it known to the public as
Fox Grandeur. He had fixed sound newsreels in the public mind
as Fox Movietone. It was the object of his enterprises to build
up a chain of theatres that would cover the forty-eight states of
the Union. Fox Film would acquire theatres from Maine to
Illinois, and West Coast would acquire them from California to
Illinois, and some day the chains would meet. He had started
school pictures, church pictures, scientific pictures. Of course
he considered himself the man to run the industry!

At the session I had with W. F. and his wife, there was an
interesting little drama. It seems that for years she had been
begging him to retire; she had had enough of being married to a
slave, and of having to turn herself into a slave in order to have
a husband. "All this fight was unnecessary," she said; "he had
promised me to retire in a year, and that year was half up."

I looked at W. F., rather puzzled. I remembered all the new
obligations he had assumed during that year, a total of $93,000,-
000; I remembered the new plans he had told me, the new companies he had bought, and his plans for amalgamation; the new
chains of theatres and their redecoration; the Grandeur pictures;
the new and cheaper projection machines and sound equipment,
that would put talking pictures into schools and churches, into
hospitals and orphan asylums, and make them as common in the
home as the radio is today. "Did you really mean to retire in
the year?" I asked. W. F. smiled a sly smile and said, "I meant
to retire as soon as I had got things fixed so that they would run
themselves." Mrs. Fox then told me a story about little Eve Leo
in the days before her marriage. She had befriended an old Irish
woman, and this old woman had made a remark which had
seemed dreadfully cynical to the little Jewish girl: "A woman
can lay her head on the same pillow with a man for fifty years
and never know what is going on inside his head."

William Fox was a man who did not know how to rest, and
who was always undertaking new responsibilities and risks. But
you will note that when he issued new stock and sold it to his
stockholders or to the public, he gave them real value for their
money. When he turned over his own theatres to the public, it
was at a proper price, based on their earnings. When he bought
other chains of theatres, he saw that he got full value, and proved

it by making these theatres earn dividends. He intended it to be that way with his next move.

Marcus A. Loew died, and left behind him Loew's, Incorporated, a holding company owning some two hundred theatres throughout the United States, also a prosperous producing concern, Metro-Goldwyn-Mayer. The widow of Loew had 400,000 shares of stock in the company, which was close to one-third, and practically carried the control. The stock was selling on the market for about $75 a share, but of course a block like this which carried the control was a different matter, and the price for the block was $50,000,000. Warner Brothers wanted these shares, and Zukor of Paramount also became a bidder.

W. F. figured what he could do with Metro-Goldwyn-Mayer if he got it. Here were two rival concerns, Fox and Metro, with duplicate plants, and 130 duplicate marketing agencies, covering nearly every country in the world; through the elimination of this waste, there would be a saving of $17,000,000 a year; in comparison with this, the price of the Loew shares was a small matter. W. F. obtained an option on the shares and set out to raise the money.

Get this layout in mind. A going concern is to be purchased— in the year 1929 Loew's, Inc., was to earn a profit of nearly $12,000,000, and the $50,000,000 purchase which W. F. is making will give him one-third of the future earnings of the company: this in addition to the expected saving of $17,000,000 a year. W. F. knows that his stockholders will welcome this proposition, and when he offers them new stock, they will buy it eagerly.

We have seen W. F. continually borrowing money from bankers. He now wants $50,000,000, which is too much for ordinary bank borrowing, or any form of amateur financing. It is a job for one of the so-called investment banking houses, and W. F has a standing arrangement with a prosperous and powerful concern, Halsey, Stuart & Co ; there is a contract, whereby they agree to do new financing for his companies. They have sold to the public $6,400,000 for a Detroit building, $4,750,000 for a St. Louis building, $4,000,000 debentures for a New England enterprise, $13,000,000 debentures for a chain of theatres acquired in New York, $4,000,000 for a bond issue for studios in California, $1,800,000 bond issue for studios in New York, and a

$2,500,000 debenture bond issue in connection with the Roxy theatre; a total of approximately $36,450,000, for which they received a commission of from 7 to 10 per cent, the total being over $3,000,000.

Now W. F. puts before them a plan for the $50,000,000 cash purchase of the 400,000 Loew shares; he shows them the lay-out, and they approve it, and with their advice he sets out to raise the money. He goes to the American Telephone & Telegraph Company, the great $3,000,000,000 octopus which owns most of the wire communications of the country, and also is manufacturing talking picture equipment, and leasing patent rights, and therefore doing business on a profitable basis with the Fox companies. It so happens that the Telephone Company is in the midst of a protracted quarrel with Warner Brothers over patent rights and licenses. The Telephone Company does not want its enemy to get hold of those Loew shares and increase its power by amalgamation. In order to keep Warner from getting them, it agrees to help Fox get them, and it lends him $15,000,000 for one year. Also it takes him to the Chatham & Phoenix Bank and arranges for that bank to lend him $3,000,000 more. Halsey, Stuart & Co. lend him $10,000,000 for a year, and the Bankers' Securities Company of Philadelphia, of which W. F. is a director, lends him $10,000,000, taking a part of the Loew shares as collateral. The Fox Theatres Corporation raises $16,000,000 by selling new shares, which makes a total of $57,000,000. That will leave a balance of $7,000,000 on hand for emergency.

This purchase of the Loew shares took place on February 24, 1929, after negotiations lasting about six months. The financing was of a temporary nature, and all parties concerned understood clearly that the Fox companies could not pay this money out of earnings, but must either sell new stock, or issue bonds or debentures to cover it. The loans for a year were to close the deal, and allow time to plan the refinancing.

A few days passed, and then Harry Stuart, who had advised and even urged the deal, and had loaned $10,000,000 to make it possible, sent for W. F. and said that he had thought the matter over and changed his mind about it. W. F. tells as follows:

"He said that I had done a terrible thing. He said, 'Here is a company that has 1,350,000 shares of stock; you have 400,000,

which is less than a third. What is to stop them from going into
the market and buying these other shares?' I told him I didn't
think Mrs. Loew would do that, that I had faith in these people.
I paid higher than the market price for them because you could
never buy this number of shares in the market, and we didn't
want a long-drawn-out process of getting these shares. I said,
'What do you want me to do now?' and he said, 'I want you to
go right in the market and buy the number of shares it will take,
so you will have a majority of the total number of shares outstanding.' When I asked what I would buy them with, I was
told that I still had $7,000,000 from the $57,000,000; that the
brokers would carry the stock on a 50 per cent margin, which
would allow me to carry $14,000,000 worth of stock. Our arrange-
ment with the Government was that we would own no more than
400,000 shares of stock. I was told to buy these in individual
names; that I didn't have to buy them in the name of the company. Stuart said, 'For goodness sake, own the majority, or you
will be wiped out here. You can see your danger.'

"Several days later the representative of the Telephone Company called and said, 'You are in a fine spot, aren't you? You
had better hurry and buy these shares before someone else does.'
I followed the advice, and bought 260,900 additional shares in
individual names, some in my name and some in the names of
my children, etc. I stripped the companies of all the cash they
had to make this acquisition, acting entirely on the advice of my
bankers and my friends in the Telephone Company. This all
occurred in the months of May and June. These shares were
acquired between February 24th and June 1st. In the meantime,
the Loew's hadn't bought a share and didn't intend to buy a
share."

So now the total of the obligations of W. F. is seventy millions. He has borrowed a great deal of money from various
banks, and is heavily involved in the stock market. He looks back
on it now and wonders, was that advice given to him by his
financiers honest advice, or were they deliberately leading him
into a trap? What shall we think about it?

Human minds are complicated, and it may be that the heads
of Halsey, Stuart & Co. and of the Telephone Company would
not themselves be able to say exactly when the dream of taking

over the "pot of gold" of William Fox first took shape in their minds, and just when and how that dream became changed into a determination. The time when Stuart advised the stock market purchases was a time when everybody in America was buying everything, in the certainty that no matter how high the price, it would go still higher. I do not know whether foxes ever run in packs, but I have read about wolves, and have learned that a wolf is not attacked so long as he is well and strong, and is running at the head of the pack. It is only when something happens to him, so that he stumbles and falls, that the other wolves fall upon him and "merge" him.

And so it was with this Fox, according to my guess. He didn't need much stimulating to lead him to buy. He had behind him those two tremendous companies with no indebtedness, and earnings of sixteen or twenty million dollars a year. Seventy million dollars of new financing didn't weigh on his mind in the least; he knew that he could offer a million new shares of Fox Film to the stockholders and they would pay $80 a share for them gladly. If any were left over, the great firm of Halsey, Stuart & Company would dispose of them to the general public. W. F. was so sure of himself, and of his great companies, and of his great bankers, that he was even willing to take one more bite.

In that spring of 1929, there came to America a man named Isador Ostrer, the principal stockholder of a concern known as the British Gaumont Company, motion picture distributors and owners of some 300 theatres in England, including the best. Owing to hard times in England this chain was for sale, and here again was a proposition of enormous importance to the Fox companies. The Fox pictures were being continuously released in Great Britain, and at a great disadvantage. The managing heads of the Gaumont concern were unfriendly to the Fox interests, and were paying the Fox companies less than $500,000 per year. But if this purchase was made, then Gaumont would run Fox pictures, and this would add about $5,000,000 a year to the income of Fox Film. The purchase price of the shares offered, an actual majority of the outstanding shares, was $20,000,000, and the Fox companies would be repaid this investment in less than five years—without taking into account the dividends earned by the British company during the period.

W. F. consulted Halsey, Stuart & Co. on this matter. Harry L. Stuart, head of the firm, was in London at the time, and W. F. had Stuart's New York office cable, and thus obtained a complete check on Ostrer and his enterprises. Before the purchase was negotiated, Stuart returned to New York, and W. F. declares that the matter was thoroughly discussed with him. Stuart arranged for various London banks to lend the Fox companies $8,000,000 towards the purchase.

Also this deal was discussed with John E. Otterson, who represented the Telephone Company. Otterson knew Ostrer well, having met him in London on a recent trip. Otterson had been trying to sell to Ostrer sound equipment for his 300 British theatres; he had failed, and so he didn't like Ostrer very much; he said that Ostrer "thought himself the czar of everything he surveyed." But if Fox would buy these 300 theatres, he would put in the Telephone Company's equipment, which at that time was costing $25,000 a set; 300 times that would be a nice little bill of $7,500,000 for the Telephone Company. More than that, the other 3,000 theatres in Great Britain would have to follow suit, and there would be a still nicer bill.

W. F. pointed out to Otterson that he already owed him $15,000,000, and had not yet made his merger, and he was timid about going forward. But Otterson said that was all right, the Telephone Company was behind him; if necessary, the note for $15,000,000 would be renewed. When W. F. hinted that he ought to have that in writing, Otterson was offended, and asked if he did not trust his friends.

So W. F. bought the Gaumont theatres, paying $14,000,000 in cash, and giving notes for six million, due in six months. Immediately the Telephone Company got its contract to install sound equipment in these theatres, and so everybody was happy. W. F. was going to make his Loew shares pay for themselves in four years, and his Gaumont shares in less time. The Fox picture business would become the greatest in the world, and that was the way W. F. wanted it.

7

REEL EIGHT

RED TAPE

WE HAVE followed through these various purchases, in order to make a consecutive story. But we must now go back to the days before the Loew purchase, in order to become familiar with another aspect of this deal.

One of the major problems confronting an American big business man who wants to incorporate some new company into his own, is the problem of coming to an arrangement with the Attorney-General's office of the United States Government. We have a law called the Sherman Anti-trust Act, a statute which has been revised and edited and rewritten by innumerable court decisions until it has become a labyrinth to which the justices of our United States Supreme Court themselves do not possess a key. We have seen that the Government has graciously permitted the moving picture makers to do the very thing which it sternly forbade the Chicago meat packers to do—that is to own and operate their means of retail distribution.

The use of this comparison brings me a letter of protest from W. F. He does not like to be compared with the "beef trust," and explains in detail the reasons which compelled him to begin buying chains of theatres. There had been formed what was practically a motion picture trust, through the alliance of the Loew family with that of Zukor, president of Paramount. These two big concerns had an understanding between them. They would run each other's pictures in their chains of theatres, but they would not run the pictures of any outsider. It made no difference how good the Fox pictures might be, the exhibitors decided that they were not worthy of exhibition. If they used Fox pictures at all, they would use them in third or fourth grade houses, and then only when the joint products of Loew and Paramount were insufficient in number to fill these houses. So of course it became necessary for Fox to get his own theatres, and when he had purchased the West Coast, and controlled everything in eleven states, then and then only was he able to make a satisfactory deal with Loew and Paramount. Says W. F.:

"I would not like to have myself presented to the public as one who hoped to stifle the middleman and destroy him for the benefit of the Fox Film stockholders; for the independent exhibitor throughout all of the United States, as well as throughout the rest of the world, knows that William Fox stood for the independence of the independent exhibitor, and fought the exhibitor's battles, beginning with the breaking of the trust in 1912. The independent exhibitors of the United States and other countries of the world recognize William Fox as their friend and not as their enemy."

I admit all that. I hope that no one will get the idea that my comparison means that I am comparing the product of the picture studios with that of the packing-houses. I am merely pointing out what seems to me an obvious fact: that in one case the Government forbade a certain group of manufacturers to own the means of retail distribution of their product, while in the case of another group of manufacturers it permitted this to happen. W. F.'s own argument concedes this, for he tells how Loew and Paramount combined to freeze him out of the means of retail distribution which they controlled. I am sure that back in the days of the fight upon the "beef trust," if you had questioned the Armours as to why they considered it necessay to set up butcher shops all over the United States, they would have answered that it was because the butcher shops owned by Swift and Morris sold only the meat products of Swift and Morris and refused to deal in the meat products of Armours.

The fact that one maker of motion pictures, William Fox, favored the independents and protected them, has nothing to do with the legal point I am making—although, of course, it is very important to this story, and I am glad to bring it out.

If you are a manufacturer of either meat or motion pictures, and desire to purchase a rival concern, what you have to do is to go and call upon the Attorney-General's office. In normal times you will find that it is a question of what friends you have, and what enemies. In abnormal times you are at the mercy of political thunderstorms. If, for example, Theodore Roosevelt is President, and is posing as the people's friend, then the Attorney-General's office will start out on a "trust-busting" campaign, and the only way you can make a merger is first to precipitate a panic, as the elder Morgan did in 1907, thus forcing from Roosevelt permission to take the Tennessee Coal & Iron Company into the steel trust. On the other hand, if the president is an easy-going boon companion, like Harding, you can do about anything you please.

The Government had made no objection to the purchase of the West Coast and other chains of theatres, because each of these was in a different locality, and no competitors were involved. But the Loew Company owned theatres in the same cities with Fox, and the Fox production unit was of course a direct competitor of Metro-Goldwyn-Mayer. So there was a chance of trouble.

During the negotiations for the Loew purchase W. F. was caught between two administrations. Hoover had been elected early in November, but Coolidge was still president until March. What was going to be the policy of the new administration was something which a great many people were anxiously trying to find out.

W. F. went to Washington to consult the Department of Justice, and was told that the person he had to talk with was Col. William J. Donovan, known to the newspapers as "Wild Bill." Colonel Donovan was Assistant United States Attorney-General, and just then, in the middle of January, 1929, was chairman of the Boulder Dam project; so W. F. went out to Santa Fe, New Mexico, and explained matters to him. Donovan said that he had his hands full with the Boulder Dam project, but that if W. F. would dictate a statement to Donovan's secretary, Donovan would send a copy of it to his assistant in Washington, Mr. Thompson, who would sit down with W. F.'s lawyer and find a way to work things out.

So W. F. dictated a statement, telling the Government that great economies were required in the motion picture business and must be made immediately.

"From our records it was clear that of the gross money we

were receiving for the pictures we made and released, at least 40 per cent came from other countries. By this time, Fox Film had a rental agency in every country in the civilized and non-civilized world other than Russia, and it had come into my mind, what was going to occur when an English-speaking picture was going to Czechoslovakia or to Hungary or to Roumania or China or Japan, from which countries we were receiving substantial revenues? It was clear we could not make talking pictures in every language, and I could see no reason why these obscure countries would change their language to suit the American producer. I reached a conclusion that it would be necessary to reorganize our entire business so as to meet this new condition. A survey had been made of the situation during 1928, and when the figures were compiled, there was a clear indication that the Loew Company and the Fox Company were wasting by duplication of their work a minimum of $17,000,000. Here was a saving that would be greater than the loss in revenue. Fox Film and Metro-Goldwyn-Mayer were running two sets of executives, two sets of studios were competing for the purchase of stories, for the price of the performer and director, and when pictures were completed, they would rent them to the exhibitors, and had some two hundred offices throughout the world in which was carried on the rival business.

"I explained to the Government that I felt there was a responsibility to retain for our country the well-earned position that it had in the making and distributing of motion pictures throughout the world. I felt that if the picture companies were deprived of a great part of their foreign revenue, they might get to a place where they could not carry on. I hoped to be able soon to make foreign language pictures, to hold our business abroad. I tried to bring these Government officials to realize that American trade follows American pictures, and not the American flag; that the Government's duty was to try to retain the supremacy of picture making in this country; that even if this consolidation did not entirely conform to laws on our books, that if a condition of this kind arose, it was their duty to help to retain this industry for America."

W. F. is a business executive, accustomed to making up his mind quickly and then acting. But now he was making acquaintance with the ways of bureaucracy. Copies of his statement were sent to the Government officials and the lawyers, and W. F. went to Los Angeles, so as to be near Donovan in Santa Fe. Time passed, and each day he called his lawyers in New York to find out what had been done, and nothing had been done. He waited in Los Angeles for thirty days and then he went back to New York. There his lawyer informed him that only half an hour ago Thompson, the department official, had consented to the acquisition of the 400,000 shares, and that the lawyer's advice now was to make the acquisition. Saul E. Rogers, the lawyer, said that he hadn't asked for consent in writing, because such consent would have been one of their stock letters with a lot of "ifs" and "ors" in it, and he would be better off without that. "I would rather have his word than a written communication, because there are no strings attached to his word." At this time it was generally understood that Donovan was to be Hoover's Attorney-General, and so everything was all right.

It was a close shave, because Mr. Schenck, the president of Loew's, was becoming impatient. When W. F. had gone to see Donovan, he had told Schenck that he would be back within eight days. Schenck's reason for impatience was that Warner Brothers had been pressing him. The Warners apparently considered that they could pull other political wires than Fox, and would be allowed to do what he wouldn't be allowed to do. Anyway, they had made an offer of $56,000,000, which would have made $6,000,000 more in Schenck's own pocket. Says W. F.:

"The Loew family had commissioned Schenck to sell these shares, and had given him an option for their acquisition at somewhere around $100 a share, and in the deal with me he was earning somewhere around $10,000,000, over and above the price he had to pay to the Loew family. If he could have carried out his Warner deal, he could have made $6,000,000 more. I carried on these negotiations for some six months and had not been pressed, but one Sunday Schenck became very impatient, and I asked him to allow me until Tuesday, and if I didn't have the money then, it was all off. On Monday I went to the Telephone Company and Halsey, Stuart, and made arrangements for the purchase."

That was on February 24th, and on March 4th, Hoover was inaugurated, and very soon his cabinet was announced, and the Attorney-General was no "Wild Bill," but a tame gentleman named Mitchell. W. F. was uneasy, and sent his lawyers to this new Attorney-General, who told them that the matter would not be handled by Mitchell, but by his assistant, who had not yet been appointed. The appointment was made in June, and it was a gentleman named John Lord O'Brian. Very soon W. F. and his lawyer went to interview this gentleman, and there were present in the room four persons, William Fox, Saul E. Rogers, John Lord O'Brian, and that Mr. Thompson who had told Rogers that it was all right to acquire the shares.

"Mr. Rogers said that we had come to visit Mr. O'Brian for the purpose of discussing the consolidation of the Fox Company and Loew's; that we had acquired 400,000 shares of stock with the consent of the department, and we would now like to discuss the method to employ for its consolidation. Mr. O'Brian, after examining the papers said, 'I see nothing in this record that indicates that we have ever consented to your acquiring these 400,000 shares; in fact, as I read this record, I find the opposite, we warned you against it.' I spoke up then and said, 'Mr. O'Brian, we don't have to refer to the records. You and I are fortunate to have in this room the very two men who reached this agreement. Mr. Rogers and Mr. Thompson met in New York, and after a long drawn-out conference for a period of thirty days, in which they discussed whether the department had any objections, Mr. Thompson told him that the department consented to the acquisition of these shares, or that the department had no objection, and based on that word, three days later I passed a check of $50,000,000 to the Loew family.' I then turned to Mr. Thompson and said, 'Won't you please talk up? Is it or is it not a fact that you came to New York and told Mr. Rogers that it was all right to purchase these shares?' He said he would rather answer that question when his chief put it to him. I then turned to Mr. O'Brian and asked him to ask Thompson that question, and O'Brian said he would ask it at another time. With that he rose, and there was nothing else left for us to do but rise and leave.

"Shortly thereafter two investigators appeared in New York

and wanted to know the complete details of the acquisition of these shares. They wanted to know the exact number of shares we owned, was it 400,000 or was it more. They wanted to know where the money came from and many other questions. I then sought the advice of some friends who knew the workings of the Government, and informed them that these men had been in New York and were making an investigation; that I felt I was being annoyed unnecessarily, and I believe we then received a letter from the Department of Justice asking us to divest ourselves of these shares."

It was necessary to use some influence, and W. F. considered that he had it. He sought an appointment with the President, and was invited to luncheon at the White House. Before we tell about this interview, it will be necessary to step back a few months and see just what had been the relationship between William Fox and Herbert Hoover. The former is an ardent admirer of the latter, and considers that Hoover did a great deal to help him. To me, having heard the whole story, it appears that Hoover exhibited his customary indecision and ineffectiveness, and that what he gave W. F. was the customary political "hand-out" of palaver and promises. In short, I think W. F. was one of many thousands of victims of the White House meal ticket system. Having received one of these meal tickets myself, way back in the "Teddy" Roosevelt days, I know how impressive they are. However, here is the story, exactly as W. F. tells it, and you can judge for yourself.

An intimate friend of W. F.'s was Albert M. Greenfield, chairman of the Bankers' Securities Corporation of Philadelphia. W. F. was a director in his friend's company, and also a debtor to the company to the extent of $10,000,000, part of the purchase money of the Loew shares. Greenfield was an active politician, and had done his best to obtain the seating of Vare, who had been elected to the United States Senate, but had been refused his seat on account of charges of election frauds. W. F. had worked with Greenfield for more than a year in the effort to seat Vare, but in vain. In the summer of 1928, prior to the Republican nominating convention at Kansas City, Greenfield had come to W. F. with a story that Mellon was going to try to nominate Coolidge at that convention, and that if Mellon succeeded in this, Vare would be kept out of his seat, because Mellon was his enemy and Coolidge was Mellon's man. Greenfield had met Hoover many times and liked him, thought he would make a great President—and also thought that he would help to seat Vare.

So W. F. and Greenfield discussed how they could bring about Hoover's nomination at Kansas City. Ever since the signing of the Declaration of Independence, the delegates of Pennsylvania had always voted as a unit, but now Greenfield thought there might be a split. He had learned that Mellon wasn't coming to Kansas City until Monday morning, and he had a plan to "dish" him.

"He proposed selling Vare the idea to let the Philadelphia Republicans vote independently of the rest, and to announce on Sunday night, the night before the convention, that for the first time in the history of Republican politics the Pennsylvania delegation had split; Philadelphia was for Herbert Hoover. He actually did that. His announcement caused the greatest excitement at the Kansas City convention, and Greenfield felt that as a result of that Herbert Hoover was nominated."

Soon after Hoover's nomination, but before his election, Greenfield took W. F. to Washington, and introduced him to Hoover. W. F. pointed to Greenfield and said: "You can blame that little bald-headed Hebrew Jew who made it possible for you to become the President of the United States." W. F. reports that "Hoover naturally was vitally interested to learn the details of how this came about."

W. F. told Hoover of his great admiration for him, and of his desire to see him elected president. In talking to me, W. F. explained his reasons in detail, and I listened with no little interest. Ever since "The Brass Check" and "The Goose-step" were published, my critics have been saying that I attributed to the masters of finance in America too high an intelligence and too clear an understanding of their own interests. According to my critics, these masters of finance just blunder along, controlling politics and education and movies and radio in their own interest, without really knowing that they are doing it, or why or how they are doing it. I am sure that William Fox in any dealings he has had with politics and politicians, has known exactly what he was doing, and why he was doing it. I am glad that he is willing to tell about it frankly.

"I told Greenfield that I was an admirer of Mr. Hoover, and that I was desirous of working for his election, and that my companies could be instrumental in his election; that the Fox Film Corporation made and released in the theatres of America the Fox Movietone News, and that I would be happy to devote it in behalf of Herbert Hoover; that the Fox Movietone News had 10,000,000 theatre patrons, and I considered it a very strong force, and a great ally for any political party to have."

And at the talk with Hoover, W. F. repeated the same thing to him:

"I told him of my admiration for him and of my willingness to work for his election. I told him frankly of my using Movietone News in behalf of his nomination, and that for the election campaign I would be glad to take the most efficient executive I had, and put him in charge of all the picture work that Mr. Hoover would like to have. Mr. Hoover replied that my offer was the most generous one that he had as yet received during his campaign, and that he appreciated it."

So W. F. spent great sums of money, and gave a great deal of time to Hoover's cause. He tells me that it was with no definite idea of asking anything in return. But suddenly he found himself in need of a return, and he was invited to luncheon with the President.

"After we had adjourned to his smoking room, I frankly told him of my great embarrassment. He listened to it attentively; he was vitally interested. The reasons for his interest were apparent—I had claimed that an injustice had been done to me by the Department of Justice. Before I had left, he had requested that my attorney, the attorney for my company, the one who had made this arrangement with the department, go back to the department some time later and have another talk. I suggested that perhaps I ought to engage some outstanding outside counsel, but he resented that. I was to incur no expense; my lawyer could do the whole thing and do it very well; in fact, that is the way he wanted it done."

So W. F. thought that he was all right. But alas for those who put their trust in princes! W. F.'s lawyer went to see the department officials again and again, but somehow or other nothing happened. "Unfortunately, I felt my lawyer was not making the progress that he should have."

W. F. was "on the spot," as the phrase has it, and, of course, it was known among his friends and associates, and also among his enemies, that he was occupying this uncomfortable position. Somebody more powerful than Herbert Hoover would have to be enlisted in his behalf—or at any rate, someone more direct and decisive.

Colonel Huston, treasurer of the Republican National Committee, came to W. F. and inquired whether he knew a man by the name of Louis B. Mayer. W. F. answered that he did, and presently he realized that he was getting a tip. Said Colonel Huston: "He seems to be a nice sort of chap. Why don't you call him up some time? Why don't you ask him to come to see you?"

So W. F. did call him on the telephone, this in the latter part of June, and four days later Louis B. Mayer came to see him. For the benefit of the uninitiated, I explain that Mayer is president of Metro-Goldwyn-Mayer; also a very prominent and active worker in the Republican party, being chairman of the California State Committee of the party, and a popular orator at conventions and banquets.

Mayer occupied just then a peculiar relationship to W. F., in that W. F. was about to merge him. You understand that Metro-Goldwyn-Mayer is owned by Loew's, Inc., and W. F. has purchased the control of both companies, and is contemplating taking over Mayer's elaborate and expensive plant in Hollywood, and his hundred or so distribution centers throughout the world, and making them all a part of the Fox system. Naturally, Mayer has not been oblivious or indifferent to such an effort. Back in February, when the news had spread that Fox had bought Loew, W. F. was asked for a conference by Mayer, Rubin and Thalberg. Says W. F.:

"These three gentlemen are the owners of a company which had leased their services to the Metro-Goldwyn-Mayer Company. They were employed there under a contract that had still two years to run. Under the terms of that contract, after $2 a share is paid on the common stock, these three gentlemen get 20 per cent of the earnings. I think under that contract in 1929 they collected about $3,000,000. They were, of course, alarmed at the acquisition of this stock. They had two years more to go and they would be materially affected by it. When they sent for me, I thought their purpose was to discuss whether or not their contract would be continued.

"They told me they had been improperly treated. Here they claimed to have built this company up and made it the great success it was, and now when $50,000,000 was paid for 400,000 shares of stock, they were not asked to contribute their stock in that sale. They were entitled to part of that $50,000,000. Schenck, having played so fair with me from the beginning, since he had a chance to sell these shares for $6,000,000 more than I ultimately paid for them, I felt I should refute any charge of unfairness on his part.

"I took the attitude that Schenck was fair. I took the position that these men had no grievance. They had an unusual contract, and I had definitely in mind the purpose to make a new deal, more advantageous for both companies. We had several conferences, and in all of them I sided with Schenck. I did, in my conversation, discover that none of them owned any stock. What they would have liked to do was to buy some of these shares on the market, and sell them for more than twice as much as they bought them for. I told them that they hadn't expressed any faith in their company, by the mere fact that they had not seen fit to invest any of their money in the stock of that company. They said they had owned some at one time, but had been advised by Schenck to sell it. As a result, I incurred their animosity in these conferences."

Now "Louis B.," as he is familiarly known in the studios, comes for another conference with the man who is planning to merge him. Says W. F.:

"It was my job now to make him my friend if I could. While no one had told me that he had anything to do with my difficulties with the Attorney-General, I surmised he had. I had reached a conclusion that perhaps Mayer, Thalberg and Rubin should have gotten some of the money in the Loew deal, although that was none of my business. Mayer, after the usual greetings, started the discussion, expressing his displeasure at the whole transaction; how hard he had worked to build up this company; that it was his great effort, and not Schenck's. He was offended at the position I took immediately after the purchase, my attacking his contract; that he was going to use every means in his power to prevent this consolidation, legally and otherwise. I said that was his privilege, if he felt his interests would be affected. But I told him that if he couldn't stop this thing legally, what was the use of doing it illegally. And finally, as he became cooled down, I said, 'I didn't ask you to come here to hear this talk. You must have realized that I had a plan in the back of my mind. I have reconsidered this transaction, and I have reached the conclusion that you have not been treated properly. I asked myself: supposing Schenck had asked $52,000,000 for these 400,000 shares—$50,000,000 was entirely an arbitrary price. There was no such value, and the only reason it had the value was because of the consolidation, and because $17,000,000 could be saved in the consolidation of these companies.'

"So I said to Mayer: 'If we can merge these two companies, I am willing to recommend to our company to pay you and your associates $2,000,000, just as though we originally paid $52,000,000. We will pay you $2,000,000, if and when this consolidation is made. We will at that time discuss with you a new contract on an entirely different basis from the present one.' He said he recognized that the contract would have to be changed, and that they were ready to change it on any fair proposal I was going to make. He said, 'You are a strange man. When I first came here this morning and threatened you, you looked me square in the eye and said, 'You can take any remedy you like and be damned.' You were as positive of your position, and I got nowhere. To me it looked as if I had made the trip in vain. Now you are making me your friend. You inform me that you are about to present me with $2,000,000; you tell me that you didn't buy the studio, but that you bought this company because of my ability. That is a compliment. You make the stipulation you will give me this $2,000,000 if and when these companies merge. You must have known that I have moved heaven and earth to prevent this consolidation. Surely you felt that someone used his influence to have the Government change its opinion with reference to the acquisition of these shares. I was responsible for that, and it was a perfectly easy matter. But now you have given me a difficult task. How am I going to get them to change their opinion back again? However, that is my task, and I think I can do it.' That concluded our talk, both parting as the best of friends."

Apparently Louis B. Mayer was able to do in the Attorney-General's office what Herbert Hoover wasn't able to do; for nothing more was heard about the order to William Fox to divest himself of the Loew shares. Instead, Colonel Huston now told him that everything was all right; only one thing was needed. There had existed some kind of contract between Loew's and Paramount, and also there had been a sort of royal alliance between the two houses. Marcus A. Loew had a son, and the president of Paramount had a daughter, and these two had been married. The Department of Justice did not require that this marriage should be abrogated, but they did want the business contract abrogated, because it would look as if Fox were absorbing not merely Loew's but also Paramount. W. F. had learned that the Warners also were anxious to have this arrangement cancelled, because they wanted to absorb Paramount, and couldn't do it so long as Paramount was tied up with Loew.

W. F. made a date to play golf with Schenck, the president of Loew's, at the Lakeview Country Club, on the morning of Wednesday, July 17, 1929. I should have told you before this that W. F. is an ardent golf enthusiast, and frequently makes his business deals on the golf course. You may be puzzled to understand how a man can play golf when he cannot lift his left arm above his shoulder; you may find it hard to believe that W. F. does his golf playing with his right arm alone. Not only does he do this, but he manages to beat most of his two-armed rivals, and proves his faith in himself by betting his money on the outcome. He told me a hair-raising story about betting $1 at the first hole, $2 at the second hole, $4 at the third, $8 at the fourth, and so on up. You can figure out according to the laws of geometrical progression what this sum amounted to at the eighteenth hole. But fortunately it all ended happily, W. F. won his money back, and so I do not have to record that any of his business difficulties were due to losses on the golf course. In the New York newspapers I read that he is credited with having three times achieved the feat of a "hole in one"—a truly amazing thing for a one-armed player.

He was never more sure of himself in his life than on that July morning as he was rolling on his way to the golf course. "While my car was riding to Long Neck, I was dreaming of the perfect conclusion. Life had just begun, and this was to be the greatest stepping-stone of my career. At fifty-one, I was to be the head of the largest company of its kind in the world."

But we know what Robert Burns says about the best laid schemes of mice and foxes. The chauffeur who was driving this Fox had lost his way, and they found themselves on an untraveled and obscure road with no cars in sight. They had reached a crossing, going slowly, perhaps twenty miles an hour, uncertain which way to turn. There was a hill which hid from their view someone coming from the left. As they made the crossing, a car came down the hill at a high rate of speed, driven by an inexperienced woman driver. The car of William Fox was almost across; in another foot it would have been safe. But that extra foot made the difference between success and failure for the dreams of W. F. There was a crash, and his car began turning in the air, and the next thing he knew he and a friend who was with him were crawling out from underneath the car.

The first thing W. F. saw was his chauffeur, dead. The car had fallen on his neck and broken it. Blood was streaming all over W. F. from his own head. He staggered to his feet, half dazed, and here is his own description of what he did: first, he kicked his right leg, and said to himself, "That isn't broken." Then he kicked his left leg, and said, "That is all right. I can still walk." Then there was only one thing to be determined. He made a swing with his right arm, and found that it worked, and he said to himself, "O. K. I will still be able to play golf!"

REEL NINE

THE VULTURES

WILLIAM FOX was carried to the hospital and had the gash in the top of his head sewed up. He had lost about one-third of the blood in his body, and had to have transfusions. After ten days he was taken to his country home at Woodmere, on Long Island Sound, and there he stayed for three months, recovering his strength.

And while he is recovering, let us make ourselves familiar with some of the complications of this story which have so far been passed over. It seemed wise to give first the main outlines; but if you are to understand everything that follows, you have to be introduced in turn to a number of persons who play parts in the drama. Some of them are friends of the Fox, some of them are his enemies, and some are persons who pretend to be friends, but prove themselves to be enemies. We shall have to go back again and again, and see how each of these persons came into the life of our subject.

Let us take first the great investment firm of Halsey, Stuart & Co., of Chicago and New York. Harold Leonard Stuart, head of this firm, was a power in the financial affairs of Chicago, having handled most of the business of the Insull light and power interests; I am assured that during the past ten years this firm has marketed not less than $5,000,000,000 worth of securities to the American public. Stuart is the gentleman of whom we have learned that he invariably wears a carnation in his buttonhole when he attends the directors' meetings of corporations. He dresses to match this carnation; always perfectly groomed and impeccable, clean shaven and almost snow white. When he is entertaining a customer whose bonds he expects to handle, he is the incarnation of goodness. If, after thinking the matter over, he should decide not to handle the bonds, he can act next day,

94

without the slightest difficulty, the part of the meanest man on earth. He has a younger brother, Charlie, and both of them are bachelors. When there is a disagreeable message to be delivered from the firm, it is always Harry who does it, since Charlie does not know how to deliver such messages.

This firm took up the handling of the Fox financing. W. F. relied upon them completely, because he himself is not a financial man, nor did any of his directors have these qualifications; they were executives, whose business it was to make moving pictures and market them.

Afterwards, when the disagreement occurred, the firm of Halsey, Stuart & Co. issued to the stockholders of the Fox companies, March 24, 1930, an open letter, in the course of which a statement was made, "Up to this date (autumn of 1928) this firm had furnished financing to the Fox companies in the aggregate amount of $23,150,000, with little profit on these transactions." Of course, the phrase "little profit" is one about which there can be dispute. All I can do is to tell you how much profit they made, and let you judge for yourself whether it is "little" or enough. The bonds sold were all first mortgage bonds, issued to cover the purchase or building of theatres, and they were all overwhelmingly secured. The bonds were sold over the course of a little more than two years, and of the total price of $23,150,-000, Halsey, Stuart & Co. kept $3,396,500.

This "little" being insufficient, Halsey, Stuart made a demand upon W. F. that he allow them an additional profit of $1,000,000 upon these transactions. They made this demand in a peculiar way—they asked W. F. to write them a letter, and they themselves drafted this letter. It was really additional commission on the last sale, of $13,000,000 worth of bonds, but they asked to have it granted, not as a commisison on these bonds, but for financial advice in previous transactions. The reason was that if the million were a commission on the last sale of bonds, it would have to be divided among a syndicate which had participated in this sale; but by having the million given for previous "financial advice," Halsey, Stuart & Co. were able to keep the entire million for themselves. W. F. assented to this arrangement, and signed the letter as requested.

Then came the purchase of the Loew shares. For this deal

8

Halsey, Stuart loaned $12,000,000, and charged a discount of 2½ per cent, plus interest of 6 per cent, so that the money was supplied at the cost of 8½ per cent for one year. In their statement to the Fox stockholders, they stated that this was really a $10,000,000 loan, and that the $2,000,000 was to retire "some other obligations of the company." This statement gives a fair idea of their frankness. What had happened was that they had purchased in the open market some of those same bonds of the Fox companies which they had sold to the public, and they now demanded that W. F. borrow $2,000,000 from them at 8½ per cent per year, and use the $2,000,000 to take back these bonds! The other $10,000,000 loan was covered by one year gold notes which they sold to the public.

Even so, W. F. thought that the genial and bluff Harry Stuart was his friend. They played golf together, and in the course of this golfing, W. F. made suggestions as to how Stuart might make more money, and these suggestions Stuart was glad to accept. W. F. called his attention to the fact that all the other bankers were creating investment trusts, and thus adding enormously to their resources. Why shouldn't Halsey, Stuart do that? W. F. urged this at several conferences, and finally Stuart followed this advice, and created an investment trust, and its capital grew to $75,000,000. When I add that it is now worth approximately $1,000,000, you can realize how the face of the world has altered in four years!

Including all the theatres he had built and the chains and companies he had bought, W. F. had obtained in the investment market something over $135,000,000 in four years. He says:

"There wasn't the slightest difficulty in borrowing this money —the credit of the company was of the highest class. Bankers were eager and seeking the privilege of underwriting or loaning money to either or both of these companies. There was a ready market for all of the securities offered, and each time the offer was oversubscribed. Again and again Halsey, Stuart would issue booklets, pamphlets, circulars and letters in which they would describe these great Fox enterprises. Again and again in their literature from time to time they would advise the purchase of these securities, and tell of the ability of William Fox; all of this they did after an exhaustive and careful investigation

of both these companies, as well as of myself. Several times
during our negotiations they would make private loans to the
companies, of sums ranging from $400,000 to several million
dollars, as a result of their belief in these companies and their
confidence in me."

An idea occurred to me while listening to this recital. I
noticed that all the other Jewish picture men dealt with bankers
of their own race. Warner Bros. had Goldman, Sachs, Paramount had Kuhn, Loeb, and Universal had S. W. Straus—all
good Hebrew names. Only William Fox ventured to deal with
haughty Anglo-Saxons such as the Stuarts, and Hayden, Stone
& Co. and the Telephone Company, represented by Walter S.
Gifford, and by John E. Otterson, late of the United States Navy.
Soon we shall see him trying to deal with Elisha Walker of
Bancamerica-Blair, and even with the great Albert H. Wiggin
of the Chase National Bank—and making matters worse by
adding an "s" to the name of the great Mr. Wiggin, which, I am
told, is the most direct and immediate way to incur that gentleman's direct and immediate hostility. I have carbon copies of
some letters which W. F. wrote to "Mr. Wiggins," asking for
help, and I could have told him the answers to those letters before
he sent them.

I asked W. F. what he thought about the possibility of an
anti-Semitic factor in his troubles. He said it might have been;
Mrs. Fox was quite sure that it had been, and Benjamin Reass
said he had heard talk about it. Very certainly we can be sure
that it played a part when W. F. appealed for help to Henry Ford.

Oddly enough, W. F. still cherishes a weakness for the genial
and bluff Harry Stuart. It seems hard for him to go on believing
evil of anyone with whom he has played golf. He thinks that
Stuart was led to plot his downfall by the more powerful Telephone Company, and he cherishes a remark which some mutual
friend brought him—Stuart said to this friend that if he had
known how matters were going to turn out, he would never have
helped to oust Fox.

For my part, I do not play golf, and feel no affection for
investment bankers who helped to unload upon the American
public the enormous pyramid of water and wind known as the
Insull securities. It so happens that I have another check-up on

Halsey, Stuart & Co.; I find them in the Congressional Record, Vol. 74, No 58, recording the proceedings of the United States Senate for Saturday, February 21, 1931. It appears that a Senate committee had been investigating stock swindling in the District of Columbia, and proposed a "blue sky" law to put a stop to the evils. Senator Blaine of Wisconsin reported to the Senate the result of an investigation of the Wardman Company, a concern which dealt in real estate, and had issued 6½ per cent gold debentures and had them put upon the market by Halsey, Stuart & Co. These bonds had turned out to be worthless, and Senator Blaine stated:

"Halsey, Stuart & Co. knew at the time they were financing this new arrangement that the Wardman properties had not been paying carrying charges. They knew that that organization was bound to fail. They could not help but know it. Yet they made representations to the public that these bonds and securities were gilt-edge, the very finest character of investment."

It appears that Halsey, Stuart & Co. had quoted an "independent engineer" as valuing the properties at more than $31,000,000. They had put $24,000,000 worth of liability against the properties, and it turned out that their true value was $17,-147,000, and Halsey, Stuart admitted that the Wardman bonds "have practically no market value at all at this time." Said Senator Blaine: "We enact laws to punish the man who jimmies the safe. We punish men for highway robbery. We punish men for forgery, and they must submit to imprisonment. Yet in the field of investment, we let the perpetrators of fraud go scot-free."

Also he said: "Halsey, Stuart & Co. cannot complain at the disclosure of these facts. Halsey, Stuart & Co. were apprised that the subcommittee would hold a hearing on a certain day at a certain time, at which they would be afforded every opportunity to appear and present their side of the matter. They failed to appear, and upon the record in this case that one investment company alone stands convicted as one of the greatest vultures in the investment field."

That seems to me to cover the case; but I cannot resist the impulse to add one item more. It seems that Halsey, Stuart & Co. has a radio hour over the coast-to-coast network of the National Broadcasting Company and associated stations. They have a famous radio person known as the "Old Counsellor," who tells the widows and orphans to buy the securities put out by them. For their program for February 11, 1931, they had as "guest speaker" none other than Martin J. Insull, president of the Middle West Utilities Company. Subsequently Halsey, Stuart & Co. printed this masterpiece of eloquence in pamphlet form, and a copy was sent to every United States Senator. The title of the address was "The Power Trust," and the purport of it was, of course, that there was no such thing. The people who had bought from Halsey, Stuart & Co. securities costing $5,000,000,-000 and had seen them drop to less than one billion, listened gratefully to Mr. Insull's wisdom, and were glad to know that everything was perfect in America.

So now we know the immaculate financial gentleman from Chicago who comes to directors' meetings with a carnation in his buttonhole. Next we have to know one of his associates, another great Chicago financier, Harley L. Clarke, president of the Utilities Power & Light Corporation, and of so many other utility corporations that it would be a bore to list them. Clarke plays a vital part in this story, and now is the time to make his acquaintance.

He had come to W. F.'s office a couple of years back, bringing a letter of introduction from Harry Stuart. It was a cordial letter, saying that Stuart would be grateful for any favors shown to Clarke. W. F. listened, and learned that by accident Clarke had taken on a side line which concerned the motion picture business; he had got mixed up in the International Projector Company, and had merged a lot of companies together, and now was making 85 per cent of all projection machines used in America. He had just created a company called the National Theatres Supplies, and as the Fox enterprises were his customers, he wished to get more of their business.

A day or two later, Stuart sent for W. F. Said he: "I am sorry you saw Clarke before I got to you. You know, we both live in the same city, and when he asked me for this letter of introduction I couldn't say no I want you to watch yourself in your dealings with him—don't trust him further than you can see. He will make every kind of promise and do nothing, so watch your step." Says W. F.: "I explained to Stuart that all

Clarke had talked about was selling our enterprises materials, and that we were now buying those materials, and was there any reason why he didn't want me to serve him in that respect? Stuart said that was all right, but if he knew that bird, he would want more than that before long."

It turned out as Stuart had said—the "bird" wanted very much more. Presently W. F. was engaged in making an experimental projection machine for the wide screen, and then Clarke wanted to go in on this enterprise. Said he: "I am in a rather peculiar way. Our business is building projection machines, and if you are going to turn the style from normal size to grandeur size, we are out of business. I see the great possibilities—I would like to do this jointly with you. We have done a lot of experimenting of our own on a wide projection machine. We have invested considerable money." That resulted in the forming of a corporation known as the Grandeur Company, Clarke's company owning 50 per cent and Fox owning the other 50 per cent.

W. F. had decided that he wanted to make his own projection machines, and he bought the Mitchell Camera Co. of Los Angeles. This concern was now taken into the Grandeur Company, and there was organized the General Theatres Equipment Company, with W. F. taking 25,000 shares of stock for the capital he had invested in Mitchell and Grandeur. So now he was on intimate terms with Harley L. Clarke, and at the same time wondering why a public utilities magnate should be fooling with pictures.

Soon after W. F.'s accident, Clarke came to his home with a new proposition. He wanted to buy W. F.'s voting shares in Fox Film and Fox Theatres. At any rate he wanted to buy a half interest in them. Says W. F.: "I said I was not desirous of selling a half interest in them. I asked him of what interest they could be to him. He said: 'I have a vision beyond yours—I believe that this is a time I could buy out the Paramount Company and others, and I would like to merge them all together.' I said he couldn't do that, because I was having trouble merging two of them now. He said perhaps he had a way without my knowing it, because in his employ there were sons of two of the U. S. Senators. Of course I was not interested in the proposal he was making. He said that that was wholly insignificant, what he really wanted to say was that he wanted to be of service to me from time to time. 'Any time you find yourself in a jam at all don't you be afraid to come to me and I will be glad to loan you money.' "

So now you see, W. F. has many powerful friends. He has the Telephone Company, which has loaned him $15,000,000 and caused a bank to lend him $3,000,000 more. He has the powerful Harry L. Stuart, head of the second or third largest investment banking house in America, preparing a plan for the refinancing of all his $93,000,000 worth of loans. And now here is the great Mr. Clarke, partner with W. F. in a big enterprise, and offering to help him out if at any time he gets into a jam.

Of course, all these powerful persons want something in return. The Telephone Company wants some patents which W. F. owns, and about which you are next to be told. Harley L. Clarke wants W. F.'s voting shares, because he has a dream of merging all the picture companies, and taking the place of William Fox. What Harry Stuart wants is not yet clear, but no doubt he will reveal it when he presents his plan for the $93,000,-000 worth of new financing.

REEL TEN

THE OCTOPUS

THERE is one more of the powerful friends of William Fox
to be told about; one of the mightiest powers in our business affairs, the American Telephone & Telegraph Company, or
"A. T. & T." It has at this time about $3,000,000,000 worth of
resources, and $370,000,000 of surplus, which it can use in an
infinite variety of ways to "rig" the market and bring profit to
itself and its officials. You may be puzzled as to just what a
telephone company would be doing in the moving picture business, and why it should be setting out to destroy a moving picture
producer. If you ask that, you will be showing yourself unfamiliar with the internal anatomy of the American Octopus, which
has a powerful digestion, and can assimilate the most diverse
kinds of food.

William Fox strenuously insists that public service corporations, occupying a special position and enjoying special privileges
from the Government, should not be permitted to enter into other
businesses and to compete with private individuals. He points
out that the Telephone Company is permitted by law to come onto
your property and claim rights-of-way. It can set up telephone
poles in front of your home, and string its lines across your
property. More than that, it is in a position where it can, if it
wishes, listen in on your private conversation and learn your
business secrets. He claims that it does frequently wish to.

The Telephone Company manufactures its own instruments
and rents them to you at an enormously high profit. For this
purpose, it has a subsidiary, 98 per cent owned, called the Western
Electric Company; and when talking pictures came into the market, the Western Electric Company began manufacturing talking
picture equipment for theatres. That seemed logical, since the
process is an electrical one, and since the sound reproducing appa-

ratus is a kind of telephone. Since the Fox companies owned many theatres, and were among the pioneers in equipping these theatres with sound apparatus, it came about that W. F. was a highly valued customer of this Telephone Company's subsidiary. Since he was friendly and agreeable about giving up some of his rights when he was ordered to do so, he was favored by the Telephone Company in many ways. Since Warner Brothers, on the contrary, were stubborn in standing up for their rights, there was bitter enmity between the Warners and the Telephone Company, and a dispute was and still is in arbitration.

There was a tangle of patent rights for the "talkies," and a vast amount of research to be done to improve the process. Accordingly there was established a concern called Electrical Research Products, Inc., a wholly owned subsidiary of the Western Electric Company. The president of this concern is John E. Otterson, and it was with him that W. F. dealt in all the negotiations concerning patent rights. Since W. F. owned some patents which the Telephone Company had failed to obtain and later desperately needed, John E. Otterson was extremely obliging to W. F., and when there was a question whether the Warner interests or the Fox interests should purchase the Loew shares, the Telephone Company assisted Fox.

This matter carries us back to the question of "sound on disc" or "sound on film." Some talking pictures with the device of the phonograph disc had been shown in the United States as early as 1905, but as they depended upon the tin horn, of course they were terrible. But then came the "orthophonic" method, and the Telephone Company was convinced that they had real talking pictures by this method, and in 1926 and 1927 their representatives were visiting all the motion picture producers and heads of theatre chains, seeking to convince them that talking pictures were here, and that sound on disc was the proper method.

The Warners took up the project and staked their future upon it. At that time their 550,000 shares of stock were worth only $8 a share in the market and they were running continuously in the red. At the instance of the Telephone Company they created a concern called "Vitaphone," and Warner Brothers presented the first "Vitaphone" pictures, and they raised new capital and went in for this process on a large scale. The trouble was that the equipment to show these pictures was very expensive, about $20,000 per theatre, and there were only about 100 theatres equipped for the process. The Telephone Company had a wonderful vision of what would happen if the 20,000 theatres of the United States could be persuaded to install their $20,000 equipment. Since the profits were enormous, it would have added $100,000,000 or $200,000,000 to the surplus of the Octopus.

Up to that time the motion picture industry had invested the sum of $1,100,000,000 in silent pictures. Most of this value had already been written off, but there was still estimated to be something like $100,000,000 of value left in the existing stock of negatives. If talking pictures really won out, the public would no longer pay to see silent pictures, and that remaining $100,000,000 worth of film would become so much junk. Everybody was in a panic, and everybody had to decide all at once. The producers who were turning out silent pictures faced the prospect of having them become junk before they were finished. But, on the other hand, if they installed new sound stages and made "talkies," where would they find theatres equipped to show these talkies? And suppose, after the work was done, they should find that they had used the wrong process?

The Fox companies were standing out for sound on film, and refusing to have anything to do with discs. When the representatives of the Telephone Company came to W. F., he told them his one hundred and one reasons why sound on disc was wrong. He told them that he was experimenting with sound on film; and since they claimed to own all the patents, they were naturally interested.

W. F. had bought the Case patents, as we have seen, and also he had bought the patents for a German process called the "Tri-Ergon"; but he wasn't sure just how valid these patents were—nobody could be sure, because it was a new field, and there were tangled claims. The Radio Corporation of America, another great octopus, also claimed to own everything. Radio and Telephone made a deal, dividing the field 50 per cent between them. While they stood together against all comers, what chance did a little fellow like W. F. have? He decided to play safe, and keep on friendly terms with this mighty combination.

So the Fox companies made a deal with the Telephone Company, whereby the latter got the benefit of six million dollars which Fox had spent in investigating and perfecting the process of sound on film. The Fox companies were to be licensed to make moving pictures for theatres on the same terms as all the other producers, but Fox was to receive the exclusive right to make sound newsreels. The Fox Movietone News was developing to enormous proportions, and all through these complicated negotiations, W. F. was told that his reward for developing sound on film and turning it over to the Telephone Company was to be that he was to have the exclusive newsreel license.

Also it was provided in the agreement that the Fox companies were to receive an exclusive license for five years to develop sound pictures for the educational, industrial, religious and scientific fields. W. F. was holding onto that dream of putting sound apparatus into every church, and having all the congregations of America listen to the twelve most "inspirational" preachers. He was going to put a sound apparatus in every classroom in America, and have the children listen to a few best teachers. Now the Telephone Company graciously condescended to say that he might have a chance for five years to develop these rights. They told him this again and again in the presence of his lawyers and others. As W. F. tells the story, they said: "There will be no other licenses. That promise we are going to carry out. When you are ready to exercise that right, we will give you the proper papers." But W. F. adds, "Although we asked for those papers every time we saw representatives of the Telephone Company, we never got those papers."

The Telephone Company sent their best experts to the laboratories of William Fox, and got everything that he had got out of $6,000,000 worth of experiments. All those Case inventions that we have read about, the canary bird singing and the Chinaman playing the ukelele, they got all that. They assured him most solemnly that the Case patents and the Tri-Ergon patents were utterly worthless, but still they had to admit that the Case people and the Fox people had really made sound on film, and the Telephone people now learned to make the apparatus for Fox, and for the Fox theatres and all the other theatres of the world. They had given a license to the Warners, whereby the

Warners could have this same apparatus, and they now proceeded to give licenses for the same apparatus to all the other picture concerns; in return they promised Fox the non-theatrical field, and also promised him the exclusive newsreel field.

But sound newsreels were in enormous demand, and the other companies wanted to make them, and presently they were making them, and W. F. learned that they had licenses from the Telephone Company.

"I was then told that the Telephone Company had reconsidered the promises made to the Fox companies, and found that they couldn't be carried out, because it wouldn't be proper for the Telephone Company to show preference; but that they would in the near future find a way of compensating the Fox companies for the time, effort, money and energy that was expended. Of course, it is clear that that was not the reason they were going to violate the promises to us. The reason was because the other producers were able to receive a license from the Radio Company, which had the identical system as the Telephone Company, and had a half interest in these patents; so that when the Telephone Company began competing for these producers to become their licensees, they had to give them that which the Radio Company was willing to give them. It is clear, therefore, that their promises were to be broken, not because they wanted their licensees to be on an equal basis, but because they found their competition with the Radio Company compelled them to do so. The only way they could have carried out their promises to the Fox Company was to buy back from the Radio Company the 50 per cent of their rights."

W. F. was going ahead making pictures of surgical operations to be used in medical schools, and he was making educational pictures to be used in the public schools. But he saw that he was going to lose these exclusive rights also—because the Radio Company would give what the Telephone Company didn't give. Here was a pretty tangle of interests, and a series of lawsuits which would have kept several firms of Wall Street attorneys "on velvet" for the next ten years.

But it happened that this was the time, February, 1929, when W. F. had to give his final decision to Schenck; that Tuesday when he had to plank down a certified check for $50,000,000 for the Loew shares, or else see them go to the Warners. He had been to the Telephone Company about it, and a deal had been argued back and forth, and the Telephone Company had offered to lend $15,000,000 for a year, provided that W. F. would agree to write a letter, finally waiving any and all claims that the Fox companies had against the Telephone Company against any promises made from the beginning of the negotiations up to the time of the loan. W. F. had to choose between a ten-year lawsuit, and the chance to take over the Loew theatres and Metro-Goldwyn-Mayer.

There was another claim which the Telephone Company wanted waived. They proposed that W. F. should surrender to them the Tri-Ergon patents, letting them reimburse him for the amount he had invested in these patents. They insisted that the patents were no good, but still they wanted them. W. F. replied that these patents were his property as an individual, he had no desire to surrender them, and if that was a condition of the loan, he didn't want the loan. If the Telephone Company wanted the Tri-Ergon patents, let them make a cash offer to W. F.

I must now tell about these patents, which have turned out to be the biggest prize of all. At the beginning, nobody realized their value, not even their owner. They were just a gamble, a chance that he had taken. But month by month and year by year their importance began to grow, and the Telephone Company began to bid, $5,000,000 cash in April of 1929, and in July a "feeler" that indicated $10,000,000 or more.

The first attempts at sound on film were made with the selenium cell, and this did not work. The successful process was the photoelectric cell, and the first persons to use that cell in the reproduction of sound were three Germans named Engl, Vogt and Massolle. They took out their patent in Germany, March 3, 1919, and made their application in the United States on April 4, 1921. Under the so-called Nolan act, their title to their patent takes date from the day of the filing in Germany. In the year 1919 the inventors of this Tri-Ergon process gave private demonstrations in Germany, and in September of 1922 they gave in Berlin the first public demonstration in the world of the use of the photoelectric cell in the making of talking motion pictures. They brought their invention to the United States, and William

Fox bought the North American rights for $60,000, and established the American Tri-Ergon Company, himself owning 90 per cent of the stock

The United States Patent Office refused to issue the patent for the photoelectric cell. Our patent laws and practices have many peculiarities. A great corporation like the Telephone Company can claim all the patents in a certain field, and denounce everybody else as a "bootlegger," and tie these persons up in a tangle of lawsuits and injunctions, and go ahead and levy tribute upon a whole industry to the extent of tens and hundreds of millions of dollars. Then, after ten years or so of litigation, it will turn out that the great corporation never had any basis for its claims; but meanwhile the little fellows will be ruined, and perhaps dead and buried.

The American Tri-Ergon Corporation brought proceedings against the Commissioner of Patents to compel him to issue the patent. It was not until December 9, 1931, that this suit was finally decided by the Supreme Court of the District of Columbia. The decision of Justice Adkins appears to be about as sweeping as the English language makes possible. After taking a whole year to study the case, the judge denies all the other claims, and states without qualification that the plaintiffs were the first to demonstrate the photoelectric cell in the process of sound reproduction. He says: "The claims here at issue are directed to a meritorious and novel invention which cannot be properly rejected on any of defendant's citations, or any combination thereof; the claims are patentable, and on the record before this court a patent thereon should be granted."

Still W. F. has not got his patent. It seems that the bureaucrats take their own time in obeying the courts. There is still some investigating to be done. And meanwhile, the Radio Corporation has played a new trick. It has managed to find another man who had some patent on file, and it has paid him $10,000 for an option, and again has tied matters up. That is what shrewd lawyers are for; and there is a big stake in this case, some $6,000,000 or $8,000,000 a year which Radio and Telephone between them are taking from the American picture industry, upon the basis of claims which are now evidently baseless.

I asked W. F. to tell me something about John Edward

Otterson, who had been arguing and fighting with him over this patent tangle for several years. I found that W. F. did not admire Mr. Otterson very ardently. He spoke of him as a "flag lieutenant," and said that he had learned his manners while bossing a gang of stokers. I asked if W. F. had made sure that bossing stokers was among the duties of a flag lieutenant, and our discussion dissolved in laughter.

As a matter of fact, Otterson was graduated from Annapolis and took a degree at Massachusetts Tech. He was in the navy for fifteen years, retiring as naval constructor with the rank of lieutenant. He was president of the Winchester Arms Company and the Simmons Hardware Company, and is now president of the Western Electric Company of Argentine, of Brazil, of Cuba, of Mexico, of Switzerland, of the Near East—all kinds of impressive posts, you see. But in spite of it all, W. F. insists that he is very dumb, and that the stockholders of the Telephone Company would be ill pleased with him if they knew how many hundreds of millions of dollars his dumbness has cost them.

Otterson's portrait, which I have before me, shows a long nose and a high forehead, a typically Anglo-Saxon face; and it may be that W. F. has anti-Gentile prejudices. He reports ex-Lieutenant Otterson as a heavy-set, powerful man with a big chin and jaw and sharp piercing eyes. "When he shakes your hand, you can feel the muscular development throughout the entire arm, and he makes sure to grasp you so that you do feel his muscular development. He never allows you to forget that he is speaking for the great and mighty Telephone Company. He is not a man who uses either tact or diplomacy; he does all things by brute force. He will give you his promise and word of honor again and again, and without the wink of an eyelash deny that he ever said so. He is as cold as ice, and feels that because he represents the Telephone Company he is privileged to break his word at will."

You see, W. F. had the task of trying to persuade the powerful John Otterson that there really was a great future for talking pictures. Otterson wouldn't believe it, and especially wouldn't believe in sound on film; when sound on film came, as a result of the labors of W. F., and in spite of the opposition of Otterson, then Otterson had to come to W. F.'s laboratories and get what W. F. had, and make him all sorts of promises, and then repudiate the promises.

Also he had to do the same with Warner Brothers. This concern had pioneered in sound on disc, and established the Vitaphone Company for that purpose, and Otterson had made an agreement with them whereby Vitaphone was to charge all moving picture companies 8 per cent of their gross royalties on sound pictures; Vitaphone was to get three-eighths of that amount, and Otterson was to get five-eighths. But when Radio began to compete with Telephone in granting these licenses, Otterson was in the same predicament with Vitaphone that he had been in with Fox.

One of the large losses that the stockholders sustained through the "dumbness" of Otterson was when W. F. got him the chance to buy the Warners outright, and he wouldn't take it. This was at the beginning of the talking picture development, when the stock of Warners stood at $8 a share or less. W. F. was asked to negotiate, and was authorized to offer the Warners $4,500,000 for the entire company, lock, stock and barrel. The Warners were to pay $3,000,000 of this for notes outstanding, and the balance would be divided among the four brothers.

The Warners made a counter-proposition: they would take $6,500,000, which would give each of the brothers nearly $1,000,000 apiece. But if they had only a million and a half to divide among the four, they would consider themselves broke, and they might as well go on. Of course, the purpose of the Telephone Company in these negotiations was to buy back the contract outstanding with Vitaphone; but their estimate of the future of the "talkies" was so low that they threw away a chance to buy Warners for $6,500,000—and two years later the common stock of Warners was selling in the open market for upwards of $240,000,000, plus $50,000,000 for the bonds and preferred shares!

But ex-Lieutenant Otterson's masterpiece of "dumbness" was in relation to the Tri-Ergon patents. W. F. had bought the North American rights to these patents, and he had an option on the rights for the rest of the world for $40,000. Again and again W. F. sought to impress upon Otterson the importance of these patents. In the year 1928 he wanted Otterson to buy the rights for the rest of the world, and what he succeeded in bringing about was, not that Otterson bought these rights, but that he forbade Fox to buy them! Says W. F.: "Because the man who was authorized by the Telephone Company to speak on this subject had a brain which was not equal to grasping this picture, the Telephone Company has lost hundreds of millions of dollars. They have already spent a million or more in litigation abroad, as a result of not owning the Tri-Ergon patents in Europe, and as a result of it they have lost the entire European field."

I expressed amazement at this story. I couldn't understand the Telephone Company forbidding Fox to take up an option which they didn't want themselves. I couldn't understand what right they could have to forbid an American citizen to make a purchase if he chose to. But W. F. explained that he was just a poor little fellow trying to keep going in the presence of the great Octopus, which could have swallowed him in two or three bites. Said the Otterson-Octopus, addressing the Fox: "We don't want you to exercise this option. It is of no value to you or to anybody. It is no good. You have made a bad investment here. If you exercise this option, we shall consider it an act of unfriendliness, because you don't intend to become either a licensor or manufacturer of equipment; that is not your function."

W. F. explained to me what had been his point of view at the time: that maybe the Tri-Ergon patents were no good, and if so, he had to have a license to produce talking pictures, and if he quarreled with Otterson, Otterson might deny him a license. It appears that the owner of a patent is not a common carrier, or anything of that sort; he can sell or he can refuse to sell at his sovereign pleasure. I suggested that W. F. might have exercised his option on the world rights of Tri-Ergon through a third party, without letting the Telephone Company know about it. The somewhat proud answer was as follows:

"William Fox has made a habit all his life in his business career, which was always a fearless one, to do everything in the open. His practice has been during his entire business career that once he stated he would not do that thing, then a thought to do it through a subterfuge or through someone else never entered his mind. It was possible for me to have a substitute in my place exercise that option, but that would not be playing

9

the game fairly, and I decided to play fair with the Telephone Company, as I felt they intended to play fair with me. I found out that I played it fairly and they didn't."

I am sorry to reveal myself as a person of low ethical standards, but I will say how it seems to me. W. F. was being made the victim of an act of tyranny and intimidation, and if he had quietly brought it about that his brother-in-law, Jack Leo, or his other brother-in-law, Joseph Leo, had quietly secured that piece of paper, and put it away in a safe and retired place, he would have done nothing of which he needed to be ashamed.

In the year 1929 Otterson was forced to change his opinion about the Tri-Ergon patents. In April he came to W. F and offered $5,000,000 for them; W. F. said he would take $25,000,-000, but Jack Leo insisted that these patents might prove to be vital to the conduct of the Fox business, and certainly the rights should not be sold without giving the Fox companies an opportunity to buy them. Shortly afterwards the United States Patent Office reached the conclusion that one of the Tri-Ergon patents was valid—the so-called "fly-wheel," essential to the operation of sound reproduction machines. Naturally W. F. wondered whether advance information had come to the Telephone Company as to the expected action of the patent office.

Here you see W. F.: at the end of February borrowing $15,000,000 from the Telephone Company, and in April refusing to sell them patents which are necessary to their control of his business. Another three months pass, and he is lying in his home prostrated after a serious automobile accident, when Otterson calls him on the telephone and asks for an appointment. Otterson comes and explains that he is going abroad for the purpose of trying to pacify producers and theatre owners, and to make an arrangement whereby European producers of pictures can bring their products to America and American producers can show their pictures abroad.

W. F. says that he doesn't think Otterson can arrange that, because the Tri-Ergon patents have been declared valid abroad, and will soon be declared valid in America, and no one will be able to use the photoelectric process in America without a license from Fox. This greatly disturbs the powerful Otterson, and he says he is obliged to use strong language. In February his company loaned W. F. $15,000,000, and promised that if W. F. was not able to pay it when it became due, they would extend the loan. More than that, they took him to a bank and arranged for a further loan of $3,000,000. And how is Fox repaying them? How is he acting since the time of the loan? W. F. reports the conversation:

"I said I didn't think I had done anything, and wanted to know in what way I had acted incorrectly. He said, 'You know darn well that had I been in America while you were borrowing this money, I wouldn't have allowed it, unless you let us buy the Tri-Ergon patents' I told him that if that had been a condition of the loan, I wouldn't have borrowed the money, and Loew's would have gone to Warners. I told him they hadn't loaned me the money because they wanted to help Fox Film, but because they wanted a general release of all the previous claims we had, for the work on which we had spent $6,000,000. If they had kept on violating the promises made to me, the value of the claims we had against the company were well over $15,000,000.

"'Putting all this aside,' he said, 'what I came to quarrel about is that you, William Fox, have dared to send a written communication to the Telephone Company, telling them that they were infringing the Tri-Ergon patents.' I told him there was no such letter according to my knowledge. He assured me that they had gotten such a letter. I told him that if they were violating the patents, then we certainly ought to claim it; but if they had gotten a letter, it was without my knowledge and consent. I called up my attorneys and inquired about such a letter, and they informed me that one had been sent. Then Otterson said, 'All right. Let us try to dispose of this whole matter. How much do you want for these Tri-Ergon patents?' I asked him to make an offer. He said I had quoted him a price before, but I told him that price was off, there was a new price for it today. After much discussion I made an offer of $25,000,000, which price was rejected, and he went abroad without acquiring the Tri-Ergon rights."

As a result, Otterson failed in his mission abroad. And you can imagine how much love he bore in his heart for the stubborn Fox, and how much of a desire to help him he brought back from Europe!

REEL ELEVEN

REAPING THE WHIRLWIND

IN telling of his battle, W. F. names three factors which brought about his defeat, and claims that all three were beyond his power to control. First, he thought he had obtained the consent of the Government to the merger of Fox and Loew, and he had no means of knowing that the Government would change its mind. Second, he had no means of knowing that an unlicensed woman driver was going to hit the rear end of his car and lay him up for three most critical months. And, finally, along with the rest of the American people, he did not know that a panic was going to prostrate the financial world at the end of October, 1929.

The first time that W. F. came to the city after his accident was on Thursday, October 24th. He came to attend a banquet given in honor of his friend, Col. Claudius H. Huston, newly appointed treasurer of the National Committee of the Republican party. This was a distinguished and exclusive affair. The Republican party, the instrument whereby big capital governs America, was here presenting its collector of funds to the men from whom the funds were to be collected. To lend formal sanction to the occasion, there came several members of the Cabinet and several of the party chiefs from the Senate and House. A list of the New York guests included the heads of every large financial group: the Rockefellers, the Morgans, the Chase Bank, the National City Bank, the Equitable Trust, and all those investment banking houses whose acquaintance we are making in this book: Kuhn, Loeb, and Goldman, Sachs, and Hayden, Stone, and Dillon, Read, and Halsey, Stuart. The august nature of the occasion may be understood from the fact that the newspapers listed those present, but were ordered not to report the speeches, and obeyed the order. This was a time when the Masters of America were

going to consult among themselves. Having been honored with
an invitation, W. F. attended, doctor or no doctor, and accounts
it a divine interposition; for if he had not attended that dinner,
he would have been a ruined man a week later.

There were a number of orators, among them James Francis
Burke, Pittsburgh lawyer, whom we shall meet later on; he was
general counsel for the Republican National Committee, and, as
W. F. reports it, "If 2 per cent of the things he said about Colonel
Huston that night were a fact, Huston was one of the outstanding men of the nation." W. F. thinks that he was, and
thinks it too bad that he became involved in a political scandal
and had his career destroyed.

But the event of the evening for W. F. was the speech made
by Secretary of Commerce Lamont. It was the most important
speech W. F. ever listened to, and after the first ten minutes
he turned to a friend and asked who the gentleman was. Said
W. F.: "That man is either the most damn' fool man I ever
listened to, or the most intelligent man I ever listened to. Which
is it?" The friend said he didn't know, but would inquire of
some of the others after the address. The others, it appeared,
were of the opinion that Lamont was a brilliant man.

What he said to the bankers of America was that the country
was in a very grave condition. "He went on to tell these men
that no nation could continue when its citizens refused to buy
bonds; that all great nations were built on the public's willingness to buy bonds, and that unless a great market could be
created for bonds, and this speculation in common stock were
terminated, the nation was threatened. He drew a picture so
black that I trembled at the thought of what would occur the
next day when these hundred bankers would reach their offices,
and when the bell would ring at 10 o'clock in Wall Street. No
one could have listened to him that night without wanting to sell
every share of stock he owned the next morning "

I can quite understand the gratitude of W F. to Secretary
Lamont for giving him that stock market tip at a critical moment.
No doubt all the bankers were grateful to him; but this is one
more case where I have to differ from my subject as to the
abilities of the political leaders of our nation. If Secretary
Lamont had made that speech to the bankers in October of 1928,

I would have considered him something of an economist and a far-seeing statesman. I would have thought it to a lesser degree if he had made the speech, say, on October 15th of 1929. But he made it on the evening of October 24th; and consulting headlines in the New York "Times" I find as follows: October 17, "Acute Weakness"; October 20, "Wave of Selling Engulfs Market"; October 22, "Continuation of Selling Wave"; October 24, "Paper Loss, Four Billion"; and while Secretary Lamont was making his speech, the headline writers of the New York "Times" were describing the events of that day in a four-column head on the front page as follows:

WORST STOCK CRASH STEMMED BY BANKS

12,894,650 Share Day Swamps Market

Really it seemed to me that it required something less than genius for a Secretary of Commerce to be able to tell the bankers of the country that their affairs were in serious danger on that night! Also I am amused to note that while the New York "Times" was suppressing the speech of Secretary Lamont (intended only for the bankers), there was being handed out to the general public the regular official "taffy," a diet of which we have since become so sick. On October 22d the front page headlines told, "Washington Holds that Situation is Sound." On Friday the 25th, the same issue which suppressed Lamont's speech, the headlines read, "Call Break 'Technical.'" On the 26th, the headlines said, "Officials Optimistic," and on October 30th, after two days of frightful panic, the public was fed on what you might call bi-partisan taffy. "Dr. Julius Klein Declares Business is Sound"—that is the assistant Secretary of Commerce, speaking for the Republicans. "Time to Buy Stocks, Says Raskob"—and Raskob is the proprietor of the Democratic party.

But let us return to the adventures of W. F. He says: "I had with thirteen brokers approximately $20,000,000 worth of stocks of corporations other than those that I controlled, and I promptly proceeded to sell them commencing Friday morning, October 25th. By Monday afternoon I had disposed of these $20,000,000 worth of stocks, as a result of what Lamont had said on Thursday night. When the bell rang in the New York Stock

Exchange on Tuesday, those $20,000,000 worth of stock were not worth $6,000,000, and had I not acted on my impulse as a result of what Lamont had said, not only would my companies have been embarrassed, but I would have been a bankrupt."

It is a curious thing to go back over the newspapers of those panic days, which now seem so far away and so naive. People were appalled, because stocks had lost $14,000,000,000 of their paper value in five hours. To give you a glimpse of events, I have taken the quotations of October 15th before the beginning of the slump, and again on November 9th, after it was supposed to be over, and everybody was getting ready for a new wave of prosperity. Fox Film had dropped from 101 to 71; Fox Theatres from $25\frac{7}{8}$ to $15\frac{1}{8}$; Loew's had dropped from $64\frac{1}{4}$ to $49\frac{5}{8}$, and American Telephone and Telegraph from $300\frac{3}{4}$ to 229. And they thought that was a panic! Not even the genius of Secretary Lamont could look forward to the end of May, 1932, when I am writing this book, and when Fox Film stands at $1\frac{1}{8}$, Fox Theatres at $\frac{1}{4}$, Loew's at 16, and American Telephone & Telegraph at $91\frac{3}{4}$.

You may remember that·W. F. had 660,900 shares of Loew stock, for which he had paid more than $73,000,000, and in the worst of the panic of Monday and Tuesday those shares lost more than half their value. Two-thirds of them were in the hands of bankers, as collateral for loans which had been incurred in their purchase; the remaining one-third was in the hands of brokers, having been purchased on margin in the name of W. F. and his relatives. The only thing that made it possible to hold onto these shares was for W. F. to sell his other stocks, and use the money as margin on the Loew shares which he was trying to hold for his companies. W. F. assures me explicitly, "I had not sold a single share of Loew's, Fox Film or Fox Theatres." Throughout all the storms and conflicts which follow, you may picture him clutching to his bosom those 660,900 shares of Loew stock which he had purchased for his companies, and the happy ending to our story is this one sentence: "I was able to hold onto the 660,900 shares of Loew stock, and I am happy to say that ultimately the Fox Theatres sold these shares for $75,000,000."

Of course when W. F. tells us that on Friday and Saturday, after hearing Lamont's speech, he got rid of $20,000,000 worth of stocks, and that all the other big bankers who had been present at that dinner followed his example, what he is really telling us is that he and the other bankers brought on the panic of Monday and Tuesday. But such is the world we live in. Its law is each for himself, and my corporation against all the other corporations. As W. F. explains it, the value of the Loew shares was constantly falling, and the money he was getting from his brokers for the sale of other shares was continually being demanded as margin on the Loew shares.

On Tuesday morning, W. F. was out at his country place, in the boathouse which fronts over the water; he was living on the first floor and his friend, Rubenstein, who had been a victim of the automobile accident with him, was living on the second. The telephone rang a few minutes after ten, and it was a call from one of W. F.'s brokers, saying that the Loew shares were still declining, and that W. F. must send him immediately a check for $250,000. He says: "I had no more than put the receiver on the hook when another broker called, and within twenty minutes the number of brokers that called for additional margins—when I totaled the sum it was more than $1,500,000. I called my office and asked them to make out these checks and have them ready for delivery. I had no sooner hung up the phone when the broker that wanted $250,000 on his first call wanted $500,000. And soon the others began to call. The funds with which I was to make these payments of additional margin were my personal funds. My telephone bell kept constantly ringing, and when all of the brokers who could possibly get me on the telephone were through calling me, it was clear that the amount of money they would require would be about $4,000,000. And this was only 12 o'clock—the market was still to run about three hours. I called my secretary and told him to tear up the checks—we would send no money to anyone.

"I was tired and weary. I was in the boathouse by myself, and took the receiver off the hook, and went on the floor above, the room that Rubenstein occupied, and lay down on the bed and fell asleep. About 3:30 o'clock I heard loud yelling, my name was called, which aroused me, and when I came downstairs, Rubenstein had returned. He was in a panicky condition. I asked him what was the matter. He said there was a panic in New

York—hadn't I heard him yelling? I told him yes, that that was what had awakened me. He said he had been yelling for a half hour and that he was frantic. The boat was not tied up to the dock, and he thought I had drowned myself. He said my room had been on the ground floor and he didn't dream of looking for me upstairs. He just found the receiver off the hook, and was making up his mind what to do."

Everybody in Wall Street was thinking about suicide that evening! Some were actually on their way to the East River, and others to the tops of high buildings from which they jumped.

W. F. told his wife that he was going to New York, there was a little disturbance in the market. His wife was ill, and he didn't want to worry her. He thought he would be back in a day or two, but as a matter of fact, he didn't return for forty-five days, and he says that in those forty-five days he slept exactly ninety hours. Fortunately he has a good digestion, and had had a long rest in preparation for this ordeal. It didn't worry him in the least. "I rather enjoyed being in difficulties; working them out was a satisfaction to me." His mother had told him when he was a little boy that "the way to judge a general is not in time of peace but in war."

And besides, it was going to be easy. Had not Harley Clarke just told him that any time he was in trouble, to call on him and he would lend him several million dollars? At that time, you understand, these two were fifty-fifty partners in the Grandeur Company; so now the first man that W. F. called on was Clarke, and he tells the story:

"I don't think Clarke ever heard such beautiful music in his life as when I told him I was in difficulties. A symphony was playing—his dream was about to be realized. Of course he wouldn't loan me any money! He didn't say that he didn't have it, or that he was affected by the crash himself, but on my plea for a loan, it was just NO. He didn't whisper the word, he yelled it. This was the day that he evidently was waiting for."

But W. F. didn't worry very much about Clarke—there were his great friends, Halsey, Stuart & Co. He sent for the manager of their New York office and told him the story frankly. The Loew shares had dropped to a point where his margin was short $10,000,000, and he wanted a loan to save the situation. The manager said he would advise Stuart at once, and he did so, and the reply was that Stuart himself was in difficulties and could lend W. F. nothing.

But still W. F. didn't worry. There were his all-powerful friends, the Telephone Company. He sent for his friend, ex-Lieutenant Otterson, and Otterson said to tell him the whole story. That was Tuesday evening, and Otterson said he would intercede with the Telephone Company the first thing in the morning, and at 10 o'clock in the morning he called up to say that he had done so, and was sorry, but the Telephone Company had loaned as much money as it cared to lend to any one man. W. F. thought it over, and called again on the telephone, and said:

"Look here, John, perhaps I had no reason to ask your company to loan me any further money, but we talked about this thing last night, and this was to be a loan without collateral, and I would like to have $13,000,000, but I don't think I should take it without collateral. I am going to give you my personal collateral. My job is to save these companies; I am not going to think about myself in this at all."

W. F. continues· "I enumerated what I owned personally and what the companies owned that was not hypothecated, and the total was $50,000,000. I asked the Telephone Company to make a secured loan of $13,000,000. He said that sounded different from the day before. But in a few minutes he called back and told me that Gifford had said no, they didn't want to loan me any more. I sensed the fact that the Telephone Company was likewise hearing a symphony. Here was Fox where he could no longer be the owner of the Tri-Ergon patents —this was the day they were waiting for."

So then W. F. went looking for the key to some other treasure chest. He had had dealings with the banking firm of Hayden, Stone & Co., and bethought himself of Richard F. Hoyt, a member of that firm. His experience with this gentleman goes back to the time in 1926 when W. F. bought his West Coast theatres. The three men who were selling it were in a hotel room, in their shirt sleeves; they were working late on a complicated deal, and had everything settled, the papers drawn and ready for signature, when two of the men who were making the deal received a telephone call, and excused themselves and left the room without their coats, and did not come back. Later they said they had changed their minds about the deal; the third man signed, and Fox got only one-third interest in the company.

Later on W. F. discovered what had happened. The West Coast purchase included 21,000 shares of First National Pictures Corporation, and when this corporation discovered that West Coast was selling out to Fox, they rushed to their bankers, Hayden, Stone, and got this concern to purchase the other two-thirds of West Coast.

So Fox took up negotiations with Richard Hoyt of Hayden, Stone to buy these other shares, and wasn't getting anywhere. Meanwhile, having made friends with the Telephone Company, he asked them to help him, and they said they would go to the Morgans about it, and have the Morgans give the orders. A day or two later Hoyt invited W. F. to breakfast with him, and was extremely angry because, as he said, W. F. had "used the big stick" upon him. The Telephone Company had called upon the all-powerful House of Morgan, and the Morgans had sent for Hoyt and told him they would consider it a favor if he could see his way clear to sell the West Coast to Fox. Hoyt was furious, and said he wasn't going to allow such methods, and that any chance that W. F. had had to buy the stock had now disappeared. It was Hoyt's intention to merge West Coast with the Stanley Corporation, a chain of theatres in Pennsylvania and New Jersey.

It happened that Hayden, the senior partner of the firm, was in Egypt He was an old gentleman, looking for a rest, and W. F. shrewdly figured that being an old-timer, he would figure that he was in the banking business, and not in the business of conducting chains of "movie" theatres. So W. F. made the mild suggestion that Hoyt should cable Hayden and tell him of Morgan's polite suggestion concerning the West Coast shares. Hoyt fell into the trap, and a few days later he sent for W. F. and said that W. F. had "tricked" him. From this W. F. knew what the reply to the cablegram had been, and he purchased the West Coast shares from Hoyt for $16,500,000.

Of course Hoyt made a big profit on this deal, probably one-third the purchase price Also he got a very good profit from Fox Film; for in order to make the purchase, Fox Film sold its stockholders $20,000,000 worth of new shares from its treasury, and Hayden, Stone got something over $3 a share, or approximately two-thirds of a million dollars on this transaction.

Then a little later W. F. made another deal with Hoyt. A group of Wall Street operators headed by W. C. Durant took hold of Fox Film stock and proceeded to run it up for their own purposes. They started it from $70 a share and ran it to $119, and W. F. knew that this was going to cause his stockholders to sell out and ultimately meet with losses; so he went to see Hoyt, and told him that he wanted to stop this rise, and that he proposed to offer the stockholders of Fox Film 150,000 shares of stock from the treasury at $85 a share. W. F. gave the orders, and the shares were put on the market, and the speculators' pool was broken—at a profit to Hayden, Stone of five or six hundred thousand dollars.

You might think from these things that Richard F. Hoyt would have cherished friendly feelings for William Fox. But, alas, there had been other developments not so pleasant. When you are taking part in this big business scramble, it is hard to keep from treading on other people's toes, and friends of one day become enemies of the next. There were the 21,000 shares of First National which W. F. had acquired along with the West Coast purchase. This common stock was supposed to be without value, but Warner Brothers bought the Stanley Company and got another 21,000 shares of First National, and if they could have got the West Coast shares, they would have had control of the company. So Hoyt came to W. F. and said, "You have had a streak of luck. I have just sold those 21,000 shares of First National for you. I have got you $100 a share, and this will reduce your cost price." But W. F.'s answer was that he was very sorry that Hoyt had made such a deal; he didn't want to sell those shares, because he had no desire to help his competitors by having Warner merge First National. Instead, he wanted to buy the other First National shares himself!

W. F. had got these shares for nothing, and here he was refusing $2,100,000 for them, and Richard F. Hoyt was losing the profit on a big deal. Worse than that, W. F. went on to build up these companies to a point where they earned $5,500,000 in one year. According to W. F.'s calculation, that made them worth $55,000,000. And Hoyt looked back on the fact that W. F. had forced him to sell them for about one-third of that price!

We come now to the evening after the panic, when W. F. is summoning Hoyt to his assistance. He is thinking of all the millions he has helped Hoyt to make; and Hoyt, naturally, is thinking of all the other millions which W. F. helped him not to make Hoyt has been to a dinner party that evening; the rest of America is in terror, but nothing troubles the elegant Mr. Hoyt, the tip-top of grace and fashion. A little before midnight he comes, in evening clothes with his shiny top hat, his silk-lined overcoat and shiny walking stick. He is a graduate of Harvard, tall, thin, clean-shaven, always smiling; he has penetrating eyes, talks fast, thinks fast, and knows the game.

He listens to the recital of how W. F. has to have $13,000,000 tomorrow. When W. F. told this story in my home, he asked the young woman stenographer please to leave the room. The young woman went out onto the porch, and closed the door, and W. F. told me the story, and said, "Now, how can you put that story into a book?" I replied that it required only one slight emendation, the changing of a word, and then it would be a perfectly proper story to put into a book. So W. F. called the young woman back, and dictated his account of his interview with Richard F. Hoyt.

"I had proceeded about ten minutes when I realized I might just as well be telling my troubles to a stone wall—that my words were falling on deaf ears. I said, 'I am sure I could read your mind.' He said, 'All right, if you think you can, go ahead.' I said: 'What is running through your mind is that you figure I used the wrong method to acquire the West Coast Theatres Company, two-thirds of which you sold to me for $16,500,000, and which is now worth $55,000,000, and that this story of troubles is music to your ears, and what you would like to do is to cut out my left kidney.' He said: 'I am glad to see you did that mind-reading act so well, because when you go broke, as you will, you will be able to earn a good living doing a mind-reading act on the stage. You have made only one mistake—it isn't the left kidney I want to cut out, but both kidneys.' At the conclusion of which he took his tall silk hat and walking stick and walked out."

So W. F. realized that he had to solve his problems without help from his powerful banking friends. He continues:

"The panic of October 29 was so severe that very few, if any, brokers in New York had gone home that night. Everybody was open so that their margin clerks could figure out the amount of margin their customers had to put up the next day. About 1 o'clock I concluded I would send for one of these brokers, one who I thought would be most friendly, and with whom my account was $1,000,000 in the red. I frankly told him what had occurred, the position I was in, and asked him whether he thought his firm would be indulgent for a day, for twenty-four hours, during which time I hoped to raise enough money to pay the deficiency. I told him it was my plan to invite the heads of my thirteen brokerage firms to my apartment the next morning at 9 o'clock; that I was going to propose they proclaim a moratorium for twenty-four hours, and that I wanted somebody to be there to urge it. He said he would. Then we called these brokerage firms and asked them to appear at 9 o'clock the next morning."

The brokers came, and W. F. informed them that he owed them a small matter of $10,000,000 and didn't have it. They had close to a quarter of a million shares of his Loew stocks on margin, and if they sold these shares, they would drive the price to nothing, and would lose their $10,000,000. He had tried to get a bid on the shares, and the best offer he could get was $5 a share. So he asked them to pledge themselves not to sell any of these shares for twenty-four hours. If they refused, W. F. would put on the market the 400,000 shares of Loew stock which Fox Theatres owned, and that would be the end of everything.

There was a long pause and finally one of the brokers said: "What are you hesitating about? If we agree not to sell these shares, he may be able to raise the money. There is a chance." So they gave him the twenty-four hours' moratorium.

I have told you that W. F. believes in special Providence, and thinks he can prove it. He offered me a number of instances in the course of his life, and this is one of them. Here he was in his apartment at the Ambassador Hotel, having to raise $10,000,000, and having no idea of how to begin, when the telephone rang, and on the wire was his friend, Albert M. Greenfield, chairman of the Bankers' Securities Company of Philadelphia. Half a year back Greenfield had been carrying on negotiations for the sale of that First National stock which W. F. had got free of charge along with his purchase of West Coast. He had added to his holdings in the meantime, and now had 25,000 shares. You recall that for this stock a short time back he had received an offer of $2,100,000 through Richard F. Hoyt representing Warner Brothers. The Warners still wanted this stock—and they were still at the height of their prosperity and had plenty of money. W. F. had forgotten all about it, because there had been no talk of the sale of these shares between the time of his accident in July and this Wednesday, October 30th.

As it happened, Greenfield didn't know W. F. was in trouble—and W. F. didn't consider it necessary to tell him. Greenfield said he thought he could get five or six million dollars for the shares, and perhaps in view of the panic yesterday, W. F. would be willing to take that. But W. F. said that was ridiculous. He didn't want to sell them at any such price. (As an aside to me, he said, "Of course, you realize that I would have been happy to sell them for any price whatever, provided it was for cash.")

W. F. told Greenfield to come to New York, and he came.

"I had rehearsed Rubenstein. I had told him that if Greenfield knew I was in trouble, the largest price I could get would be the five or six million dollars he had told me about over the phone. I said to him, 'I would like to have you agree with Greenfield in whatever he says, and disagree with me.' It was so rehearsed. Greenfield called for dinner, and before we had gone half way through the meal he referred to the First National shares. I said, 'You know we have always quoted the $15,000,000 price. I realize there was a panic yesterday, and if these men still want these shares they can get them for $12,500,000.' Greenfield went from $5,000,000 up the scale to $10,000,000, and finally said to Rubenstein, 'Don't you think if I could sell these shares at $10,000,000 today that would be a fine piece of business for Fox?' Rubenstein said yes, he thought it would be. I told Rubenstein I wished he would keep out of this deal, that this was not his affair. So we got into a terrific row. I said to Greenfield, 'I think you can sell these shares for $12,500,000.'

Greenfield came back that night at midnight with an offer of $10,000,000. He said he would consummate the deal the next morning."

The next morning at 9 o'clock the thirteen brokers reappeared, and W. F. informed them that he had the money in sight, and if they would indulge him for another twenty-four hours, everything would be all right. That day the Loew shares were rising. On October 29th the firm of Loeb, Alsberg & Co. had tried to get a bid for W. F., and the best offer was $5. On October 30th the official quotation was 32, which W. F. says was because all the shares were held off the market. This price was just about 50 per cent of the price before the panic. But on November 1st, they came back to 50¼. In the meantime, Greenfield had consummated his transaction, and at midnight on Thursday he brought W. F. $7,500,000 in cash and $2,500,000 in Warner Brothers' notes.

The Stock Exchange was closed Friday and Saturday to give a breathing space, and on Friday morning W. F. called his brokers and put up new margin, and they agreed to hold the shares until the end of the year on the basis of a margin of 35 per cent of the market price. Greenfield got a commission of half a million dollars, and everybody went away happy. As for W. F., having had two years and a half to contemplate these events and decide what he thinks about them, here is his conclusion, which requires no comment from me:

"It is clear that my help came from God Almighty. Men hadn't helped me—they were planning to destroy me. The Lord didn't want me destroyed. He wanted to save me. Why these fools went out that day and borrowed $10,000,000 to buy these shares I never could figure out. Eight hundred thousand was what I paid for them—what right had any man to believe he could sell for $10,000,000 what he had purchased for $800,000? Is it humanly possible for me to believe otherwise than that God inspired them to the point of wanting to buy these shares? As events have proven since, they would have been better off if they had never bought them."

W. F. did not explain why he thinks that God should have been so hard on Warner Brothers.

REEL TWELVE

THE FOX TRAP

THE whirlwind had passed; and those Wall Street navigators who had not jumped overboard now looked around them, and set to work to repair their shattered fortunes. William Fox was saved; but he saw that he had obeyed his doctors too well, and rested too long; he must set to work without another day's delay at the refinancing of his Loew and Gaumont purchases. It was now November, and the Telephone Company loan was due in February, and the Halsey, Stuart notes on April 1.

During the period of his rest, Harry Stuart had come to his home to call on him. Stuart wanted some advice about the new $75,000,000 securities company he had arranged; also he wanted to talk to W. F. about the refinancing which his firm was to do. W. F. had said that he was ready to go ahead, and Stuart had promised to prepare the plan. The situation with the Government was all right now; as soon as W. F. had rested, he would get Schenck and Zukor to abrogate their contract, and the Department of Justice would be satisfied.

Having placated his brokers and some of his bankers with the money got from Warners, W. F. went to see his friend Harry Stuart and tell him the good news. To be sure, Stuart had just refused him help, but that had been during a panic, and no doubt Stuart had needed his cash to save himself. But now the panic was over, and Stuart would remember that he had sold $40,000,000 worth of Fox shares to his customers, and would be concerned for the safety of those shares, and glad to know that Fox had managed to ride through the whirlwind. Stuart would proceed to the task which he himself had urged—the preparation of the new issue, and the introducing of them to the investing public.

So W. F. went to call, accompanied by his friend Jacob L. Rubenstein. As he describes the interview to me, he found "Dr. Jekyll Stuart" transformed into "Mr. Hyde Stuart." This new Stuart could see nothing good in anything that W. F. had done or that he proposed to do. He insisted that the sale of the First National shares was a breach of his understanding with W. F., because it diminished the assets of the Fox companies, upon which Stuart had made an unsecured loan of $12,000,000.

Stuart had just talked with Otterson of the Telephone Company—the first time these two gentlemen had met, it appears. They had met for the purpose of discussing the Fox enterprises and their various ramifications. They had reached the joint conclusion that W. F. was a reckless man; he had had no business to take on the English commitment. In making that commitment he had put in jeopardy the $12,000,000 Stuart had loaned and the $15,000,000 the Telephone Company had loaned, and Stuart wanted nothing more to do with the Fox enterprises. On April 1, 1930, he would expect his $12,000,000. So far as he was concerned, W. F. could do his financing wherever he wished; the firm of Halsey, Stuart wanted nothing further to do with it. W. F. was released from the preferential contract he had with them. Stuart had reached the conclusion that Fox was not what he always thought he was.

This was an astonishing experience to W. F. He says: "From time to time during my career I had been humiliated in one way or another, at least I thought I had been humiliated; but never in all my life had I received such humiliation as I did that day from Harry Stuart. He seemed to gloat over the fact that I was in difficulty."

And W. F. goes on to speculate—what could it have been that happened in that conference between Otterson and Stuart? Obviously, it has occurred to someone among these powerful groups that the Fox is down and can be dismembered and "merged." If he cannot get the cash to keep those Loew shares margined, he will lose them, and will not be able to repay the money he has borrowed from Stuart and Otterson. His companies can be thrown into bankruptcy, and those who have the cash—that is, Stuart and Otterson—will be able to buy them. The bankruptcy proceedings will automatically wipe out the voting shares—a much cheaper way than that proposed by Stuart's friend and associate, Harley L. Clarke. Whether the plan to lead the Fox into a trap was deliberately conceived or not, here is the creature actually in a trap; and to Harold Leonard Stuart and John Edward Otterson, devout Episcopalians, and to Harley Lyman Clarke, devout Christian Scientist, it must have seemed beyond question Providential.

How did it come about? Did Harold Leonard Stuart say to John Edward Otterson, "See here, this fellow is a Jew, and he wears a sweater and white socks, and doesn't allow his bankers a sufficient profit on his new issues. If you will stand by us now and not lend him any more money, we have got him where we want him." Or did John Edward Otterson say to Harold Leonard Stuart, "See here, this Jew who talks about himself too much wants to own patents and control the talking picture industry, which belongs to us. He has had the insolence to notify us that we are infringing his fly-wheel patent, and if you will just stand by now and refuse to raise any money for him, we can get those Tri-Ergon patents, and you will find that the Telephone Company has more valuable financing to do than the Fox." Or did Harley Lyman Clarke come to John Edward Otterson and Harold Leonard Stuart and say, "See here, I have decided to go into the moving picture business, and you know that a public utilities financier is a safer person to deal with than a little Jew upstart who won't take orders and wants to merge everything in sight. If you will help me hold him down while I get his voting shares away from him, I will see that Stuart gets the new financing, and that the Telephone Company gets its patents."

Which of these three things happened is a mystery which may never be solved; but that one of the three did happen is as certain as anything can be in human affairs. If you have read the theologians, you know the so-called "argument from design" of Dean Paley; if you found a watch on the seashore, you would know that a man had been there, since the parts of a watch could not assemble themselves by accident. In the same way, when you see a large group of men all acting in concert—when you see hundreds of different actions contributing towards the same end —you know that those actions are not arising by chance, but that somewhere a guiding brain has conceived a plan.

Let me anticipate to the extent of stating that while much of the evidence in this case is circumstantial, and while a great deal of it rests upon the unsupported testimony of William Fox, the main facts of the conspiracy were publicly admitted by the conspirators themselves, when they appeared by their attorneys in open court, and stated that they were not satisfied to get back the money which W. F. owed them; in fact they refused to take the money which he owed them, and demanded the control of his properties. I shall quote the exact words of these attorneys in the proper place; I only refer to them here, lest it may appear to you that W. F. was over-suspicious, and that his case is being built out of inferences.

W. F. picked up a hint here and a hint there. About ten days after Harley Clarke had refused help, there came a telephone call from Chicago. Clarke had something urgent to say, and he asked that it be kept strictly confidential.

"He had indirectly learned that the Telephone Company and Halsey, Stuart had merged their interest, so far as concerned the Fox companies, and he thought it was a downright shame. He wished to repeat to me what he had said during the summer, that he would like to acquire all of the voting shares of both companies, and if perchance I couldn't see my way clear to sell all of them, he would buy a half interest in them. His banking facilities were large enough to supply all the money the companies needed. But the question was, how could he inject himself into the picture. He didn't want to incur the animosity of the Telephone Company and Halsey, Stuart, and therefore he wanted me to suggest to them that they let him make a twenty-four hour investigation of our books, to get a quick picture of the whole condition; he would then refund the debts of these companies, so that we could repay the amounts due to the Telephone Company and to Halsey, Stuart.

"I was amazed at this statement; it was news to me. Up to this time I hadn't known that there was a merger of these two interests, and couldn't understand why the consent of the Telephone Company and of Halsey, Stuart was necessary to raise funds for my companies, and I so told Clarke. I told him I would ask no such permission from Halsey, Stuart. He called me back sometime that day, and said he had finally persuaded

Halsey, Stuart to permit him to make an examination of our books, and that the time they allowed him to reach a decision was forty-eight hours. If within forty-eight hours he couldn't make up his mind to supply the necessary funds for financing these companies, he was to step aside and stay out of the picture.

"His accountants went to work on our books, and forty-eight hours later Clarke called on me in the Ambassador Hotel. He said his people were fully prepared to take over these companies; he had a sufficient financial backing to supply the necessary cash, but that he was not interested in the project unless he could buy the whole of these voting shares. I told him that that was contrary to what he had said over the telephone; that he had then said he was interested in buying half, and that the management would remain in my hands. Now he had changed his attitude, and I was not interested in any proposal to sell."

W. F.'s immediate task was to find some bank to take the Loew shares out of the hands of the brokers, and make Fox Theatres a loan upon them. W. F.'s friend Rubenstein came to him with a message from one of the vice-presidents of the Public Bank, located at the lower end of Broadway. This gentleman wanted to see W. F., and when W. F. called he was introduced to the president of the bank, named Gersten. W. F. told Gersten the whole story, and told what he wanted; he had had an account with the Public Bank for many years, and Gersten expressed his appreciation of that account, and said that while he wasn't in position to take the Loew shares, he would like to have W. F. increase his line of credit. At present Fox Film owed the bank $450,000, and the president asked him to increase the amount to a million, as they had a lot of idle money in the bank. So W. F. borrowed the money, and gave a note for four months; and early in January, when the first note for $450,000 fell due, the Public Bank insisted upon immediate payment, and forced the receivership proceedings against W. F. Naturally this led him to wonder: was their invitation to him to come and increase his credit a part of the effort to lead him on and get him into the hands of the banks?

I have a copy of the letter which W. F. wrote to Gersten, and I have Gersten's reply. His defense is that at the time he loaned the additional $450,000, W. F. had told him nothing about his troubles. As a rule when you go to a banker and tell him your troubles, there are no witnesses, and if afterwards the banker chooses to say that you deceived him, your denial has no value. But it happens that in this case, Jacob L. Rubenstein was present at the interview. Mr. Rubenstein and his father had been depositors in the Public Bank since the day it was organized, and in a letter to me he states: "Mr. Fox went into great detail regarding the trials, difficulties and tribulations he had encountered."

W. F. now began making the rounds of the banks with which his companies were doing business. He happened to know very well the president of the great Chemical National Bank, for this gentleman had called at his office and informed him that he had followed the career of W. F., and in some respects it was like his own; he too was a self-made man, and would like to have W. F. tell him the story of how he built his great organization. W. F. never objects to telling that story, and he told it to the president of the Chemical National; the president of the Chemical National in turn told his story to W. F., and they were a pair of cronies. The president of the Chemical National liked to do business with self-made men, he declared, and gave the Fox companies a fine line of credit.

So now, of course, W. F. thought he had another friend, and went to see this Mr. Percy Johnson and told him the situation. W. F. knew that this bank constantly loaned money to Wall Street; in fact, Johnson had in his vaults part of those Loew shares which had been hypothecated by the brokers. W. F. showed him the balance sheet of Loew's and the fine condition that company was in; it was paying regular dividends of $3 a share, or $2,000,000 a year on the shares which W. F. held. But that meant nothing; Percy Johnson was sure that his bank could not do what W. F. wanted.

So our Fox traveled from bank to bank. In each case he would say if they didn't take all the shares, let them take part; let them say how many they would take. But nobody would take any. Some mysterious influence was at work—and of course W. F. did not forget how it had been when he had wanted to buy the West Coast shares from Hayden, Stone & Co., and

Richard F. Hoyt wouldn't agree to it, and W. F. had gone to his friends, the Telephone Company, and got them to go to the Morgans, and the Morgans had dropped a hint to Hoyt, and Hoyt had been furious, accusing W. F. of "using the big stick" on him. Now suppose it should be that someone having influence with the Morgans had been using it *against* W. F. instead of *for* him! Suppose that "big stick" was hanging over the head of the Fox!

W. F. hated to believe that, of course. He thought maybe it was because his proposition was too big for the smaller banks. He must go to a big one. His friend Greenfield had introduced him to Hugo E. Scheurman, a vice-president of the Park National Bank, who had extended to W. F. a line of credit of $3,000,000. This had been back in February of that year, and in the meantime Scheurman had become a vice-president of the Chase National; and surely here was a big enough one—the biggest bank in the world!

So W. F. went to see Scheurman, and told him his troubles, and told him of his visit to the other banks Scheurman told him to stop visiting the other banks, the Chase National was big enough to handle the whole thing. The Chase National was liquid; the great Mr. Wiggin, its chairman, had had foresight before the crash, and now he would have the money to make this desirable loan. W. F. was to come back after luncheon and get the final word.

W. F. is sure that his friend Scheurman was sincere in the matter; he just didn't happen to know what was running through the head of Albert H. Wiggin, chairman of the Chase National Bank and of the Chase Securities Corporation. W. F. did not know it either. It was only later that he learned that Wiggin and Clarke were intimate associates and partners in all kinds of undertakings, and that for anything Clarke wanted to do, the money of Chase National and Chase Securities was available, while for anything that Clarke wanted not done, the money was absolutely non-existent. W. F. saw the results after luncheon, when his friend Scheurman told him that he was very sorry, but the bank could not take any part of the loan.

All this visiting and shopping and telling of troubles had taken a couple of weeks; and now W. F. saw clearly that he could not get what he wanted from a bank, but must find a new investment house to offer a new issue of Fox shares to the public. Harry Stuart had thrown him out, and wanted nothing more to do with him; very well, he would find another firm.

For several years he had been dealing from time to time with Dillon, Read & Company. He had had a fuss with them at the time he had acquired the Loew shares, because this firm had been the bankers for Loew's, and considered that Schenck had double-crossed them in selling the shares without their getting a profit. First Mr. Miller and then Mr. Phillips of the firm had called and entered a strenuous protest. W. F. had tried to explain to them that he was not to blame for what Schenck had done; and he had promised them that when he was ready to do the new financing, Dillon, Read would be "in the picture."

And now here was a fine chance for Dillon, Read to be the whole picture, all by themselves. W. F. called on Mr. Miller, and said he wanted to have a conference with Clarence Dillon, head of the firm. Miller said he would be glad to arrange it, and the next day there was a luncheon at one of the luncheon clubs, attended by Dillon and several other members of the firm, and also by W. F. and his friend Rubenstein, who apparently knew all the bankers in New York, and was traveling around with his friend Fox, trying to help.

So now we make the acquaintance of another big investment house. Dillon, Read & Company had shot to the front in the past few years, among the new crop of wizards who were creating millions upon millions overnight. They bought the Dodge Company from the widows of the owners for $146,000,000, and they waved their wizard hands and overnight there was a new corporation, and a profit of $34,000,000 for the financiers. From that time on the Dodge Company began to slide, and in the end Dillon, Read put it off on Chrysler. Wall Street men now point to the Chrysler Building and remark, playfully: "That was Chrysler's commission on the Dodge deal."

Clarence Dillon is one of those Jews who have forgotten the fact. He is tall, good-looking, egotistical, a rapid talker, and you get the impression that he knows what he is talking about. W. F. says it is hard not to believe that he is a kind man; which, of course, is a useful impression to give in Wall Street. I happen to know someone whom he employed in a confidential capacity, and I asked this person about his character, and the answer took only two words: "Wholly unmoral."

At this luncheon Dillon gave W. F. the impression of being extremely nervous. The lunch was an elaborate one, and everybody had enough to eat, including Dillon; but in the center of the table was a massive bunch of grapes—there for an ornament, which, as a rule, nobody bothers. But all during the conference, which lasted for an hour or two after the luncheon, Dillon kept picking at the grapes, and by the time the conference was over he had cleaned up the massive bunch. W. F., watching him closely, was trying to figure out what his nervousness was about.

Afterwards, when the conference was over, W. F. saw clearly. Dillon hadn't come there to negotiate a business deal with a new and valuable customer. Dillon had come under orders from somebody higher up, to tell W. F. that he must part with his voting shares. And Dillon perhaps didn't like that job so much; he might have preferred to be a financier, instead of an errand boy for a conspiracy.

However, Dillon did the job very tactfully. He told W. F. that he was vitally interested in W. F.'s proposition; since Halsey, Stuart had abandoned their preferential contract, Dillon, Read would be glad to do the Fox financing. There was only one thing that stood in the way of the deal, and that was the voting shares. Dillon didn't consider such voting shares the proper way of controlling a company. Couldn't W. F. see his way to dissolve them?

W. F. was puzzled by this statement, and called Dillon's attention to the fact that he was the last man in the world to make such a request. When he had bought Dodge Brothers, and sold it to the public at a profit of $34,000,000, he had vested the control in half a million shares of voting stock, and kept all this for his own firm. Dillon, a banker who had never been in the automobile business and knew nothing about it, held the Dodge voting shares; so how could he recommend that Fox, who was in the motion picture business and knew all about it, should dissolve the Fox voting shares? Dillon's answer to this is told in W. F.'s own words:

"He then told me I had better dissolve those voting shares and do it voluntarily, because if I didn't I might be compelled to.

I might find my company controlled some day by someone I knew nothing of. I paid no attention to all that—to me it sounded like idle talk. Only later when I learned from his own lips that he was Wiggin's best friend and adviser did I recall that I was then talking to a man who most likely had discussed the Fox situation with the Chase crowd, and that Dillon was thoroughly familiar with this man who was not in the motion picture business who was going to succeed me if I didn't voluntarily dissolve these voting shares. In any event, he must have known that these companies were about to be taken away from me, and he knew it was by a man not in the motion picture business. True to his prediction, the man who acquired the business was never in the motion picture business. Dillon said that of course unless I agreed to dissolve these shares, his good firm couldn't lend itself to the enterprise."

When W. F. went away and thought this over, he realized for the first time that there was a movement on foot that was not intended to be of help to him. Until then he had been living in a fool's paradise, but now he saw that he was in serious danger. He saw that he had only one real friend left, the great Telephone Company which had loaned him $15,000,000. So he sent again for John E. Otterson, and told him how the banking world had closed its doors to him, and he must have the aid of the Telephone Company. This company had on deposit several hundred million dollars in the New York banks, and if the Telephone Company would say, "Lend this man some money," no banker in New York would say no. W. F. tells about this interview:

"Otterson said of course they would help me. I told him I had had lunch with Clarence Dillon; that Dillon wanted these voting shares dissolved, the thing I wouldn't do. He said there was no reason for dissolving them, and asked me did I want the firm of Dillon, Read to do this banking. I said yes, because they would play an important part in the consolidation of the Loew and Fox companies, they being the bankers for the Loew company. He said, 'All right. I will arrange that the firm of Dillon, Read gives your matter careful consideration. We have a private opinion of that firm, but under instructions of the Telephone Company there is no danger of them doing any harm here. However, we will insure that. I am going to arrange for Mr. Bloom to take lunch with Dillon tomorrow and tell Dillon of the interest of the Telephone Company in this matter.' "

"Mr. Bloom" is Edgar S. Bloom, president of Western Electric, and next to Gifford the big man in the Telephone Company; so this meant that Otterson was really going to put things through. Says W. F.:

"I was informed by Otterson that Dillon and Bloom had had lunch, and that the firm of Dillon, Read was now prepared to give me the financial assistance I required. I met with Miller, and he actually prepared a plan for the financing of the Fox enterprises that involved the issuing by the company, the purchasing and marketing by Dillon, Read of $75,000,000 in preferred stocks at a price that was most attractive to the company. I was met in the most friendly spirit. All my troubles had vanished. Dillon, Read were happy and proud to be the bankers for these institutions. They gave me the memorandum that showed the type of securities they were going to have issued and sold. To me it sounded like Aladdin and his wonderful lamp, and it looked as if we had consummated the transaction. Otterson was in the room all of the time."

But then came a sudden turn in the conversation. "I then called Miller's attention to the fact that one of the Fox subsidiary companies had a $500,000 note that was falling due the next day, and in view of the fact that we had gone along so well, and that this plan was so wonderful, perhaps Dillon, Read could find itself in a way to loan the company $500,000, so that our contract wouldn't go to protest. Up to this time, no obligation had fallen due and was unpaid; the record was clear from the day the company was created until the day I stood in this room in the office of Dillon, Read. Miller inquired as to what collateral I had for this loan. Fox Film still had six notes left that the Warners had given it when the First National shares were purchased. I told him so. I told him the notes were in my pocket. He wanted to see them, so I showed them to him.

"The face value of two of these notes was $500,000. He took the six notes out of my hand, and said what right had I to walk around the streets of New York with these notes in my pocket— didn't they belong in the vaults of my company? I told him that I was trying to sell them and raise some money. He said to leave all six notes with him and they would loan me $500,000. I told him that that would be a value of $1,500,000, and that I needed the other four in order to raise another $1,000,000. He told me they would loan me $500,000 on all six notes but not on two of them.

"So it was clear to me that this was not a friend at all; this was a foe. His whole attitude toward making this loan, the questions he asked, indicated clearly to me that I had spent a day in vain; that the memorandum he had prepared was a subterfuge; they had no intention of selling $75,000,000 worth of bonds and stocks for me. I asked him for a copy of the memorandum of the plan he had just prepared, and I left there and never went back."

The working out of a big financing plan such as this is, of course, a highly confidential matter. It is something like going to a clinic to have your inwards examined; you have to submit to a rigid inquisition, and tell all your secrets. If W. F. had gone on with Miller, he would have had to turn out all his pockets and open all the safety boxes of himself and his companies. His books and accounts would have been gone over by a firm of certified accountants, an elaborate process which takes at least a month, and perhaps two or three. He would have revealed to his enemies every secret of his business, every bank where his companies had a deposit, both at home and abroad; every broker where they had an account—and so on through a long list of affairs.

Most crucial of all was the time involved. If a banking-house agrees to finance you, and really is your friend and means to do what it says—then you are lucky. But if a banking house promises to finance you, and then stalls you along, promising to have papers ready this week, and then putting it off until next week—well, that is the very essence of this conspiracy; the way in which the banking business is turned into the business of highway robbery. For while you are led along, waiting and hoping and living on broken promises, precious time is passing, and your notes are falling due at the banks; the first thing you know the banks have come down on you, and there are suits for a receiver.

How dangerous this game is you can see from what happened in the case of Halsey, Stuart. W. F. had never doubted that this great firm was his friend, and had given them a preferential contract to do the future financing of his companies. This was a written document and Stuart had it. Now he had kicked the Fox out and told him to go elsewhere; but that was not a written document, and presently we shall find Stuart repudiating it, and his firm in open court standing on their preferential contract, and denying the right of the Fox companies to have their financing done by anybody else. When your one purpose is to delay a man until his obligations fall due at the banks, any sort of pretext will do, no matter how clumsy; and this clumsy pretext was enough to keep W. F. tied up in a tangle of litigation, and to make it practically impossible for anybody else to do business with him.

The Fox was thoroughly frightened now, and wouldn't go ahead with Dillon, Read in spite of Otterson's insistence. Two months later he realized what a narrow escape he had had, for he met Clarence Dillon again, and Dillon told him the truth. Let W. F. tell this in his own words:

"Dillon expressed great sympathy for the predicament I found myself in. I said, 'You know, Clarence, it is strange that you predicted it—that if I didn't dissolve my shares, some stranger would take my place. Of course you know that about three days after we met I went back to your firm and Miller had prepared a very comprehensive plan. Otterson told me that he got you to change your mind; that they had solicited your good will in behalf of my companies; that you had lunch with Bloom and he requested that you play square with me.' Clarence became incensed with that, and if ever he told the truth, I know he told it then when he said that if the Telephone Company had reported that in that lunch there was any discussion for his firm to treat squarely with me, I was to take it from him it was a dirty lie. He said, 'I can't tell you what was said then, but it was not that I should treat square with you.'

"Dillon furthermore denied that he knew anything about any plan that Miller had prepared. He said I was telling him something he now heard for the first time. He laughed at the very idea that Dillon, Read contemplated the issuing of $75,000,000 worth of securities. It is clear to me that the idea was to have me go along indefinitely, until these obligations became due and I no longer had time to turn anywhere."

REEL THIRTEEN

THE FOX HESITATES

WE have come now to the latter part of November. It is important to bear in mind that the panic had been over for two or three weeks, and conditions were gradually returning to normal. The government and all the organs of public opinion were proclaiming that the slump had been an accident, a passing flurry, and all but a few Socialists and cranks accepted this. Stocks began gradually to climb again. At their lowest official quotation during the panic, the Loew shares were close to 30. A month later they had come back to 45, and in three months more they were at 70, and a month after that at 76. American Telephone & Telegraph, which had dropped close to 200, at the same intervals climbed to 224, 241, 264. This latter stock is representative, and shows the trend of the market.

Understand, therefore, that throughout this winter and spring of W. F.'s desperate battle, he was not trying to save himself in the midst of a depression, but on a rising market. There was plenty of money again for everybody—except the Fox which had been marked for destruction. If any investment banking house had wanted to sell a million shares of Fox Film and Fox Theatres to the stockholders, to finance the purchase of the Loew and the Gaumont shares, that transaction could have been put through without the slightest difficulty, and the concern in question could have made $5,000,000 out of it. But no banking house would take this $5,000,000, at the price of incurring the displeasure of the Telephone Company, Halsey, Stuart & Co., and the Chase National Bank.

W. F. wasn't going to get an honest schedule of new financing from any investment house in New York, nor was he going to get credit from any bank in New York. There was only one way he could save himself, and that was by selling some of the things

140

which his companies owned. What did he have? Well, he had 660,900 shares of the common stock of Loew's, Inc.; but he had paid $125 a share for 400,000 shares, and upwards of $70 or $80 a share for the remainder, and at present his companies would have had to take a huge loss, which W. F. would have held to be a deep disgrace.

But also he had the shares of West Coast Theatres. He had had this concern long enough to build it up, and its shares were now worth about three times what he had paid for them. That was W. F.'s notion of the proper kind of sale to make, and he turned his thoughts thereto.

He remembered his friend Albert M. Greenfield, chairman of the Bankers' Securities Corporation. Greenfield was a true friend; also, he was involved in the matter, because his concern had loaned W. F. $10,000,000, and as it was a small concern, the amount loomed enormous in Greenfield's thoughts. Just recently he had made the $10,000,000 sale of First National shares for W. F. and he had not forgotten the two notes of Warner Brothers, each for $250,000, which he had earned in this transaction. Certainly Greenfield would be glad to undertake another deal between W. F. and the Warners.

Greenfield's wife was now in the hospital, ill, but after a couple of weeks W. F. learned that her temperature was normal, and he urged his friend to come to New York. Greenfield said he would come, with the understanding that he could leave within one hour after his arrival. It takes two hours to come from Philadelphia, and two hours to get back, and five hours was as long as Greenfield would stay away from the bedside of his wife. So W. F. said all right. Greenfield was to arrive at seven in the evening, come to W. F.'s hotel and eat dinner with him, and get back to the Pennsylvania Station in time to take the 8 o'clock train. Dinner would be waiting, and everything would go through on schedule.

Up to this time Greenfield had been told nothing about W. F.'s troubles, and W. F. thought it would be better for him to hear the bad news after he had had dinner. W. F. urged him to eat first, and take the 9 o'clock train; but Greenfield said no, he must take the 8 o'clock train. You may picture him seated at that dinner table, "this little, bald-headed Hebrew Jew," as W. F.

described him to Herbert Hoover; short, solidly built, smooth-shaven and very white of skin, wearing glasses, an alert and keen business man, waiting now for a proposition. Let W. F. tell the story:

"I can recall that he had a mouth full of food, eating very rapidly, and insisting that I tell him what I had on my mind. When I informed him about my companies, that they were in serious difficulties, that there were rumors that a receiver might be appointed, it may be that he swallowed the food that he had in his mouth; I am not sure, but I know he became violently ill. We sent for a bell-boy to get all kinds of medicine. He didn't go back to Philadelphia for at least fourteen days thereafter, and that night when he engaged a room on the floor above me. he asked my friend Rubenstein to sleep with him, to see that nothing happened. I thought that was a fine plan, because I felt that Rubenstein himself was contemplating suicide, and they would be watching each other, and nothing would happen to either one."

The next morning Greenfield felt better, and he remembered that Warner Brothers had large sums of cash on hand; surely they would be glad to buy a chain of 500 theatres, including the best in eleven states west of the Rocky mountains! What would W. F. take for the West Coast Company? W. F. figured that the value should be decided on the customary basis of ten times the company's earnings. West Coast had earned $5,500,000 during 1929, and therefore the price should be $55,000,000. The purchaser must guarantee to use Fox Film productions in the theatres, and give to Fox Film in rentals an amount equal to what it had received in 1929.

The idea of getting a commission on a $55,000,000 deal looked fine to Greenfield. He went up to the home of the Warners, and came back that night and said they were vitally interested. It would be the greatest coup the firm could make. They talked to their bankers, Goldman, Sachs, which was marketing Warner bonds as fast as it could turn the handle of the bond-making machine; these bankers said that they would be very glad to put up the money. The news that the Warners had bought this huge chain of theatres would boost their stocks to the sky, and there would be no limit to the new bonds that could be sold.

But now came a peculiar development. Otterson of the Telephone Company found out about these negotiations. Of course, there couldn't be any negotiations with any investment house in New York that the Telephone Company didn't hear about it promptly. Otterson came to see W. F., and then later came Harry Stuart, and later came Otterson and Stuart together.

You may ask, what did these gentlemen have to do with W. F.'s proposition to sell the West Coast theatres? If he got $55,000,000, he would pay off the $15,000,000 he owed to the Telephone Company, and the $12,000,000 of the Halsey, Stuart notes, and the $3,000,000 which the Telephone Company had persuaded the Chatham & Phoenix Bank to lend him—$30,000,-000, plus interest, and then he would be through with Halsey, Stuart & Co. and with the Telephone Company, and these gentlemen would not have to come to see him any more. So what was the matter now?

Otterson explained what was the matter. He said that W. F. was under obligation to the Telephone Company, and couldn't get away from that obligation. The company was asking a favor —the first favor it had ever wanted. It didn't want Warner Brothers to get the West Coast theatres. The Warners were its enemies, and it didn't want its enemies to get this great advantage.

Warner had suggested buying a half interest in the West Coast at half of W. F.'s price; and W. F. now told this to Otterson, and Otterson asked, would W. F. be willing to have Zukor of Paramount as his partner in the enterprise instead of Warner? W. F. said it would be all the same to him. Let him tell the story:

"Said Otterson, 'We will do more than that for you. I want to prove our friendship. We will buy the whole thing for $55,000,000, and sell Zukor half of it; the Telephone Company will own the other half, and it will give you three years to regain it.' Again I fell into a trap. That sounded wonderful to me. I authorized him to see Zukor. I told him we would sell it to him for ten times the earnings. Our accounts would be certified by an accountant of his selection."

Stuart came in; both he and Otterson were enthusiastic over the deal, and asked for authority to negotiate it, and went off to

11

attend to it. But then came Greenfield, and Greenfield was not so pleased. Said Greenfield:

"In the transaction over the First National I was a broker and wanted a commission. But then I didn't know you were in trouble. Now you are in trouble and I am no longer a broker but a friend. I say to you now that if I make a sale, I will not ask for a commission. But as a friend, I think you are walking into a trap. I think you made a mistake to authorize Otterson and Stuart to buy these shares. I have a feeling that this thing is not going to come out right, and I had better keep on dealing with Warner Brothers, because I think these men are stringing you. Will you please let me continue to hold onto the Warners for you? I have an engagement and want to continue these negotiations; in fact, Harry Warner is now in my room upstairs at this time and I want you to come upstairs and meet him."

So W. F. went upstairs to meet Warner, and Warner had changed his mind again, and wanted to buy the whole thing. But the price was too high. W. F. told of the proposition which was being made to Zukor, and Warner thought he might take half with Zukor. They argued back and forth but did not come to a settlement. Let W. F. continue the tale:

"I went back to my apartment. A few minutes later Stuart and Otterson appeared and said we had done the most contemptible thing they ever heard of. We had authorized them to make this sale, and while they were talking with Zukor, Greenfield and I were talking to Warner upstairs. They said Zukor didn't want any part of it now, and Warner didn't want any part of it now. They both withdrew from the room for a moment, and when they returned Otterson acted as spokesman for the Telephone Company and Halsey, Stuart. Otterson reminded me that the Telephone Company was a creditor of Fox Film Corporation for $15,000,000 and that he was also talking for the firm of Halsey, Stuart, who were a creditor of the company for $12,000,000. They had both reached a conclusion that these companies of mine were insolvent, and he said he now demanded in behalf of the New York Telephone Company and Halsey, Stuart & Company a proxy of my voting shares. He said they wanted the power of attorney to run my companies from now on. 'The firm of Halsey, Stuart and the Telephone Company will now

take your companies over.' He went into a tirade that lasted ten
minutes. I thereupon left the room, went into an adjoining bedroom, and lay down and went to sleep."

The next day the two gentlemen came back. They were in a
more polite frame of mind, and Stuart said he was sorry for his
attitude of yesterday, but he still thought that the best interests
of W. F. required that he enter into a voting trust agreement, and
turn over to trustees his voting shares which controlled Fox Film
and Fox Theatres. Says W. F.:

"Stuart made a careful explanation of a willingness and
desire to be of great service to these enterprises, and said that if
I would consent to Otterson being one of the trustees and Stuart
being the other trustee, then the firm of Halsey, Stuart, with the
aid of the Telephone Company, would undertake the refinancing
of these projects. He said they wanted to make little or no
change in the present running of the organization; that I had no
right to suspect that this was anything else but a friendly gesture,
and to prove how friendly it was, it was the intention of the
Telephone Company that when it had received its $15,000,000
back, to surrender the trusteeship of Otterson, and that then his
brother, Charles Stuart, would receive the trusteeship that Otterson would surrender.

"I told Stuart I saw no difficulty in the whole matter. I said,
'You have expressed to me in the most friendly terms the wish
to help my enterprise. I have had the most friendly relationships
until the crash; I have had no reason to distrust you except for
your attitude since the crash; I am perfectly willing to create this
trusteeship, with the distinct understanding that there is to be
little or no change in the set-up of these organizations, and that I
have no objection to the firm of Halsey, Stuart having two of
the trustees after the Telephone Company receives its money'."

So Stuart and Otterson gave W. F. a memorandum of the
conditions under which they were jointly willing to save the Fox
enterprises. He was to give the trustees a power of attorney
without limit of time, and the trustees were to be free to make
such changes as they thought advisable. There was to be a new
board of directors, and Fox, as president, was to remain subject
to the option of the powers of attorney. The memorandum added,
"May ask for more," and also it added, "Are Warner notes in

treasury?" These were the notes which W. F. had been so indiscreet as to display at *Dillon, Read's* in the presence of Otterson. W. F. took this home to think it over, and the more he thought about it the less he liked it.

It was after this that W. F. decided that he needed a lawyer. "Up to this time," he says, "I had not taken the advice of an attorney. I was conceited enough to think that I could work myself out of this difficulty. But now for the first time I had been definitely confronted with a clear, precise understanding of what the Telephone Company was desirous of accomplishing. And at this stage I felt that I must promptly be advised of my legal rights."

One of the bankers to whom W. F. owed a couple of million dollars suggested Col. Joseph M. Hartfield as a Wall Street lawyer competent to deal with this situation. W. F.'s friend and family lawyer, Benjamin Reass, ratified this suggestion, so Hartfield was sent for, and made himself familiar with the difficulties, and consented to act as attorney for Fox Film and Fox Theatres.

Colonel Hartfield is a figure well known in Wall Street, and a favorite subject for the sketch artists of newspapers. He is not much more than four and a half feet high, and when he sits in a chair his little fat legs do not come anywhere near the floor, so he has a way of tucking them under him. W. F. first estimated that he is as broad as he is long; then he qualified by estimating that his circumference is equal to his height. He is a bachelor, a devotee of the sporting world, and frequently seen at race tracks. "He lets no conference go without commenting on his popularity with the ladies. Each conference would end with the same statement: If it was in the afternoon, he was going to have tea with charming ladies; if it was evening, he was going to have dinner with charming ladies. I have no reason to suppose he was not telling the truth."

Hartfield is what is known as a "Kentucky colonel"; he was born in that state, and does not mention that he is a Jew unless you cross-examine him about it. He has the Southern twang, and says "you-all" this and "you-all" that. He is humorous, and carries a charming smile, even when he is angry. You may picture him, a dark smooth-shaven gentleman, fat and jolly, with not much hair left, and a thin voice. He possesses a brilliant mind, and W. F. says: "If a client could be sure that he was really representing him, I believe the client would be adequately represented."

The trouble with Colonel Hartfield would seem to have been that he is a Wall Street lawyer, and all those big lawyers who were fighting W. F. were his bosom friends, and those big banks and investment houses which were trying to break W. F. were the kind of clients he had always had in the past and expected to have in the future. W. F. agreed to pay him a million dollars if he could salvage the Fox companies, but apparently that million dollars didn't look as big to Hartfield as it looked to W. F. Says the latter:

"It was soon apparent that Hartfield was distinctly a Wall Street lawyer, for every once in a while he would make some sort of suggestion that would appear as if he were fighting with the Telephone Company and Halsey, Stuart. I called this fact to the attention of Mr. Reass, but he said not to pay any attention to it; that that was just a habit of rehearsing things in his mind; that he was a man who would stand by you; that he had great influence; he had the entree; he was general counsel for the Morgan bank known as the Bankers Trust Company, one of our large banking creditors."

Each day W. F. became more suspicious, and less satisfied with his high-priced Wall Street lawyer. There was so much at stake, he must have the best there was. So he consulted with Reass some more, and demanded to know who was the greatest lawyer in America, and Reass asked what he thought of Charles Evans Hughes. This was about two months prior to Hughes' appointment as Chief Justice of the United States Supreme Court. Hughes had been a justice of that court for six years, up to 1916, when he had resigned to become the Republican candidate for president against Woodrow Wilson. He had been Secretary of State in the cabinets of Harding and Coolidge. For the past four years he had been practicing law in New York, and to such a loyal Republican (in national affairs) as W. F., he would naturally seem one of the most august and impressive persons in the world.

But even so, W. F. wanted to make certain. He insisted that his friend Reass should make a complete list of all the banks and bankers and banking houses and corporations which he now believed were allied to destroy him. Reass took that list to Hughes, and Hughes went over it and said there was no name upon it which would make it impossible for him to accept a retainer. Reass said that Hughes wanted to see W. F.; and when Hartfield was told about it, Hartfield said that was all right, so W. F. went to see Hughes.

"On the morning of Monday, November 25th, I called on Mr. Hughes and gave him a complete recital of everything that involved my companies; the episodes beginning with the seeking of the approval of the Department of Justice and the acquisition of the Loew shares, until the day I appeared before him. I was confined with him in his room for more than three hours. He was as vitally interested in my recital as you have been. When I concluded, he extended his hand and the palm of it was wet with perspiration. I felt a grip of friendship. He asked me to dismiss the matter from my mind, and indicated that he had broad shoulders, and was willing to have this burden placed upon his shoulders."

Nothing could exceed the relief of W. F. at this development in his affairs. At last he had a real friend, and a real supporter. The greatest lawyer in the United States had taken charge of his destiny: Charles Evans Hughes, ardent reformer and enemy of corruption and crime; for two terms Governor of New York state on a reform ticket; for six years a justice of the United States Supreme Court; for four years Secretary of State of the United States; holder of twenty-one college degrees, and for the sixty-seven years of his life a member of the Baptist Church.

Judge Hughes spent some time in telling W. F. of the great disputes he had had to settle and the great tangles he had had to resolve in the course of his career: all the things he had been obliged to do when he was Secretary of State of the United States. He had had to settle great wars, one in particular between China and Japan. Surely W. F. could believe that a man who had settled a war between China and Japan would be able to settle a war between William Fox and the Telephone Company, the Chase National Bank, and Halsey, Stuart! W. F. said to his new friend:

" 'Mr. Hughes, from October 28 until today I have had an average of no more than two hours sleep a night. My brain is so tired, I can't think any more. I don't seem to be able to go any further.' To this Hughes said not to worry, that from now on he was going to do the thinking for me. He said he could imagine me being tired; who wouldn't be tired, going through a thing like this?

"I couldn't think; I was worn out. I had not only my business troubles, but I had illness at home. Mrs. Fox was confined to her bed at our country home throughout the whole period. I couldn't go to that home, and I didn't dare talk over the telephone, because I believed that every word I uttered was being listened to. At no previous time during my career, if I was within a hundred miles of New York, did I fail to take the train and sleep in my own home. But now I couldn't go. Now I was just a pathetic old man. I was fifty years older than my years. I am sure that if my health is spared until I am a century old, I shall never feel as old as I did then. It was because of that that Hughes took my challenge and said, 'Let me think for you.' "

W. F. went to his hotel and had a little sleep on the strength of this new-found security, and then next day he went to his office, intending to go from there to another conference with Judge Hughes. But in his office a strange bit of news was brought to him. The Jones ticker had just issued a statement to the effect that the United States Government had begun an action against William Fox, Fox Theatres, and Fox Film, requiring them to divest themselves of the Loew shares.

What a strange thing! These shares had been acquired in February, and it was now the beginning of December, and in all that time no legal action had been begun by the Government. The last that W. F. had heard about the matter was the message brought by his friend, Colonel Huston, treasurer of the Republican National Committee, to the effect that the Government would be satisfied with W. F.'s plans provided that the Loew contract with Paramount would be abrogated. But now here were the legal representatives of the United States Government filing a suit against the Fox Theatres Corporation, and so soon after William Fox had told all the details of his affairs to Charles Evans Hughes. A most singular sequence of events—the full singularity of which you cannot appreciate until you are reminded of one fact: that the name of the Solicitor General of the United States Government at the time was Charles Evans Hughes, junior!

What was our friend Fox to make of this astounding development? Was he to consider it a pure coincidence, one of those amazing coincidences which do happen sometimes in the affairs of men? Or was he to figure that there had been a flash of telepathy between the elder Hughes in New York and the younger Hughes in Washington? Or could it be that this flash had traveled, not by telepathy, but by the wires of the American Telephone and Telegraph Company?

The confidences between a lawyer and a client are supposed to be as sacred as those between a Catholic confessor and a penitent. But also, of course, the ties between a father and a son are often very close; and what would be the reaction of a devoted father who suddenly got news that his son was on the point of being involved in a serious scandal? Can we imagine that a telephone connection was established between the law office of Hughes, Schurman & Dwight in New York and the Solicitor General's office in Washington, and that words something like the following were spoken over that telephone line:

"Charlie, I have just received some information about the case of Fox Theatres Corporation and its purchase of a majority of the shares of Loew's, Inc. There may be a court fight between Fox and his creditors any day, and it is certain to make a disagreeable story in the newspapers. It appears that the Government is in a ticklish position in the matter, because Fox offered $2,000,000 to influence the Department of Justice to consent to the merger of Loew's with the Fox companies. The Government was threatening an action last July, but it hasn't taken any action, and if this story should come out, it will be the general assumption that someone in the Department has been influenced. I don't want to see your name involved in a scandal of that sort, and in order to keep yourself safe, I think you should bring an action against the Fox companies without a moment's delay."

Could any such conversation have taken place? W. F. was suspicious about it at the time, and he is still more suspicious about it now. You will not be interested in any speculations of mine on the subject, but you may be interested in some facts which for the past twenty-seven years have conditioned my thinking about Charles Evans Hughes.

It happened that during the revelations of life insurance corruption which took place in 1905, I was a good friend of James B. Dill, author of "Dill on Corporations," at that time the highest paid corporation lawyer in New York, and an "insider" on all the big deals of the time. Dill had just been appointed a judge of the Court of Appeals of the State of New Jersey, the highest court in that state. But in spite of that fact, he was the freest talker I have ever known. He told me the insides of New York finance and politics of those days, and a great part of the material of "The Metropolis" and "The Moneychangers" came from him, and all my later books have been colored by his revelations. From him I learned that perjury and jury-bribing, wire-tapping, burglary, arson and even murder, are part of American big business technique, and that nothing you could make up for a melodrama or a movie would be as "raw" as the reality of Wall Street.

It so happened that the enormous funds of the life insurance companies were in the hands of "irresponsible" men—which meant, in those days, men who were not responsible to the elder Morgan. One of them was "Jimmie" Hyde, who spent a lot of money on chorus girls, which made him vulnerable in the newspapers. Morgan wanted the control of those funds, so he fed the life insurance scandals to the New York newspapers and thus forced an investigation by the State Legislature. The man whom Morgan employed as his attorney to do this job was Dill. Morgan had previously paid him $1,000,000 to organize the Steel Trust, and make it law tight. (Morgan said, "I don't employ lawyers to tell me what I can't do. I employ them to tell me how to do what I want to do.")

Twice every day, early in the morning and late in the afternoon, the reporters for the New York newspapers came to the office of Dill, and got their latest supply of inside information about chorus girls and other breaches of trust. And sometimes I had the privilege of being in the office, and of staying after the reporters had left, and hearing inside stories about the newspapers. Not long ago some person writing in some "kept" magazine challenged the truth of my statements about Dill, and I took the precaution to get a letter of support from Lincoln Steffens, who also was one of Dill's confidants, and has told a good deal about Dill in his autobiography. I submitted this manuscript to Steffens, and he writes: "The impression you give of Hughes is the impression I have long had." And further: "So with Dill, what you give bears out very really my picture of that little genius. What a man!"

The Republican party machine in the New York Legislature, of course under the direction of Morgan's lawyer, Judge Dill, employed a high-class and upright Baptist lawyer to act as counsel for the legislative committee investigating the abuse of life insurance funds. The name of that lawyer is Charles Evans Hughes, and this was the beginning of his public career. His becoming Governor of New York State for two terms was on the basis of his conduct of that investigation. And here is the crucial and dominant fact; that investigation continued, and the exposures were kept upon the front page of the newspapers, up to the day when the control of life insurance funds was taken out of the hands of "Jimmie" Hyde and other "irresponsible" persons, and placed in the hands of Morgan and of Morgan's bankers and agents. From that moment the publication of life insurance scandals ceased, and the investigation came to an end, and the public has heard and thought no more about the matter. The use of life insurance surpluses to further stock speculations was ten times as prevalent in 1929 as it ever had been in 1905, and Charles Evans Hughes knew all about it, but if you had used a crowbar, you could not have got him to open his mouth on the subject.

REEL FOURTEEN

THE FOX ENTERS

ANOTHER and quite curious development comes at this point of my story. It has to do with John D. Rockefeller, jr., and I have to go back and tell you of relationships which had been established between our subject and the crown prince of American finance. You see, our little Fox has a kind of power of his own; he has been in all sorts of unexpected places, and met the greatest in our land, and found occasions when he could be of service to them.

The story takes us back a matter of twelve years. America is at war, and W. F. is enthusiastic in his country's cause, and is putting all sorts of patriotic material into his pictures and news-reels, and giving most of his time to raising money for the Red Cross. He has told me a number of stories about his adventures, and they are interesting stories, revealing a sense of drama, and making it plain why he was such a success as a creator of pictures for the masses. He has repeated several of the speeches he made at banquets where the great ones of the land had come, and a little Fox was selected to conjure the millions out of their pockets. He really did get the millions—I have looked up the figures in the newspaper files of that time!

In the spring of 1918, W. F. was at White Sulphur Springs in Virginia with his family, and he read in the New York paper that the Red Cross was starting a "drive" of twenty teams. They got these "drives" up in military style, with "captains" of the different teams and a "general" over them all. Morgan was one of the captains, and Rockefeller was one, and Schiff, and George Baker, and an Astor and a Gould—all the big names were there. There was a team to collect money from the banks, and one from the corporations, and so on—but no team for the theatrical people. W. F. went up to New York and pointed out this over-

153

sight, and proposed to organize the "Allied Theatrical Motion Pictures Team." Each team was supposed to raise $200,000. With the idea of frightening Fox away, they raised the demand to $400,000; but W. F.'s reply was that the Allied Theatrical Motion Pictures Team would raise $750,000. He offered to leave a check with the Red Cross for the full amount, and let them take out any deficit if he failed in his job. That was his way of talking. The board went into executive session, and faced the fact that if it added a twenty-first team, it would have to destroy all its printed stationery. It voted to destroy the stationery.

Nobody was allowed to start work until after breakfast on Monday morning. There was a gathering of captains at luncheon and W. F. was called on for a speech. He was much frightened, for he has a tremendous respect for these famous financial names —Morgan, Rockefeller, Schiff, Baker, Astor, Gould. However, he made a speech, in his direct and straightforward way, and explained the embarrassing fact that theatrical people don't get up in the morning, and so this luncheon was his breakfast, and all the money he had to report was $1 which had come in the mail, sent by an old woman who said it was half of everything she owned in the world.

John D. Rockefeller, jr. also made a speech, and explained that he also had the habit of going to bed and getting up late. He had only raised $7,000 so far, but he pledged himself to report at least that much every day in the future.

The drive came to an end, and it seemed to W. F. that the Rockefeller family was being badly treated, because the Rockefeller Foundation's large contribution could not be credited to the Rockefellers; it was given by a corporation, and therefore was credited to the team which was collecting from corporations. So W. F. decided that it was his duty to let the Rockefeller team come out No. 1. When it came W. F.'s alphabetical turn to report, he said that his report wasn't ready yet, and he waited until the report was made for the Rockefeller team; it was $1,026,000. There were tremendous cheers for Rockefeller; and then W. F. got up and reported that the Allied Theatrical Motion Pictures Team had obtained contributions from 75,000 persons, and that the amount totaled $1,023,000. As a matter of fact the Allied Motion Pictures team had raised $1,100,000, and W. F.

sent the remaining $77,000 to the Red Cross afterwards, in order
that the Rockefeller team might have the glory of being No. 1.
Afterwards W. F. received a letter in Rockefeller's handwriting,
congratulating him upon his achievement, and revealing between
the lines that Rockefeller had some idea of what W. F. had done.

Just before the end of the war came another drive, and this
time Rockefeller was the "general." I will let W. F. tell that
story in his own words:

"When it was announced that this drive was to be held, I
received a telephone call. The voice on the 'phone said, 'I am
Mr. Rockefeller's secretary, and he would like to know when it
would be convenient for him to call on you.' I told him to let
me know when it would be convenient for him and I would go
to his office. But he said, 'No, Mr. Rockefeller says that this is
a matter that concerns him, and he wants to call on you. How
would 11 o'clock do at your office tomorrow morning?' I said
that would be fine. What a thrill! The richest man in the world
calling on me on a matter that concerns *him!* I was in early
next morning to clean up my desk and my work as promptly as
I knew how. I left word with the girl at the desk that when
Mr. Rockefeller came, to come and knock three times on my
door, and then show Mr. Rockefeller in—all this so I would
know it was he, and so that his name would not be spoken and no
fuss made.

"I waited for him in my office. I watched the clock, and
when it got within about three minutes to 11 o'clock, I had an
idea that I had made the wrong arrangements. My door should
be wide open. As I opened my door, there he was sitting among
the other people and salesmen waiting in my office. I asked him
to please step in. He said he had come a little early."

There were some negotiations, in the course of which the
great Rockefeller paid another visit. W. F. became one of his
"captains," and he saw to it that the outcome was the same as
before; the Rockefeller team was first, and the Fox team was
second. There is yet another story, which W. F. shall tell in
his own way:

"Some years later I read in the newspaper that John D.
Rockefeller with his wife and Rockefeller, jr., were going to
China to dedicate a medical college. Having met him as I had

during the war days, I had great admiration for him, and felt that if he was going to China to dedicate a hospital, a permanent record of it ought to be made, and without his knowledge. In fact I was quite sure that if he knew about it he would object. Therefore, the day they left their home, he didn't know there was a camera concealed in a wagon across the street, and we photographed him as he left; he didn't know when he got off in the Grand Central Station there was a camera at hand; he didn't know we had cameras in the station and near the platform. He didn't know when he boarded the boat to go to China that our cameras were photographing him. A morning or two later he did know that a man with a camera was trying to take pictures of him. On questioning the man, what he was trying to do, and upon the man replying that he was ordered to take as many pictures of him as he could, Rockefeller replied, 'Don't you dare take any pictures. If you do that I will have you thrown off the boat.' The young man replied, 'If you throw me off the boat, I am a good swimmer, and I would still continue taking pictures. My assignment comes from Fox; I am supposed to photograph anything of interest.'

"And we did photograph. He and the cameraman became very friendly, and he let us take our pictures. We photographed the dedication of this hospital and him receiving a degree of doctor. We photographed them coming home, a few days before Christmas. When the pictures were developed, I called up Rockefeller's secretary and said, 'We have made the most beautiful pictures of Mr. Rockefeller's trip. Don't you think he would be interested to show these pictures to his children?' The secretary called me back and said by all means he wanted to show them to his children, and he had selected the next evening, Christmas Eve, to show them. We set up a machine in their little private church, and my operator tells me those children cheered and made just as much noise in the joy of seeing their parents as any other children would have done. I then suggested that Mr. Rockefeller would receive as a gift a set of these films, and asked if there would be any objection to our using some of the scenes for news items. He accepted a set of these pictures, and we did use many of the items in our newsreels later. We had spent several thousands of dollars in photographing these people."

Now the time had come when W. F. had to claim a return for these favors. He wrote a polite note to John D. Rockefeller, jr., saying that he asked for a brief interview in order to obtain Rockefeller's advice about his affairs. In reply he received a cold and formal note informing him that "for many years we have confined ourselves in our investments to certain classes of enterprises, with which we are more or less familiar, and with which it is relatively easy for us to keep in touch." I have had the privilege of inspecting the original of this letter, and saw the signature of John D. Rockefeller, jr., for the first time; I was interested to note that it is a signature which would be duplicated by a majority of the children in any grammar school in the United States. A curious thing, that this immature bit of handwriting should be the most powerful bit that you could find anywhere in the whole world!

W. F. wrote again, explaining politely that he had not asked Rockefeller for any money, and had not intended to ask for any. Again he asked very humbly that he might have a few minutes of Rockefeller's time.

Of course, what W. F. wanted was obvious enough. The Chase National Bank is a Rockefeller institution, and if he could have gained Rockefeller's ear and won his sympathy, he would have had to have only three words written to Albert H. Wiggin, three words followed by that child's signature: "Lay off Fox. John D. Rockefeller, jr."—and all of W. F 's troubles would have been over, and I should not have been writing this book.

But Rockefeller knew exactly what W. F. wanted, and didn't intend to lend his ear and have his feelings harrowed. Princes and potentates cannot do that sort of thing. If every time a prisoner of war was marked for execution, he was allowed to make personal appeal to the commanding general, what would become of the general's peace of mind, and where would be the fun of a military career?

"Young John," as he is known in Wall Street, wrote advising W. F. to consult his brother-in-law, Winthrop Aldrich, who then was president of the Equitable Trust Company, and now is president of the Chase Bank, since the merger of these two institutions. Which brings us back to take up the thread of our story in the office of the law firm of Hughes, Schurman & Dwight.

For W. F. told Hughes that he had written to Rockefeller, and when the reply from Rockefeller came, he took it to Hughes and asked Hughes' advice.

"Hughes looked at the name of Aldrich and said for me not to keep that appointment. He said: 'You know Rockefeller is a Baptist and so am I, and we Baptists stick together and understand each other. If he wanted to help you, he would have sent you to Mr. ——. He is the yes man. But Rockefeller has sent you to the no man. You will just be wasting your time.'"

Unfortunately W. F. has forgotten the name of the "yes man," an item of information which would have greatly increased the sales of this book in Wall Street!

W. F. took the advice of his great new lawyer and did not go to see Winthrop Aldrich. He was in that terrible state of exhaustion where he could not think for himself. But now he looks back upon it all and wonders, did Hughes really know that Aldrich was the "no man" and not the "yes man," and what would have happened if W. F. had gone to see Aldrich and told Aldrich his troubles? Would Aldrich have written the three magic words? Would Aldrich have said: "The Equitable Trust will furnish the money and save these two prosperous companies from destruction?"

W. F. does not know, and never will know; it is one of the riddles with which you, the reader, are left to amuse yourself.

But meanwhile here is our Fox, hesitating in front of the trap, trying to decide whether to enter or to run away. He has put himself into the hands of his great lawyer, and his great lawyer soothes and comforts him. Everything is all right. The action of the Government was a coincidence, and that matter can be attended to. As for the Telephone Company, there is surely nothing to worry about there. The great lawyer understands the Telephone Company. He has represented it many times, and knows Gifford, the president, very well. But W. F. need not be troubled about this intimacy; Hughes has been on both sides, for them and against them. He thinks there is a basis on which an adjustment can be made, both with the Telephone Company and with Halsey, Stuart. Their demand for powers of attorney is unjustified, but their proposition can be modified, and by means of a voting trusteeship the matter can be worked out and all dangers eliminated.

The Fox has to make up his mind quickly, for new troubles are gathering like storm clouds over his head. His English notes are coming due, and he is in danger of losing the whole Gaumont purchase. There are notes due at the banks in New York; and above all, there are those Loew shares in the hands of the brokers. The contract with the brokers provides that they are to hold these shares until December 31, but only on condition that W. F. can keep a margin of 35 per cent. If the shares go below a certain point, the brokers are free of their agreement; and if any one batch is thrown upon the market, then all the shares are gone.

At this time Wall Street was full of rumors of impending collapse of Fox Film and Fox Theatres. This is a regular part of the system; when a concern is to be raided and destroyed, these rumors appear magically and spread like wildfire. There are innumerable "dope sheets" which publish them, and if you are willing to put up the price, you can have anything published you want. As I am writing this book, there are exposures in Congress from which it appears that not merely do the scandal sheets take bribes, but the financial writers of the biggest and most respectable New York newspapers take bribes. And, of course, if the men who desire to beat down a certain stock are in position to have inside information as to a company's business, it is an easy matter for them to prepare tricky statements, and make the soundest company in the world appear to be on the verge of ruin. How could the little investors all over the country who had put their trust in Fox and his companies, understand that his difficulties were due, not to the fact that he had managed his companies badly, but to the fact that he had managed them too well? They were so prosperous that greedy men had banded together to take them away from him.

If anyone were trying to force the Fox into the trap, what would he have done? One thing, to force down the price of the Loew shares! Who was doing it, W. F. never found out, but a friend of his, an insider in Wall Street, brought him the news that a pool had been organized, and a raid on Loew's was to begin on Monday morning. The tip reached W. F. on Friday,

12

and he set out in desperation to find some one who would protect the stock. He had the printed balance sheet of the company, showing how far below value the stock was selling. Loew's, Incorporated, was not involved in any of W. F.'s troubles; it had more than $10,000,000 cash on hand, and its statement at the close of the last fiscal year showed it had earned more than $10,000,000—the largest profit in its history.

W. F. went to see Felix Warburg, one of the senior partners of Kuhn, Loeb & Company. Mr. Warburg had the money, and W. F. had been intimate with him during the war drives, and had had many assurances of his regard. Here was a stock which was selling at $40 a share, and was going to earn $11 a share during the coming year; its true market value therefore was $110. If Warburg would place an order for 50,000 shares of this stock, he would save W. F., and incidentally make an enormous profit. But he refused, and others likewise refused. What they lost by their refusal is evident from the figures. The Loew shares on April 1 were at 70 and on May 1 at 76. In the summer they reached the high mark of 95.

W. F. was trying to borrow money, so as to protect the shares himself. He thought of the Eastman Kodak Company, from which Fox Film was purchasing enormous quantities of supplies. He went to the selling agent of that company, and told his troubles, and the agent agreed to leave for Rochester that night and see the executives of his company. Saturday was a short banking day, and he could hardly raise any money before noontime, but he would spend all day Saturday and if necessary all day Sunday with the Eastman executives, and do his best to have some cash in W. F.'s hands before 10 o'clock Monday morning.

These Eastman executives would, of course, know that Wall Street did not want any money loaned to Fox He was asking for $6,500,000, and in order to make it easier for them, he suggested that they purchase Loew shares, and give Fox Film the privilege of repurchasing these shares within twelve months at cost plus interest. Loew's was likewise a heavy purchaser of Eastman films, and this subterfuge would look plausible.

On Friday evening W. F. had a distinguished caller—none other than Will H. Hays, head of the Allied Motion Picture

Producers' Association. This makes it necessary for us to go back again in our story, and see what had been the dealings of W. F. with this well-advertised gentleman.

Will Hays had been national chairman of the Harding campaign, and W. F. had learned to know him well at this time. After the campaign, W. F. told Hays he was wasting his valuable talents on politics. W. F. was building up a great corporation, and he invited Hays to become one of its executives. But Hays answered that he expected to become a member of the Harding cabinet. W. F. inquired as to whether he would be able to live on that meager salary. Hays replied that he was not financially independent, but still he wanted to become a member of the cabinet.

He became Postmaster-General, and, as you know, got his hands badly smeared with oil. This was embarrassing to W. F., who thought he ought to help his friend to get out of that mess. Just then it was necessary to form an association of the motion picture producers and distributors, for the purpose of avoiding Government censorship of their product, and W. F. urged that some outstanding man in the Republican party should be put in charge. He was asked to suggest a list of men, and he put the name of Will Hays at the top. As a result, Hays got the job, with a salary of $100,000 a year—which was $25,000 more than President Harding was getting. A little later his salary was raised to $250,000 per year. For this increase W. F. was directly responsible; and naturally, therefore, he thought that Will Hays was his friend.

Three times during this long ordeal, the eminent Will Hays came to call upon his tortured friend, Will Fox, and each time he came with one purpose: he knew a man who would be willing to buy the voting shares, and he urged his friend to sell them to this person. In the old days, Fox had told Hays of his ambition to manage the greatest moving picture organization in the world, and Hays had told Fox that he had a right to that ambition; Hays had met and knew intimately all the heads of all the motion picture companies, and no one among them was better qualified than Fox. But now, evidently, Hays had changed his mind as to who was the best qualified person. He had found a man who was better qualified than W. F. This mysterious person wanted to buy the shares on one condition—that Fox would state his price to Hays confidentially, and the unnamed man would promptly say yes or no. Fox asked many questions, and after a while was able to discover the name of this mysterious person: Harley L. Clarke of Chicago!

W. F. began to see the cat in the picture. Will Hays was no stranger to Harley L. Clarke. Hays was an intimate friend of Senator Watson—the two of them ran the politics of Indiana, and Watson was Clarke's political man. So Clarke was sure that he could merge Fox and Loew—and Paramount too, if he wanted to. Clarke had his political man in Washington, and he had a big financial man in New York, Albert H. Wiggin of the Chase National Bank and the Chase Securities Company. Could it be that Clarke and Wiggin had organized a raid on the Loew shares for Monday morning, and then had sent Will Hays to interview the harassed Fox on Friday evening?

Traps on every side of him, and no way of escape! Perhaps it would be just as well to sell out, and end his troubles once and for all! Let W. F. tell this extraordinary story in his own words:

"I gave Hays the price that night. I told him that before the crash Clarke once inquired if my voting shares were for sale, and I told him then that I had no intention of selling them, but if I were, the price would be $100,000,000. In view of the difficulty I was in now, I would change that price and take a third of $100,000,000.

"The next day, Saturday, Clarke telephoned me from Chicago. He said that price was all right; he would pay me a third of $100,000,000. 'I will come to New York on Monday and consummate the transaction with you.' I said I was sorry, but I didn't know whether this thing would hold until Monday. I said, 'I am in more serious trouble now than you know'—that is, I thought he didn't know. He asked me what the trouble was. I said: 'I am told there is going to be a raid on the Loew shares on Monday morning at 10 o'clock, and I need enough money to lift these Loew shares out of the hands of the brokers. First my enemies will raid the shares to make the brokers throw them over, and then the banks will have to throw them over. That will be total destruction to the Fox companies. Now you are talking about friendship, you can prove that you are buying me out just to be of service. You loan the company the sum necessary to lift these shares out of the brokers' hands.'

"He said all right. He said that of course all the banks were closed now and wouldn't open until Monday. He said, 'I will have an official of Chase Bank call on you tomorrow, Sunday, and give you a written communication indicating that there will be $6,500,000 to your credit on Monday morning when the bank opens.' I told him it happened that Richard Dwight, Judge Hughes' partner, was sitting alongside of me while I was having this conversation with him—would he please repeat to Dwight what he had just said to me. He evidently did repeat it, for the next day, Sunday, Dwight called again at my apartments in the hopes of meeting this executive of the Chase Bank.

"Instead the telephone rang again: Clarke on the 'phone from Chicago. He had changed his mind about doing it that way. He would take an early train out of Chicago. He would take a train immediately after he hung up the telephone, a train that would bring him to New York at 9 o'clock—he would be at my apartment at 9:15, and bring with him the certified check for $6,500,000. This check would be certified early Monday morning and he would bring it to my hotel and be there at 9:15.

"In the meantime, no word from Rochester. This was Sunday morning. I had told no one about the Rochester deal. No Chase Bank check for $6,500,000 from Clarke. Everybody I knew to whom I could possibly go for financial aid was exhausted. I remembered that my name was Fox, and I remembered reading somewhere that if there is a group of foxes in the woods, they are all good friends. If one of them happens to fall and break his leg, they all turn around and devour him. Then they go on and are good friends again."

But again W. F. had that blind trust in Providence. He did not know what was the basis of his assurance, yet he felt safe. "Somehow, some way, I didn't know where from, I knew that when that bell rang at 10 o'clock Monday morning, there would be no raid on those shares.

"Monday morning—9:15. Mr. Dwight at my offices was waiting for Harley Clarke. I watched the clock, and never saw minutes travel so fast. Nine-thirty and no Clarke. I 'phoned to the New York Central Station to see if the train was late. No, it was on time—it had arrived about 8.45. Clarke could have walked to my office and have been there twenty minutes ago. What had been his purpose in calling me on the 'phone at all? What had been Hays' purpose? Maybe I had made a mistake when I told him there would be a raid on these Loew shares. I could close my eyes and see the New York Stock Exchange, with all these brokers hustling and bustling, taking their positions at their various posts. I had a clear vision of the bell that was there. Here were these companies which I had built, the result of an effort I had made from the time I was five years old until now when I reached the age of fifty-one— forty-six years of building and constructing, all of which was going to be destroyed at the stroke of 10. Nine-forty-five, 9:50, 9:51, 9:52, 9:53, 9:54—and the telephone rang at exactly 9:55, the agent of the Eastman Kodak Company calling from Rochester, and saying 'There is placed to your credit $6,300,000 at the Bankers Trust in New York.'

"There He was! There was this God Almighty of mine, saving me again! Now it was necessary to 'phone thirteen brokers: 'Suckers, deliver those shares to the Bankers Trust.' They were no longer the brokers' property. A half dozen of our people who had 'phones in their rooms each took a couple of names, and we got busy. About 10 o'clock the majority of these brokers knew that they were to take these shares out of the banks where they had them hypothecated and deliver them to the Bankers Trust and receive cash for them."

So the plans of the bear raiders were thwarted. W. F. tells how at three minutes after 10 o'clock, the friend in Wall Street who had tipped him off as to the plans of the raiders, called him on the 'phone and asked: "What have you done? What has happened? Those fellows had the scene all rigged and staged, but something has gone wrong. What is it?"

W. F. was at his office in consultation with Dwight and his friend Reass; and at 10:30 Clarke arrived. W. F. tells me that if the matter had been left to him, he would not have told Clarke of his $6,300,000; but Dwight, his lawyer, considered that it was his duty to start the conversation, and to state that W. F. had been so fortunate as to secure the money at the Bankers Trust Company. Of course it would be an easy matter for Clarke to ascertain that the money thus placed to the credit of W. F. had been supplied by the Eastman Kodak Company.

Clarke showed no surprise; he apparently knew everything about the affairs of W. F. He volunteered no apologies for not appearing at 9:15 as promised, nor did Dwight consider it necessary to ask him. Said Clarke: "I am prepared to buy the voting shares of Fox Film and Fox Theatres, and I am prepared to pay for them one-third of $100,000,000. I have here a memorandum containing my proposal." He handed over the memorandum, which contained a long, confusing statement, describing the terms as to how the money was to be paid.

"One glance at the memorandum showed that his proposal to me was impossible. His plan required me to authorize the Board of Directors of Fox Theatres to sell to Clarke the 660,900 shares of Loew stock at a price of $33,045,000, which was $40,000,000 less than the company paid for them. The amount he was to pay my company, $33,045,000, plus the $33,000,000 he was to pay me—the combined figure would be $7,000,000 less than the price we paid for those shares! I didn't even stop to consider the thing. In fact, Dwight called his attention to the fact that his proposal was preposterous. In the light of what had happened since, in that Fox Theatres sold these 660,900 shares of stock and received for them in cash $75,000,000, or $42,000,000 more than Clarke's proposal—I could well understand his offer of $33,000,000 to me.

"Of course, it looked like a simple proposition to carry out this plan with Clarke, because at this particular time the market on the Loew shares was approximately $40 a share, and Clarke was proposing to buy them at $50 a share. Fox could have claimed justification for selling these shares at more than the market value. Fox Theatres would have been able to pay $33,045,000 to its creditors. The offer to Fox was a darn tempting one. You must remember that I eventually sold out for $18,000,000, and that was $15,000,000 less than I could have received at this time. Also I should have been spared all the agonies of hell that I had to go through between this time in November and April 5, 1930. And yet I have to say that if I had to do it all over again, rather than lend myself to a transaction which would have robbed my companies, I am sure I would do the same thing over again. I am that stubborn, I would have held onto my shares until hell froze over; I knew I would have held them, even though they would be wiped out in the end.

"Clarke could have bought my voting shares first, and have then carried out what he proposed in that agreement; but then he would have been making the deal with himself, and perhaps that wouldn't have been looked upon as a perfectly proper transaction. But if he could have got Fox to make the sale, while Fox was still in control of these companies, then the burden would have fallen on Fox's shoulders, and not on Clarke's.

"In his telephone conversation from Chicago, Clarke was coming down to give me one-third of $100,000,000. My guess is that he had more than this one memorandum in his pocket. Had the stock market raid taken place, the other memorandum would probably have contained an offer of $1,000,000 for my voting shares."

W. F. now looks back upon that episode and finds it one of the mysteries which will never be solved. Did Clarke really expect him to put through that deal? To take a bribe of one-third of $100,000,000, for selling out his stockholders and robbing them of $42,000,000? Or was it just another device to stall him along? Or, still worse, was it a plot to ruin him? Were they going to get him to sign this agreement, and then take it to the newspaper men, or possibly even to the District Attorney's office, or to the grand jury, and get this tough, tenacious Fox safely caged in Sing Sing prison?

REEL FIFTEEN

THE TRAP SHUTS

THESE negotiations with Harley Clarke had not helped our
Fox with his problems. One crisis came upon the heels of
another. There were still some Loew shares in the hands of
brokers; there were the notes falling due at the New York
banks; and the English creditors were threatening foreclosure.
W. F. must have another $4,000,000, and there was no way
to get it except by the trusteeship agreement, into which the great
lawyer Hughes and his partner Dwight were gently shepherding
him.

Stuart and Otterson, the principal creditors of the Fox companies, in order to save the companies and get their money back,
were proposing to enter into an arrangement with W. F., whereby
the three of them would form a trusteeship, to which he would
turn over his voting shares. The trustees would "endeavor" to
prepare a plan for the refinancing of the companies; they would
pledge their good faith to this end, and the great lawyer Hughes
assured the harried and exhausted Fox that he could so word
this agreement as to protect the interests of both Fox and his
stockholders, and that this was the only way by which this situation could be saved.

Stuart and Otterson, as the principal creditors of the companies, were the ones who had an interest in saving them, and
they had the money to save them; but of course they could not
be expected to put up money unless they had the financial control
of the companies until their money had been returned to them.
That was a fair proposition, and a quite customary arrangement,
said the lawyer; and W. F. answered, humbly: "Of course, Mr.
Hughes, anything you say is all right. I trust myself entirely
in your hands. There is no use in my coming here if I am not
going to act as you advise."

167

So the great legal minds set to work upon the voting trust agreement. It was ready; and then came a singular thing—one of the strangest developments I remember ever to have heard of in business or legal affairs. Hughes sent for W. F. and said: "Now that the agreement is ready for signature, you have to make a choice. Shall I continue to be your lawyer, or do you wish my firm to become the attorneys for the voting trusteeship?" It happened unfortunately that when this question was put to W. F., his friend and lawyer Reass had stepped out of the room for a few minutes. W. F. was surprised by the question, and didn't know what to say. He narrates:

"I told him I couldn't decide, he would have to decide for me; as I had told him the day before, I couldn't think, and I didn't know what to say. I said that whichever he thought was the best for me I wanted him to do. He said no, I must decide now whether I wanted him to remain my attorney, or whether I wanted his firm to be attorneys for the trusteeship. I then began to reason this thing out. If this trusteeship was to be that which was represented by Hughes, which was being created for my benefit—if these two men were going to be the kind gentlemen they said they were going to be, then I wouldn't need a lawyer beyond that. I wouldn't have any use for a lawyer. What I needed more than anything else was to have Mr. Hughes be attorney for the voting trustees, to see that no trouble came to me. He was our lawyer—the three voting trustees. He, the man who said he would work this thing out for me, the man who had actually drawn the paper which was being submitted to me now for my signature, still he was my lawyer—and what better could I ask than to have him the attorney for the voting trustees, to carry out the terms of this agreement as he had conceived it? Who was better qualified to be the attorney for the voting trustees?

"At any rate, that is how my mind operated then. I released him as my attorney and accepted him as attorney for the voting trustees. The basis on which these voting shares were to be dissolved was to be submitted to Hughes or his firm for his approval; therefore, I was gaining two things—one, he was going to protect me on whatever basis they were going to dissolve my shares, and second, he understood what the voting trusteeship intended to be, because he drew it himself. I decided that the obligation was greater on his shoulders when his firm was to become the attorney for the voting trustees."

W. F. was right when he said that his mind was not working on that occasion. It took him only a few days to realize what he had done: he had hired the greatest lawyer in the United States, and promised him an enormous fee, and taken him into his confidence, and told him all his troubles—and then turned him over to his enemies, to become the attorney for these enemies, to use all his power and all his knowledge in fighting and trying to destroy the man who had employed him! As I say, the oddest development I remember ever to have heard of.

The great Hughes had given much time to these personal conferences with W. F.; but from this time on W. F. never saw him again. The handling of the case was turned over to Richard Everett Dwight. Mr. Dwight is a graduate of Princeton and a very fashionable lawyer; W. F. thought that his face looked familiar, and after a week or so he remembered where he had met him, more than twenty years back. Dwight was seventy-five pounds heavier, but still the same person who had represented the General Film Company, that motion picture trust which in 1908 had cleaned everybody else out of the field. Dwight had sat up all one night with W. F, negotiating a settlement, and had handed over a check for $350,000. A great humiliation for a rising young lawyer! Could it be that Dwight cherished the memory, and was not sorry for the development which in a few days placed him at the head of the enemies of William Fox?

The negotiations concerning the trust agreement took place in the presence of Hughes, Dwight, Reass, Hartfield, Otterson, Stuart and their lawyers. W. F. agreed to turn over to a trusteeship of three persons, Otterson, Stuart and himself, his voting shares of the Fox Film Corporation, 50,101 shares out of the 100,000 Class B shares; also 100,000 Class B shares of the Fox Theatres Corporation, which is 100 per cent of the voting stock. These shares were to be turned over to the Bankers Trust Company with an escrow letter. W. F. agreed to deliver to the trustees the resignations of all the directors of the companies, and of such officers of the companies as the trustees might request, with the exception of the president; also the resignations of directors in fully controlled subsidiaries, and of those directors who represented the interests of Fox in the partially controlled subsidiaries.

The crucial paragraph of the agreement was the third:

"The trustees will endeavor to prepare a plan of reorganization and refinancing of the companies and in the meantime will undertake negotiations with a view to preventing the sacrifice of the assets of the companies, including particularly securities pledged. The trustees will also undertake to negotiate with creditors and other persons interested in the situation with the view of obtaining their forbearance and co-operation during the period of the preparation and submission and adoption of any such plan."

It was furthermore provided that Hughes, Schurman & Dwight should be the counsel for the trustees, and that "no plan of reorganization or financing of the companies shall be finally submitted to the creditors and stockholders for approval and adoption until all the legal questions involved therein shall have been approved by such counsel." It was furthermore provided that "the action of any two of the trustees with respect to any of the matters embraced in this agreement shall be deemed to be the action of the trustees."

I hesitate to put myself in the position of criticizing the legal work of the great Charles Evans Hughes, but I cannot refrain from calling attention to a peculiar provision in this agreement in the second paragraph: "Fox agrees to deliver to the trustees forthwith the resignations of all the directors of the two companies." The eleventh paragraph declared: "It is understood and agreed that the resignations of a majority of the directors of the Fox Film Corporation and Fox Theatres Corporation are to be accepted forthwith and Fox covenants and agrees that he will forthwith cause the remaining directors to elect in the place and stead of the directors whose resignations are accepted persons nominated by the trustees."

It seems that this eleventh paragraph makes it clear that Fox is to have a minority of directors representing him; but if so, why should the second paragraph provide that Fox should deliver the resignations of *all* the directors?

The voting trust agreement lay on the desk. W. F. had read it, as well as he could in his exhausted state; but he wasn't so much concerned about its phraseology as he was about having a gentlemen's understanding among the trustees, made in the presence of their lawyers and his. These understanding gentlemen promised him that he was to remain as president of both the corporations, and as a director of each. Also that his brother-in-law, Jack Leo, should remain as a director, and two others of his employees, Sheehan and King, whom he counted as his loyal friends. W. F. had withdrawn from the room with Hartfield and Reass to study the voting trust agreement, and Hartfield made a written memorandum of the gentlemen's agreement which W. F. wanted to have stated. These propositions were stated by W. F. to Stuart and Otterson and all the lawyers, and they all agreed that they were gentlemen, and that this was their agreement.

Of course, everything connected with this voting trust arrangement depended upon the good faith of the two men who were to constitute the acting majority of the trustees and in whose hands lay the whole conduct of affairs. W. F. was parting with his two most precious pieces of paper, and the two companies, Fox Film and Fox Theatres, were placed at the mercy of Otterson and Stuart. They assured him that they had no desire to run his companies or to interfere with his running of his companies. He was earning dividends and they were satisfied with what he was earning. All they wished to have was the handling of the financing of the companies, so as to get back their $30,000,000. If they were to sell new securities to the public, they must have the administering of the finances until this had been accomplished. That was their only purpose in entering into the agreement, they declared; and if that was so, then they were gentlemen, and their undertaking was a legitimate and honorable one. If, on the other hand, they wanted to disrupt W. F.'s management of the companies, to take them away from him and make them their own, then they were conspirators and bandits. Which were they?

On the day after the signing of the agreement, the three trustees had their first conference. W. F. suggested that they should meet at the offices of the Fox Film Corporation, but he was promptly told that the trustees had no intention of ever meeting at the offices of the Fox Film Corporation. The headquarters for the conduct of Fox Film and Fox Theatres in the future would be at the corner of Dye Street and Broadway, the offices of the American Telephone & Telegraph Company.

W. F. describes his physical condition on that day:

"During the month of November, 1929, it was common to read in the newspapers of men who had met with reverses during these thirty days, resorting to every known means to bring life to an end. During this period there were suicides daily, and in each instance there was a Wall Street record behind it. In jest I have often heard that Wall Street winds crookedly, with a river at one end and a cemetery at the other, and now this became a reality to me. During these thirty days I had exactly sixty hours of sleep. I was mentally tired and physically worn out. I am not exaggerating this in the slightest degree when I tell you that when I attended the first meeting of the trustees, if I sat down in a chair I fell asleep and if I stood up I felt like falling down. I was bewildered."

Here is the scene of the first meeting:

"When we gathered at the offices of the Telephone Company and when I arrived, there were present Dwight, Charles Stuart, and a lawyer who was to act as secretary. One chair was at the head of the table, the others were arranged on each side. Dwight greeted me very cordially as I came in, and escorted me to one of the chairs, where he had decided I should sit. That gesture was wholly without significance to me. Otterson came in next. The chair at the head of the table was still unoccupied, and Otterson took it. The first thing that had to be done was to elect a chairman, a chairman of the trustees. Dwight pointed to Otterson and said, 'You are occupying the chairman's seat now, I presume you are to be the chairman'; and then turned to Charles Stuart to see whether that was agreeable to him. Charles Stuart said, 'These stocks don't belong to us; it strikes me it would be more appropriate to have Fox the chairman of the trustees for his own stock.' Dwight's plan was foiled, of course, because it took two of the three trustees to elect a chairman. When he heard Charles' view, he promptly said, 'I suppose then under those circumstances Fox ought to be the chairman.' "

Hartfield came, and the trustees got down to business. The first announcement was that before the meeting could go forward, William Fox must give them a statement of the assets and liabilities of William Fox. He found this demand surprising, for he had been under the impression that it was the Fox companies which were in financial difficulties, and not Fox himself. The trustees were supposed to administer the voting shares of Fox for his benefit; but here they were proposing to strip him of everything he owned. He asks:

"Were they inquiring to know all my personal assets so that they could give me further aid if necessary? I soon found that was not so. Their questions were directed at me because they claimed that $4,000,000 was necessary, and if I had $4,000,000 anywhere, anyhow, or had properties that were worth $4,000,000, they should know it. If I had it in cash I ought to loan the company $4,000,000. If I had it in personal properties, I should give it to them as collateral for the $4,000,000 required. The fact that the companies had unencumbered assets of more than $30,000,000, which the companies were perfectly free to pledge for anything necessary, did not concern my trustees at all. The main purpose here was to take from Fox everything he had. As tired and as weary as I was, I knew that that was not for my benefit, and I protested.

"From time to time I have read newspaper accounts of a third degree at Police Headquarters in New York. I had seen scenes portrayed in pictures of a prisoner receiving his third degree in an effort to make him break down and obtain a confession. Here I was getting a third degree as hard as it was possible. By whom? Otterson representing the Telephone Company, Charles Stuart of Halsey, Stuart, and Dwight of the firm of Hughes, Schurman & Dwight, who only twenty-four hours before was my personal attorney. I resisted this third degree, and soon I found my other honorable lawyer, Hartfield, asking me to step into another room—he wanted to have a talk with me. We did, and he spent a half hour or more trying to convince me that what these gentlemen were asking me was perfectly proper and right, and I should give them this memorandum indicating what my assets and liabilities were.

"When this trouble first began, I realized one of the things

I had to have was as much available cash as possible. I had a large equity or loaning power on my life insurance policies, and I had promptly applied to the life insurance company for loans against my policies. It was on this particular morning that my secretary handed me a batch of checks that we had received as loans on my life insurance policies, amounting to approximately $490,000. How Otterson, Stuart, Dwight and Hartfield found that out, I have been unable to discover up to this day. This was the $490,000 that really belonged to my widow and orphans if I were to die, for I had insured my life for their benefit. That conference did not end that morning until I took from my pockets this $490,000 worth of checks and turned them over to my companies. It was only after I agreed to do that that my trustees would arrange to take from our brokers the stocks that were there and which the brokers were carrying on margin, to lift the balance of these shares out of the hands of my brokers and place them with two banks."

There was an important point to be noted here. Very soon when the break comes, we shall find Harry Stuart and Otterson declaring that they obtained money to save W. F., and that this is one of the reasons why they have acquired an interest in the trusteeship agreement. We shall find Harry Stuart and Otterson declaring under oath that they endorsed notes for this money— and failing to say a single word about the fact that they required W. F. to put up collateral to cover every dollar of these loans. In the charges and counter-charges in which presently we shall find ourselves entangled, it will be important to bear this detail in mind. Again and again in this book we have read accounts of interviews in which W. F. was alone with Stuart or with Otterson, and in which he declares that promises were made; we shall find them declaring in their affidavits that no such interviews took place and no such promises were made; and which are we going to believe? Here is one place where we can judge. Says W. F.:

"Neither the Telephone Company nor Halsey, Stuart ever loaned these companies a single dollar in this emergency where they were trustees. In their affidavits they said the Telephone Company endorsed a note. They didn't tell you in that affidavit that that note was accompanied .by collateral traded in in the

New York Stock Exchange, and that for nearly $4,000,000 these two men had obtained, we had deposited approximately $6,500,-000 worth of New York Stock Exchange collateral: $1,000,000 of Warner Brothers notes, and the rest shares of Loew's, Fox Film and Fox Theatres. They were not required to lend their names to these loans. They told the banks to take the collateral and make the loans—just as up to this time they had told the banks *not* to make loans, regardless of collateral. Neither of these trustees had guaranteed anything or put their hands in their pockets for a penny. The communication of Stuart, in which he said that the voting trust had come to an end and that he would no longer put up any money, meant nothing, because up to that time he hadn't put up a dollar. True, he told us what banks to go to to get this money; but that is what banks are for."

There was the problem of the English obligation:

"It became necessary to call London on the telephone, which we did from the Telephone Company's offices, and carry on quite a lengthy conversation with the Telephone representative in London, who was handling the English creditors, knowing them all. His suggestion was that approximately $1,000,000 was necessary at this time to temporarily tide over the requirements in England. There were one or two more trustees' meetings, all concerning the English situation, and the arrangement was to take collateral belonging to Fox Film and Fox Theatres and hypothecate it for the loans from banks designated by Stuart and the Telephone Company. I believe the last of these meetings was conducted about Friday or Saturday of that week.

"Much of the time was spent in discussing how promptly these meetings were to be held. It appeared that Otterson and Stuart wanted to reserve for themselves the right to call a meeting to be held in the Telephone Company's offices at an hour's notice. After a very lengthy discussion on this subject I convinced them that that was wholly unfair, that I might be uptown and couldn't arrive downtown in an hour, and after long debate, it was finally consented that—I believe it was either two or two and a half hours' notice to be given. It was clear to me that I was going to spend the remainder of my time in running the affairs of Fox Film and Fox Theatres by attending trustees' meetings."

13

Next came the problem of the New York bankers. All these gentlemen had wanted their money from W. F., and had refused to hear to any extensions, or to accept any of the collateral which W. F. kept pressing upon them. But, of course, it was an entirely different matter when the outlaw Fox was taken over by great and respectable concerns such as the Telephone Company and Halsey, Stuart & Co. The bankers were invited to the offices of the Telephone Company, and they assembled and listened to an address by Otterson, in which he informed them of the new voting trust arrangement. The Telephone Company would consider it a favor if they would be indulgent, until a plan of financing could be worked out whereby everyone could get his money. Everyone was pleased, and everyone was indulgent. There would be no further trouble from the New York bankers.

There were several of the executives of Fox Film and Fox Theatres who were supposed to be the friends and supporters of W. F., but who, as he was now discovering, had been won away from him by his enemies. He learned that two of these men, Sheehan and King, were having secret conferences with Stuart and Otterson. He thought that if there were to be conferences of executives with trustees, he, as the third trustee, should be present. He consulted Hartfield about this, and Hartfield reminded him of the gentleman's agreement which had been made when the voting trust was signed. W. F. recited his understanding of this agreement—that his four directors, Fox, Leo, Sheehan and King, were to remain on the board; that Fox was to remain the president of both companies, and that Otterson was to withdraw when his money was repaid. Hartfield said that he had had the same understanding, and had made a memorandum of it; he showed the memorandum to W. F.

But now it appeared that Stuart and Otterson were denying any such understanding, and were preparing to remove Leo from the board of directors. W. F. asked Hartfield the reason for this, and Hartfield answered, because Leo was too close to Fox. That indicated clearly that King and Sheehan were *not* close to Fox, and showed definitely what had been going on at the private talks of King and Sheehan with Otterson and Stuart. Says W. F.:

"I said that would be all wrong; Mr. Leo must be retained, because his executive position was about on a par with a car-

buretor of an automobile. What could these men be thinking of
doing, that they didn't want Leo to know and didn't want me to
know? I said to Hartfield, 'I didn't understand that these two
men were to run the companies. It was only to enable them to
do the necessary financing, and while the trust agreement didn't
obligate them to do the financing, at least they were going to try
to do it. That was all the voting trust was for.' Hartfield said,
'I don't know what they have on their minds any more than that
they don't want Leo for a director—he is too close to you. If he
is a director, you will know everything that happens, and they
don't propose to have that.' "

After that conference W. F. went to his home on Long Island.
He was ill, and his doctor was sent for, and reported his temperature at 103½. He stayed in bed for five or six days, and in
that period of time the other two trustees were able to hold
meetings without being burdened by his presence. One of the
things they did in the interim was to summon from Los Angeles
Harold B. Franklin, president of West Coast Theatres. This
corporation, you must be reminded, is a wholly owned subsidiary
of Fox Film. At the time W. F. bought the concern, Franklin
had a contract for $150,000 per year, plus 10 per cent of the net
profits of the corporation. W. F. doesn't approve of those 10 per
cent arrangements, but there was no way to get rid of the contract. He had brought the earnings of West Coast up to $5,500,-
000 in the year 1929, and therefore Franklin was about to receive
$550,000—bringing his total compensation to $700,000. That
would seem to be ample, but apparently it did not seem so to
Stuart and Otterson, for W. F. now learned that they had brought
Franklin on to make him a proposition that he should become
also the president of Fox Theatres, and receive a further salary
of $150,000 a year in that capacity, plus 10 per cent of the net
earnings of Fox Theatres, which during the year 1929 were over
$2,000,000.

But how could they offer this new post to Franklin when it
was already held by W. F.? Why pay a man $350,000 a year
for doing a job, which another man was doing faithfully for nothing? Could it be that working without salary was considered to
be setting a bad example in Wall Street?

And also, what about the gentlemen's agreement? Could it

be that the agreement had been made under a misapprehension? That the wearing of a carnation in one's buttonhole when attending directors' meetings, or being a graduate of Annapolis and a lieutenant and naval constructor, does not necessarily imply that one is a gentleman? Says W. F.:

"There came to me a clear realization that I had made a terrific mistake; that I had taken that which I had earned by the sweat of my brow as a result of hard labor for twenty-five years, and that I had parted with it, and that the two men who now had charge of it were not going to be trustees for my estate or for my property, but intended to disrupt, disorganize, and ruin the venture that I had built over a period of a lifetime. It was now up to me to try to confirm if I was right in my contention."

W. F. consulted his friend, Benjamin Reass, and on Friday evening, the fifth day of his illness, Reass came to his home with Hartfield.

"There were present at this conference Mr. Reass, Jack Leo, Colonel Hartfield, Mrs. Fox and my daughter, Mona. I didn't know what the conversation was in the lower end of this building; I was confined in my bedroom. I was later informed that Hartfield had expressed to my wife his regrets for the great difficulties her husband found himself in, and paralleled this to a general in the army. He said when a general in the army plans a battle and loses it, he must expect to be deposed. He told Mrs. Fox that her husband had carried on a battle here just as a general in the army did, and having lost a battle, he must expect the same fate as a general in the army.

"I heard loud voices downstairs and rang the bell and asked them to please come up. Mrs. Fox didn't tell me of this talk while Hartfield was there. I now wish she had done so. Hartfield said it was important that I promptly meet with Dwight.

"One of the things that my lawyers had failed to include in the voting trust agreement was my definite understanding that when the Telephone Company was reimbursed for the $15,000,-000 they had loaned to the company, Otterson would resign as a trustee. One of the thoughts in my mind was that I wanted the Telephone Company out of my business as soon as I could get it out. I didn't want the Telephone Company running my business—particularly in view of our controversy over the Tri-Ergon patents. Hartfield had failed to include that in the voting trust agreement. I had said to Hartfield that I thought I would be well enough to come to New York on Sunday to have the conference he suggested, and I did go to New York that Sunday evening to hold a conference at which were present Reass, Newman, Rubenstein, Hartfield, Dwight and myself. I had gone in to recite what had been brought to my attention during that week. I openly charged the contemptible things these trustees were doing while I was ill in bed.

"Dwight defended the trustees, saying that what they did they had a full right to do. I told Dwight that when this trust agreement was drawn, his firm had failed to include in the voting trust agreement that Otterson was to resign as a trustee as soon as the Telephone Company had received its $15,000,000. That was discussed. Dwight took the position that there was never such an understanding, and that his client expected to remain the trustee for those shares which belonged to me, and that if I insisted upon that being done, if I insisted that Otterson resign when the Telephone Company was reimbursed for its $15,000,000, then the whole deal was off; we could dissolve the voting trust agreement—he knew his client would never agree to anything like that. Dwight left the room, calling the trust agreement off; it was ended as far as he or his clients were concerned. Hartfield tried to persuade him to come back, and suggested that perhaps it would be an easy matter for him to get the Telephone Company to agree to withdraw upon the receipt of their $15,000,000. But Dwight insisted nothing doing, and finally left."

So that is what has become of all W. F.'s bright hopes in connection with the law firm of Hughes, Schurman & Dwight! Three weeks had passed since he visited the great Charles Evans Hughes, and told him all his troubles, and received many firm pressures from his hand, and been told that the great man's shoulders were broad, and that from now on he would carry the burdens of the little Fox. Charles Evans Hughes, for four years reform governor of New York State, for six years a Justice of the Supreme Court of the United States, for four years Secretary of State of the United States—this world-famous statesman had agreed to protect William Fox from his powerful and dangerous enemies, for a fee which turned out in the end to be

$520,000; and his partner, Richard Everett Dwight, would earn that fee by the bitterest opposition to every interest that the Fox has and to every right that he claims! Do you agree with me that this is an odd development of a legal bargain?

Looking back on the events from a distance of two years and a half, W. F. records this opinion:

"It was not a trusteeship agreement. The title was entirely wrong. Stuart and Otterson never intended to be trustees—they intended to be destroyers of what I had built up. They didn't intend to protect me, they intended to wreck me and take my property. And when Mr. Hughes helped to draw this paper, no one knew better than he that he had prepared a paper that would not act in the interest of William Fox; that he was not protecting Fox, and that these men were receiving powers not accorded to trustees. I don't want to find fault with Dwight; I didn't talk to him. But I had my confidential talk with Judge Hughes, and he extended me his hand as a friend, and said he would assume the burdens and responsibilities from then on; that my troubles were over. Didn't he know that that wasn't a trust agreement to protect my property? Of course he did; he must have known it."

Also, let us say a few words about the difficult situation of Colonel Hartfield from Kentucky. The colonel has undertaken to become the lawyer of W. F., and to be paid $1,000,000 if he can succeed in saving the companies from receivership. In this effort his opponents are the big bankers whom he has hitherto been representing, and the big lawyers with whom he has hitherto been associated; they are the bankers whom he will be representing in the future, and the lawyers with whom he will be associated, when this one little misadventure is over. His firm, White & Case, was counsel for the Bankers Trust, one of the creditors, and the bank which had the voting shares in escrow.

Hartfield's embarrassing position was set forth at one of the conferences with the bankers—the speaker being a young lawyer who had not yet learned discretion. Said this youngster: "Colonel, isn't it rather peculiar for you to be on the other side of the fence? I have never known you to be for the debtor—you are always for the creditor. You were always a bankers' lawyer." Hartfield turned this off with a laugh, as he so well knows how to do.

Whatever the reason may be, through most of these negotiations Hartfield considered it his duty to advise W. F. to do the things which his enemies wanted him to do, rather than the things which W. F. himself wanted to do. But then, when the situation grew too bad, Hartfield would become conscience-stricken, and remember who it was that was paying him. One of these occasions had been on the previous Sunday, when he had met W. F. at the Ambassador Hotel, and agreed with him about the gentlemen's agreement, and told him that the trustees were planning to remove Jack Leo from the board of directors of the two companies. A second occasion was here, a week later, after Dwight had made his announcement that the trust agreement was off for good and all. Says W. F.:

"In the presence of Benjamin Reass, Jacob L. Rubenstein and Emanuel Newman, Hartfield said that he had withheld this information, but now that the whole thing was terminated, he ought to tell me what had transpired during the week I was lying in bed. One, they had no intention of electing Jack Leo as a director. Two, they had no intention of retaining me as president. Three, Harry Stuart had suggested that I ought immediately to leave the country, and stay for at least six months, because the disgrace and humiliation showered on me would be so great I could never stand it."

So there at last the cat was out of the bag! The Fox knew the whole program now; and next morning the whole of New York knew it. For when he picked up the New York "Times," for Monday, December 16, he read a front page story "according to an authoritative source," setting forth that "a new holding company has been definitely decided upon by the trustees," and that there was to be "wider participation of Class A stock in management"—which meant, of course, the dissolution of W. F.'s voting shares. He says:

"Under the trust agreement, if it became necessary to dissolve these B shares, they were to give me 1½ shares of A stock for each share of B stock. Had they done that, they would have given me 75,000 shares of Fox Film at the then market price of $20 a share, and 150,000 shares of Fox Theatres at $8 a share; so I would have shares with a market value of $2,700,000. That was the price they were to pay for taking over the companies and throwing me out—a price that was $30,500,000 less than Clarke had offered me a brief two weeks before! This would of course have put the companies entirely in the hands of the Telephone Company; they were going to be in the motion picture business. And it wasn't going to cost them anything; they were getting the business practically gratis.

"We inquired from Hartfield as to how that article appeared in the newspaper—who issued that story? He disclaimed any knowledge of it at all; in fact, no one from Dwight on down knew anything about it. They said the story must have been given to the New York 'Times' by me, and I must have had a definite reason for giving it to them; what was my purpose?

"During all these trials and tribulations one of the editors of the New York 'Times' constantly kept in touch with me, and insisted that I tell him all I could as the case progressed. I asked him to call on me at my home the next night. I realized that in his sober senses he would give me no information, so together we split a quart bottle of Scotch, and we both became talkative. Then I said, 'I always thought that you were my friend, but you played me a dirty trick. When I gave you that plan that appeared in Monday morning's paper I gave it to you with the understanding it was strictly confidential. Now I find you are around squealing on me.' He said, 'Who said you gave that story to me?' I said, 'Didn't I? Well, who did?' He said, 'It was given to me by your bankers. It came from them.'

"So you see that on Sunday night when we met Hartfield, Reass, Dwight, myself and others, they were cocksure of their position, that there would be no difficulty with the trust agreement, and promptly on Monday morning appeared this article of the dissolving of my shares. They felt that they had captured these companies—there was no doubt in their minds. It was probably given to the papers Saturday morning, with instructions to release on Monday morning—too late to recall, because our conference broke up about midnight and the 'Times' was already printed."

Let us now run over the whole chain of evidence in consecutive order, from December 3, when W. F. signed the voting trust agreement. First, Stuart and Otterson have searched the pockets of the Fox and taken out his $490,000 worth of life insurance

money. Second, they have taken $1,000,000 worth of Warners'
notes and sold them—something he could just as well have done
for himself. Third, they have taken about $5,000,000 worth of
additional collateral from him. Fourth, they have won Sheehan,
King and other employees away from him. Fifth, they have
brought Franklin from California, to make him president of Fox
Theatres in W. F.'s place. Sixth, they have decided to remove
W. F.'s brother-in-law as director of both companies. Seventh,
they have told Hartfield that they are going to remove W. F. as
president of both companies, and that the wise thing for him to
do would be to go away immediately and stay for six months.
Eighth, they have given the New York "Times" a detailed story
to the effect that W. F.'s voting shares are to be wiped out, and
that his compensation is to be $2,700,000 worth of stock. W. F.
decides that this chain of evidence is conclusive, and that he will
travel no further under the guidance of such "trustees."

REEL SIXTEEN

THE FIEND INGRATITUDE

YOU will note throughout this story that both Stuart and Otterson apparently considered they had a right to withdraw at any time, and then come back. They would say that they were through with W. F. forever, and had no further interest in his affairs, and then the next day they would expect everything to go on the same as before. Now it appeared that Richard Dwight claimed the same privilege; on Sunday he had called everything off, and on Monday he appeared with a letter from Otterson, agreeing to withdraw as trustee as soon as the Telephone Company had got back its $15,000,000.

They assumed that W. F. would accept that; not knowing, of course, that in the meantime Hartfield had "spilt the beans." Never again would Stuart and Otterson be able to pose as friends of the Fox! He consulted lawyers, and was told that he no longer had any legal obligation under the trust agreement, but should declare the agreement at an end. He so notified Dwight, and resisted Dwight's arguments and importunities.

The first consequence of this refusal was that he received a collective letter signed by the six principal executives of his two companies. This was the famous "round-robin" letter, much exploited in the press. It was a dignified and high-minded communication, in which these gentlemen assured their chief of their deep loyalty both to him and to the companies. They pointed out that it had been he himself who had announced to the public the trusteeship plan as his solution of all the troubles; and now the announcement that he had withdrawn would have a disastrous effect upon the credit of the companies.

This round-robin letter was one of the bitterest things that ever came to W. F. It was not the product of sudden impulse upon the part of these six gentlemen. A long story of intrigue lay

184

behind it. W. F. thinks that his enemies had begun the process
of buying his executives immediately after the Wall Street panic;
as soon as the bankers had realized that he was in trouble, and that
they might be able to get his properties. The method they used
was a different one in each case, so there are six separate stories.
I shall tell only two, which are of special importance.

We have already met Saul E. Rogers, vice president and
general counsel of Fox Film and Fox Theatres. He is that
lawyer who had charge of the negotiations with the Government,
and to whom Thompson, representing the Government, gave the
assurance that the merging of Fox and Loew's would be permitted. He is the person who, immediately after the panic,
Otterson and Stuart insisted must be eliminated from the companies, and who W. F. insisted should be retained. Saul E. Rogers
had been the personal attorney of William Fox since about 1905.
When Fox Film was organized in 1915 he became its general
counsel. His salary at that time was $30,000 a year. It had
been raised to $60,000, and to a person of my humble notions
that would seem sufficient to live on, even in New York. But
apparently Rogers had not found it so. Says W. F.:

"In August, 1929, a month after my accident, Rogers called
at my home at Woodmere, Long Island, and informed me that
his contract was to expire on December 31st of that year, and
that he wanted a new contract. Fox Film had acquired the
400,000 shares of Loew stock in February, and had as yet not
merged the companies; in fact, we had been informed that no
consent had been given by the Government to the acquisition of
these 400,000 shares. Under no circumstances could the Fox
companies get along without the services of Rogers, to be a
witness as to the acquisition of the 400,000 shares. Fox Film or
Fox Theatres could not afford to have Rogers become forgetful,
as men sometimes do. I asked him what salary and for what
period he wanted a new contract. He wanted $156,000 a year,
for five years, and he was not requesting it, he was demanding it;
I could hear that by the tone of his voice. There was a clear
indication in his voice on what he was basing this salary: $60,000
a year for salary, and $96,000 for remembering that Thompson
told him to acquire the 400,000 shares of Loew stock. There was
no use discussing the price, so I asked him to draw a new con-

tract, and I signed this contract, I considered, under duress. I figured I would argue that out at another time, when the Loew matter was settled; for that reason I never submitted that contract to the Fox Film or Fox Theatres board of directors, and they never did approve the contract.

"When the company got into these difficulties, I sent for Rogers and recited the fact that he had been my personal counsel for twenty-five years, that he had been the lawyer of these companies from their very inception. The mere fact that some of the executives were not going to stand by meant nothing; the one man I had a right to expect to stand by was himself. Here was a chance to prove I had not made the wrong selection of a lawyer twenty-five years ago.

"He asked me to tell him how I expected to get out of this difficulty. I went on to tell him of at least six different methods. He rejected them all; none of them could possibly save the situation. I was in difficulty, and the only people that could possibly save the situation were the Telephone Company and Halsey, Stuart, and I ought to go along with any proposal they made. I repeated to him that these were the two men who made a condition, the very first time we met, that he be thrown out; that Otterson disliked him, because he caused the infringement notice to be sent him, and that Stuart hated him, because he was insistent that Stuart's lawyer be eliminated, and so Stuart thought he was insolent. These people had charged him with retarding my progress, and I had defended him against all that. I said, 'How can you now tell me that these are the people I must ally myself with; how can you possibly sell your soul, which you have done? Where must I turn now? In all these years you were my counsel.' There was no response to all that, and without much apology or ado he took his hat and coat and left; and he became one of the six signers of that round-robin letter. In fact, I think he was the originator.

"It came about that in the following April, after Clarke bought me out, Clarke said to me: 'You know, Fox, I have enough intelligence to know that you have been shamefully and brutally treated by men who had your confidence. These men had been in the employ of your company since its very inception, had worked themselves up into these high posts, and then double-crossed you. I could forgive them all if it had occurred to me, except Rogers, your lawyer. If my lawyer did that, I would kill him as sure as God made little green apples. I don't understand how you had this blind faith in this man, and why you increased his salary from $60,000 to $156,000.' I told him of the necessity of doing that; that this was a hold-up contract, but that I had no choice, and I told him of the fact that having recognized it at the time I had signed the contract, I never had the contract approved by the board. He said: 'It is approved by the board; it is in the minutes.' I told him if it was in there, it didn't belong there. He pointed it out to me in the minutes.

"I then sent for the former directors of both companies and read to them this resolution. They informed me that they had never heard of the resolution; it had never been brought up in the meeting. I asked how it got in there—they didn't know. On talking later to one of my confidential men, he told me that one of my employees, a lawyer under the supervision of Rogers, had had the minutes changed at the request of Rogers, confirming Rogers' contract. I have been reliably informed that this lawyer has made an affidavit in which he acknowledges the fact that he had these minutes changed at the request of Rogers; that sometime in February he had rewritten the minutes of November.

"Of course, by this time Clarke was through with Rogers, and what he wanted to do was to get rid of him. Clarke was frank enough to say to me: 'You don't believe I am going to have a bit of faith in any one of the men who signed the round-robin letter, do you? I have enough sense to know that if these men double-crossed you, they would soon double-cross me.'

"Clarke tolerated Rogers for a year after I had sold out, and then one morning he went to his office and put padlocks on the door. When Rogers arrived he couldn't get in. He was then told that his services were no longer required—they were through with him. They didn't care anything about the five-year contract Fox had given him. Rogers is now suing to recover on that contract."

The other signer of the round-robin letter whose story we must hear is Winfield R. Sheehan, vice president and general manager of Fox Film. Sheehan also had entered the life of W. F. quite early. He had begun as a reporter for the New

York "World," and had become private secretary to Police Commissioner Waldo of New York City, at which time he had become a friend of W. F. In 1910 or 1911 there was a murder brought about by the graft situation in the police department, and the newspapers were looking for a "man higher up" in the department, and were beginning to mention the name of Sheehan. Sheehan appealed to W. F. for help, and W. F. took him into Waldo's office, and asked Waldo whether he meant to stand by Sheehan. W. F. said he knew that Sheehan had nothing to do with the murder, and that Waldo must know it, and that if Waldo would not stand by Sheehan, W. F. was prepared to spend a million dollars in his defense: a service much appreciated by Sheehan in this time of danger.

I have before me some clippings from the New York newspapers of September to November, 1912. There is a scandal in the police department, having to do with the collection of graft for promotions. Winfield R. Sheehan, secretary to Commissioner Waldo, is involved in these scandals, and is summoned before a committee of the Board of Aldermen. The counsel of the committee asks him if he will waive immunity, and he pretends not to understand. He says, "I haven't asked for immunity and I do not want it." Says Emory R. Buckner, counsel for the committee, "That answer is what is called in police parlance bunk. Now I ask you if you will sign away your immunity." The discussion continued:

" 'I don't want any immunity,' the witness replied. 'I don't think you have any power to grant immunity.'

" 'The committee has nothing whatever to do with it,' Mr. Buckner declared, 'and it doesn't make any difference whether you want immunity or not. If you are sworn by this committee and testify, you get immunity automatically, unless you waive it. Now, are you willing to waive it?'

" 'No, I am not,' the witness said.

" 'Then you think that if you are indicted by anybody, you might need the immunity you would get here?'

" 'I won't sign a waiver,' Mr. Sheehan declared."

In April, 1914, there was another investigation of police graft of a still less pleasant sort. In the New York "Times" for April 30, 1914, I find these headlines:

CALLS W. R. SHEEHAN THE MAN HIGHER UP.

Alice Walker Testifies She Paid Graft to Supposed Agent of Waldo's Secretary.

Alice Walker, it appears, was the keeper of a house of prostitution, and she testified that she had paid $100 through a police
agent, who told her that he represented Sheehan.

Sheehan resigned as secretary to Waldo, and became secretary to William Fox at a salary of $100 a week, the highest he
had ever earned. Sheehan proved his ability, and two years later
was made vice president and general manager of Fox Film at a
salary of $20,000 a year, and ten years later was earning $45,000
a year, in charge of production in Hollywood. At the time of
W. F.'s troubles his salary was $130,000 a year, without counting
the many extras. W. F. declares that he had made him personal
gifts of many thousands of W. F.'s own shares of stock. At the
time when Durant was running up Fox Film in the market, W. F.
called Sheehan, then in Hollywood, on the long distance telephone
and said, "Where have you got those Fox Film shares? Now
is the time to cash in." Sheehan sold his shares, the greater
portion of which represented W. F.'s gift, for $1,450,000. W. F.
declares that Sheehan repaid him for this service in the following
way: Sheehan asked W. F. to lend him $400,000 and invest it
for him, which W. F. did. Subsequently, when the shares went
down, Sheehan denied that he had authorized W. F. to buy
them.

Winfield R. Sheehan is a short and plump gentleman with
blond hair and prominent eyes of a color which his press agents
describe as "baby blue." He is a jovial person, and suffers from
liver trouble. In October of 1929 he had gone abroad for his
liver. There was another employe of W. F.'s, one Blumenthal,
whose story we shall hear in a moment, also in England at the
time of the panic. These two came back together, arriving in
New York on the evening of the signing of the trust agreement.
Sheehan and Blumenthal had been bitter enemies, but now they
had become fast friends, and W. F. speculates as to what they
talked about on the boat. Blumenthal had gone over to the
enemy, and did he point out to Sheehan that W. F. was to be
deposed, and that there would be a new president of Fox Film,

and that in this capacity Sheehan would have for the first time an opportunity to display his full abilities?

Anyhow, it was a new Sheehan who landed in New York. He went at once into conference with Otterson and Stuart. He spent six hours with them, and was to have another conference with them the following day. Naturally, W. F. became concerned. He thought that if the trustees were going to consult with executives of the companies, the third trustee should be present. When he learned that Stuart and Otterson were going to throw Jack Leo off the board, but retain Sheehan and King, he knew that Sheehan and King had gone over to the enemy. He summoned Sheehan to his home, and Sheehan said he had a terrific pain in the back of his head, and they had to arrange a place for him to lie down. Now, as W. F. looks back upon it, he strongly suspects that the purpose of that headache was to enable Sheehan to avoid remembering what he had talked about with Otterson and Stuart.

"I said: 'Look here, Sheehan, every so often you have caused the employes and executives of our corporation to present me with testimonials of loyalty and devotion. The last one you gave me was only a year or so ago; it was printed on beautiful paper, and the first signature on it was yours, and the testimonial goes on to state the great executive head that I am, how all you men appreciate the efforts I have given to these enterprises, and what I have done for you all, and you express a great sentiment of appreciation and loyalty. When these were given to me, I was proud of them, but this last one has really been of little or no value, for it was during prosperity while the company was flourishing. Now we appear to be in a little financial difficulty; now I would like to have a resolution as to who is going to stand by and who is going to run out. I want you to call the executives together and propose to them now to sign a letter expressing their loyalty.'

"He said he didn't think it was practical at this time; that it would be a mistake on my part to try to get it. I said: 'I don't want to make an effort to get this. I never did before—it always came voluntarily. This is the first time I have asked for any support.' It was apparent that there was to be no such conference of executives, and if there was to be an executive conference, Sheehan's signature would not be on any such letter.

That further confirmed the rumors I had heard about him and Otterson and Stuart."

This was the bitterest part of W. F.'s experience. To have these men who had been his intimates turn against him, one by one, and join the conspiracy of his enemies, and sign their names to slanders and falsehoods about him! In the course of this trouble, the New York "Evening Telegram" published Sheehan's picture on the first page, and in large type above it just one word: "INGRATE."

There seems to be only one thing more to say, to state the price of Sheehan's services to the enemies of W. F. Instead of his pittance of $130,000 a year, his new contract with Fox Film Corporation, made after W. F. was out, provided for $250,000 the first year, $300,000 the second year, $350,000 the third year, $400,000 the fourth year, and $500,000 the fifth year. If you add those items together you find they amount to $1,800,000, whereas if W. F. had stayed in power, Sheehan would have had only $650,000. Says W. F.: "*Of course* it was a new Sheehan!"

While we are on the subject of these old-time friends, we have to make the acquaintance of one more, Alfred Cleveland Blumenthal by name. There was a time when I used to see signs all over Los Angeles: "This property for sale. Apply to A. C. Blumenthal." If you applied, you met a little man well under five feet, quite pale, and feminine in appearance; he was close to fifty, but you would have taken him for thirty. Looking back on him, W. F. reports that he is as sharp as a steel trap; he deals very much in innuendoes, and never says anything kind about anyone. He has the habit of telling you what someone has said about you, and whether this is true or not, it causes you to say what you think about the other person. He then takes this back to the other person, and causes the other person to say what he thinks about you. Thus he collects a great deal of information.

Blumenthal came to New York and appealed to W. F.'s sympathy. There had been a slump in Los Angeles real estate, and Blumenthal had been wiped out. He offered W. F. a ground lease upon some land, and W. F. took this lease, and recently built upon the spot the Los Angeles Theatre, which he believes to be the finest in the world. Blumenthal had the idea that he might arrange for W. F. to buy the West Coast theatres; but

14

before he could deal for them he had to have his debts paid off. He owed hundreds of small creditors, the total amount being over $50,000. W. F. put up the money out of his own pocket, and paid Blumenthal's debts, and they formed what they called the Foxthal Company, with Blumenthal having a half interest, and Fox Theatres having the other half. This company was to get all the commissions which Blumenthal might earn in purchasing theatres or stocks of theatrical corporations. What this amounted to was an arrangement whereby Blumenthal was to act as a real estate agent for Fox Theatres, getting half the commissions himself and giving the company the other half.

Blumenthal of course was extremely grateful, and became a friend of the Fox family. He took to addressing Mrs. Fox as "mother," which conferred an air of respectability upon him. To the Fox family he became "Blumy," and when Blumy's mother was about to return to California and told Mrs. Fox that the next day was her birthday, and that she was to spend it on the train, Mrs. Fox and her husband proceeded to get a New York jeweler on the telephone, it being Sunday, and the jeweler came and opened his store, and Mrs. Fox selected a bracelet costing $10,500, and W. F. paid for it as a birthday gift for Mrs. Blumenthal.

Many important deals were put in Blumy's way, and everything went pleasantly—except that, so W. F. declares, Blumy had a way of finding an excuse to hold out his commissions. He always needed the money for some purpose or other, and the Fox Theatres Corporation would get it later. It was Blumy who got word that Schenck was willing to sell the Loew shares, and W. F. arranged for Fox Theatres to pay the Foxthal Company $3 a share on the 400,000 shares, which meant $600,000 in Blumy's pocket. Later on W. F. decided to buy a chain of New York theatres, and he turned this job over to Blumy, and Blumy's commission was a million and a quarter. Then came Ostrer to New York, and Blumy got in on that, and was to go to London to conclude the negotiations. W. F. suggested that before he went he should give the Foxthal Company an accounting, but Blumy gave the excuse that the British-Gaumont purchase was very urgent, and he went to England and earned a commission there of a million and a quarter. Altogether he owed

the Foxthal Company close to $3,000,000. Of course if it should
happen that somebody would offer him an opportunity to escape
having to pay all that money, Blumy would be strongly tempted
to favor that person.

After the panic, W. F. was asleep in his bed, and woke up
with a yell. His wife asked what was the matter, and he told
her he had just dreamed that Blumy had double-crossed him.
But Mrs. Fox said for him to go back to bed and stop dreaming.
She said, "All the others that you have faith in may double-cross
you, but never Blumy." She looked upon him as if he were her
son. But W. F. and his wife had had psychic experiences
before, so the next day W. F. decided to make a test. He telephoned to London, and said to Blumenthal that there was serious
trouble in New York, and Blumenthal had close to $3,000,000,
half of which belonged to Fox Theatres; would he please cable
it, because it was badly needed.

"He said yes, he would do it tomorrow. But tomorrow—
no money. Again I telephoned. He was just making up the
accounts; tomorrow. But tomorrow, no money. I said to Mrs.
Fox, 'We have been double-crossed. That was no dream at all.'
I soon got the kind of cables from Blumenthal that indicated
clearly he was acting under an assignment from the Telephone
Company; that he had a mission to perform over there."

That was the time while Sheehan was in London, having his
liver cured, and during one of the telephone calls, Blumenthal
said: "Here is Sheehan sitting alongside me. Do you want to talk
to him," That sounded strange to W. F., because if ever two men
hated each other, it was Blumenthal and Sheehan. Sheehan was
always saying, "He is going to double-cross you." But now here
they were friends, and they came back from England together.
Blumenthal had gone in July, in a great hurry, and he and his
wife had taken just a couple of suit-cases. Says W. F.:

"This night when he returned to the Ambassador Hotel, vans
stopped and eighteen or twenty trunks came in. I was meeting
a new Blumenthal. I naturally felt that the first thing he would
do would be to tell me about the things that had transpired.
Instead he begged to be excused—he must have dinner, and then
he wanted to do some unpacking. He couldn't any longer look
me in the eye. I knew that night clearly that Blumenthal was

no longer for me, but was in the employ either of the Telephone Company or Harley Clarke.

"It appears I made the right guess, because sometime later, maybe several months later, Blumenthal called to see me and one of my attorneys at the Ambassador Hotel, and said that what he would like to do was to acquire the voting shares of Fox; that on his word of honor he was not to receive a penny of commission on this transaction. He just wanted to be of help. When the thing was finally concluded, we learned that all the time he had had a contract in his pocket signed by Clarke to pay him 5 per cent up to $12,000,000 as a commission if he could induce Fox to sell his shares. Certainly he was employed by Clarke now. It is clear to me now the purpose of that connection. If Fox remained in business, Blumenthal would have to return half of the $3,000,000; if Fox went out of business he would have an arrangement with Clarke that the entire $3,000,000 belonged to him. Not only didn't he return any part of the $3,000,000 he had in his pocket, but sometime thereafter Clarke made a settlement with him and paid him an additional $500,000 by note, the greater part of it yet unpaid.

"Soon after I sold out, I wrote Clarke a letter and told him I wanted him to know the relationship between Blumenthal and the Fox companies. I recited our relationship and warned them against giving Blumenthal any part of this money, and that I, Fox, as director of the company, was demanding that the proper settlement be made by Blumenthal—all of which was disregarded, because there was an agreement, there must have been an understanding that Blumenthal could keep this money."

At the time of Blumy's return from London, he still owed his friend W. F. $40,000 out of the $50,000 which had been put up to pay his personal debts. Also he owed the Foxthal Company $3,000,000, of which half was to go to Fox Theatres; and W. F. was desperately combing the city, trying to borrow a few hundred thousand here and a few hundred thousand there to meet his obligations. There was a note due and payable at a bank in Boston, on a contract which Blumenthal had consummated, and W. F. didn't want that note to go to protest.

This was while he was home ill, early in December, and Mrs. Fox, having heard the whole story, decided to send for the man who had been calling her "mother" for so many years. He came, and W. F. had an interview in his sick room, and asked Blumy to return the money which belonged to Fox Theatres. Blumy said he wouldn't do it. Then W. F. asked that he repay the $40,000 of the personal loan. This Blumy said he would do. Then W. F. asked that he lend $400,000 temporarily, so that W. F. could meet the note of the bank in Boston. Blumy refused.

W. F. didn't know that his wife was standing behind the door, listening to this conversation. But now he heard a sound behind the door, and he guessed, and ran out of the room, and found his wife standing there with a bottle of vitriol in her hand. Mrs. Fox told me how she had bought this, because she had become convinced that her husband was going to be killed in this terrible struggle, and she did not mean to survive him. But now, listening to this man, Blumy, and realizing the extent of his perfidy, she said: "I am going to blind him. This dog who has called me mother—if he is going to destroy my husband, I am going to destroy him."

There was not much of an argument. W. F. pushed her into a room by force, and locked her in, and then got rid of Blumy as quickly as possible. Wherever Blumy may be, when he reads this story, he will be interested to know what a close escape he had.

Just one more detail, and then we are through with this little gentleman. In April, when W. F. was finally forced to sell out to Harley Clarke, he went to Clarke's office, and there was Blumenthal. W. F. tells of the scene:

"I said to Clarke: 'I didn't know you were going to have this man here, but now he is here I have some questions I would like to ask him in your presence. I don't know what he has told you about me, but I would like to tell you something about him. Before he gets in your good graces, you had better hear from my lips just what he is. After I get through telling it to you, you will throw him out of this room, because if you don't, there will be no deal.' Then I proceeded to tell Clarke what I thought of Blumenthal and how he had withheld money that belonged to these companies. At the conclusion of this I demanded he be ordered out, which he was. Clarke was not going to lose this deal with me."

REEL SEVENTEEN

BANK SOLIDARITY

W. F. realized now that he had lost the eminent firm of Hughes, Schurman & Dwight, and was soon to lose Colonel Hartfield. He must have another lawyer, and he chose Clarence J. Shearn, who had until recently been a judge of the Appellate Division, and before that, had been counsel for William Randolph Hearst. Judge Shearn is a very little man, frail and slender, clean shaven and extremely nervous; he has a kind face and is sympathetic, and readily expresses his sympathy. He was brought to W. F.'s home by Reass on a Sunday afternoon, and listened to W. F.'s story, and was so much interested that he called off a dinner engagement and spent the evening. He begged W. F. not to tell his story to anyone else, because the telling was emotionally so destructive to him. Shearn himself had recently lost his wife, and said he was so depressed that he had planned a six months' trip around the world; but he decided that he could just as well forget his troubles by fighting W. F.'s battles, and he went to work on the case the very next day.

That was December 23, and there was a meeting of the bankers at the office of the Telephone Company. Shearn addressed this meeting, and told the bankers that W. F. had neither moral nor legal obligation to go on with the voting trust agreement. He pleaded with the bankers to extend the loans, which amounted to about $6,800,000 unsecured. He pleaded, and W. F. also pleaded, with the balance sheets of his companies before him. He showed that the companies had properties against which there were no mortgages, and with a value of approximately $20,000,000. Said W. F.: "Gentlemen, doesn't it seem peculiar to find a man with $20,000,000 worth of valuable property, and not able to raise any money? I would like to make you a proposal. Since the voting trust agreement has been abro-

196

gated, the only interest you can possibly have is for these companies to return the money that is due you. We can't give it to you in cash, we haven't got it. What we have got is $20,000,000 worth of property unencumbered. You form a committee amongst yourselves, and you have that committee pick out of it $2 worth of collateral for every dollar we owe you. We will make you a secured creditor. Instead of your bank's money being in jeopardy, we want to guarantee now that we are going to pay it."

The dominating factor at this meeting was Sherrill Smith, one of the vice presidents of the Chase National Bank. For some mysterious reason, Chase National was recognized as the leader of the pack, and every time W. F. or Shearn made a point, Smith would find some technical or legal objection. Because of the fact that the Fox companies owed twelve million to Halsey, Stuart, they could not give their properties as collateral. But there was nothing in the agreement with Halsey, Stuart to forbid this. The agreement forbade only new obligations; it did not forbid collateral to cover old obligations. But everybody agreed with Smith; they would not take collateral for their loans, and it was plain enough that they were all under orders. Says W. F.:

"This meeting was really a great farce. The session opened with Dwight announcing that under the circumstances of my attitude and my actions, the trustees wished to withdraw. Some of the banks who had not been in the full confidence of the Telephone Company inquired why Fox was asking for the voting trust agreement to be abrogated. I suggested to Dwight that he tell them why. I said: 'They asked for it—tell it to them.' But no, he would rather not; in fact he wouldn't. I said: 'Gentlemen, we are in the offices of the Telephone Company, and they know the reason why I am withdrawing from this as well as I, and I feel it is their obligation to tell it to you. You came at their invitation. If they don't tell it to you, I won't. But they know why, and let them tell it to you.' They never told why."

W. F. then went home and wrote a letter to the thirteen banks which were his creditors, renewing his offer to put up collateral. This letter brought no help, so he requested another bankers' meeting, this time at his own offices on January 2. He again reiterated his offer to give $2 worth of collateral for each dollar's worth of loans, but all in vain. On January 5, Heppenheimer and

Marcus, two presidents of creditor banks, came to W. F. and informed him that it was the intention of the banking creditors to apply to the courts to appoint a receiver for the Fox companies.

On January 6, W. F. made a new proposition: since the banks were unwilling to take property of Fox Film and Fox Theatres, would they take the personal property of W. F. as collateral? He had millions of dollars worth of real estate scattered throughout the country. He was trying to sell it but couldn't. He now offered it as collateral, but in vain. Nobody wanted any property belonging to Fox. For some reason or other, it was all poison. The banks demanded their money, and if Fox couldn't pay their money, they wanted to throw the companies into receivership and ruin them.

You will remember my reference to Paley's famous watch which is found on the seashore, and which proves that a man has been there; the man in turn proving that there is a God who created the universe. Observe now the complete harmony of action of thirteen New York bankers attending business conferences and writing letters. Normally no banker ever refuses to accept collateral for a loan. Some one banker may refuse to extend a loan which is properly secured, but thirteen bankers do not all unite and refuse to extend loans which are properly secured, unless there is some powerful motive, some powerful force which brings about that solidarity. W. F. tells of visiting executives of many banks, and they were all personally friendly, but no one of them would lend him a dollar, and no one would extend a note. One of the bank presidents went so far as to tell him confidentially that he would like to do something, but that his hands were tied.

"He told me he couldn't do anything except what the Chase Bank was asking to be done; that the Chase Bank was the leader in this movement; that regardless of what his attitude was in these bankers' meetings, I would have to understand that it was not what he wanted to do, but what he was compelled to do."

One of the creditors was Edward Rothschild, president of the Chelsea Bank. He was the employer for whom W. F. had been working for a salary of $17 a week, three years prior to his marriage. So for thirty-one years W. F. had been his friend, and he had watched the great enterprise grow. He had loaned money to Fox Film, and also to Fox personally. The personal loan was never pressed; Rothschild said that he couldn't do what he wanted to about Fox Film, but he offered W. F. a receipted bill for the personal loan if he wanted it.

"Rothschild did more than that. He asked me to come to his apartment one day, and he had a group of men in the room. He inquired of me how could he be of financial service to me. I told him that what I would like to do would be to take these 280,000 odd shares in the hands of brokers and park them somewhere; that I was willing to pay a substantial price for the accommodation; that I would like to have someone buy these shares for $50 a share, with an agreement that the Fox companies would have the right to recapture these shares with a premium of $10 on or before a year from the date that they were acquired from us. In addition to that to pay 6 per cent per annum for the loan. If the companies had the ability to re-acquire these shares at the end of twelve months, it would net the bankers 26 per cent per annum. I was to pay $10 a share premium for the recapture of these shares any time during the year.

"I naturally had the fondest hopes that I could work this thing out in three months or perhaps six months at the longest. If I could work these difficulties out in three months, the banks would earn approximately 80 per cent profit in three months, or 40 per cent in six months. The proposition surely was attractive, and this group of men thought they could swing this deal. They did take it up with Field, Glore & Company. A mutual friend, who was present at the meeting when this proposition was being discussed with Field, Glore & Company, reported that the members of this bank were willing to go forward. The deal looked like it was going to be consummated. There was no reason why this was not a good piece of banking business, and while the conference was at its height, one of the bankers was called to the 'phone, someone from Morgan & Company was on the wire. He left the room for less than five minutes, and when he returned he had no interest in the matter. He was sorry, but his firm had no interest.

"Of course, it was commonly known by Field, Glore & Company that this proposal was being made by my friend, Rothschild. Whether or not the closing of his bank shortly thereafter, and then the opening of the bank shortly after that with Rothschild entirely eliminated from the bank, had anything to do with his wanting to help me, I don't know. Offhand, I would say that that was the price he paid for his willingness to help Fox.

Another curious story about a creditor, the Bank of the United States, to which Fox Film owed $1,600,000 unsecured, and W. F. personally owed $1,000,000 secured. Marcus, the president of that bank, told W. F. that he could not help so far as concerned the Fox Film loan, but as to the personal loan W. F. need not worry.

"Somehow or other the Chase Bank did discover that I had a personal loan at that bank, and shortly thereafter I met with Marcus, and he informed me that for reasons he was unable to name, it became necessary for me to supply more collateral. I could understand that, and deposited more collateral, and again he informed me that that was not sufficient, and that for reasons he was unable to explain I must give him more collateral. He thought his bank needed at least $500,000 more collateral. I told him of two pieces of property I owned—in one I had an equity of $600,000 and the other was a piece of property for which Rockefeller had offered $1,450,000, and which had mortgages of a little less than $625,000. I told him to take his choice. He said that what he would have to do would be to have these properties appraised, and then he would make his choice. Day, a prominent real estate man in New York, appraised these two pieces of property. On his appraisal there was no more than $500,000 equity in both. I put up both pieces of property as collateral.

"In the spring of 1931 I met Day—that was after the Bank of the United States had closed its doors. I said: 'When I was in difficulty you had a chance to serve me and you didn't do it. You were elected as an appraiser of two pieces of property I had.' He said: 'I knew all about them. I will frankly tell you about it. I had had business arrangements with Marcus in every real estate enterprise. When he asked me to make these appraisals, he told me the exact amount he wanted these appraisals for.'

"I said: 'You must have known their value, because Rockefeller had already announced that he was building the Rockefeller Center, and that I owned the only 110 feet of property that was not included in his purchase. You must have known the real value of that lot. You must have known that I had an equity of more than $800,000 above the mortgage.' He said: 'Yes, I know, but Marcus told me the amount he wanted these properties appraised at, and I appraised them that way.' Perhaps he could justify his appraisal by saying he was not concerned in the Rockefeller Center; that he was only concerned in that piece of property on that day regardless of the Rockefeller interests.

"This was Marcus who at the beginning of this transaction expressed a spirit of friendship; it was he who recommended that I engage Colonel Hartfield as my lawyer; it was he who continued the $1,000,000 loan when it was uncollateralized. Whether he was punished for that by the closing of his bank later, I don't know. But it is strange that the only two banks of the thirteen banks I was associated with, and which had my personal loans, had their doors closed shortly after I sold out."

Since I have referred to the piece of real estate in Rockefeller Center, let me complete this curious story. The property is on Sixth Avenue, between 48th and 49th Streets, and is included in three square blocks bought by Rockefeller, on which the new Radio City, or Rockefeller Center, is being built. Just before the panic, the representatives of Rockefeller tried to buy this property, offering $1,450,000 for it, but W. F. refused, because he thought it would be a good thing to have a building on that site and call it the Fox Building.

But then came the panic and all the troubles, and W. F. sent for the head of his real estate department and said, "All right, I will sell that piece of property for $1,450,000." But then it turned out that the offer was withdrawn; the maximum price was $800,000, which was only a little more than the mortgage. The Fox was down, and Rockefeller also was going to take a bite out of him.

While we are moving in such distinguished company, let me tell also the story of the Honorable Reginald McKenna, formerly First Lord of the Admiralty, then Home Secretary, then Chancellor of the King's Exchequer, and now Chairman of the Midland Bank, one of the five great banking chains which rule Great Britain. This eminent British statesman and financier had been interested in the Ostrer deal, and had loaned £800,000 to make the deal possible. Also, at the instance of W. F.'s agent, he had purchased 6,000 shares of Fox Film for $150,000. As soon as the panic came, McKenna became disturbed and asked to be relieved of his purchase. W. F. remembered the £800,000, and returned the $150,000 at once.

But then on December 30, 1929, the £800,000 was due, and W. F., having called off the voting trust agreement, no longer had any credit in London. He sent a cablegram to McKenna, a copy of which I have. It gives a detailed statement of the financial position of the Fox companies, their earnings and resources and lack of obligations. It is a most eloquent cablegram, and may have shocked a reticent and prudent Englishman by its extravagance, for it contained close to 700 words, and cost about $150   The reply came promptly, and read as follows: "Telegram received but bill must be met today. McKenna."

W. F. asked me what I thought of that reply, and I said that the Englishman also could be accused of extravagance; the first three words of the cablegram were superfluous. W. F. calls my attention to the intimacy of relationship between the Chase Bank and the Midland. They were associated in many American enterprises, and McKenna and Wiggin were intimates. Also Stuart and Clarke had told W. F. of their close friendship with the great British statesman and financier.

The bill was not met that day, and McKenna proceeded next day to attach all the funds of Fox Film in London. At this time you must understand the weekly business of Fox Film in England amounted to about $100,000, and three-fourths of this amount was being cabled to America each week. W. F. had offered to liquidate the loan, on the basis of the difference between the English income and expenses. If McKenna had consented to do that, the $4,000,000 would have been paid off in twenty-five weeks. But that was not satisfactory to him; he preferred to bring legal proceedings and cripple the American organization.

He went farther, and instructed the Hon. John W. Davis to commence an action in New York. Oddly enough, he claimed the full £800,000, without making any allowance for the amount that he had already got by attaching the Fox Film money in England. This was extremely fortunate for W. F., for if McKenna had sued only for the money that was actually due, W. F.'s lawyers could not have filed an answer; but as he sued for too much, it was possible to file an answer, and thus keep the suit from coming to trial for a long time.

Also, there was the great National City Bank of New York. This great bank has branches all over the world, and W. F. was one of their depositors all over the world. They showed their appreciation of his business, and their desire to assist his companies, by attaching all the money which the companies had on deposit all over the world, and applying this money week by week to $400,000 which W. F. owed in New York. This, of course, was intended to cripple the business abroad, since the companies had to have their foreign money to pay their foreign debts; but the fact was that Fox Film was so prosperous that in spite of all these funds being taken away, it was able to carry on and pay its current debts.

The three largest banks in New York are the Chase National, the National City and the Guaranty Trust. We have still to hear from the third of these. Fox Film had used the Guaranty Trust as its depository in Paris for all the money it collected throughout France. "We owed nothing to the Guaranty Trust—we had never borrowed a dollar from them. And we had had this account for many years. But during this difficulty I was advised by our French agent that he was sent for by the manager in Paris and told to take the damned account out of the bank; they didn't want any Fox account in the bank. We had to comply with the request. That did us no injury, but it indicates the spirit of co-operation between these large banks in New York and these foreign banks."

Also there was Ostrer, seller of the British Gaumont theatres. Ostrer had got $14,000,000 in cash, and had $6,000,000 still due him. As soon as Ostrer learned that W. F. had broken with Halsey, Stuart and the Telephone Company, he saw his chance:

"He would declare a default, recapture the two and one-half million shares we had purchased, have his shares back, keep the $14,000,000 already paid to him, and most likely sell these shares at public auction for the best price he could get. I don't know how much he could have gotten for them at that time. Perhaps there would be no other bidder but himself. If he was successful in having no competition, he could probably have gotten the shares for $1,000,000. Here he could have his shares back,

$14,000,000 we had already paid, and a deficiency judgment against these companies for $6,000,000 more—of course, it was good business on his part."

In the midst of these harassments, with bankruptcy and destruction hanging over his head, W. F. remembered that it was the 31st of December. He had not been home since the 15th, that Sunday when he got up out of his sick bed to attend the conference at the Ambassador Hotel. But now came this triple date, his birthday, his wedding anniversary, and New Year's Eve, and he put everything behind him and went home. His wife had been gravely ill, and he was trying his best to keep his troubles from her. Over the 'phone he did not dare discuss his affairs, because he was certain that every word was listened to and recorded. In talking to his wife he says that he "lied like hell." He told her that his affairs were getting better every day; but this valiant lying did no good, because she got the truth from her brothers, Jack and Joseph Leo.

She had got out of her sick bed on the night that Hartfield had come to her home and so gently and tactfully told her that when the general of an army has lost a battle, he must expect to be deposed. After that her illness became worse; and now on the night of this triple anniversary her husband came home, ill himself and dazed with exhaustion. This was the occasion about which W. F. tried to tell me, but broke down and could not. "Here was this poor soul suffering the tortures and agonies of hell; and unfortunately for me I misconstrued her attitude. I had almost felt that this episode in my life was going to estrange me from the thing that I had loved most."

Apparently he suggested something to the effect that she too was going to turn against him. Anyhow, it was something he could not bear to remember or to talk about. The outcome was this: "Mrs. Fox said she could be just as ill in New York, and she would no longer be separated from me and left out of my troubles."

In spite of all suffering, Eve Leo came to New York, and thereafter her place, while her husband was in conference, was standing behind the door of the room listening. No telephone message came without her being on an extension 'phone; if the telephone company could listen in, so could a wife! She no

longer trusted her husband or her brothers to tell her bad news;
she got it for herself. She would judge the persons with whom
her husband was dealing, and after they had left she would
express her opinion of them; many times it turned out that her
opinion was better than her husband's. He says:

"At one time my wife's doctor advised her that it was necessary to undergo an operation. She would be confined to her bed
for only three or four days, but she had to have it done. Before
going to the hospital, she made me promise that Otterson and
Stuart would not be trustees of my shares. I gave her my sacred
word that I would do nothing about it without first going to the
hospital and talking it over with her. Everything was prepared
for the operation. She went there the night before. In the
morning she was being wheeled out of her room to the operating
room, and in the hallway some friend or relation told her that
he had just heard that I was settling my affairs by allowing
Otterson and Stuart to revive the trust agreement. That ended
that. She insisted upon being wheeled back into her room—no
operation was going to take place. She dressed, ordered her car,
and came back home. She said: 'Here I have just turned my
back for one night and you have already weakened.' I tried to
assure her that it was not true, but she knew it was true, or this
party would not have told her so. I told her to go back and have
the operation done, but she didn't care about an operation, death,
or anything—here I was doing the very thing I had agreed not
to do!"

One of the ways in which W. F. has spent his leisure time
and money has been the making of an art collection. He has
many treasures in his Park Avenue home, and thinks he has one
of the best collections of paintings ever seen in one room. He
and his wife began this collection about the third week after their
marriage, which was when they were living in the railroad apartment in the Myrtle Avenue tenement in Brooklyn, at a rental of
$11 a month.

"I had passed a store where an auction was being held, and
a dirty-looking picture was being sold. It was up to 80 cents
when I joined the bidding; it was finally sold to me for $1.
With great pride I presented it to my wife and it has always
occupied a place of honor at my home. It was the first piece of

art that I was interested in, and from then on until this very day we have from time to time bought treasures and added to our collection. For some individual pieces of art I have paid up to $100,000. The $1 picture was a horse in a stable with a cat standing on its back and some chickens and dogs and other animals around it.

"At one time a friend came to the house and he frankly expressed himself, that this battle would be my ruination, and then pointing to all my art treasures, he said: 'Now you know you can't go on like this. All these things are going to end in the public auction-room; you know they are going to strip this home.' Mrs. Fox was again standing behind the curtain. When this address was being made, she appeared and went into a frenzy, saying she didn't want a piece of it, it could all be sold. She was willing to go back to an $11 apartment again. She knew $11 a month now could only rent a hall bedroom, but just as long as I had not committed an act that was dishonorable, she was willing to go on with me. The only thing she wanted to take along with her, she said, was the little picture I had bought her three weeks after we were married."

It was a time of intense and devastating emotions. W. F. was holding on like grim death to his voting shares and his control of the companies. It was not merely the treasure involved—it was his name, his reputation, the faith he wished to keep with his stockholders. That these things really were involved was made plain by the outcome; the fact that the enemies of William Fox, when they got his companies away from him, proceeded to loot them and deprive the stockholders of everything.

REEL EIGHTEEN

FORD JOKES

OUR Fox was conferring every day with his lawyers, Hartfield, Shearn, and Reass, as to the means of staving off bankruptcy and receivership. Hartfield was still urging his client to go back to the trust agreement with Stuart and Otterson. Even though he had so plainly revealed the ruin that was planned, he kept on urging this course, insisting that the agreement could be modified so as to protect W. F. Hartfield was trying to win Shearn over to this way of thinking, and there was a conference at lunch at W. F.'s home, attended by Hartfield, Shearn, Reass, and Rubenstein. Says W. F.:

"With all the power I possessed, I tried to make my case clear to Shearn and keep him from thinking in Hartfield's direction. I would get Shearn to think my way, and then I would leave the room and lie down, and by the time I came back I would find Shearn thinking in the direction of Hartfield. I would again open the subject, and bring Shearn back to my way of thinking, and then go in and lie down again. I would come back an hour later and there was Shearn almost in accord with Hartfield. This continued until about 5 o'clock. I then turned upon Hartfield and called him all the vile names that it was humanly possible to call another man, and concluded by saying: 'Why the hell aren't you man enough to step out of this case? Why don't you resign? I ought to blow your brains out.'

"After this tirade, which lasted for a half hour or more, and which Hartfield tried to smooth over, he said he would take it up with his firm, to see if they would let him resign. Of course, he was thinking of the million dollars I had promised his firm if they could salvage the companies. If we fired him, we might be liable for a suit; so it seemed to me it was better to have him resign. I said everything I could to make him do so. This, of course, was in the presence of Shearn, who was horrified by it all. This meeting finally broke up, and Shearn and Hartfield got into their automobile and rode down town together.

"Shortly thereafter Ben Reass said: 'I have just had a terrible experience today. Shearn, who claims he 'phoned me today and that I was not available, reached the conclusion that we were working on matters without taking him into our confidence, and under those circumstances wishes to withdraw from the case.' Here was a man who thought he could forget the death of his wife in our work better than by a trip around the world! Ten days later, having heard the arguments of Hartfield, who didn't even try to defend himself, Shearn stepped out of the case. That was a pretext he gave—that we were not conferring with him in all matters. Of course, there is no doubt in the world that he and Hartfield had got together."

And so once more W. F. was without a lawyer, save for his family friend Reass. Judge Shearn had seen what an ugly fight it was going to be; he had seen how many powerful interests he would have to antagonize, and he discreetly and quietly stepped out.

W. F. refused to have any further communication with Hartfield, and I asked whether Hartfield ever brought a suit for his money. The answer was that he didn't have to sue; he was paid out of the funds of the companies. All the lawyers were paid out of the funds of the companies; not merely Hartfield, Hughes and Dwight, but all those various firms which were soon bringing actions for receivership, the Berenson brothers, and Kresel—and we shall find the Fox companies paying them for their success in ruining the Fox companies!

The story that W. F. had withdrawn from the voting trust agreement was, of course, no secret. The newspapers made much of it, and the talk of receivership and bankruptcy for the Fox companies. One of the consequences was a visit from W. F.'s friend, Col. Claudius C. Huston. Huston came up from Washington to express to W. F. the regrets of Herbert Hoover at the difficulties in which W. F. was involved. Huston wanted to be of help if he could, and said he would be willing to live in New York for a week, a month or longer if necessary, to be at his side and act as his advisor. Here is a significant story:

"I told him it was not advice I needed; there was a conspiracy to drive me out of my business, and one of the conspirators was Albert H. Wiggin of the Chase Bank. All that Huston had to do, representing the White House, was to go to Wiggin and say, 'Stop. The administration resents this.' On Christmas day he actually went to Wiggin's home in the country to take Christmas dinner with him, and there expressed to Wiggin the dissatisfaction of the administration at the attitude of the Chase Bank. A day or two later Huston told me that Wiggin had sent word to him that he, Wiggin, resented the White House interfering in the business of his bank, and that Huston had better go home and mind his own business."

It was here again that W. F. and his historian join issue over the problem of Herbert Hoover. W. F. thinks that this was a great proof of friendship on Hoover's part, while I think it was one more proof of Hoover's indecision and ineffectiveness. What more could Hoover have done, W. F. asks, humbly. I answer that here was supposed to be a conspiracy to deprive an American citizen of his property, and it would have been a simple matter for the President of the United States to instruct his Attorney-General to consider the bringing of criminal proceedings against the conspirators. The merest hint of such a course from the White House would have brought the conspirators to their knees, and the money to save the Fox companies would have been forthcoming from the New York bankers. W. F. kept urging his high-priced lawyers to consider taking action under the criminal law, but in this he was not successful. These Wall Street lawyers will tell you that they don't practice criminal law; the reason being quite obvious. So many of the things they do are criminal, that there has to be a gentlemen's agreement among them that the criminal law does not exist.

Herbert Hoover had a great deal at stake in this case. A receivership for the Fox companies, with assets running into hundreds of millions, would certainly have smashed that little sprout of prosperity which the administration was trying so hard to nourish into life. At this time receiverships for industrial corporations were extremely rare. Says W. F.: "During 1929, after five years of prosperity for all corporations, the word receivership had almost been forgotten. It was easy to see that if, in the middle of December, a brief six weeks after the financial earthquake, we were to go into the receivership period, particularly with a company of this size—you see what horror it would have caused. The only time a receivership had occurred in the last generation where $91,000,000 worth of liabilities was involved was in a railroad receivership; so this would have been the largest industrial failure in the history of American affairs."

So here was Huston, treasurer of the Republican National Committee, most anxious to help his friend W. F. in any way that would not offend Wiggin or Morgan, and the other great bankers from whom Huston had the job of collecting campaign funds. "He thought the first thing to do was to try to adjust these difficulties amicably. He suggested that perhaps a modification could be made in the voting trust. Would I be willing to make a modification? He said that, in view of my former experiences with these people, I ought to be able to protect my interests. Huston felt the first gesture for the adjusting of this matter should come from me. He ought to be able to report, when he returned to Washington, that he had made an honest endeavor, and that Fox was willing to go along."

So on December 22, W. F. prepared a memorandum, of which I have a copy. The essence of it is: "that no new plan of consolidation or financing can be adopted that contemplates the dissolution of the present outstanding voting shares without the consent of William Fox. . . . I will not permit the powers that I have as president to be modified in any other respect, except that I am willing that there should be a finance committee created, and this finance committee can have full power to attend to the financing of the company."

Of course, Stuart, Otterson, and Wiggin would not accept any such arrangement: one that would save the Fox and leave him in control. Colonel Huston traveled back and forth; he stayed with W. F. morning, noon and night, and tried in every way to adjust the situation. He even went so far as to appeal for help to his personal friends. He knew a man who had just received $30,000,000 in cash, and that would have been very useful; but he could not succeed in interesting this friend.

Then one day W. F. made a curious suggestion: why not appeal to Henry Ford? Some eight or nine years back Henry

Ford had had the fangs of the bankers in his leg, and he knew how it felt. Could Huston get to Ford? Could he say that he had come at the suggestion of Hoover, or with Hoover's approval? For it was not Hoover alone who was interested in the return of prosperity. Ford had just as big a stake involved. Ford wanted to stem the tide of destruction and bring business back.

"Finally we agreed that we would send to Ford and lay before him a picture in the following continuity: first, convince him beyond the shadow of a doubt that the supplying of money to these enterprises was good business, convince him that this was not to be a charitable venture, or one in which he would take any risk, convince him that more than ample securities could be given him for every dollar he was asked to put into the enterprise; second, explain to him the avariciousness of this banking group and of the Telephone Company, trying to parallel this story to the difficulty he had been in; third, convey to him the importance of saving this company, the fact that this was to be the largest receivership in the history of American industry; and when these three things were fully presented to him, if he showed the slightest sign of interest, then and only then could we say to him: 'The President of the United States is vitally interested in this thing, and if you will call him on the 'phone, he will tell you that the administration would consider it a service, if you will help in this emergency.'"

They found an emissary, David A. Brown, a Jewish banker and philanthropist, whose brother was Ford's architect. This emissary went to Detroit, and came back and reported that "the old man was kind of foxy"; he didn't really believe that the emissary had authority to speak for the White House. So another mission was sent, this time Huston, Brown, and a professor of accounting at the New York University who was familiar with the affairs of the Fox companies.

"A talk was had with Henry Ford. He appeared to be vitally interested in the matter; he said he would go over the figures, and if the transaction justified itself, he would be glad to give it careful consideration. He was then urged to please call the White House, which he said he would do as soon as he had examined the figures. We waited for a day and a week. We no longer could get in touch with Ford, we could only find his secretary after that; and at the end of a day and week there appeared in New York a gentleman who said he was Ford's confidential man, and wanted to get my story first hand. I gave it to him, and I thought I was able to recite it very well at that time. After listening to me carefully, he finally suggested that he and Ford were on very friendly terms with the Telephone Company, and that if I wished, he would be glad to take the matter up with Gifford. Here he was, the confidential man of a chap who had had an experience almost as bad as mine—and now he was going to occupy the position of a steerer! I was to be steered back to the Telephone Company. It reminded me of the saying: 'All roads lead to Rome.' I informed him that I needed no introduction; I had had the pleasure of meeting Gifford; and so the conference terminated.

"We then could understand why Ford had never 'phoned to the White House. If he had, and the request had been made for him to do this thing, he would have been in the position of having disregarded a request made of him by the White House. If he didn't 'phone, he was disregarding no one but myself. Of course, I only had this man's word that Ford and the Telephone Company were very friendly. I don't know whether his reason for declining was a personal acquaintance with Gifford, or stock ownership, or because he reached a conclusion that he might be playing with fire if he was going to displease the Telephone Company. He must have to have a clear picture in his mind of what the penalties might be. I don't believe it would do for Ford to have someone listen in on all his telephone conversations. He reached the conclusion, and perhaps wisely so, that this Octopus was too large for him."

I asked W. F. what had been his previous experiences with Ford; for I had noted my subject's peculiar way of forgetting the enemies he has made, and how he has made them. I succeeded in dredging out of his memory three Henry Ford stories. Two of them have nothing to do with this book, but may serve some future historian with a taste for oddities. The third I think explains completely why W. F. didn't get the help he sought.

The first story carries us back to the summer of 1916. "A lady called on me and said she was Mrs. Rosika Schwimmer, and she asked me the following questions: 'How would you like to

have your name on the front page of every newspaper of the
world? How would you like to have your name discussed at
every dinner table? How would you like to be the most talked-of
man in the history of the world? How would you like to sell
twenty times more pictures than you do now?' I said there was
only one of those things I was interested in, and that was how
would I like to sell twenty times as many pictures as before.
How could I do that? She said: 'I have a plan. I have char-
tered a boat and I call it my peace ship. In reality it isn't any
peace ship at all. I would like you to finance it. You must
provide the food and the crew. From the time this ship starts,
it starts the four things I have just named.'

"I asked if she hoped to bring peace. She said: 'You know
we can't do that. But the mere fact that the newspapers will be
printing about it and people will be talking about it will get
people to thinking about it, and that may result in peace.' I
asked her to leave the manuscript of her plan with me, that I
would like to think it over, and for how long would she give
it to me with an option? She would give it to me for a week.
About three days later, she came back all excited—what could she
do, all her plans were being upset. She said: 'You know I have
given you an option, and I didn't tell you that before I had a
conference with you I went to Mr. Ford and asked him the same
questions. And the strange thing about you two men is that he
also said not to mind the rest, but tell him how he could sell
twenty times as many cars as ever before. I got a telephone
call this morning that he has accepted it, and wants to close the
deal. What shall I do?' I told her I had given the matter consideration and didn't want to do it anyway. Eventually that
was the Ford 'Peace Ship.'"

As you know, the ship did not succeed in stopping the war,
and America went in to make the world safe for democracy.
W. F. became chairman of the Allied Theatrical Motion Pictures Team for the Red Cross, and as part of their drive they
arranged a mammoth concert at the Metropolitan Opera House.
For the first and last time in history John McCormack and
Enrico Caruso were going to appear upon the same stage. A
remarkable achievement in diplomacy—they had sent someone
to Caruso to say that McCormack wanted the honor of appearing

upon the stage with Caruso, and they had sent someone to McCormack to say that Caruso wanted the honor of appearing upon the stage with McCormack. Caruso fell at once, but McCormack tried to bargain; he would appear provided Kreisler was invited. Kreisler, an Austrian, was an enemy alien, and barred from American platforms. They hunted Kreisler out, living with his wife in a hall bedroom, destitute. He would play, but he hadn't his violin; his violin was pawned, and the pawn-shop was closed because it was after 11 o'clock on Saturday night. They couldn't find the pawnbroker, and so Kreisler couldn't appear, and finally McCormack consented to appear with just Caruso.

It was a grand occasion; the tickets were beyond price. United States Marshal McCarty made a bid for funds, by auctioning off a gold cup which the Kaiser had presented to some American citizen for winning a yacht race. It was five feet high, a marvelous trophy made of solid gold. It had been on display in one of the large theatres, with four soldiers to watch it, two by day and two by night. It had become quite a feature in New York life, having been put up at a public gathering and sold at a high price, and then the bidder had returned it and let it be sold again. Thus it had been sold and given back a dozen times at various gatherings. But now it was announced that the cup would be sold for the last time—the purchaser would not be asked to return it. Amid great excitement, Marshal McCarty lifted the huge object to show how heavy it was; it was too heavy, and slipped from his hands, hit the stage and broke to pieces! It was not gold at all, but a fake!

The concert was a kind of circus affair. Everybody was there to make a contribution for the relief of the war sufferers, and to do it in a conspicuous way; everybody was entering into the spirit of the occasion, and those in charge were getting as much money as possible, and repaying in publicity and fun. Says W. F.:

"I sat in the box at the left hand side of the house with Mrs. Fox and my family. All at once there was a commotion, and Al Jolson, who acted as one of the ushers, ran down the aisle and interrupted the marshal in what he was doing. He said: 'I have a great bit of news. Who do you suppose we have in the house?

Mr. Henry Ford and his wife and son!' The operator threw
the light right down on them. The marshal began making his
address of welcome, praising this genius who gave employment
to a million men and brought comforts to all the peoples of the
world, a benefactor. The marshal said: 'Mr. Ford, I know you
have contributed liberally to the American Red Cross, that you
have contributed in Detroit where your contribution belongs.
But this is the City of New York, the city that probably has
more Fords that any other city in the country. The people of
New York City are proud to ride in a Ford car. The people of
New York would be glad if you could see your way clear to
make a nominal contribution to this New York sum. Won't
you please name to these wonderful men and women here, an
amount, be it ever so small, just so that we can record your
name on our books?'

"By this time every eye was turned on Ford. He had risen
from his seat, in spite of his wife and son both trying to keep
him in his seat; he pulled loose and strode out of the theatre.
I quickly left my box, and went outside, where I found him
telling his troubles to a couple of chauffeurs and a policeman.
He said that he had bought his ticket and had a right to sit in
peace."

And now for the third story, which I think explains so
completely the attitude of Henry Ford to William Fox:

"Ford started a weekly paper, the Dearborn 'Independent,'
bought and read mainly by people who were unfriendly to the
Jews. It greatly aroused the Jews of New York. Indignation
meetings were held, and consultations were had as to how to stop
the attacks. I met with Louis Marshall one day and said to him
that all our methods were wrong. I told Marshall the peace
ship episode, and said: 'Now, just as this Rosika Schwimmer
asked him how he would like to sell twenty times more cars than
he was selling now, in exactly that way somebody walked into
Ford's place and said: "There are 120,000,000 people in America,
and only 6,000,000 of them are Jews. So the Jews comprise only
5 per cent of your customers. If you begin a campaign against
the Jews, you will lose that 5 per cent of customers, but you will
gain 25 per cent from the other people of America." That is why
Ford started these attacks.'

"That is what I said to Marshall. I gave no more thought to the matter until one day a man came to me and said: 'You are going to be in the Dearborn "Independent" three issues from now.' So it was to be myself! The shoe was threatening to pinch. I found a mutual friend of Ford and myself, and said, 'You like Ford very well?' He said yes. I said: 'All right, there is to be an article appearing about me in this paper. There has been a campaign conducted against my people—I resent it strongly, and I have made up my mind to throw a little searchlight on Ford, and see whether or not he is without a weak spot. In the short time of my investigation I find that there are more accidents where people are killed who are riding in Ford cars than in any other car made. That is probably because he has more cars being used. We have hundreds of cameras from coast to coast. From now on they are to be instructed that wherever they learn of an accident in a Ford car, they are promptly to go to the scene of action and find out what people were killed, how many dependents were left, and so on. They will then get an expert to make an analysis of the car, and have him swear as to what had snapped in this car, if there were any defective parts, etc. We will probably get a hundred of these accidents a week from now on, and I am going to take the best ones to appear in our newsreels, one on Monday, and one on Thursday in all my theatres. The first two or three weeks, I don't believe the people in our theatres will pay any attention to it; but after a few weeks I just don't know how many people will want to ride in Ford cars. It may and it may not hurt Ford.'

"This man said: 'I suppose you want me to tell this story to Ford.' It was then about 3:30 in the afternoon. He left immediately for Detroit, and returned saying he had told the story to Ford, and said: 'While you didn't authorize me to say it, I made it clear that that is your plan unless he abandons this attack in his paper. He agreed to do this; not only to abandon the attack, but he will let you select an editor of his paper, and he will pay the man's salary. Your editor will pass on every piece of copy that goes into that paper.' I said I didn't want to assume that responsibility. But the attack was stopped, and that was the end of that publication.

"I thought that Ford and I had settled that difficulty in an

amicable way. The request to discontinue the attacks on the
Jews came from everywhere—it came from the President and all
kinds of societies throughout the country. When Ford finally
saw that the sales of his cars were going to be attacked, that the
estimate of increase of sales supplied to him was incorrect, he
wrote a personal letter to every protestor, saying that he was
discontinuing the attacks as a special favor to that protestor."

So much for Ford stories; and now while we are in the company of the great ones, let us spend a short while with two others.

Soon after the panic W. F. had made an appeal to his friend,
Bernard M. Baruch, with whom he had been associated in a
business undertaking. Baruch is a stock market operator and
prominent Democrat who became an admirer of Woodrow Wilson, and during the war was chairman of the War Industries
Board. "Bernie" Baruch is now a benevolent-looking gentleman
with snow-white hair; very tall, slender, and stooping slightly
to meet his fellow mortals. His judgment about an investment
proposition is respected by everyone in Wall Street, and when
W. F. found himself in trouble, he remembered the great pleasure
he had given his friend by collecting the old negatives from the
morgue of Fox Film dealing with episodes in the life of Wilson,
and putting them together into a picture. He knew Baruch was
close to the Chase Bank and an intimate friend of Wiggin—this
before W. F. had come to realize that Wiggin meant to gobble
him up.

Baruch called upon W. F. one evening at the Ambassador
Hotel, and examined the figures revealing the growth of Fox
Film and Fox Theatres and their tremendous earnings. Baruch
is a man who is able to understand corporate figures, and he
expressed amazement that institutions so sound should be in
financial difficulties. Says W. F.:

"After two or three hours of examination of the figures I
presented, he became wildly enthusiastic about the whole enterprise. He could readily see from these figures that the common
stock was selling on the basis of one year's earnings. It was
customary at that time for common stocks of corporations to sell
at ten times their one year's earnings, and therefore he stated
that the figures he had read made this proposition 'a pot of gold';
that it was customary for him to find projects of this kind and

present them to his friends, the bankers, and he was so impressed with the figures presented to him that he himself would make a $10,000,000 investment. He said he knew that if proper finances were provided and proper banking facilities afforded, with the force he knew I possessed, this could be made a most unusual enterprise.

"He explained to me that during the entire panic he was the confidential advisor of Albert Wiggin; that Wiggin was his personal friend; that both Wiggin of the Chase and Mitchell of the National City rested on his advice, and that the matter which confronted me was insignificant, and there would be no difficulty in straightening it out promptly. Also he added that there would be no trouble with the Telephone Company, because Gifford was his personal friend.

"I naturally was filled with hopes. This occurred very early in this difficulty, sometime between November 2 and November 10. As a result of the most kind and friendly interest Baruch had taken in the enterprise, particularly his assertion that this enterprise resembled 'a pot of gold,' I took the liberty of calling at his home on Fifth Avenue several times. It was on my last visit to his home that he informed me that he had discussed the matter downtown, and that the Stuart brothers had requested that they be permitted to call on him. I warned him against this meeting. He said their attitude would make no difference, but he felt that he ought to hear their side of the story, and their appointment was on this particular morning—they would be coming along at any minute. We concluded our conferences, and I left, and waited directly across the street from his home, and within a few minutes thereafter saw the Stuart brothers enter Baruch's home.

"What transpired at that conference I don't know, but I know that from that time on Baruch was no longer available to my telephone calls; my requests that he permit me to see him again were denied. I presume that from the lips of Stuart he heard that this difficulty I was in was going to make it possible for the Telephone Company and the Chase Bank to capture my business. I can readily see that when Baruch had to choose between Fox and his friends Gifford and Wiggin, he was no longer on my side."

Very soon now we shall see a new banking group coming forward to do the Fox financing. This group will be looking for trustees, and will be so indiscreet as to suggest in court that either Bernard M. Baruch or his son should take the place of Stuart or Otterson as a trustee. Says W. F.:

"Baruch was infuriated at the thought of their using his name in any matter that concerned me. He wanted nothing to do with the enterprise that only a few weeks before he considered 'a pot of gold.' He wanted nothing to do with the enterprise that, only a few weeks earlier, he had expressed a willingness to participate in to the extent of $10,000,000 of his personal fortune. Whether or not he did participate in the financing that resulted after my companies were acquired by Clarke, the Chase Bank and Chase Securities, I was never able to learn. It is probable that he had a participation in the enterprise; and if so, he lost his money."

The other great person whom we have the honor to call upon is Charles M. Schwab, chairman of Bethlehem Steel, and granddaddy and Santa Claus to all American big business. My first acquaintance with this benevolent orator of optimism and prosperity was back in 1906, when one of his former employes placed in my hands a mass of documents having to do with the Carnegie Steel Company, which some time before had been making defective armor plate for American battleships. Charlie at this time had been one of "Andy's boys," the shop foreman or superintendent; and here were shop-records doctored in those same shops, and proving that certain plates which had been placed in the turrets of the battleship "Oregon" were full of air bubbles, and would have splintered like glass if they ever had been struck by a shell. Fortunately for Charlie, the aim of the Spanish fleet was bad; no less fortunately for Charlie, all these documents were burned in the Helicon Hall fire in the spring of 1907, and can never be produced at any of the banquets of financiers and executives where Charlie makes speeches bubbling over with patriotism and loving-kindness, telling them how prosperity is just around one more corner.

It happened that the contracts of Mayer, Rubin and Thalberg with Metro-Goldwyn-Mayer came up for renewal. Schenck of Loew's desired to renew them, but W. F. didn't think that the contracts ought to include 20 per cent of the net earnings of the Loew Company, because this included not only the earnings of Metro-Goldwyn-Mayer, which the three gentlemen were running, but also the net earnings of a chain of 200 theatres which the gentlemen were not running. Schenck, in his efforts to convince the stubborn and penurious Fox, invited him to pay a visit one evening to the home of Charlie Schwab.

As a youth I can remember very well surveying this $3,000,000 French chateau, made all of brownstone, with innumerable towers and turrets, and securely protected against prowlers on Riverside Drive by high iron spikes. Perhaps Schenck thought that W. F. would be overawed by this royal splendor; or perhaps he thought that W. F. would fall in love with the soft caressing voice and loving smile of Charlie. Anyhow, Charlie spent an evening convincing W. F. that this bonus arrangement was not unusual; all the executives of Bethlehem were getting it; Grace, the president, was receiving a small salary and a bonus on the profits amounting to more than $1,000,000 a year. This, of course, was before the stockholders got on to that little scheme, and made such a fuss that Charlie and his boys had to back down. W. F. makes the unloving suggestion that executives of corporations who take a bonus on the profits ought to pay the companies a bonus in years when there are losses. This one sentence is enough to explain to you why W. F. was driven out of Wall Street.

Of course W. F. did not find himself in this palace, in consultation with the benevolent Charlie, without telling that seventy-year old philanthropist his troubles and asking for help. Charlie expressed sincere sympathy and regret for his difficulties, and made him a free gift of the hope that he might ultimately find a way out of them. W. F. adds: "I was amazed to learn recently that Schwab, at the request of Pynchon & Co., and of Wiggin of the Chase Bank, of which Schwab is a director, had invested $2,500,000 in the enterprise to drive me out." Of course, Charlie lost this money, and W. F. would be superhumanly loving if he were sorry.

REEL NINETEEN

THE REPTYLE

AGAIN our Fox was hunting for lawyers. Through Huston he retained James Francis Burke of Pittsburgh, general counsel for the Republican National Committee, to help him in his negotiations with the Government. But he must have another lawyer in New York, and he found himself thinking about Samuel Untermyer. A curious circumstance—Wall Street knew he was going to retain Untermyer as soon as Reass began talking to Untermyer over the telephone. W. F. began to try experiments, making over the telephone statements which were not true, and then seeing them appear in the gossip-sheets of Wall Street. He interprets this as one of the reasons why so many of the great ones, both financiers and lawyers, backed out of the case when they discovered the grim antagonism of Otterson and Gifford. Few indeed are the persons in Wall Street who would be willing to have all their conversations "listened in on"!

Samuel Untermyer is an elderly Jewish lawyer, greatly dreaded by the money power of this country. The reason is that he is the one independent man who knows the game inside and out. He was the only one who ever had the nerve to put the elder Pierpont Morgan on the witness-stand and ask him real questions; the fury of the old wild boar of Wall Street over this experience is one of the great stories of American history, and will be told in all school-books when we have real historians in America. Meanwhile, perhaps you can find in your public library a copy of the so-called Pujo report, which is part of the Congressional record for the year 1912.

W. F. had thought about the terrible Untermyer, and had been warned against having anything to do with him; the chief warner being Charles Evans Hughes. Says W. F.: "I distinctly recalled when I first met Judge Hughes, telling him that some people were urging Untermyer to be taken into the case, and asking if he had any objection if we asked Untermyer to help him. He didn't want Untermyer. He said Untermyer was the lowest type of human that ever lived; he called him a reptyle."

In his sore distress our Fox now recalled that Untermyer was representing Warner Brothers in a long drawn out fight with the Telephone Company. What W. F. wanted more than anything else in the world was a lawyer who was willing to fight the Telephone Company! Then one day Reass told him that Untermyer had said: "You ought to bring that Fox case over to my office." Another day Untermyer said: "Fox will never get out of his difficulties until he calls on me, because I am the only man who has no strings on him." W. F. mentioned the idea to Colonel Huston, and Huston said that if Untermyer came into the case he would have to retire, because Untermyer was a prominent Democrat, and Huston was treasurer of the Republican National Committee. Confidentially, Huston added that Untermyer was the one man "the gang down town" was afraid of.

So now Fox traveled down to Atlantic City, where Untermyer occupied a penthouse on top of a hotel in an effort to help his asthma. And now at last he had a man who would stand by him and fight his fight through. I was happy when he told me this, for I am under a debt of obligation to this hard-hitting lawyer. Thirteen years ago, when I was publishing "The Brass Check," and the Associated Press and the paper trust had put a boycott on me, so that I couldn't find a wholesale paper dealer in the United States who dared to sell me a scrap of paper, a friend in Boston agreed to make a carload of book paper if I would put down the cash with the order; and it was Samuel Untermyer who loaned me the $4,600 required for that deal. Also Untermyer was kind enough to read the manuscript, and tell me that it couldn't possibly be published, because it contained fifty criminal libels and not less than a thousand civil suits. I published the book, and did not go to jail, and nobody even threatened a civil suit. So now I smile at Untermyer, and tell him that he is a better lawyer than prophet.

At this same period, early in January of 1930, our Fox had conceived the plan of going over the heads of the bankers, and dealing directly with his own stockholders and theatre owners.

He remembered how Henry Ford had saved himself from the bankers in 1921, by going to the Ford dealers, requiring them to order a certain number of cars and pay for them in advance. W. F. was supplying pictures to approximately 8,000 theatres in America and as many more throughout the rest of the world. At least half of these theatre owners depended for their livelihood upon the Fox pictures. Surely it would be to their interest to save the Fox companies!

W. F. consulted Professor Madden of New York University, who had gone to interview Ford with Huston and David Brown. Madden, whose specialty is accounting and finance, worked out a plan for a $35,000,000 bond issue, and the Fox accountants made a complete survey of the assets of the company. It was arranged that there were to be $2 worth of security for every dollar of the bond issue. If each of the 16,000 exhibitors were to take $2,000 worth of Fox bonds, the problem would be solved. That was just about the amount which these exhibitors were paying to the Fox companies for films in a single year.

This was to be a perfect bond, designed not by a banking group, but by a dean of a university! This dean had published articles warning the bankers that the security for the South American bonds which were being sold to the public was wholly insufficient. He had told W. F. of an incident: the House of Morgan had written him, resenting his attitude towards a South American bond issue which they were about to put out; and Madden had called Morgan's attention to the fact that the country in question had already defaulted in one or more bond issues.

Here was to be a model bond, prepared by a model professor of finance. It was to be issued by a newly formed company called the Fox Securities Corporation. This, of course, was a terrible thing for the "gang downtown." Here was this lawless and disorderly Fox proposing to raise capital without bankers! He was going to sell $35,000,000 worth of bonds without giving the customary rake-off to an investment house! Just as Ford had escaped from their hands, so the Fox was going to escape; and who would be the next one?

The Fox Securities Corporation was formed, and the circular for the bond issue was ready. "I had the first group of exhibitors, thirty or more, come from various parts of the country to
16

try the plan out, to see whether or not it would be practical to sell these bonds. While we hoped for an average of $2,000 per theatre, we soon found our calculations were all wrong. There were many of those who came amongst the first group of thirty who were prepared to buy substantial blocks of these bonds. This was a bond of a company they were thoroughly familiar with; a company that they wanted to keep in business.

"One man called to see me, Pat Powers, who had been in the motion picture business at least twenty-five years, and whom I knew very well. He wanted to know all about the bond issue, and he wanted to subscribe to $1,000,000 worth of these bonds. He had read about the difficulty I was in. There were others in the room when Powers offered to take $1,000,000 worth of these bonds. There was a report made downtown that thirty men were enthusiastic about it, and that instead of an average of $2,000 apiece we could probably sell these men $1,500,000 worth. There was a clear indication that we could sell $130,000,-000 worth of bonds if we had enough collateral to collateralize that many bonds."

At this time W. F. was in communication with Giannini, the California banker, to whom he had appealed for financing. Giannini had sent his New York man, Elisha Walker, president of the Bancamerica-Blair Corporation. The name "Elisha" suggests a patriarch from either Palestine or New England, but, as a matter of fact, this Elisha is a graduate of Yale and of Massachusetts Tech, and a thoroughly modern "go-getter," hard and cold. I happen to know about him because a friend of mine, a young man here in Southern California who was working for the Bank of America as a salesman, was ordered to assist in a manipulation of "Transamerica." Walker was supporting this stock, buying it, and trying to persuade the public to help him. He came to Los Angeles and made a speech to all the bank salesmen, telling them what a great bank it was and what a wonderful issue. My friend said to me: "I won't trust that man and I won't trust his stock." He went to his superior in the bank and was told that this was the stock he was hired to sell, and he would either sell it or resign. He resigned; and the stock slid from 45 to 2½. Walker split with Giannini, and ousted him, and then the stockholders reversed the procedure.

Early in January of 1930 Elisha Walker came to our Fox, to discuss the proposition of doing the Fox financing for a very high fee. He came with a son of Giannini's, and W. F. told them his story, and Giannini's son was sympathetic; but, to quote W. F.'s words, "Walker is of a more practical type." He came again and again, "and each time he would have under his arm all the papers I had given him to study. To me it looked like he was not interested in my proposal, and that he was calling for the purpose of discontinuing the negotiations. Else why was he carrying these papers around with him? If he was interested in doing the financing, the papers belonged in his office. Every time I saw him with these papers, I was sure he had come to call off the deal."

Now came this dangerous and terrible proposition, a Fox Securities Company to do the financing of the Fox companies, and there must have been some word passed by the powers of Wall Street. At all hazards the Fox bond issue must be stopped, and legitimate bankers must do that financing. At any rate, they must pretend that they were going to do the financing, until they had succeeded in blocking the independent plan.

Which was it? W. F. wasn't sure, and isn't sure today. To realize the complications of the mystery, you must note that Elisha Walker was at that time a director of the Chase Bank. Wall Street friends of mine tell me that Blair and Company have always been known as the "back-door" of the Chase: that is to say, if the Chase turns you down, you go to the Blairs, and they take your proposition at a higher price, and Chase lends the money to Blair, and some Chase officials get a "rake-off."

Elisha Walker came one day and said, "We want to do your financing." Also Untermyer reported that he had taken the proposition to the firm of Lehman Brothers, and they agreed to come in. Subsequently "Bobbie" Lehman told W. F. that before the decision was taken, he consulted the House of Morgan, asking for permission to join in the enterprise, and received it. You can see what a scare the Fox had thrown into them; also you can see who it was that had been blocking the Fox companies from credit!

It was to be a job paying $10,000,000 in commissions, and there weren't many such jobs lying around Wall Street in

January of 1930. Nevertheless, it was a great favor the bankers were doing, so they all considered. Once more W. F. was summoned to a third degree, to have his pockets searched, and if possible picked. Once more the swarm of accountants and lawyers—fifty-eight accountants and twenty-two lawyers—invaded the offices of the Fox companies, and as W. F. says, "for thirty days and thirty nights they made an exhaustive search of every transaction, of every directors' resolution, from the very inception of this company, to discover one misdeed on the part of Fox. These auditors and lawyers never went home to sleep. They remained locked in this building of ours, and delved and searched in the hopes of discovering one thing that this man Fox had done with which he could be charged."

You must get the peculiar position of our Fox at this moment. His securities plan is failing, but so far he has managed to keep that fact from the bankers   The reason of its failing, he declares, is that the practical work was dependent upon the Fox executives, those very same gentlemen who had signed the "round-robin," and who were now working in the services of Otterson and Stuart and Harley Clarke. Pat Powers had promised to buy $1,000,000 worth of the bonds; but then pretty soon "W. R. Sheehan learned about Pat Powers, and from then on I no longer had the $1,000,000 subscription."

The day after the first conference gathered, W. F. asked Grainger, the American sales manager, if he had got those subscriptions. "There was an excuse made as to why each one would have to go home and consult his partner, wife, father, mother, brothers, sisters—all kinds of alibis were given me. It appeared clear to me that the sale of these securities to my customers was not going to be as easy as I thought it would be. Grainger was Winfield R. Sheehan's most intimate friend, and he was to handle the American exhibitors; Clayton Sheehan, Winfield's brother, was to handle the foreign exhibitors. Confidentially it was reported to me that neither Grainger nor Clayton Sheehan intended to do anything that would result in this venture becoming successful. In fact, they were spreading secret propaganda that no one should buy any of these debentures."

So W. F. went ahead with the bankers. He insisted on taking in Dillon, Read & Co., because they were the bankers for the

Loew Company, whose friendship was needed for the consolidation or merger. Clarence Dillon must be a friend to the enterprise if it was to go through; on the other hand, if it was just one more bluff, and if it was not going through, then it was obvious that the Fox was completely helpless, and would have to sell his voting shares, and in that case Dillon would be in the group that would buy them. Dillon, you recall, had eaten all the grapes at the luncheon, and had been very nervous, and had warned W. F. that he was going to lose his voting shares, and that someone who knew nothing about the picture business was going to be put in charge of the Fox companies. Dillon was a director in the Chase Bank, as was Elisha Walker.

W. F. was sure that the Halsey, Stuart and Chase Bank crowd would know everything that he was doing anyhow, and it was better to have them in the picture. When I asked about this, he said: "Never avoid your enemy. Always meet him face to face. I can fight him better if I see him every day, than if I have shut him out where I can't watch him."

The accountants had finished their work, and the time had come for the final picking of pockets, which took place at the home of Elisha Walker. There was a lawyer named Swaine, representing the Bancamerica-Blair, and one named Royce representing Lehman Brothers. Says W. F.: "As long as I live I shall never forget the grueling that I received at the hands of Royce and Swaine. Royce soon made it evident that he was representing something else besides the bankers. 'The Tri-Ergon patents? Why, they belong to the Fox Film Corporation,' was his attitude, and, 'We insist upon you turning them over to it.' The Grandeur Company, of which I was a half owner, belonged to the companies; he insisted that I return it to the company. Although from my books they could readily learn that I had invested $600,000 of my own capital, that didn't make any difference. Mr. Walker was telling me on the side that of course he had no control of these bankers; that was their recommendation, and we needed their names as having approved the form of financing. They took the attitude that the interest I had in the Fox Movietone News belonged to the company."

The answer of W. F. to all this was that if he was going to be tied up with the bankers for ten years or so, he ought to have a salary. He hadn't received any for the past four years, you will remember. But no, there wasn't any need for him to get a salary. What Elisha Walker was going to do was to avoid any written contract on the subject.

"Finally a compromise was made after much discussion—after my pointing out to them that we were paying three or four or five thousand dollars a week for performers who had no knowledge of the picture business when we began, and that Zukor was probably getting five or six hundred thousand dollars a year, and that my salary ought to be the same. A salary of $150,000 a year was to be paid to me; a free license was to be given to the companies of my patents of Grandeur and of Tri-Ergon; and I was to return the 25 per cent interest I had in the Movietone News department. That was as far as I would go; they knew I would go no further, and they made their contract on the best basis they could.

"How can I indicate more clearly to you that when they were making this deal they were representing Clarke, than to tell you that later on, when Clarke bought me out, he insisted that I turn in my shares in the Movietone News, that I give him a free license for the Grandeur Company, and that I give a free license for the Tri-Ergon patents? In other words, in January these bankers and lawyers were extracting all that they knew they could get, so that when Clarke took control he would have no bargaining to do."

Now came the question of the trustees who were to control the voting shares during the period of financing. It was arranged that there were to be three: one was the president of a bank controlled by Bancamerica-Blair; another the president of a bank controlled by the Lehmans; and the third was to be named by Clarence Dillon. Whereupon Dillon arose with a new and brilliant plan. These banking firms would be very pleased to form a syndicate, to sell $65,000,000 worth of Fox securities for a 10 per cent commission; but he felt that the number of trustees was insufficient, and that the number should be increased to five; there should be added Harold Leonard Stuart of the firm of Halsey, Stuart & Co., and John Edward Otterson of the Telephone Company.

All along W. F. had felt certain that the great Clarence Dillon was representing these groups, and so he was not surprised by this proposition. Everybody else in the room seemed to think it was a fine idea, including even W. F.'s lawyers, James Francis Burke, Samuel Untermyer, and Alvin Untermyer, his son.

"Clarence Dillon carefully explained to me that no harm could come through my consenting to this new arrangement, because after all the Telephone Company and Halsey, Stuart were going to be in the minority. They had only two votes out of five. Of course, the fact of the matter was that they would have at least three votes out of five, for surely Clarence Dillon's vote would always belong to the Telephone Company. This conference, as it appeared to me, was for no other reason than to again steer me back into the spider's web.

"I thought that with this new formed banking group it would be better if I did not strongly oppose this new recommendation, which had been fully concurred in by everyone present. It is rather a strange feeling to sit in the room with twenty presumably brainy men, all of them agreeing on a plan, and for one individual to say, 'No, that doesn't suit me.' Such an action would, of course, clearly indicate that they were dealing with a stubborn man.

"I felt that I could well afford to risk agreeing with the plan, with the reservation that it must be consented to by Mrs. Fox. I felt reasonably sure in my own mind that there wasn't the slightest chance of Mrs. Fox agreeing to this proposed plan, in which the Telephone Company and Halsey, Stuart were again to become the trustees of my shares. I said: 'Gentlemen, this is a perfectly simple matter. You have a telephone here. Let's call Mrs. Fox on the 'phone and ask her to come here.' 'No,' said Clarence Dillon, 'this is a sort of stag party and I don't believe she should be asked to come here.'

"Samuel Untermyer then volunteered that he go to my home, and talk to Mrs. Fox and explain to her the necessity of consenting to this arrangement. I suggested that it would be bad policy for Untermyer to accompany me, for if she objected to the plan, and he used his persuasive powers on her without success, it would result in her losing confidence in him, and therefore I would suffer as a result of it. I suggested that one of the bankers come along with me, or one of the lawyers for the bankers. No, they would prefer not doing that. It was then suggested that James Francis Burke, who said he knew Mrs. Fox very well, that he had met her often, come along.

"So James Francis Burke and myself left the bankers and lawyers at Dillon's home and proceeded to my home. I promised him that when we entered the house I would do no more than say good evening to Mrs. Fox, and I would do that within his presence and within his sight, and that he would do all the talking, and I would be perfectly quiet. This plan was carried out just that way. Mr. Burke began the conversation. He spent ten or fifteen minutes explaining the great danger of William Fox; that without a banking group this meant total destruction. Mrs. Fox became uneasy and said: 'Why, I can't understand it. I can't quite understand what you are talking about. Mr. Fox has a banking group now. Why, Mr. Fox had created the Fox Securities Corporation, and was prepared to sell $35,000,000 worth of bonds. He was requested by this banking group not to do that, although he was assured of ·success. Now, is there any doubt about this banking group going forward with this proposal?'

"It was then that Burke told her, no, they just wanted a very slight modification—to increase the trustees to five. Mrs. Fox said: 'Well, there's no objection to that. Whom do they propose for the additional two?' She suggested that perhaps they were kind enough to see the justice of nominating me as one. Who would the fifth one be?' 'No,' said Burke, 'the plan is to give these two trusteeships to Stuart and Otterson.'

"Well, the scene that followed that was just as though a volcano had burst forth. She ran to the door and locked it, ran into her room and put her hat and coat on. When she came back again, nothing would do but to take her to Clarence Dillon's home. She wanted to meet these honorable bankers and these lawyers. She was perfectly willing to see William Fox ruined, but the Telephone Company, so far as she was concerned, never again were they to have anything to say in Fox's business. That was about 1 a. m. We persuaded her to please stay at home and let us go back.

"Well, we returned. I said to Burke: 'I will remain in the lower hall while you go up to the conference room to explain this scene. I would rather not be present. You will probably be able to explain it more satisfactorily with my not being in the room.'

"Of course Burke had spent considerable time explaining to Mrs. Fox that this meant ruination to me, and meant the withdrawal of the banking group. But a few minutes later Clarence Dillon came from the upper floor downstairs to where I was waiting, and took me into a separate room and said: 'Fox, I have seen all kinds of deals here in Wall Street. I have never seen one just like this. You and your wife display more courage and more nerve than I have ever seen expressed before in a Wall Street transaction. Your courage deserves great consideration on the part of your bankers, and now that we know the true sentiment that exists with you and Mrs. Fox, we will manage to go forward and just leave three trustees.'

"In other words, Dillon had played his last card for the Telephone Company. Dillon wanted to be able to say honestly and truthfully to Albert Wiggin and to his friend Walter Gifford that he had done everything in his power to put Halsey, Stuart and the Telephone Company back into the picture. But he had failed."

REEL TWENTY

LEGAL ACTIONS

IT is impossible to know what was going on behind the scenes during this crisis. There is no complete solidarity among banking groups; they rebel against authority, fight one another, and steal one another's loot. The stakes here were huge ones, and it looks as if the Elisha Walker and Lehman crowd had made up their minds to take the Fox away from the Stuart-Telephone-Chase Bank crowd. The latter crowd, on the other hand, were determined to hold onto their prey, and they went ahead with plans to tie up the new financing arrangements.

There began a series of legal actions intended to throw the companies into receivership. The method pursued in such cases is that of suits by stockholders. It happens at rare intervals that a stockholder's suit is genuine, but ninety-nine times out of a hundred, these suits are arranged for by rival financial interests, seeking the control of a company, or the manipulating of its stock. A lawyer is told to find a stockholder who is willing to let his name be used, provided that all the costs are paid.

The lawyer who brought the first receivership action against the Fox companies was named Berenson, and came from Boston. He had appeared in the New Haven Railroad receivership, representing a few shares of stock, and had finally worked himself into a position where he received a fee of $1,000,000. Our old friend Blumy had relatives in Boston, and knew Berenson well; and, as we know, Blumy had become a retainer of Harley Clarke of Chicago. W. F. ventures a guess that Clarke may have asked Blumy to find a lawyer who would start an action against the Fox companies. That Berenson was working in the interests of Clarke is proved conclusively by the fact that after Clarke had come into full control of the Fox companies, these companies paid Berenson's fee, amounting to more than $250,000.

Berenson in his action claimed to represent 620 shares of stock, the value of which on the day of filing the action was less than $12,000. Berenson's complaint charged all kinds of gross mismanagement of the companies against their president. He charged that W. F. had incurred a mass of financial obligations which he could not meet; that he was about to pay large sums of money to himself and to the stockholders as dividends which the companies could not afford. Accordingly it was prayed that the United States district judge would appoint a receiver to take over the affairs of the companies and protect the stockholders.

This complaint was filed January 14, 1930, and shortly afterward came a complaint of Mrs. Susan Dryden Kuser. Mrs. Kuser is the widow of that Newark friend who had invested $200,000 in Fox Film in 1915, and had had the money repaid to him with 8 per cent interest in 1917, and in the course of fourteen years had received about $10,000,000 in dividends. The bulk of the fortune which Kuser left his widow had come from the Fox enterprises. Says W. F.:

"Anthony Kuser was one of the best friends I had, a great believer in me and in the Fox enterprises. Any time he wanted $100,000 or $500,000 or $1,000,000, he simply sold some of the shares that he had got for nothing. When this difficulty came up, his widow had still a substantial block of these shares. There were at least fifteen or more Kusers who are stockholders in the Fox enterprises, and who had made this tremendous fortune. The Kuser family were united during all of this difficulty behind Fox. The only one of the family who appeared dissatisfied was Mrs. Susan Kuser. I don't believe she was really dissatisfied. I believe someone had gone to this widow and incited her to become adverse to my interests.

"General Heppenheimer, president of the Trust Company of New Jersey, one of the thirteen banks from which I had borrowed money, was the confidential advisor of Mrs. Kuser. I presume that either the Telephone Company or the Chase Bank at one of the bank meetings asked Heppenheimer, didn't he know a substantial holder of Fox Film stock who would start an action. He must have said, 'Yes, I know Mrs. Susan Kuser.' General Heppenheimer is the same chap who called with B. K. Marcus, president of the Bank of the United States, as a committee of two to inform me that it was the intention of the bankers to apply for a receiver. To Marcus' bank, Fox Film owed $1,600,-000. It was the largest bank creditor. Marcus' interest should have been to protect that money. But he was evidently under orders from Chase Bank, and on his shoulders fell the obligation of supplying the lawyer who would begin an action for receivership for a lady by the name of Kuser, whom Heppenheimer must have produced."

The lawyer who brought this suit for Mrs. Kuser was Isador Kresel, general counsel for the Bank of the United States, the Marcus bank. Also he was a director in that bank. W. F. owed $1,600,000 to this bank, and he would have thought that Kresel's first interest would be to the bank. In bringing suit against the Fox companies to ruin them and destroy their assets, he was certainly not performing a good service for the bank. W. F. speculates:

"Perhaps he was told by the Chase Bank and by the Telephone Company: 'Mr. Kresel, if you take this case, so far as the $1,600,000 that the Fox Corporation owes your bank, you can dismiss it from your mind. Under any circumstances, we will pay that note.' How could a man take a case like this with any other understanding? Of course, when my stock was sold out to Harley L. Clarke, we found a check drawn to the order of Isador Kresel out of the treasury of the Fox Theatres Corporation for the sum of $50,000. Again I wish to call your attention that Kresel's bill first should have been paid by Mrs. Kuser, if Mrs. Kuser had retained him; second, if she had not, and if Harley L. Clarke asked Kresel to serve as the attorney for Mrs. Kuser, then the bill was due from Harley L. Clarke. If, on some theory, Clarke could justify Kresel's services being paid for by the very company that he, Kresel, was trying to ruin, then the bill should have been paid by Fox Film. But on what kind of reasoning was it possible to imagine paying Kresel's bill out of the funds of the Fox Theatres Corporation, for whom he had never performed a service? That is beyond my understanding powers."

In order to complete the story of Isador Kresel I mention that he has since been indicted on many counts in connection with the closing of the Bank of the United States, and as I write these words he is on trial for perjury in connection with this matter. Says W. F.:

"Of course, when I learned that Kresel had started an action for Mrs. Kuser, I confronted Marcus, and charged him with having supplied his personal attorney, the general counsel for the Bank of the United States and a director of that bank. Of course I found fault with him for allowing Kresel to lend himself to a dirty action of that kind. Marcus tried to get out of it, but I said: 'If you don't see this man at your bank, he lives with you in the same building. I take it for granted you are in constant conference. He couldn't have taken this retainer without your knowledge. In fact, I believe you asked him to take it.'

"I made a rather strange prediction to Marcus sometime in January or the early part of February, 1930. I made this prediction to him across a dinner table; there were four of us dining—he, his brother-in-law, a friend of mine and myself. He was constantly urging me to go forward with the trust agreement, that was my only salvation. I had listened to him and taken his advice, until the day when he asked for more collateral for my personal loan. Then I felt free to speak to him as follows:

" 'Now, Bernie, I don't believe you think you are fooling me. I know definitely you are now in the employ of the Chase Bank and the Telephone Company. You are acting under orders. They are telling you what to do. I would like to make you this little prediction. Some day the Chase Bank won't like what you do. Some day the Telephone Company won't like how you did this job. Whenever they reach that conclusion, there are going to be two things happen to you. Only one thing is happening to me—my business is being taken away. But two things to you: one, they will take your bank away and shut its doors, and two, they will indict you and send you to jail as sure as your name is Bernie Marcus.' It was less than a year afterwards that they closed his bank, indicted him and sent him to jail. Many a time while sitting on a bench inside those prison walls, he must have a vision of me, and remember the words I sang in his ears. The Chase Bank and the Telephone Company were through with him, and ended him just as I told him they would."

W. F. consoles himself with the idea that Mrs. Kuser never saw the charges which stand in her affidavit. He thinks that Kresel, attorney for his enemies, prepared these charges, and that Mrs. Kuser just signed the document put before her. Among the charges was that Mrs. William Fox was a grafter; that she had performed work in designing and decorating the theatres of the Fox Corporation, and had received profit therefrom. Soon after these charges had been filed, and when it began to appear that a receiver was going to be appointed for the Fox companies, W. F. received a call from a son of Mrs. Kuser, State Senator J. Dryden Kuser of New Jersey. Says W. F.:

"He told me that his mother had made a great error, that she had been informed that this was a suit that was only begun for the purpose of permitting the Telephone Company and Halsey, Stuart to do the financing; that she now learned she had been tricked; that the facts were that she became a plaintiff in an action by subterfuge, and what could he do to remedy that condition? The truth of the matter was that his mother hadn't any feelings against Fox and his family, and his mother appreciated the millions that Fox had made for her and her husband."

As a result of this there was placed before the court an affidavit of ten members of the Kuser family declaring their support of W. F.; and when in March there was a meeting of the stockholders of Fox Film to decide the future of the companies, the stock of Mrs. Kuser was voted for William Fox.

Concerning the charge against Mrs. Fox, W. F. adds as follows:

"The truth of the matter was this: Mrs. Fox had spent from 1915 until April, 1930, fifteen solid years of labor, day and night, sometimes until the small hours of the morning, giving the best that her brain had, for which she had never received a penny of compensation. For example, when we were building our theatre in St. Louis, Missouri, it was a common occurrence for her to commute from New York to St. Louis all during the hot summer to carry on her work. Her purpose was to eliminate graft by anyone to whom we may have let the contract."

W. F. told me how it had come about that Mrs. Fox took up this work. There were two concerns which had been doing the work of redecorating Fox theatres, and these rivals were bidding for a certain contract, and had got into a quarrel, and W. F. didn't fancy the job of deciding between them. As he phrased it, it was a question of the Rolls-Royce style of theatre decoration as opposed to the Hispano-Suiza style. Rather than make this choice, he requested that this theatre be decorated according to the Eve Leo style. She did so well and saved so much money that she had a new job.

In my long talk with Mrs. Fox she told me more about these activities. She told how she had climbed the stairs of factories and lofts, to see with her own eyes the making of furniture and chair covers and decorations. She told of the many problems involved in choosing durable materials; chair covers have to be tested for the effects of human grease and sweat, and for wearing qualities in relation to expense. Always, of course, there were efforts being made to cheat the companies, and the saving of the companies' money was one of the life passions of her husband.

She told me how the dealers would try to buy her with petty graft. When a new contract was being considered, they would take her and show her some beautiful thing which they had in stock, and which they thought would catch her fancy—a piece of tapestry, a chair, or what not. They would offer her this as a present, and Mrs. Fox would say, "What is the price of this?" They would answer $150, or whatever it might be, and Mrs. Fox would say, "All right. If you can afford to make me a present of that value, you can afford to take that amount from the company's bill. Please do so."

I asked what could have started the rumors of graft, and W. F. told the story of the Altman Art Galleries:

"Some years ago, it came to Mrs. Fox's ears that it was the common practice of our studio employes here in Los Angeles to hire furniture and furnishings to dress the sets in which the pictures were made, and on one of her visits she had seen some of the bills for rentals we were paying. This is the way it was: a piece of furniture would be brought in and the owner would value it at say a thousand dollars, and the company would pay 10 per cent of its value per week for its rental. Sometimes it would stay in the studio four or five weeks, and the company would pay $400 or $500, without putting a touch on that piece of furniture—it would be just as good the day the art gallery got it back as when they loaned it to us.

"She said: 'You are throwing temptation in the way of the employes. In the first place, you are paying too much for the lease of the furniture, and there are so many places that this furniture can be leased, it occurs to me that someone is receiving graft in connection with the hiring of it. You ought to try to eliminate that.' I asked her how. She said: 'Commission me to buy for the company $100,000 or $200,000 worth of art objects and furniture. I will spend a long time gathering it, going to every auction sale that occurs in New York of all the wealthy people, and inside of six months or a year, I will have the finest set of art objects and furniture in California.' I authorized her to do it, and she spent close onto a year, going to these auction sales two or three times a week, acquiring the finest art objects there were.

"Well, after all the purchases were made, I reached the conclusion that this furniture was by far more than we could use at our own studios. The trick was then to rent these things to all studios. If it were known in California that this belonged to Fox Film, no other company would hire it. So we created the company known as the Altman Art Galleries. No employe knew it belonged to Fox Film, but all of the stock was subscribed for and owned by Fox Film; it was a wholly owned subsidiary. We shipped the goods out here to California and engaged quarters on Sunset Boulevard. They are still there. The Fox Film Corporation was instructed that they should not lease or hire a single piece of furniture from anyone but the Altman Art Galleries.

"Someone around the studios immediately must have conceived the idea that that was a business belonging to Mrs. Fox. She was no more the owner than you or this stenographer here; but one of the charges of graft was that that was her business. Of course, Clarke and his crowd knew it wasn't, because Clarke and his crowd had all the stool pigeons in the world in our employ, who went on his side just the minute I found myself in trouble, and he definitely knew that the Altman Art Galleries belonged to Fox Film. Saul E. Rogers, our general counsel, had created that company, and he was one of Clarke's henchmen."

After he was out of his companies, W. F. wanted his wife to bring suit for slander against Mrs. Kuser. But his lawyer, Benjamin Reass, informed him that he was without redress, either against Mrs. Kuser or against the newspapers that had published the charges. Reass made a statement on the subject, which I quote:

"This is how a newspaper can destroy a man without redress. A complaint is filed and the allegations are always based on information and belief, and under that category you can make every accusation that comes to your mind. The plaintiff in such an action as well as the attorney have complete exemption from responsibility, because once they come into court and file it, they can't be held chargeable. In other words, that is the one place in which you can libel a man without the slightest evidence or proof and no responsibility on your part. The newspapers are also exempt; they simply report what the complaint charges, and you are left without redress and without a defense. These allegations were all used as the basis for a newspaper article, and when I saw this thing about Mrs. Fox, and when Kresel said that in court, that was one of the occasions I lost my temper. I strutted across the courtroom and I told him the others had adopted the usual methods of slandering Mr. Fox, but that there wasn't one that had brought a woman into the matter yet. I didn't exactly call him a liar, but I used every other phrase I could think of to give the same idea, and I told him I would make him apologize for it."

These two law suits were the first sprouts of a large crop. Altogether there were some twenty-five legal actions brought in the matter of the Fox companies. They were brought in Federal courts and in State courts, and there were charges and counter-charges, and pleas and counter-pleas, and injunctions, and stays of execution, and arguments of counsel as to the rights of Federal courts as against State courts—I have many millions of typewritten and printed words in a full suitcase and two large desk drawers. I doubt if any one human being ever read them all. As I turn their pages, looking for this or that, they loom in my mind as a monument to the wastes and imbecilities of our capitalist society. All these highly paid lawyers, these hundreds of skilled stenographers and typists, these filing clerks and court

17

clerks and messengers and bailiffs and policemen and judges—all this apparatus of chicanery and red tape for the purpose of determining the ownership of two pieces of paper which controlled a treasure chest—and when the issue was settled and the ownership was determined, the treasure was gone, and nobody but the lawyers and the bankers had anything!

The bankers of the new group—Bancamerica-Blair, Lehman, and Dillon, Read, were meeting with W. F. and working out a new financing plan. (Hereafter we shall refer to them as the Lehman group, and the plan as the Lehman plan.) Their accountants were making their investigation of the Fox companies, and W. F. was scurrying around trying to raise a little money, and his lawyers were arguing in court trying desperately to avert receivership action, which would have ruined everything. If the business of the Fox companies had been confined to New York, the situation might not have been so bad, because you can sometimes get a friendly receiver, and save at least a part of your properties. But here was a concern doing business all over the world, and there would have had to be a receiver in a score of countries, and W. F.'s life work would have been turned over to a swarm of vultures to pick its bones.

The judge who had the deciding of the question was Frank J. Coleman of the Federal District Court. Judge Coleman is a Republican and a Catholic, having studied in his early years to be a Jesuit. He had a most difficult problem put before him, and heavy pressure was brought to bear to persuade him to throw the companies into bankruptcy. The story of his attitude, and of the various hearings and arguments, is a fascinating one, and the outcome has the qualities of a movie thriller.

Let us get the situation clearly in mind. The issue is the stubborn refusal of William Fox to go on with the voting trust agreement with Stuart and Otterson. He has been supposed to turn over to them the resignations of his directors, and he refuses to do it, and the receivership threat is held over his head as a club to frighten him. Halsey, Stuart & Co. are demanding the receivership, and at the same time claiming that the responsibility for this danger rests with W. F., because of his stubborn refusal to go ahead with them.

It is the claim of Stuart and of Otterson that W. F. is bound by agreement to their method of financing. They have never brought forth any plan, but they now insist that they want to do so, and that nobody else has a right to do so. At the bankers' meeting of December 17th, in the presence of about thirty men, their lawyer, Richard Dwight, had stated that it was their intention to retire from the whole affair; and as Dwight's clients were present when this statement was made, the statement was binding upon them. But they now claim that the word "retire" meant that they were retiring from the room, not from the trusteeship. The fact was that they didn't retire from the room, but stayed right there, and the court had before it the affidavits of Benjamin Reass, Jacob L. Rubenstein, and Prof. John T. Madden, declaring that everyone present had understood that Otterson and Stuart were through with the Fox companies and their financing forever.

But now they are back again, and Stuart is standing upon the agreement whereby he has preferential rights to the Fox financing. He claims that Fox cannot have his financing done by anybody else, because an agreement forbids him to issue long term securities having priority to the Halsey, Stuart loan. Of course the purpose of the new financing is to pay off that loan, and to pay off the Telephone Company's loan, and all the bank loans. But the high-priced lawyers of Halsey, Stuart are not able to understand this detail, and they don't expect the court to understand it.

But all the thirteen banks to which Fox and his companies owe money have brought court actions and are demanding receivers, and the danger is imminent and deadly. Even Samuel Untermyer is frightened by it, and has written a letter in which he urges his client, "with all the power he possesses and with all the sincerity he can muster," to preserve the companies by going forward with the Stuart-Otterson trusteeship. Greenfield also writes urging this—Greenfield, of course, has the job of collecting $10,000,000 for his securities company. Only W. F. and his wife stand out and refuse to yield.

The lawyers appear before Judge Coleman, and tell him about this insane stubbornness; they have public hearings and private hearings, and word is brought to W. F. that the judge insists on his agreeing to three trustees for his voting shares and turning in the resignations of his directors. If he refuses, Judge Coleman will act at once. All the judge has to do is write his name at the bottom of a paper, naming a receiver, and W. F. is out of his companies, and the courts of the entire world will proceed to hand their friends jobs at the expense of the Fox stockholders. But W. F. stands like a rock, insisting that if a receiver is appointed and the companies destroyed, it will be because Wall Street forces it, and not because he consents. He says:

"I knew better than all the Untermyers and all the judges in the world that our companies didn't need receivers, because I knew their earning power, and there was no way of my understanding that any judge who meant to be fair and equitable could dream of a receivership here."

One day W. F. received a telephone call, ordering him to come to Judge Coleman's chambers. A judge is permitted to talk with the defendant in a case, provided the lawyers of the other side consent. W. F. suspected that his own lawyers had consented also. He pictured Untermyer as saying to Coleman: "I can't control my client. You call for him." The idea was that the court was to act as a mediator, to persuade Fox to go along with the voting trusteeship.

W. F. was summoned for 1 o'clock. It so happened that he had made an engagement which he considered very important—a friend whom he had to consult was going out of town. The result was that W. F. did not reach Coleman's office until 1:45; and court was to convene at 2. Let him tell in his own words the story of this curious adventure:

"This court room was not located in a building where justice is supposed to be dealt out, but rather was located in an ordinary loft space. Judge Coleman was holding court in a room in the Woolworth Building, and it was filled to suffocation by lawyers and curiosity seekers and newspaper men. The corridors leading to this room were lined with men mumbling and talking. Everyone seemed to know that Fox had been sent for, and that the judge was waiting for him; that he was supposed to appear at 1 o'clock, and here it was 1:45 when he walked in. I can imagine the speculation that was going on as to whether he was coming at all. The atmosphere was tense, but I was managing to be calm. Again and again I reminded myself that God had been good to me, and that I knew He was not going to desert me now. I knew I had no occasion for excitement. The whole world, the judge, the attorneys, and my opponents could be excited, but I had to remain calm.

"Many years before, when one of my girls was twelve and the other was nine, foolishly the older was being taught how to drive an automobile. We lived at the time at Mt. Hope in the Bronx. There was a steep hill, and this child was driving the car down this hill. Instead of applying her brakes when she noticed a street car coming, she stepped on the accelerator. Instead of the car being stopped, it came down faster. The motorman had seen this car racing down, and when the two vehicles came to a stop there was not an inch of space between the automobile and the street car. My younger daughter sat in the rear seat, and that night I heard her say to the sister: 'You make me sick. You always do that. You became frightened; you took your hands off the steering wheel, threw them up in the air and shrieked. What is the use of having a head if you lose it just when you need it the most?'

"Here I was going down town to meet Judge Coleman, and I heard clearly this child saying: 'What is the use of having a head if you lose it just when you need it the most?'

"While riding down town, I was accompanied by Harry Sundheim, one of my lawyers, and he was rehearsing me as to what to say to the judge. He said: 'I know, W. F., your inclination to become loud, and you may irritate the judge. Be sure you don't do that. If his judgment sounds wise, follow it.' He gave me a line of talk I was to have with this judge, none of which was of any value to me, none of which would have helped my situation. So when I entered this building and arrived on the floor where this court room was, I found a pitch of excitement so intense that my good friend Reass was walking along this corridor, and I wanted to greet him, but he didn't see me. I thought he looked me square in the face, but he was so wrapped up in what he was going to do when court opened that he didn't even see me. I met Untermyer, who was all excited, and he told me the judge was upset because I was late.

"I was ushered into a room which I should say was about ten feet long and five feet wide. This was the room where the judge and I were to have this confidential talk. He was annoyed, irritated, and excited at the fact that I had disregarded his instructions to be there at 1 o'clock, and this was 1:45. He inquired how dared I disobey his instructions. Didn't I know he had the power to sign a set of papers which had been submitted to him and which would be the doom of my companies? I was exactly the type of man that had been described to him by the people who were applying for receivership, and now that I had delayed the thing, he would talk very hastily.

"The judge is a man about six feet tall, and wears glasses; he has a head of gray hair and is clean-shaven. Perhaps I am prejudiced, but if I were asked to describe him in full, I would say he was saintly. He was taller than I, and I looked up to him. When he was angry his face was flushed. We sat down; I was sitting so close to him that our knees touched, and I could look him right into the face. He wanted me to place in his hands the resignations of my directors at once, and unless I did that and did it immediately, or unless I promised to do it immediately, he would walk right into his court room and appoint a receiver for these companies. He talked for ten minutes, and I listened to him. I still remembered what my little girl had said, and I didn't propose to lose my head. I moved nearer to him, as close as possible, and I looked him square in the eyes and said: 'Look here, your Honor, I have a very high regard for you and for your court, and no threats that you make to me have any effect on me at all. You are not going into that room and sign an application for receivership—you have no intention of doing it—you are not that type of a judge.'

"All the while I felt my bones up against his. I said: 'If you were sitting in that court room in there and trying a case that involved $1,000, you would sit there calmly and carefully until the plaintiff had presented his complete case, then you would listen to the witnesses for the defense, and at the conclusion of that you would go to your private chambers and give the matter careful consideration before you rendered a judgment which involved $1,000. This case involves hundreds of millions, and all you have heard are those who want a receiver. You have not heard my side of the story. Even if I had come at 1 o'clock I could not have told it all to you. I am not going to give you any resignation or papers, and I dare you to go into your room and sign an application for receiver.'

"He drew back and said, 'I warn you that I will appoint a receiver when I walk out of here.' I said, 'Oh, no, you're not going to sign an application for receiver until such time as you have familiarized yourself with every fact in this case. This morning you have had no such opportunity.' Judge: 'Will you go through with this trusteeship in modified form?' Fox: 'No, sir.' Judge: 'I will sign this application for receivership.' Fox: 'No, you won't.' It was with 'Yes, I will,' and 'No, you won't,' that he walked out, and of course he didn't sign the application for receiver.

"I had never met him before that day and have never met him since. He asked one of the lawyers in court, 'Have you ever had the privilege of talking to Mr. Fox?' and added, 'Well, I have.' What impression I created at that conference I can't imagine. Whether it is because he is a good judge of human nature that he never did sign an application for receivership; whether it was because of his contact with me or not, I don't know. Whether my pressing my knees to his and penetrating right through his brain, whether looking into my eyes he felt and knew that I was not deserving to be destroyed, and that I was worth helping and protecting by the powers he possessed as judge of that court, I don't know. If I had hypnotized him that day, he had months to get over the spell and change his mind. If I were asked now as to why he so staunchly stood by to save these companies for the benefit of their stockholders, I would have to say that it was because he read in the eyes of the lawyers of the Telephone Company that their words were insincere, that their purpose was to capture these companies, that they had planned my destruction, and that he was not going to permit the power of his court to be used unjustly.

"When I got downstairs I met my Philadelphia attorney. He was anxious to know whether I had followed his instructions. He said: 'I was standing right outside of that door, and while I could not hear what you were saying, I knew that you were talking too loud, and you must have disobeyed my instructions.' I told him what I had said, and he heartily disapproved. He said, 'Long before we get back to your headquarters you will read in the papers that a receiver has been appointed for your companies.' He anxiously waited, and after court adjourned he found that no receiver had been appointed."

One most curious detail in connection with this duel of wills: the behavior of the stock market in relation to it. Judge Coleman's court was not the only place that was crowded; so also was the trading post where Fox Film shares were sold on the floor of the Stock Exchange. A total of 494,000 A shares were sold on that day—and with only 820,000 A shares outstanding! At the outset, the price of the stock was 22. On the report that W. F. had consented to deliver the resignations of his directors, the price rose to 34. On the report that he had refused, the price sank again to 25!

REEL TWENTY-ONE

THE SCALES OF JUSTICE

LET us now go into the court room, where the eminent counsel were assembled before Judge Coleman for a hearing on motions for receivership. The date was January 27. There were three lawyers, Berenson, Kresel, and Lazarus, representing groups of stockholders; Bogue representing Halsey, Stuart, and Pratt representing the Telephone Company; Swaine representing the Lehman group, the new bankers; Untermyer and Reass representing the Fox companies. Untermyer presented to the judge the resignations of the directors of Fox Film and Fox Theatres, but upon important conditions: they were deposited with the court, to be held until the court received the resignations of Stuart and Otterson, the abrogation of the voting trust agreement, and the depositing of the Fox voting shares with the court. There were to be new trustees named, and these trustees were to elect a new board of directors.

All this, of course, was to be part of the new financing arrangement, the Lehman plan. Untermyer explained that it was the result of "a week of constant effort by day and night." This plan was going to save the companies, he said, and he assured the court that there could be no question of "their overwhelming solvency. Their earnings in the past two weeks are said to be the largest in their history." He went on to express his amazement at the attitude of Halsey, Stuart:

"Messrs. Halsey, Stuart & Company have brought suit and are pressing for payment, although by their terms, the notes are not due until April 1st. They claim that the giving of obligations by the Film Company, having more than 120 days to run, on the purchase of the English chain of theatres, constituted a default that matured the notes before their due dates, although I understand, and the papers submitted to you show that they were not

247

only familiar with but assented to the deal to consummate the English purchase, and in a sense, participated in the negotiations."

Halsey, Stuart answered through their attorney, Morton Bogue. He spoke of this "very elaborate gesture." What it came to was that Stuart and Otterson were asked to get out. He found fault with the plan because it was indefinite. "There is no money in sight, and I do not see why we should be asked to forego our interests or to desert the other creditors and consent to a new management where there is no promise before the court that our debt will be paid or that anybody else will be paid."

Bogue had been invited to a conference with Swaine, representing the new bankers, but he had considered that "a preposterous suggestion. I saw no point in getting into a discussion representing bankers and those supposed to have an interest in the new financing, and being there in a position to help Mr. Fox break his agreement with my clients." His clients would have nothing to do with this Lehman plan, not even to the extent of getting out of the way of it. "It is not our financial program, and although we are here trying to protect, and we want to protect all creditors, we would rather have the receivership immediately, and if this plan could be worked out, the receivership can be terminated quickly."

In other words, here was the attorney for Halsey, Stuart, stating in open court that they preferred to throw this concern into bankruptcy, rather than permit another banking group to finance it. They were proposing to throw it into bankruptcy, because of notes which did not fall due for more than two months. They had rented a house to a tenant, and now they came to court and asked the court to throw the tenant out and put his furniture on the street, because they did not believe the tenant would be able to pay his next installment of rent when it came due!

The court was adjourned until the next day, to give the lawyers a chance to consult with their clients. At this second hearing, Untermyer read to the court the new voting trust agreement, and Bogue again refused to present his clients' resignations.

"So far as my clients are concerned, they feel that they should not withdraw from the position they took yesterday in requesting a receivership, because they feel that there is a possibility that no plan will be presented, and we will be that much further behind; and they feel also that there may be a plan which will not be agreeable to Mr. Fox, and we will be that much further behind, and we may come to a point where we will have to have a receivership at a very unseasonable time of the year in the film business."

The case was adjourned for two weeks to give the Lehman group a chance to complete their financial plan. Two weeks later a still larger group of Wall Street lawyers assembled, and Swaine presented the complete Lehman plan, providing for the issue of $65,000,000 worth of new securities of Fox Film and $40,000,000 of Fox Theatres. There was to be a 9 per cent underwriting commission, and in addition the banking group were to receive 135,000 shares of stock. They had tried to get the Tri-Ergon and Grandeur patents, and had obtained a free license under these patents.

By this plan the Halsey, Stuart notes and the Telephone Company note and all the banking obligations with which these companies had any concern were to be paid in full, principal and interest. So they should have been satisfied—or should they? Could it be that their dissatisfaction was stimulated by a revelation made by Untermyer: "We have a statement here showing that the Fox Film Corporation earned over $2,000,000 the last four weeks, and that its business is greatly on the increase, notwithstanding the troubles that it is having now in the way of financing."

Next Berenson addressed the court; the Boston lawyer who was a friend of Blumy, the agent of Harley Clarke, and who was subsequently paid a quarter of a million dollars by Harley Clarke out of the treasury of Fox Theatres. The basis of Berenson's objection was that this plan was going to cost the stockholders too much money. On one computation it was $20,000,000, and on another computation it would run up to as much as $35,000,-000. He was figuring in the 10 per cent redemption fee of the bonds. Said Untermyer: "Do not the stockholders get the premium if they take the bonds?" So Berenson dropped that argument. He figured another large sum by taking the value of the shares at their book value—about three times their market value. The court asked if Berenson had any suggestions as to how else to raise the money, and Berenson pleaded for a receivership, so that the assets in the companies could be sold. The Loew shares, for which W. F. had paid $75,000,000, could now be sold by a receiver for $23,000,000. That was the Boston lawyer's idea of how to protect his clients, the owners of 620 shares of stock!

Who else had a plan, asked the court, over and over again, and Berenson suggested that Bogue, representing Halsey, Stuart, should be asked whether his clients had a plan. And so came a repetition of the extraordinary scene of two weeks back, when Bogue refused to give up his clients' rights under the preferential agreement to do Fox financing. "The new plan is taking the only free asset that Fox Theatres has, the Loew stock, and proposing to pledge this equity." That this equity was being pledged in order to pay for itself—that Fox Theatres didn't really own the equity but merely owed for it—this was a detail beyond the comprehension of a great Wall Street lawyer. Samuel Untermyer had to remind him: "They are pledged now."

Said the Court: "Will you consent that your arrangement for future financing be withdrawn? Will you consent to that if the present bankers go ahead with the plan?"

Said Bogue: "I am not prepared to say that."

He went on to explain that he would like to consult with his clients. And now came that dangerous "reptyle," Samuel Untermyer, tearing at the veil which covered this dark mystery. Said Untermyer: "But, your Honor, this proposes to pay these gentlemen every dollar of their debts. What are they doing there? What is it they want? They do not want their money. Evidently they want something else."

And again:

"Mr. Untermyer: This is a matter of some importance, your Honor, and I think we should be heard upon it.

"The Court: Yes.

"Mr. Untermyer: Your Honor realizes, of course, that so far as these gentlemen are concerned as creditors of these corporations, this plan proposes to pay them principal and interest.

"The Court: Yes, that is apparent.

"Mr. Untermyer: Your Honor realizes that the securities that they may have issued on various theatres in the past and on their own footing; that they are very much increased in safety by the furnishing of this additional money to the Theatres company.

"The Court: I understand that.

"Mr. Untermyer: They are not jeopardized. They are helped and materially helped by that fact, so that there must be something else behind this. Let us see what there is behind it. These gentlemen have a bankers' agreement for a fifteen-year preferential contract. It is a most unusual thing. In other words, the Fox Film and the Fox Theatres could not do any financing for the next fifteen years without first giving these gentlemen the opportunity to do it; and they also have—I do not want to create any ill feeling here—they have another arrangement which—

"The Court (Interposing): Mr. Untermyer—

"Mr. Untermyer: I am not going to go into that.

"The Court: It is my judgment that we ought not to."

So you see we are not allowed to tear the veil! The dark mystery must not be shown to our eyes!

There was an adjournment for a couple of days, and again we find Bogue trying to block the proceedings, and Untermyer probing the mysteries:

"Mr. Untermyer: I do not understand Mr. Bogue's attitude, your Honor, and I would like to be heard on it. I understand Mr. Bogue is representing Halsey, Stuart. This plan proposes to pay them in cash for notes that have been selling at 50 cents on the dollar and now are selling at 70 cents on the dollar, for which their clients are to get 100 cents on the dollar. What is this policy of theirs? It looks a good deal like a dog in the manger policy, and that is all there is to it, I think.

"The Court: I do not think you ought to characterize it, Mr. Untermyer.

"Mr. Untermyer: They said this—

"Mr. Bogue: Just one second, please.

"Mr. Untermyer: May I finish?

"The Court: Yes.

"Mr. Untermyer: The position taken by Mr. Bogue is an

extraordinary one. He said that in years past, Halsey, Stuart have made loans on various pieces of real estate, have issued bonds that have gone to the public of the Theatres Corporation—by the way, it is not here—the Film Corporation is here, but they have made a loan. Now, then, they seem to think that a receivership will be better security for those underlying loans than would the putting of $35,000,000 behind them."

Bogue objected to having his position stated by Untermyer, and so he stated it himself. His clients refused to give up their preferential option. His clients were prepared to submit a plan more favorable to the interests of the stockholders. If Fox would not agree to go on with the trusteeship agreement with Halsey, Stuart, that was Fox's lookout, and Halsey, Stuart could not be penalized for that.

Then came another lawyer, Pratt, representing Otterson and the Telephone Company, and presenting one of the most extraordinary arguments that I ever read in a legal document. Said he: "In spite of the fact that this plan provides the payment of our amount in full, we object to the plan for this reason: we have a fifteen-year contract with the Fox Company, covering the talking motion pictures, and we do not feel that this plan provides sufficient latitude for future financing for them to properly carry on the business that is contemplated by that contract, and that it is necessary to work out a plan which is comprehensive for the future, as well as taking care of the present needs."

One important point to note: Mr. Pratt's clients did not have this fifteen-year contract with Fox Film. The contract had been negotiated but not signed, and the Telephone Company knew that if W. F. succeeded in paying off the debt to them, he would never take a lease on their patents, but would proceed upon the basis of his own Tri-Ergon rights.

In order to get the full meaning of this claim of the Telephone Company, made in open court, let us bring it down from the misty regions of high finance to the level of ordinary human affairs. You are running a small corner grocery, and one day, because you want to enlarge your store, you borrow $1,000 from your wholesaler, and give him a note for a year. Some time before this note falls due, the wholesaler decides that you are not going to be able to meet the note, and proposes to move in and take possession of your business. When you assure him that you have a plan by which you will have the $1,000 in a few days, and will pay off the note, he answers that that is not satisfactory to him, because you have contemplated signing an agreement to purchase groceries from him for the next two or three years, and he is afraid that under this new plan you will conduct your business in such a way that you will not be able to buy enough groceries from him, and "to properly carry on the business that is contemplated by that contract."

Study this, you little business man of America, and learn how precarious is your hold upon your enterprise, when you come within reach of the tentacles of the great Telephone Octopus! And especially when your earnings are increasing at the rate of half a million dollars a week! It seems to me that this statement made by George C. Pratt in open court justifies and proves every charge of conspiracy which William Fox has made and which I have repeated in this book.

And then another odd coincidence: the very day after Pratt's first appearance in court, and his demand for a receivership on behalf of his client, the Telephone Company, the president of that company, Walter S. Gifford, appeared in Washington to testify about another matter before the Senate Committee on Interstate Commerce. A senator asked him a question, what about the loan his company had made to the Fox companies; and Gifford answered that he was not worried about that, he knew the companies were perfectly sound. If he knew that, why was he sending a lawyer to court to state exactly the opposite?

The reply of the Court to this demand was: "Mr. Pratt, I am absolutely convinced from my talks with Mr. Fox and my observation of his conduct in this case that he never will consent to entering into an agreement with Halsey, Stuart & Company and with the Electric Research Laboratories. The plan that you suggest as possible can only be worked out by means of receivership. I am convinced of that."

Judge Coleman went on to pin the lawyers down on this point. Fox was blocking the Telephone Company from taking possession of his business through the voting trust agreement. Said the Court: "Can you point out any way in which I can prevent him from blocking it except by means of a receivership?

"Mr. Pratt: I cannot, sir.

"The Court: There is no way, is there?

"Mr. Pratt: There is no other way."

And here is Untermyer again fighting for a hearing: "I object to the responsibility for this situation being placed to any extent upon Mr. Fox or his unwillingness to go on with Halsey, Stuart & Company or anybody else. The responsibility for this situation rests right at the door of Halsey, Stuart & Company, and now of the Electric Research Laboratories.

"The Court: No, Mr. Untermyer, I cannot permit you—

"Mr. Untermyer: Your Honor does not seem to want to permit me to be heard. I want to be heard.

"The Court: I want you to be heard on matters that are up for discussion. On those matters I am glad to hear you, but on matters that we cannot do anything about I think it would be a mistake to attempt to deal with them.

"Mr. Untermyer: But, your Honor, you started by saying that Mr. Fox would not do this and Mr. Fox would not do that, and these gentlemen have made certain objections and I am answering them. A week ago or two weeks ago Mr. Bogue stood up here and said that he wanted a receivership for Halsey, Stuart & Company. This is about as extraordinary a situation, I think, as has ever been presented in a large transaction. Here are two creditors, one for $12,000,000 and the other for $15,000,-000, who are confronted by a plan of three of the most reputable banking houses in the country to pay their principal and interest in full, and they are objecting to that plan."

But Bogue and Pratt will not give way. They will not cancel the voting trust agreement. They will continue their "dog-in-the-manger" attitude. Then comes a new lawyer, Conboy, representing some more stockholders, and he is indignant because Fox presumes to block the Halsey, Stuart plan, and he says that his clients prefer the alternative of a receivership. "That might be an alternative that would be the lesser of two evils, because if your Honor appointed a receiver for this corporation, then there would be somebody who would have in mind not merely Mr. Fox's individual and personal and selfish interests, but the interests of all parties who are concerned with this corporation."

Judge Coleman made his attitude perfectly plain. He would not appoint a receiver if there was any possible way to avoid it. The Lehman plan seemed to offer a way out, and he would give the Fox companies an opportunity to submit this plan to the stockholders. The court would not make any recommendation to the stockholders, but the stockholders would decide whether or not they wished to approve this plan. If Halsey, Stuart had a plan, and wished to tell the stockholders about it, that was up to them. If anyone else had a plan that would avoid a receivership, the court would hear it.

This was on February 11, and on March 5 the stockholders held their meeting. I shall tell about this in detail, but first I think I shall finish with Judge Coleman. On March 27, the final hearing was held, and since the judge could not be moved from his determination not to throw these two prosperous companies into receivership, Halsey, Stuart resorted to the desperate step of having their attorney, Bogue, bring a charge of prejudice against Judge Coleman, and thus take the case out of his hands. The law governing this proceeding is peculiar. Judge Coleman was not permitted to deal with the truth of the charges, but merely to decide whether the charges, if true, would disqualify him to deal with the case. He was then obliged to retire, and turn the case over to another judge.

When he did so, an extraordinary scene occurred in court. Robert T. Swaine, attorney for the Lehman group, asked permission to make a statement. He was very careful and polite about it, but the substance of his remarks was that an affidavit had been filed which everybody knew to be false, and that Swaine's desire to maintain his own dignity must yield to his "public duty of protecting the good name of the United States District Court, and of a judge who has been tireless in his energy, and honest and upright in his efforts to save this vast enterprise from the disasters of receivership into which the filers of this false affidavit would plunge it."

Swaine went on to tell how his clients had come into the case, and the substance of his story was that they had done so only after conferences with the Stuart and Otterson crowd and their lawyers, and after having had positive and repeated assurances that Stuart and Otterson only wanted their money, and would

18

not stand in the way of any plan which would get them their money. Said Swaine:

"I regret exceedingly to have to violate the confidence that is supposed to exist between lawyers and personal friends, for Mr. Bogue is one of my closest personal friends, and even those events do not shake me in that attitude. I went to Mr. Bogue and I asked Mr. Bogue if his clients had any interest in this situation if their indebtedness was paid off. I understood Mr. Bogue to assure me that their interest in this situation was the payment of the $15,000,000 obligation to the Electrical Research Products Company, the $12,000,000 of notes issued by Halsey, Stuart & Company, and $4,000,000 of bank debt which had been guaranteed by Halsey, Stuart & Company and Electrical Research Products Company. I also understood Mr. Bogue to believe that Mr. Fox would never co-operate in putting through any plan, but I equally understood him to say that if Mr. Fox did co-operate in putting through a plan which would take care of that indebtedness, no obstacle would be raised.

"I talked to Mr. Pratt, counsel for Mr. Otterson, within an hour of the time I came to your Honor to present a plan. I had from Mr. Pratt personally, over the telephone, the assurance that if he paid the indebtedness to the Telephone Company there would be no trouble about the B stock."

Swaine went on to tell how Elisha Walker had consulted Otterson and Charles Stuart, and had received the same assurances. The Lehman group had therefore gone ahead with their plan—and then, when they brought it into court, the other side had broken its word.

You have noted through this book William Fox many times accusing Stuart and Otterson of making false statements: for example, of withdrawing from his affairs, and then the next day denying that they had done so. Most of the time these charges have rested upon the word of W. F. In a few minutes I shall show you Halsey, Stuart mailing a pamphlet to all the Fox stockholders, full of charges against W. F., and W. F. mailing a pamphlet full of countercharges; and you will be uncertain which to believe. Do not overlook the fact that here in the court record is the charge, made by an obviously high-minded lawyer, of false dealing on the part of Halsey, Stuart, and Otterson, and their lawyers. This charge is all the more impressive because the man is making it with reluctance and pain, concerning an intimate friend.

I was interested in the ethical problem here involved, and after my reading of the court record, I questioned W. F. and his attorney, Reass, about it. Here is this discussion as the stenographer took it down in my home:

"Sinclair: Now about Mr. Bogue. He is a very important person in that procedure before Judge Coleman. He is accused of having lied. Swaine accused him of it.

"Fox: Swaine is expressing his regrets for the removal of Coleman from the case. Morton G. Bogue is of the firm of Beekman, Bogue & Clark. I had met Mr. Bogue before this difficulty, in connection with bond issues that Halsey, Stuart had underwritten for the Fox subsidiaries, and my relations with him were rather pleasant. I presume he was doing nothing more or less than any lawyer would do under the instructions of his client, Halsey, Stuart & Co.

"Sinclair: Does a lawyer make an agreement with another lawyer of the other side and then break it?

"Fox: The lawyer should not do that, but I take it for granted that whatever agreement he made with the other side, he had received instructions from Halsey, Stuart not to carry it out. Of course, it would have been a nice thing if he had retired from the case rather than break his word.

"Reass: They don't make agreements that their clients do not approve of, and when he broke it, it was because his clients wanted it broken. He wasn't making agreements with Swaine without authority—adhering to them for weeks and then breaking them at the last minute.

"Sinclair: Was there no penalty or disgrace attached to such procedure?

"Reass: There are no penalties for anything Wall Street does. Lawyers' ethics are for the poor lawyers, but it has nothing to do with Wall Street. They have a code all their own.

"Sinclair: Have you a code of your own? Your office is not very far from Wall Street.

"Reass: That is the reason I can speak with authority.

"Fox: What Mr. Sinclair wants to know is this . . .

"Sinclair: The reason I asked about Bogue and Swaine is this: here is one lawyer accusing another of highly unethical conduct, and I wondered what the consequences were. Can those two men say things like that and then go out to lunch?

"Fox: They are probably the best of friends.

"Reass: Swaine represented one banking group; Bogue another. He tried to tell the court the agreement, and the court interrupted him. The court wasn't concerned with these quarrels. Swaine refused to get into a squabble there.

"Fox: That isn't what Mr. Sinclair wants. He wants to know is it customary for two presumably reputable lawyers to stand in open court and charge each other with breaking faith with each other, and then continue to be buddies and pals afterwards. Mr. Sinclair, that is absolutely customary.

"Sinclair: Here am I prepared to present this story to the public, and this deposing of Judge Coleman is one of the most dramatic chapters in the story. Here are these two men in this fight. I have to tell the public what that story means. Is this a picture of everyday Wall Street ethics? Is it proof of the extremes to which these men were going in their effort to break Fox, or is it just ordinary? Is it the way they do business all the time?

"Reass: It is not the way they do business. You can fairly take the attitude that it is just the sort of rascality of Halsey, Stuart to carry out their plans.

"Fox: You will find they are social friends and business friends. My experience with lawyers isn't that animosity that occurs in a court room between them continues by them in their private life after the case is over. My experience is that, regardless of how they fight in court with each other, when the case is to the end, that is the end of the controversy, and the relations are re-established and the pleasantries continue as heretofore. A lawyer usually treats a matter in court as just another case."

REEL TWENTY-TWO

A JUDGE IN BUSINESS

IN order to follow through the hearing before Judge Coleman, we have skipped ahead of our story. We must now return, to attend one of the sessions of our Fox with the new bankers, the Lehman group, who are going to finance his companies. We have seen these bankers in court, represented by their high-minded attorney, Swaine, who tells the court that his clients came in "to assist this situation solely for the purpose of endeavoring to save it." Bankers with such altruistic motives are not common in Wall Street, so it will be interesting to sit in with them, and observe their altruism at work.

You remember that we left Ostrer, the English theatre magnate, in possession of $14,000,000, which W. F. had paid him, and with $6,000,000 still due, and a chance of foreclosing on his Gaumont shares and buying them in for a million or so, and without losing his claim for the $6,000,000. If the Bancamerica-Blair, Lehman Brothers, Dillon, Read crowd really want to "save the situation," here is the place to get to work. They are advised by W. F.'s attorneys in London that no more delay will be permitted. Unless Ostrer has the money in hand before 3 o'clock on the following day, he will foreclose on the Gaumont shares. Three o'clock London time is 11 o'clock New York time.

So W. F. begs the Lehman group to lend Fox Theatres $6,000,000 for forty-five days; that being the time between the date of the conference and April 15, when the bankers are pledged to supply $65,000,000. The negotiations are carried on all day, and adjourned to the Fox Building at 850 Tenth Avenue, and continued all night. Here is a story with a human touch; showing you what great financiers and Wall Street lawyers go through, the price they pay for their large incomes.

259

"Alvin Untermyer, one of the lawyers for the Fox companies, was present. Samuel Untermyer, who at this time resided at the Ambassador Hotel, was asked to remain at the hotel, in case his son had any questions he would like to ask him. The discussion during the night was what charge should my bankers make for the loan of this $6,000,000. From time to time Alvin would call his father on the phone. The last time we called him was about 4:30 a. m. At the conclusion of that we had not reached a determination. It was suggested at 5 a. m. that we call him again. I refused to have him called again—we had annoyed him sufficiently during the night, and he certainly ought to be allowed to go to bed, so he would be fit the next day to carry on his work in the behalf of my companies. The next day at 8 o'clock I called at the Ambassador Hotel, and proudly stated the fact that I had refused to have him called, to which he replied: 'You didn't do me a bit of a favor. Why didn't you call me? If you had, we could have settled the matter then and I could have gone to bed and slept. As it is, I have not slept a wink.'"

So now we can understand why Samuel Untermyer suffers from asthma, and has to come out to Southern California to spend his winters! Also, we can understand why the hearing before Judge Coleman of February 13, 1930, opened with the following dialogue:

"The Court: What have you to report, Mr. Untermyer?

"Mr. Untermyer: Just a moment, your Honor, until I get up. I am not feeling so well—I am in pretty bad shape today."

The end of the all-night conference was that the Lehman group agreed to lend $6,000,000 for forty-five days at a price of $600,000. Ten per cent interest for forty-five days is .222 per cent per day, and if you multiply that by 365 days, you get 81 per cent per annum. In addition to that, they added the legal 6 per cent—of course, it wouldn't do for great bankers to fail to charge the legal rate of 6 per cent interest. The rest of the amount was a fee, or a premium, or bonus, or some other fancy thing, having nothing to do with interest.

But whatever you call it, it was 87 per cent profit on the loan; and, would you believe it, there was a Wall Street financier to whom that amount seemed insufficient! None other than our friend Clarence Dillon, who had eaten all the grapes at the

luncheon, and told W. F. that if he didn't dissolve his voting
shares, his companies would soon be in charge of someone who
was not in the moving picture business. W. F. says that he had
brought Dillon into the picture in order to find out what was
Dillon's real attitude. And now he found out—when Dillon's
firm would not "take this risk." Says W. F.:

"The risk involved was to receive for collateral the stock
that we paid $20,000,000 for, and any other collateral that the
company may have had; collateral against which Dillon, Read
had signed a commitment to sell to the public $65,000,000 worth
of securities. It doesn't need any argument as to why Dillon,
Read didn't want to go along with this. Dillon, Read had instructions, perhaps from the Telephone Company, that the Gaumont
property should be sacrificed—that was one of the ways of
destroying the Fox companies. So the $6,000,000 loan was
actually made by Lehman Brothers and Bancamerica-Blair.
When the new financing was done, the bankers on or before the
15th received back their $6,000,000, and made their profit of
87 per cent in the interim."

Here is a second story of the Lehman group, and the assistance they gave to the Fox companies:

"It appears that my enemies weren't just satisfied to instruct
the banks to sue and get a judgment, but when the Public Bank
secured its judgment for $450,000, they gave the execution of
that judgment to a sheriff, who promptly presented himself at
the Fox Film Corporation's offices and took possession of the
entire plant. He was there to levy on the apparatus, the machinery, everything that we had, so as to be sure that the corporation
could not function any longer. These people who were planning
our destruction were annoyed by the fact that after they had
attached the cash of the Fox Film Company, of every bank
account in New York as well as every bank account in every
country in the world, the corporation was still going on and
doing a prosperous business; the receipts from its American business were sufficient to take care of all its current operations.
There was no surplus left over, of course, with which to pay
$450,000 judgments. They knew that the surest way to destroy
the earnings was to publish the fact that a sheriff had entered the
premises and attached everything that his eyes surveyed.

"By this time the Bancamerica-Blair group were in the picture. I asked them to please loan the company the money to satisfy this judgment, so that we could remove the sheriff from the premises; that unless that was done, there wasn't any financing to do. It was finally accomplished by my giving my personal note—not the note of a corporation, but my own note—to the Bancamerica-Blair group, and they in return gave me the necessary money on the discount of my note, and took as collateral the judgment that the court had rendered against the company, and in that way we paid this judgment and removed the sheriff."

One of the difficulties standing in the way of the Lehman plan was the action which the Government had started against W. F. and his companies, requiring them to divest themselves of the Loew shares. Colonel Huston had been doing his best in Washington to have this suit discontinued, using the argument that the only alternative was the throwing of the company into receivership and thus risking another panic. Says W. F.:

"I then suggested that perhaps the Department of Justice would see its way clear to give me a letter that I could exhibit to my bankers, indicating a plan that would be agreeable to the Department of Justice, and stating terms under which these companies would be permitted to merge. Huston asked me to come to Washington. He would propose my suggestion to the then Attorney-General, Mr. Mitchell.

"The day I left for Washington I informed the Lehman bankers and their attorney, Mr. Swaine, and Swaine offered to wager me $10,000 or more that I was going to Washington on a fool's errand; he was familiar with the policy of the administration, he had tried again and again to discuss consolidations and mergers, and the administration was unwilling to discuss them. He called my attention to the fact that promptly after taking office, Mitchell had made an address declaring that the department no longer would meet with heads of companies to discuss mergers, that the companies must find their own lawyers, and their lawyers knew what was legal and what was illegal. In this public address he made it clear that the department intended to stand by that, and if these mergers were legally arranged, there would be no interference from the Government, but if they were illegal, the department would take such action as it deemed necessary.

"On the morning I was leaving for Washington I had received a letter from Senator Thomas Walsh of Montana, whom I had known, expressing his regrets for the difficulties that I found myself in, and as this letter appeared to me, it was an invitation for me to come to Walsh and tell him what my difficulties were. While the letter didn't directly so state, I construed it, however, as an invitation to call, so that when I arrived in Washington to meet Huston, I showed him this letter from Walsh. He is the senator who carried on the oil investigation during the Harding administration, and was then a man to be reckoned with; he was powerful, and his reputation was always for the under dog. Huston asked me to permit him to please keep the letter during that day. Later that evening, Huston, all elated, brought me a letter signed by Mitchell, the Attorney-General, in which the Attorney-General outlined the plan of the method that could be employed to consolidate the Loew and the Fox companies.

"Huston's statement to me was that this was the first letter of the sort that Mitchell had written from the day that he had taken office; that it was contrary to the policy of the Department of Justice or the Attorney-General's office to advise any corporation of what method to employ for consolidation; that an exception to the rule had been made in this emergency."

The Lehman plan was ready, and the next step was that it should be submitted to the stockholders of Fox Film and Fox Theatres; so Judge Coleman directed the calling of a meeting on March 5. Stuart and Otterson were now concentrating their efforts upon the balking of the Lehman plan, and part of their program was to rush forward a plan of their own, in which they offered the stockholders better terms. Inasmuch as W. F. refused to deal with them, and as W. F.'s directors refused to endorse the plan or put it before the stockholders, Halsey, Stuart & Co. were forced to offer the plan directly to the stockholders, and they set out to collect proxies in their interest. W. F.'s brother-in-law, Jack Leo, also began a campaign, and the stockholders all over the country were deluged with literature, which they must have found puzzling, because of the diametrically contradictory statements contained.

The by-laws of the companies provided that new financing

must be approved by a two-thirds vote of the stockholders, and as the day for the meeting drew near it became evident that the decision would be close. W. F. came to the meeting with a total of 62 per cent of the proxies. Halsey, Stuart had about 7 per cent, and 26 per cent were in the hands of a stockholders' committee which had been organized independently, and concerning whose attitude W. F. had no information. The remaining 5 per cent of the stock was the voting shares belonging to W. F., and this was in escrow with the Bankers Trust Company, held in the interest of the trusteeship. If W. F. could vote these shares, he would have 67 per cent, and the matter would be settled. As soon as he realized how close the issue was to be, he brought a motion before the Supreme Court of New York State, asking an order permitting him to vote his shares at the stockholders' meeting.

This was accompanied by the affidavit he had prepared in answering the complaint of Mrs. Kuser, and he added many exhibits, including the text of the Lehman plan, and financial statements of Fox Film, Fox Theatres, and Loew's. Stuart and Otterson came back with an answering affidavit, and W. F. made a replying affidavit, and an additional replying affidavit. Halsey, Stuart submitted their plan, and also a so-called "stockholders' plan." The whole makes a sizable book.

I have studied these various documents carefully. I note in them a number of direct contradictions: Fox says one thing, and Stuart and Otterson say the opposite, and it could not have been an easy matter for a judge, unfamiliar with the case, and having only a brief time at his disposal, to distinguish truth from falsehood. It so happens that my eyes have been trained to pick out the rascalities of big business, and I note in the answering affidavit of H. L. Stuart and John E. Otterson a subtle piece of fancy work which I will point out to you, so that you may understand just why Wall Street lawyers are paid retaining fees of one or two hundred thousand dollars, and a million or more when the case is won.

At the hearings before Judge Coleman, Stuart, represented by his attorney Bogue, and Otterson, represented by his attorney Pratt, had pleaded for the throwing of the Fox companies into receivership. These hearings had been of two kinds: one kind in open court, at which stenographers were present, and the second kind in the judge's chambers, of which no record was made. At both kinds of hearings Bogue, representing Stuart, had pleaded for receivership; but Pratt, representing Otterson, had not directly demanded a receivership at any open hearing; all that he had done in open court was to object to the Lehman plan. Perhaps it was intentional that he confined his advocacy of receivership to Judge Coleman's private chambers. That he did there argue for receivership is testified to in an affidavit by Alvin Untermyer, who was present.

The time comes when Stuart and Otterson are jointly making an affidavit before Judge Levy of the State Supreme Court. It is their tactics to persuade this new judge that they have not ever asked for a receivership, but that the blame for the receivership danger rests entirely upon W. F. What they, Stuart and Otterson, are doing is offering a better plan than the Lehman plan, more advantageous to the stockholders; so they ask Judge Levy not to let Fox vote his shares for the Lehman plan, but to let them vote Fox's shares for their plan. Their affidavit is a joint one; all through its text the two men are speaking together of their common actions and their common interests. But when, they come to the delicate receivership question, there is a deft switch in the process: the defendant Stuart disappears behind the curtain, leaving the defendant Otterson to hold the stage by himself.

The reason for that is clear enough to eyes which have been trained to the arts of diplomacy. The defendant Stuart dares not swear that he did not urge a receivership, because he knows there is a record of the open hearings before Judge Coleman. Therefore the defendant Otterson alone takes up the argument.

And now let us see what his argument is. Otterson quotes the affidavit which he made in the proceedings before Judge Coleman, as follows:

"It is essential, in my opinion, that in the interest of stockholders and creditors alike, the business (of Fox Film Corporation) be conserved through receivership or trusteeship or some other form of conservation."

The defendant Otterson then goes on to explain to the new judge exactly what the above request meant. He says:

"At the time of the execution of said affidavit by the defendant Otterson, no plan of reorganization of the Fox companies had even been suggested. Mr. Fox had refused to go through with the trust agreement and it seemed at that time to the defendant Otterson that, in the absence of some other method by which the assets of the Fox companies could be preserved for their creditors and stockholders, a receivership was inevitable.

"This is the extent to which the defendant Otterson has urged a receivership. He does not favor a receivership, if the same can be avoided, and is not defending this action or interposing the counterclaim herein for the purpose of bringing about a receivership, or bringing about the ruin and disruption of the Fox companies, but on the contrary is anxious that said companies shall be rehabilitated and successful, to the end that the interests of creditors and stockholders shall be properly protected, including the interest of the plaintiff as such a stockholder."

So you see the clever trick! Judge Levy of the State Supreme Court will read that statement, and will entirely miss the fact that Stuart is saying nothing, and will get the impression that the two men are not now urging a receivership, but are urging the Halsey, Stuart plan! You will see in a moment the judge actually admitting in his decision that he had not had time to read the law in the case; so perhaps it will escape his attention that the phrase used by defendant Otterson "through receivership *or trusteeship or some other form of conservation,*" is a pure piece of verbiage. There is no "other form of conservation" recognized by the law, and a receivership is the only possible outcome of the action which the defendant Otterson has been and, at this very time is supporting and urging before Judge Coleman of the United States District Court!

Let me give you one more example of what Stuart and Otterson told the Supreme Court of New York State. They told how in August of 1929 the Fox had foolishly bought the Gaumont shares, without the approval of Stuart or Otterson. Under oath they stated: "Not until in or about the month of November, 1929, did either of these defendants learn of said obligation in connection with said Gaumont chain."

I asked W. F. for a written comment on this, and he gave me a detailed account of his negotiations with Halsey, Stuart concerning the Gaumont deal in July and August of 1929, before the purchase was made. He says:

"This matter was discussed at great length with Mr. Ernest Niver, manager of the New York branch of Halsey, Stuart & Co., with whom I had almost daily contact, not only in this matter but in other matters, and he was the authorized agent at all times for Halsey, Stuart & Co. It was he who sent cables about this matter to Harry Stuart while Stuart was in London, and received replies and informed me of them. It was he for the firm of Halsey, Stuart & Co. who urged as hard as he knew how that the acquisition of the Gaumont Company be made. . . . When Stuart returned from abroad and called on me again in August, as he says he did, the matter of the Gaumont acquisition was fully and completely discussed. He commented on the cables he received and sent, and inquired whether the information he had transmitted through his office was of any assistance to me."

W. F. goes on to inquire what would have been the chances of the London bankers lending the Fox companies $16,000,000, without taking the trouble to consult the New York banker of the Fox companies, who happened then to be in London, and who happened to be their business associate and personal friend. W. F. invites me to try to borrow $16,000,000, and see if the bankers do not investigate my financial standing, and particularly if they do not consult the banks with which I am regularly doing business. He says:

"You will please bear in mind that neither Fox Theatres nor Fox Film had ever before borrowed from the English banks. It did, some ten years ago, take a mortgage on its building in London for approximately $100,000, but had since paid it off. Here was the first time that Fox Film was seeking a loan in London for $16,000,000, two and one-half times as much as the total amount Fox Film owed to all the thirteen banks in America. Is it possible that they would extend that kind of credit without making an inquiry of our bankers here? Is that the usual practice of a bank to loan a firm $16,000,000, a foreign concern, and make no inquiries from its bankers, as to whether or not the company is worth such a risk?"

It was Blumenthal who was in London, negotiating the Gaumont deal as a representative of W. F. Blumenthal went to see the bankers, and can we believe that he failed to tell them that Halsey, Stuart & Company was the concern through which the Fox companies did their financing? Is it then thinkable that the London banks did not consult Harry Stuart, and make the fullest inquiries of him as to the standing of W. F. and his enterprises? One of the men who advanced the money was Reginald McKenna, and I have previously stated that this great banker and statesman was intimate with both Harry Stuart and Harley Clarke. Here was Harry Stuart in London; and we are invited to believe that McKenna loaned £800,000 to the Fox companies without taking the trouble to call Stuart on the telephone and say: "What is your opinion of those companies?" Common sense forces us to believe that such a loan would never have been made unless Harry Stuart had replied: "The Fox companies are our clients; we have sold more than $30,000,000 worth of their bonds, and their position is excellent."

Incidentally, I have inspected a dozen copies of the motion picture trade papers, the "Exhibitors' Daily Review," "Motion Pictures Today," and the "Film Daily," which reported the details of the Gaumont deal from June to October of 1929. These papers are followed closely by all persons who trade in film stocks, which includes the clients, employes, and members of the firm of Halsey, Stuart & Company. It also includes Otterson, Bloom, Gifford, and other officials of the Telephone Company. Fox was at this time their heavy creditor, and it is contrary to common sense to suppose that they were not following Fox affairs thus made public.

Such were the statements made to the court by Stuart and Otterson, seeking to prove that William Fox was unfit to vote his shares at a stockholders' meeting. In seeking a judge to decide this issue, the lawyers representing the two sides went hunting through the corridors of the court house. Judge McCook disqualified himself because his wife owned stock in the Telephone Company. They went to two or three more, and finally came to Judge Aaron J. Levy, who agreed to hear them and took the papers for study. His decision was rendered just a few hours before the stockholders' meeting, and is a most curious one. Judge Levy makes the statement: "As to the various questions of a legal nature which have been raised, it need only be pointed out that no proper opportunity was here afforded to appropriately inquire into them and so they must of necessity be left for the trial of the action." Having thus admitted that he is not able to render an intelligent decision, he proceeds to pass judgment upon the moral character of William Fox.

"It is said that of little acorns great oaks do grow. Here we have a little $1,600 acorn which grew into a sturdy $300,000,000 oak. Why was not well enough left alone? The very Fox chopped down this healthy thriving tree with his own hatchet. The world knows much about avarice and cupidity, and I wonder if this is not another illustration. May he now be heard to complain? Has he placed himself in that position which justifies his assault upon the character of men? I think not."

And because Justice Levy considers that "the very Fox" is an avaricious Fox, he denies him the right to vote his shares at the stockholders' meeting, and rejects with contempt his claim to be "the unfortunate victim of a malevolent conspiracy to seize control of the companies from him for the iniquitous purpose of bestowing it upon Halsey, Stuart & Co. or Electrical Research Products, or both."

When I first read this document, I said, "This is not a legal decision, but a venting of spite." I was sure there must be a story behind it, and asked W. F. The first detail I got was that Levy is an intimate friend of W. R. Sheehan. The second detail was that Levy is an active Tammany politician, and that just at this time Sheehan gave an important position at a high salary to a friend of Levy's, another Tammany politician. The third detail was: "Three months later, when all the clouds had blown away, we were advised that Judge Levy's brother, Lloyd Levy, had received a position with Fox Film at a salary of $150 a week. Harley Clarke had brought him out to California and given him this position."

I wanted to know more about Levy, so I wrote to a lawyer friend in New York, who replied:

"In 1921 Aaron J. Levy was a justice of the Municipal Court and a procedure was brought to remove him. By law justices are forbidden to engage in any other business. It was claimed that he did engage in business, that of ladies' tailoring and dressmaking, the business of exhibiting motion picture plays, the business of printing and publishing a newspaper known as the 'Wahrheit,' and that of owning, managing, directing and controlling a corporation, H. Milgrim & Brothers, Inc., engaged in ladies' tailoring. Judge Levy admitted that he was a stockholder in H. Milgrim & Brothers, Inc., and that he spent a considerable part of his time at the office of the corporation. The court held that the term 'carry on a business' implies such a relation to the business as identifies the person with it, and imposes upon him some duty or responsibility in connection with its management. The court found there was no evidence that Judge Levy actively engaged in the conduct of the business. The petition was therefore dismissed. The case is reported in 198 N. Y. Appellate Division, 326."

I read this letter to Benjamin Reass, and he made a sarcastic comment, that the basis of Justice Levy's acquittal was that he didn't try the dresses on the customers of Milgrim Brothers. W. F. had something to contribute to this story of the Milgrim concern, as follows:

"During an intermission of the stockholders' meeting, one of the employes of Fox Film, William Brandt, asked to see me privately, and told me that Levy had just rendered a decision forbidding me to vote my shares at the meeting. Brandt then told me of Levy's connection with the Milgrims, and added that Mrs. Milgrim's brother had a chain of theatres which he had recently been engaged in selling to the Fox Metropolitan Company. The price was to be determined upon the basis of ten times the annual income, and the legal or accounting department of the Fox company discovered that there had been misrepresentations made with respect to the figures. So the Fox company refused to go on with the purchase, unless there was a re-accounting. Judge Levy then came to see William Brandt in connection with the matter. He notified Brandt to tell me that he, Levy, was interested in that theatre, and had money invested in it, and wanted the thing to go through. The matter was not taken to me, and the deal did not go through."

Judge Levy gets into trouble frequently, it appears. I find that early in 1931 former Supreme Court Justice William N. Cohen, chairman of the Committee on Courts of the Bar Association, addressed to the president of the association a letter reciting two charges against Judge Aaron J. Levy. It appears that Levy had heard two cases against the Bank of the United States, and had decided one case in the bank's favor, and had the other before him, when the Brooklyn "Daily Eagle" published the fact that Levy was a borrower from the bank, owing it the sum of $143,015.92, upon a loan secured by stocks worth on the market only $40,000. After this exposure Levy decided, "for certain reasons," not to go on with the case.

REEL TWENTY-THREE

THE STOCKHOLDERS MEET

WE are now to hear about the critical stockholders' meeting of March 5, 1930. Before discussing it, we should know something about the previous meetings of Fox stockholders, since the first one in 1916. Says W. F.:

"There were fourteen annual meetings of the Fox Film Corporation, and there was present at each of these fourteen meetings, other than the officials of the company, one lone stockholder. He was a doctor, and lived in Newark, N. J. He considered himself, and so did I, as the mascot stockholder of Fox Film.

"At every annual meeting we were prepared for the ceremonies, and provided a large room where many people could gather, and after waiting for the time to come for the meeting to open, this little doctor would walk in, this lone stockholder. He was one of the original stockholders when the company was formed, and I presume being a doctor by profession he had spare time so that he could come to these meetings. The value of his holdings had jumped so between the first annual meeting and the second one that he perhaps came the second time to express his appreciation, and then each year the earnings grew and the value of his holdings became larger. When 1929 arrived, he had a substantial fortune in the value of the shares that he received as a bonus at the meeting of 1915.

"I knew him and learned to like him. He is a most charming little man, not more than 5 feet high. The number of shares he had was very small, but he would go through all the formalities proper to a stockholder. We usually had the proxies of the other shares; they would be given to one of the officials of the company, and this little doctor would be one of the tellers. He would count the votes and he would count the proxies plus

272

his vote. We usually had a very fine meeting, and occasionally had lunch together before the meeting.

"When the doctor attended the first meeting of the Fox Film Corporation on February 1, 1916, the company was a private company. Its securities were not listed on any stock exchange. William Fox owned 50 per cent of all of the outstanding stock, and the other 50 per cent was owned by a group of some fifty stockholders, one of which was the little doctor. The annual meetings from then until May, 1925, at which the little doctor attended each meeting, the stockholders were still not more than fifty; it was in 1925 that Fox Film had its stock listed on the New York Stock Exchange, and offered some of the shares to the public. At the meeting of February, 1926, our stockholders were perhaps 2,000; but when the stockholders' meeting was held, the only one of the 2,000 who attended was our little doctor. In 1927 we perhaps had more than 3,000, but when the meeting took place, the only stockholder that attended was the little doctor. At the meeting of 1928 we perhaps had more than 4,000 stockholders, but when that meeting was held the only stockholder who was present was the little doctor. When the meeting of February, 1929, came, I did not attend, because I was then busily engaged with Bill Donovan, trying to secure his consent to the acquisition of the 400,000 shares of Loew stock. I was informed, however, that the annual meeting was conducted, and although the number of Fox Film shareholders at that time was more than 7,500, the only stockholder who was present was the little doctor."

But now came the meeting of March 5, 1930, a great contest featured in the newspapers, and a crowd of people attended. On the top floor of the Fox Building are two spacious rooms, one 100×175 and the other 100×125. Many thousands of people came crowding to these rooms. Says W. F.: "Not so many stockholders as there were agitators representing the Telephone Company, whose job it was to hooray everything the Telephone Company wanted and shout down everything that Fox wanted."

"This wasn't to be the kind of a stockholders' meeting where one person living in the state of New York and forty-nine living in Newark, N. J., would cause their votes to be cast to elect directors for the ensuing year. This was a stockholders' meeting intended for the purpose of approving the plan of refinancing proposed by Bancamerica-Blair, Lehman Brothers and Dillon, Read & Co. The purpose of Otterson and Stuart in attending this meeting was to prevent the stockholders from approving a plan that would avoid these companies being thrown into receivership. The purpose of Otterson, Stuart, the lawyers, and the 'plants' attending this meeting was to make impossible the Fox Film Corporation repaying to them the money that it owed them —$15,000,000 to the Telephone Company plus interest past due, and $12,000,000 declared due by Halsey, Stuart in January, although not actually due until April 1, 1930.

"The one spark of human kindness that I could find at this stockholders' meeting was when my eyes became riveted on the face of that little doctor! But at this meeting the doctor wasn't going to be the teller. This meeting required ten tellers. This wasn't the meeting where the doctor, being appointed the teller, would drop his one vote into the hat, and find every other vote in accord, and declare the vote. This was to be a meeting where it would take ten men, and did take ten men the greater part of the day to examine all of the proxies and to certify under oath that they had examined the proxies, in the manner in which the stockholders had voted. This was a new sensation, this meeting.

"There were some nice people there who were stockholders and came to the meeting. There were ladies and gentlemen who were honestly stockholders of the companies, and who came to hear the fate of the companies in which they had invested their hard-earned savings. There were pathetic old ladies and some young ones who had their savings invested in the enterprise created by William Fox, and who had invested their hard-earned dollars because of William Fox. There were men in the audience who had the greater part of their fortunes invested in the enterprise. The room was packed to suffocation, and the number who actually were stockholders in my opinion were less than 5 per cent of those who were in the room.

"Amongst those who attended the meeting were Winfield R. Sheehan, James Grainger, Clayton Sheehan, and Courtland Smith —all actively engaged in mingling with the stockholders, urging them to give their proxies to Halsey, Stuart. In one case that comes to my mind a stockholder whose name was Madden, a professional bookmaker at race tracks, had brought his proxy already made out to the order of William Fox. When the proxies were later examined, the name of Fox was crossed out, and I was told that Winfield R. Sheehan had met Madden in the meeting room and had him change his proxy from Fox to Stuart. Other changes were made in the meeting, not quite as clumsy as that; the proxy they had was destroyed and a new proxy offered them for signature.

"The group that I controlled, and that was seeking proxies in my behalf, was the group headed by Jack G. Leo. Leo knew before the meeting opened the exact number of proxies I had, and the number that he had obtained totalled less than the two-thirds required. The shares necessary to make up the difference lay in the 50,100 shares of stock that I had deposited with my trustees at the Bankers' Trust Company. Every one of my attorneys felt confident that the decision of Judge Levy would be in my favor, and that his injunction would restrain the Telephone Company from voting my shares, and that the Court would order that the shares be given to me so that I could vote them. Had Judge Levy's opinion been that way, our troubles would have been over. But within fifteen or twenty minutes before the meeting really opened, Richard Dwight of the firm of Hughes, Schurman & Dwight, proudly announced that he had just been informed that Judge Levy had rendered a decision leaving the shares that belonged to me with the Bankers' Trust, and that Halsey, Stuart and the Telephone Company intended to vote my shares against my plan to save our companies, and to prevent our companies from paying them the $27,000,000 plus interest that we owed them.

"It was in that frame of mind that I sat down to open this meeting. You must picture me on October 28th as a man weighing 182 pounds, and on March 5th sitting down at this meeting weighing less than 150. You must picture my appearance by the fact that I had had no new clothes made between the time I weighed 182 and the time I weighed less than 150 pounds, a brief four months thereafter. You must picture me when I weighed 182 pounds as a man robust and healthy, as against the man haggard and tired and worn, with not enough vitality left to assert himself and his rights—but rather happy and glad that he was still alive, and wondering whether he would be able to finish it out; whether he would be able to complete the job before his widow and orphans would hear the Rabbi say: 'And here in this coffin lies William Fox. He wasn't a bad man. He lived a righteous life.'

"The controlling votes, 26 per cent of the outstanding shares, were in the hands of the stockholders' committee. They were represented and sat at the table. I tried my level best to discover how this 26 per cent would vote. One-half hour before the time for the opening of the meeting, Mr. Untermyer stated that it would be necessary to gather the directors together in the directors' room of the Fox Film Corporation. We did. Winfield R. Sheehan was there—the same man whom I had picked up some time in 1912 or 1913, and had rescued from the murder charge they were making against him as secretary to the Police Commissioner, and had offered to spend $1,000,000 of my money to protect him against the charges they were making against him.

"Another director was Saul E. Rogers, my personal attorney and counsel for twenty-five years, to whom in August, 1929, I had given a contract for a five-year employment at $156,000 per annum. He took the leading oar, and said that they had in their pocket a plan of refinancing submitted to them by Halsey, Stuart & Co.; that they were desirous of presenting this plan at the stockholders' meeting, and therefore would like to have the board of directors consent to the plan offered by Halsey, Stuart & Co., so that it could be presented to the stockholders. This was the first time that I had officially heard that Halsey, Stuart had a plan and really were willing to finance these companies.

"Of course, it goes without saying that the majority of the board of directors declined to entertain any plan of financing by Halsey, Stuart The majority of the board of directors of Fox Film viewed this as just one more trick on the part of the Telephone Company. The majority of the board felt that even if it wanted to abandon the Lehman plan and accept the Halsey, Stuart plan, when the showdown came there would be a reason found why Halsey, Stuart could not undertake this obligation, and that the purpose of proposing the Halsey, Stuart plan was to destroy the relationship between the Fox companies and the group of bankers who seemed to indicate a strong desire to do this financing. If the Fox directors would lend their ears to the Halsey, Stuart plan, and if the directors approved and the stockholders took that plan, in place of the Lehman plan, then the Bancamerica group would have received 1½ per cent of the $65,000,000, or about $1,000,000 for the services they had rendered, and they would be out of the picture.

"Our board of directors' meeting adjourned without giving consideration to the Telephone Company-Halsey, Stuart plan, and we went to the floor above, where the annual meeting of the stockholders of the Fox Film Corporation was to take place. It was during this intermission that William Brandt asked to see me privately, to tell me about Judge Levy.

"Well, here I was, my whole career lying in the hands of this stockholders' committee, which had the balance of the votes. I don't know how this committee came into being. These stockholders' committees spring from nowhere. If they cast their votes for the Halsey, Stuart plan, then the stockholders were without financing, for the Halsey, Stuart plan could not be considered by the court, unless it was first approved by the board of directors, and the board of directors, previous to the opening of the meeting, had refused to do this.

"You will recall my telling you that the attorneys who brought these suits against the Fox companies, all those who were demanding and crying for receiverships, were actually paid out of the funds of the Fox companies. All these attorneys were now present at this meeting, representing the Telephone Company, Halsey, Stuart, and Harley Clarke. In reading the minutes, bear in mind that all of the questions asked and answered were asked and answered by lawyers who were paid by the wreckers of the companies. I don't believe you will find a single lawyer that asked a single question at that meeting who didn't, after I sold out, receive a check in payment for services rendered out of the funds of these companies."

I have before me the minutes of the stockholders' meeting, some 50,000 words of text. Human nature is always interested in a fight, and I derive amusement from this conflict of gladiators. You may remember Martin Conboy, whom we saw appealing to Judge Coleman for a receivership. Conboy is a graduate of a Catholic college and a Knight Commander of the Order of St. Gregory the Great—I believe you kiss the Pope's toe for that. He was a captain in the New Jersey National Guard, and counsel to the Judiciary Committee of the New York State Assembly which kicked out the Socialist assemblymen during the war. He is a Tammany politician, and what is known as a "silver-tongued orator"; soft-spoken, polite, always smiling, apologizing for the deadliest blow. All through this meeting we find Conboy sparring with Samuel Untermyer. Throughout the fight they never forget that they are members of a privileged caste; they never fail to greet each other before they fire, and when their volleys have been delivered, they pay each other jovial compliments upon their accuracy of aim. " 'Am I right about this, Mr. Conboy?' says Untermyer.

"Mr. Conboy: Not entirely, Mr. Untermyer. You are partially right and you are partially wrong.

"Mr. Untermyer: That is what most of us lawyers are.

"Mr. Conboy: Well, you are right most of the time, you know.

"Mr. Untermyer: Thank you. So are you, Mr. Conboy.

"Mr. Conboy: Thank you, sir. You blow my horn and I will blow yours.

"Mr. Untermyer: Well, you are getting ready to blow another horn.

"Mr. Conboy: And you are getting ready to blow yours, too."

Pretty soon arose Mr. Berenson from Boston, and made a long and bitter speech, full of attacks upon the Lehman plan and upon William Fox. He refused to permit his time to be limited. He stated that he wanted a receivership, and from that time he lost out with the stockholders. " 'I say that under such circumstances as that it is better for every stockholder in the corporation to stand behind the petition for the appointment of a receiver under the guidance of the United States Court.'

"(Hisses and cries of 'No, No.')

"Mr. Berenson: Wait one second—

"(Renewed hisses and cries of 'No.' 'Choke.' 'Sit down.')

"President Fox: Now will you please sit down, Mr. Berenson. You are out of order.

"Mr. Berenson: I am not out of order. I decline to sit down. I am going to be heard. There are stockholders here that want to hear me.

"Mr. Untermyer: No, there are not.

"(Cries of 'No.' 'Sit down.')

"President Fox: Mr. Berenson, just a moment. Is there anybody in the room who wants to hear Mr. Berenson further?

"(Cries of 'No, put him out.')

"A Voice: Who ever heard of him before this?

"Another Voice: He has been on the first page of the New York 'Times.'

"President Fox: Won't you please, Mr. Berenson, sit down?

"Mr. Berenson: I will not sit down. I am going to be heard.

"(Cries of 'Put him out.' 'Sit down.')

"A Voice: The man has a legal right. Let him say it.

"President Fox: Mr. Berenson is your man, gentlemen. (Laughter.)"

This went on for several minutes. Berenson demanded seven minutes more and got them. Finally he subsided and Conboy arose and stated his objections in detail. He put in a jovial word for Berenson:

"It has been stated by poor Mr. Berenson—he got an awful razzing because he just mentioned receivership cursorily, and everybody hissed him, and I thought for a time they were going to tear him apart—

"A Voice: You seem to like him.

"Mr. Conboy: Well, I am not an enemy of his. I like you too, from your appearance from here.

"Mr. Untermyer: But, Mr. Conboy, you ought to have a great deal of sympathy with Mr. Berenson, because you, too, asked for a receivership.

"Mr. Conboy: There is not any question of sympathy. I did not ask for a receiver.

"Mr. Untermyer: You did.

"Mr. Conboy: I told the court there were worse things than a receiver. Don't interrupt me with statements of that kind. You know that is not quite an answer to what I am saying. We are talking about receivers for a minute.

"Mr. Berenson: He wants to razz you, too.

"Mr. Conboy: God bless my soul, you talked for quite a while, and I thought you were going to talk so long that Mr. Untermyer would not let me talk at all, he charged your consumption of time up to me.

"Mr. Untermyer: No, I didn't.

"Mr. Conboy: I knew you wouldn't."

All so jolly and friendly, you see. A minute or two later Conboy is saying: ". . . when he went into court last week with Mr. Untermyer as his counsel—and he could not get a more astute or better counsel in the City of New York, or any place else than you, Mr. Untermyer—(Applause) we all know you to be as formidable, if not the most formidable man who goes into a court room—I pay you the compliment without hesitation—

"Mr. Untermyer: But that is taking your time, Mr. Conboy.

"Mr. Conboy: I will give more time to it, if necessary, to make the statement."

There arose the counsel for the stockholders' committee: Emory R. Buckner, formerly assistant district attorney of New York County. He was that Buckner whom we saw acting as counsel for the police investigation in 1912 and 1913, before whom Winfield R. Sheehan had been haled and accused of taking graft. Buckner, you may remember, invited Sheehan to waive his immunity, and Sheehan pretended not to understand what he meant, and Buckner called that "bunk." Now he represents the Stern committee, which controls 26 per cent of the outstanding stock and has the decisive vote. W. F. has had no hint as to what will be Buckner's attitude, and he described to me with dry humor his varying emotions while Buckner was making his speech. It was a case of "off again, on again, Finnegan."

Said Buckner: " 'In that letter the Stern committee said that up to the present time as it was writing these letters the Bancamerica-Blair (Lehman) plan seemed to be the only practicable plan or best plan, because of the necessary co-operation of the Fox directors and of Mr. Fox personally.' " At that moment the hopes of W. F. went high. But then a moment later they sank again. " 'The committee said, however, and has reserved its right to use its influence for the adoption of any plan which is the best plan, but always to avoid a receivership. (Applause.)' " Then they went up again. " 'There may be those who have Mr. Berenson's fancy for a receivership, but I think that stockholders are ill advised if anything they can do to prevent a receivership is left undone. Because we lawyers know, even if you have not had experience, that in a receivership it is mostly the lawyers and the trustees and new bankers or new organizing gentlemen that come around that do nearly all the receiving, and the common stock is generally wiped out in order to make a reorganization more practicable.' "

Buckner read the correspondence with Fox and with the directors of Fox Film, in which they stated that they were convinced that the Halsey, Stuart plan was not made in good faith, and that they would have nothing to do with it. Buckner said that his committee had no interest in the quarrel and no knowledge as to what had happened; their only concern was to find a way to save the companies. In the end he came out with the announcement that the committee would cast its votes for the Lehman plan.

Now arose Richard Dwight, member of the firm of Hughes, Schurman & Dwight, representing the trustees of the voting trust, or rather a majority of them, Stuart and Otterson. You will recall the strange circumstances whereby Dwight was employed by W. F., and then authorized to represent the trusteeship, which made him the opponent of W. F. from that time forward. Here Dwight addressed the stockholders, and told them he assumed that he was acting "at Mr. Fox's request." There came a passage at arms between Untermyer and Dwight, in which you will once more hear two eminent and high-priced lawyers accusing each other of lying.

"Mr. Untermyer: I am afraid Mr. Dwight is just a trifle disingenuous. He says Mr. Fox is one of the trustees, but the trustee agreement says that the two other trustees can vote without him, so that he is in a peculiar position.

"Mr. Dwight: It says nothing about that in the voting trust agreement.

"Mr. Untermyer: It does say that any two or a majority can act."

"Mr. Dwight: Not the voting trust agreement."

"Mr. Untermyer: Yes, and so much so that this Halsey, Stuart plan which has the approval of the trustees and is really made by the trustees was considered and put out in your office.

"Mr. Dwight: That is correct.

"Mr. Untermyer: Yes, without even letting Mr. Fox know. So he is a funny kind of a one trustee, isn't he? (Laughter.)"

Here again, fortunately, we have the means of pinning down the issue, and seeing whether it is the Fox or his opponents who tell the truth.   It is embarrassing to me to have to state that a graduate of Princeton University and the New York Law School, a law partner of the Chief Justice of the United States Supreme Court, made a false statement to the stockholders of Fox Film Corporation; but it happened to be false, and common sense compels us to assume that it was deliberately so.   Three months ago Richard Dwight had helped in the drafting of that voting trust agreement; it had been prepared by his firm, as a result of the solemn promise of Charles Evans Hughes to support W. F. and help him out of his troubles, and prepare the agreement in such a way that his trust could not be abused.   For three months Mr. Dwight had been carrying on a long and hard-fought contest over that voting trust agreement.   For six weeks he had been discussing before Judge Coleman the carrying out of the agreement, and explaining its provisions to the judge, both in chambers and in open court.   Can you believe that he had forgotten what was in it?   Are you not, on the contrary, compelled to believe that he knew it by heart?

This clause of the agreement is crucial, because it has enabled Otterson and Stuart to do what they please, regardless of the Fox.   And now Dwight assures the stockholders of Fox Film that this passage is not in the agreement.   Here is the passage, as short and sweet as it could be written: "Fifth: The action of any two of the trustees with respect to any of the matters embraced in this agreement shall be deemed to be the action of the trustees."

The lawyers presented their arguments to the stockholders, and at last it was time for the vote.   Before the proxies were taken, Martin Conboy challenged the vote of the Stern committee, cast by Buckner; 'and this led to a very funny scene.   Conboy demanded that Buckner be sworn, according to section 20 of the General Corporation Laws; a provision requiring that those casting a proxy vote shall take the following two oaths: first—"I do solemnly swear that in voting at this election I have not, either directly, indirectly or impliedly, received any promise or any sum of money or anything of value to influence the giving of my vote or votes at this meeting or as a consideration therefor."

And second: "I do solemnly swear that I have not either directly, indirectly or impliedly given any promise or any sum of money or anything of value to induce the giving of a proxy to me to vote at this meeting, or received any promise or any sum of money or anything of value to influence the giving of my vote at this meeting or as a consideration therefor."

Having obtained that oath from Buckner, Conboy demanded it from Swaine, who had cast the proxies collected by Fox and Leo. Swaine said all right, and then Samuel Untermyer suggested that they ought to have the same oath from Otterson and Stuart. Then came Alvin Untermyer with a highly inconvenient suggestion.

"Mr. Alvin Untermyer: And are you voting, too, Mr. Conboy?

"Mr. Conboy: Yes.

"Mr. Alvin Untermyer: We might have one from you, too."

There was some delay while the forms were being read to the inspectors and signed, and that gave Conboy time to realize that he had got himself into a predicament. Said Conboy: "I move the swearing be closed." But W. F. was not ready to have it closed. He asked that Otterson and Stuart should take the oath, and then he turned to Conboy again. But, as I said, these lawyers belong to a privileged caste, and Untermyer also had come to realize the predicament of his friend, Conboy. Said he: "I think we will waive Mr. Conboy's oath anyway." To which Conboy replied gratefully, "You relieve me from a lot of embarrassment."

"Mr. Untermyer: Especially that part of it as to any promise of anything of value.

"Mr. Conboy: Certainly.

"Mr. Untermyer: If we put you on oath and asked you from where the thing of value came it might be very embarrassing.

"Mr. Conboy: Yes, very embarrassing."

But now spoke up Stern, chairman of the stockholders' committee which was represented by Buckner. Said Stern:

"We are reputable bankers and Mr. Conboy is a reputable

lawyer and I think if he wants our oath he should be compelled to take one himself.

"Mr. Conboy: I will withdraw my proxy before I sign any oath. I am a member of the bar, and I am here as an attorney at law representing interests, and if I have to take an oath with respect to compensation I am not going to do it, and Mr. Untermyer knows that I won't do it. That is all there is to it."

See what a chance that gave the Fox. All day long he had been sitting here, being baited and sneered at by these high-priced lawyers, and now he had one of them hung up by the heels. Let us follow the dialogue:

"President Fox: Now I think that is terrible, Mr. Conboy.

"Mr. Conboy: Do you?

"President Fox: Yes.

"Mr. Conboy: Well, I don't.

"President Fox: No one here in the room wanted that oath signed but you.

"Mr. Conboy: That is all right. If anyone challenges my vote—

"Mr. Untermyer: Don't let us bother. We are wasting time.

"President Fox: If that is not gall I don't know what it is, Mr. Conboy.

"Mr. Untermyer: Call it what you please, but it is not necessary.

"President Fox: It is perfectly awful. You want the law against anybody except yourself.

"Mr. Conboy: That is right.

"President Fox: That is wonderful. I think, Mr. Conboy, we ought to let you withdraw your ballot.

"Mr. Conboy: You do think so, do you?

"President Fox: I do. Would you care to withdraw it?"

How funny to see that jovial Martin Conboy suddenly turning pale, and seeking shelter behind his big brother, Samuel Untermyer, the chief of the sacred caste—to whom he has been paying nice compliments all day! Says Conboy:

"It is all in the hands of Mr. Untermyer.

"President Fox: I am running this meeting. I happen to be the chairman.

"Mr. Conboy: No, Mr. Untermyer is running it.

"President Fox: Wait a minute. Which would you like to do, withdraw your ballot or take the oath?

"Mr. Conboy: I have told you what I wanted to do.

"President Fox: What is it?

"Mr. Conboy: I have told you.

"Mr. Untermyer: Now let us get on.

"President Fox: Mr. Untermyer, now wait a minute. Mr. Conboy, what would you like to do, take an oath or withdraw your ballot?

"Mr. Conboy: I have told you.

"President Fox: Please repeat it.

"Mr. Conboy: I told you that if my vote was challenged I would withdraw my proxy.

"President Fox: Unless you take an oath like I did, I challenge your vote.

"Mr. Conboy: All right, if Mr. Untermyer thinks I should, I withdraw my proxy.

"Mr. Untermyer: I don't think so. I would not do it.

"President Fox: I bow to your judgment, sir. (Applause.)

"Mr. Untermyer: This is a brother member of the bar and a very good friend of mine.

"Mr. Buckner: Lawyers should never work for nothing. Mr. Fox is trying to create a precedent, that lawyers should work for nothing.

"Mr. Conboy: I hope he won't create that precedent, and I don't think that you will let him. Mr. Untermyer certainly does not. It is much more important to him in this connection than anybody else.

"Mr. Buckner: That is why he sides with you.

"Mr. Conboy: I thought so too. I thought I was in safe hands.

"Mr. Untermyer: But you did start something, didn't you?

"Mr. Conboy: Didn't I?"

Such is the lawyer's comment on the matter; and may I add a few words from a mere layman? It seems to me that if there is such a thing as stating a plain intention in plain language, the corporation statutes of New York State undertook to prohibit and do prohibit a paid attorney from casting a proxy vote at a stockholders' meeting. But all the attorneys ignore that law, and intend to go on ignoring it, and therefore Samuel Untermyer stepped in and prevented William Fox from pinning Martin Conboy down on a dangerous issue.

The votes were counted, and next morning there was another meeting, and the tellers reported the result, which was that the resolution in favor of the Lehman plan had been carried by a vote of 914,405 against 33,085 shares. The meeting was declared adjourned; but Richard Dwight wasn't satisfied to have it adjourned, and retired into a corner and continued the meeting all by himself. In the meantime, at the request of the stockholders, William Fox made a little speech:

"I cannot promise you that I am going to work any harder from now on than I have in the past, because I don't believe I have the same vitality left. After all, I gave this company my best years, from twenty-one to fifty-one, and I do not believe that I have got thirty years more left, and I am sure if I had they won't be years with as much energy as I was able to expend in the last thirty. But all that I have belongs to these companies, I pledge you that." (Applause.)

REEL TWENTY-FOUR

THE JAPANESE MEETING

OUR Fox had his vindication, and was very happy, for a few days. He had his bankers, and his plan, and his stockholders' consent, and in a month or so he was going to have $65,000,-000, and pay all his debts, and consolidate his companies, and double their income through a saving of $17,000,000 a year. Incidentally he would fire all his traitor executives, and clean house, and start life over again—such was his fond dream.

But he was reckoning without the Telephone Company, Halsey, Stuart, and the Chase Bank. They had no idea of letting go their hold upon the Fox, and they sat down with their shrewd attorneys to figure the next step in the process of hamstringing and paralyzing their victim. They decided that the time had come for Winfield R. Sheehan to earn the $1,800,000 of new salary. On March 18, in the Supreme Court of New York County, Winfield R. Sheehan, being duly sworn, deposed and said that he was the plaintiff herein, and was vice president and general manager of the Fox Film Corporation, and had been such for the past fifteen years, commencing with the inception of that corporation. He went on blandly and serenely to tell the world in substance that he was Fox.

"I was the responsible general manager and chief executive of this company, and under my management and supervision, the company has prospered enormously. . . .

"With the exception, however, of theatre expansion and financial arrangements and laboratory work, I was responsible for all of the business activities of this company.

"I have a more intimate knowledge of the general business details, production details, distribution details, and all other fields which are under my supervision, than any other official, executive, or employe of the company."

20

Sheehan told the world exactly how "enormously" the company had prospered under his "management and supervision." He cited "the aggregate gross annual business of the company derived from the distribution of pictures produced by it":

$$1925\ldots\ldots\ldots\$21,321,869.59$$
$$1926\ldots\ldots\ldots\ 23,547,633.92$$
$$1927\ldots\ldots\ldots\ 25,542,718.66$$
$$1928\ldots\ldots\ldots\ 66,525,737.48$$
$$1929\ldots\ldots\ldots\ 72,000,000\ 00\ \text{(approximately)}$$

"Based on my knowledge of the plans and arrangements made for production for the year 1930, I have every reason to believe that the rate of increase of gross business and net profits for that year, will be approximately 25 per cent more than for the year 1929."

This affidavit of Sheehan was not merely filed in court, but was printed in a pamphlet by Halsey, Stuart & Co., and sent to all the stockholders of the Fox corporations. W. F. promptly printed an answer and sent it to the stockholders, and stated the true figures of the income of the company derived from the distribution of pictures, as follows:

$$1925\ldots\ldots\ldots\$20,230,007$$
$$1926\ldots\ldots\ldots\ 20,639,363$$
$$1927\ldots\ldots\ldots\ 22,847,131$$
$$1928\ldots\ldots\ldots\ 26,263,210$$
$$1929\ldots\ldots\ldots\ 31,317,648$$

You will note that to the last two years' items, Mr. Sheehan added, out of his imagination, a trifle over $40,000,000 per year. He got these millions partly out of the receipts for theatre admissions of the Wesco Theatre Company, a concern with which he had absolutely nothing to do, the concern being managed by Harold B. Franklin.

It is interesting to take up the annual report of Fox Film of December 27, 1930, which was after W. F. had been ousted. At the time this report was issued, Sheehan was still vice president and general manager, and a director of the corporation. He must have read this report and approved it. Does he there tell the world what he told in his affidavit of March 18 of the same year? Does he there say that the "aggregate gross annual business of the company derived from the distribution of pictures produced by it was $66,525,737.48 in 1928, and approximately $72,000,000 in 1929"? No, he gives a table of "gross rentals," which is the same thing, and he there shows for 1928 $22,626,747, and for 1929 $30,803,974.

And what about his serene prophecy for the year 1930— "based on my knowledge of the plans and arrangements made for production"—that the gross rentals would be $90,000,000? For some strange reason, the 1930 report of Fox Film stops its table of gross rentals with the year 1929. The corporation under the Clarke-Sheehan regime apparently is not proud of its record made in the year 1930, and deftly side-steps the issue. Nor can I tell you the gross rentals for the year 1931, because they now tell the world only their total gross income, which includes theatre receipts. The reason for this is very simple: they have increased the number of their theatres, and therefore the gross total of theatre receipts shows an increase, which automatic increase they use to conceal the fact that their receipts from film rentals are steadily declining!

After telling how Sheehan had run Fox Film, the affidavit goes on to tell how Fox very foolishly failed to consult Sheehan about financial matters. Fox failed to inform him as to how the Loew purchase was to be financed. All that Fox did was to inform Sheehan "in a general way of his intentions." To this I quote Fox's answer, as follows:

"The fact is that Sheehan was in New York when this transaction was being negotiated and consummated. At that time it became necessary to interview Mr. William Donovan, the then Assistant Attorney-General of the United States, who was then Chairman of the Boulder Dam Project and was residing at Bishop's Lodge, New Mexico. I took Mr. Sheehan with me to visit Mr. Donovan. We traveled together for three days and three nights to Bishop's Lodge to see Mr. Donovan. During the long journey we talked about nothing except the purchase of the Loew stock. We had seen Mr. Donovan, and from Bishop's Lodge, New Mexico, Mr. Sheehan and I traveled to Los Angeles. We continued to talk of barely anything else except the purchase of the Loew stock and our conference with Mr. Donovan. Mr Sheehan remained with me in Los Angeles for a week or ten days thereafter, and we spent much of our time continuing the discussion of the Loew purchase. Mr. Sheehan was enthusiastic about making the purchase; urged it in the strongest terms, and traveled more than 7,000 miles to assist me in consummating that purchase."

Having recited many other blunders of his employer and former friend, Sheehan got down to the earning of his increase in salary. He asked the Court to kill the Lehman plan, and force W. F. back into the arms of Stuart and Otterson. He prayed "that this Court decree specific performance, compelling Mr. Fox to carry out the conditions, terms and covenants of the trust agreement, and I ask that this motion for temporary injunction be granted, restraining and enjoining the defendants (other than Halsey, Stuart & Co., Inc., Stuart, Otterson, and Electrical Research Products, Inc.) from going through with the Bancamerica-Blair plan, or issuing any securities thereunder, or doing any act or thing to interfere with the trust agreement."

At the same time with the Sheehan suit came a flood of new receivership actions by various creditors in the State courts; also, in the Federal courts, the affidavit of Harold L. Stuart, alleging prejudice on the part of Judge Coleman. This affidavit recited a long list of the things which Coleman had done, and a number which he had not done, to favor Fox and hinder Stuart; it concluded by asking that Judge Coleman "enter upon the records of this Court the certificate of disqualification"—that is, his own disqualification. This was done, according to the law, and a new judge was appointed, and the whole complicated proceedings had to begin all over. The new judge, Knox, had to study the case—and how long would this take, and what would the creditors do in the meantime? It was Halsey, Stuart's trump card, and a knock-out for our poor little Fox.

Consider the situation which confronted the Fox. He was not admitted to the secret conferences of either his enemy-bankers or his friend-bankers, but he knew them and could guess what was happening. We also know them by now, and can guess. Did Harry Stuart and his lawyer Bogue first go to Elisha Walker and his lawyer Swaine? Or did the Walker-Swaine pair seek out the Stuart-Bogue pair? We cannot say; but remember that Swaine has said in open court that Bogue is one of his "closest personal friends," and that he expects to keep him as such, even though he has called him in open court a breaker of pledges. Remember also that Swaine has stated that the Lehman group took up the new financing plan only because they had been assured that Halsey, Stuart would make no objection to their undertaking. Now they have learned that Halsey, Stuart make violent and furious objection, and are going to fight them bitterly. Remember, also, that Walker and also Dillon are directors in the Chase Bank, and that Blair & Company is known as the "back door" of that bank. It has been a family quarrel.

Since the Walker-Swaine pair have shown themselves the more polite and conciliatory, let us assume that they make the first move. Let us picture them inviting the Stuart-Bogue pair to a luncheon, with perhaps Bobbie Lehman and Clarence Dillon —another luncheon where Dillon will be nervous and eat all the grapes. Or perhaps, since it is now the end of March, the grapes from California will be replaced by strawberries from Florida. They ask whether it may not be possible to come to a friendly understanding; and Stuart-Bogue make reply as follows:

"Look your proposition over and see what you have got: a tangle of law-suits and no possible way out. Judge Coleman was your one best bower and you have lost him. We are going to get an injunction in the State Supreme Court on the Sheehan motion, and you won't be able to do any financing. Judge Knox will be forced to appoint a receiver. And whether he is your man or our man makes no great difference, because we have got the contract for the preferential financing, and whatever financing is done, we will do it or we will tie up the receiver.

"In short, there isn't any way out for you, and it only goes to show what we told you in the beginning, that you were foolish to butt in on this job. This is our Fox; we had him hung up all ready for skinning, and why should you horn in and take him away from us? You are breaking all the rules of the game, and making yourself a lot of enmity that some day you will regret. We all agree that we don't like this little Fox from Hungary or Jerusalem or wherever it is. He does a lot of his financing for himself, and you can see what a dirty crook he is from the fact that he got up this Fox Securities Corporation and proposed to sell $35,000,000 worth of debentures without any bankers at all! Why in the world should we gentlemen go on fighting each other and let this little blankety-blank get away with a whole skin?"

So much for Stuart-Bogue. We can imagine Walker-Swaine-plus-Lehman-Dillon making reply: "There's a big 'spread' in this financing, and there ought to be enough to go around. Will you let us in on it?"

Says Stuart-Bogue: "We might give you a share—say one-fourth."

"The hell you say!" says Walker-Swaine-plus-Lehman-Dillon. "If that's the best you can think of, this luncheon might as well stop with the cocktails."

They argue all the way through the cold consomme, and the olives and celery, and the filet of salmon. By the time they get to the broiled spring chicken and peas, Stuart-Bogue have come to the point where they are offering one-third of the financing; and that proposition stands until Clarence Dillon has eaten the last of the Florida strawberries, and everybody has smoked a couple of cigars or half a dozen cigarettes. It is only when Walker-Swaine-plus-Lehman-Dillon have got up to leave in disgust, and after the Stuart-Bogue group have telephoned to Otterson-Pratt and to Wiggin-Chase Bank that they finally settle the matter upon the basis of 50-50.

Understand just what these gentlemen are bargaining over. There is going to be something over $100,000,000 worth of new Fox securities sold to the public, and these gentlemen are to do the selling, and pay themselves a whole string of commissions and stock allotments, some of them secret, so that it is impossible to estimate the totals. But Stuart-Bogue plus Wiggin-Chase Bank expect to get not less than $40,000,000 for their job of stringing up the Fox, and the Lehman group are demanding half of this for not stealing him away. Otterson and his Telephone Company will get the Tri-Ergon patents, provided they can manage to frighten them out of the Fox in the course of the deal.

All of these gentlemen agree in not wanting a receivership, because they might not be able to control the receiver. Obviously, it is cheaper and safer to buy the Fox out. If they come to an agreement among themselves, they can force him to sell, for he will no longer have any bankers, nor any hope of being financed, and a receivership would wipe out his voting shares automatically and leave him nothing. Therefore he will sell; and the bankers will find somebody to buy, and will lend the money for that purpose, charging another commission. The buyer will have the privilege of looting the companies of whatever the bankers have left.

As I say, I don't know just how this deal was made; I don't know who made the first move, nor where the luncheon was held; the menu I have given here is based on what I have observed at similar affairs. But before long you will see it admitted that a deal has been made; and you will see its terms embodied and fixed in court records and issues of stocks and bonds.

What would be the first hint that W. F. would get of such a bankers' deal? In the course of his negotiations with the Lehman bankers they had raised one very important consideration. Suppose that while they were going ahead with their plans for new financing, and incurring the animosity of the all-powerful Chase Bank and the all-powerful Telephone Company—suppose that Fox should decide to sell his voting shares, and thus terminate his relation with his companies? Again and again he had assured them that he would not do it without consulting the Lehman group. But they weren't satisfied, and required him to write them a letter in which he assured them that he would not offer these voting shares for sale.

And now suppose that a bankers' deal was made, such as I have described at the imaginary luncheon—how would W. F. know that? The answer is easy: he would get a letter from the Lehman group, informing him that they no longer held him bound by his promise not to sell the voting shares! A day or two after Judge Coleman was taken out of the case, W. F. received such a letter. And the very day he received that letter, came his friend Albert Greenfield from Philadelphia. Greenfield, you remember, had been W. F.'s representative in several deals. He had sold the First National shares for him just after the panic, and he had tried to sell the Loew shares and the West Coast shares. So he was known to Wall Street as W. F.'s "contact man." And now comes Greenfield again, and wants to know, would W. F. care to sell his voting shares? W. F. says no, he wouldn't care to sell them.

You recall that the Lehman group, under their agreement, were to do their financing not later than the 15th of April. But all these legal entanglements have delayed them, and it is now the end of March, and there is no sign of financing, and Judge Coleman is out, and W. F. says to Untermyer: "It looks to me as if this law business is going to take a long time, because Judge Knox will have to become familiar with the case. And here in two weeks the commitment of my bankers will expire. It seems to me you ought to give me some idea how long you will take in court, and then we ought to meet these bankers and get an extension of time." Untermyer said he thought the legal proceedings would take until June, and W. F. asked him to get the bankers together in one room and ask for an extension of the Lehman plan until June 15.

It was Monday, March 31. W. F. remembered the date because the following day was the birthday of that little daughter of his, who had made the remark about not losing your head when you need it the most. W. F. with Samuel and Alvin Untermyer called by appointment at the offices of Bancamerica-Blair Corporation and, to their surprise, they were kept waiting in the outer office for nearly an hour. That isn't usual, because "Papa" Untermyer is a very distinguished old gentleman, and his time is worth a lot of money. W. F.'s suspicions were aroused, and he said: "I think we ought to plan out our program when we go in there, and I wish it would be followed as I suggest—that neither Alvin or myself open our mouths, but that you do all the talking, and we be allowed to observe the banking group and their lawyers." That was agreed to, and W. F. narrates:

"After waiting an hour we were ushered in. There sat this group of men, I should say fifteen in number. As I came into the room, they appeared to me as though they were all Japanese. Every man in the room, as I watched him, was wearing a Japanese mask; all their faces were tense. I could understand why we had been kept waiting outside—they had been rehearsing this play that was about to take place. Every man in that room knew that Judge Coleman was no longer in the case; that Halsey, Stuart had filed the affidavit of prejudice; that the court that had held this thing together was no longer there to do it. I felt that every man in the room knew that Halsey, Stuart had played their final trump, and won the game. As I observed each of the faces of the men in the room, I was receiving mental communications that something had gone wrong. I was not in the presence of the tremendously friendly group who had been arguing in court that their plan should be the only plan submitted to the stockholders. At the stockholders' meeting these men had been like schoolboys in a contest. What in God's world could they be thinking about now?

"While all this was in my head, Untermyer said: 'Gentlemen, because of this great amount of litigation, and because of the removal of Judge Coleman, Fox has requested that we have this meeting to inquire from you whether or not you would be willing to renew your contract to supply this financing for sixty days longer.' There was dead silence, and at the other end of the room Mr. Swaine, attorney for the Bancamerica-Blair Corporation, asked Untermyer a wholly irrelevant question."

This question had to do with certain law suits that were pending. What would be the effect of them, and how was Untermyer going to go about it? This, of course, caused Untermyer to go into a lengthy explanation, wholly immaterial to the question about an extension of time. It took Untermyer fifteen minutes to answer, and when he had finished, he asked again whether these men would be ready and willing to extend the financing contracts to June 15th.

"Mr. Royce, a lawyer representing the Lehman group, then asked Untermyer a question, again a carefully prepared one, and again it took Untermyer fifteen minutes of explanation before he could conclude the answer. Not a sound out of all these bankers; not a word, not an eyelash movement—they were just Japanese diplomats! You couldn't read what was in their faces at all, you had to guess at it. And then Untermyer for the third time asked whether they would extend the contract, and this time Swaine, who had asked the first question, began asking a second question. I went over to Alvin and said: 'Go and tell your father not to ask our question again, but to leave with our question unanswered'; and so we did leave. It was never replied to."

Our Fox did not tell his lawyers what was in his own mind. He went off and worked out the problem himself. The birthday of his little girl was the day that he needed his head, and on that day he telephoned to his friend Greenfield to come up from Philadelphia. Yes, said W. F., he would be willing to sell his voting shares. Who wanted to buy them? Greenfield answered that the person who wanted to buy them was Harley L. Clarke of Chicago.

You have not forgotten, I am sure, how the great utilities magnate had come from Chicago two or three months back, and offered W. F. a third of $100,000,000 for his voting shares— on condition that W. F., before making the sale, would sell to Clarke the Loew shares, owned by W. F.'s company, at a price $40,000,000 below what the company had paid for them. Now Clarke comes again, and this time he says he is willing to pay $15,000,000 cash, and with no strings tied to it. W. F. says "O. K."

And so, on the fourth day after the "Japanese meeting," Clarke and his lawyers are in conference with W. F. and Alvin Untermyer in a hotel room. It is a Saturday morning—our Fox has waited until "Papa" has gone down to his penthouse retreat on the roof of a hotel in Atlantic City. It appears that "Papa" is still trusting the Lehman bankers, and his client thinks he mightn't approve this deal, so he isn't to be told about it until it is over.

You may recall the story about A. C. Blumenthal—how when W. F. went to Clarke's office with Greenfield to discuss the terms of the sale, he found little Blumy there, and he told Blumy's life story to Clarke, and then demanded that Clarke order Blumy out, which Clarke did. W. F. was interested to learn afterwards that Clarke had promised Blumy a commission of $500,000 on this deal—always, of course, out of the treasury of the Fox companies.

There is another interesting story connected with these preliminary negotiations. W. F. noted that every item in the demand of Harley Clarke had already been prepared in the demands of the Lehman group. Clarke wanted W. F. to surrender his Fox Movietone stock, and his Grandeur patents, which were his personal property. Also Clarke wanted him to surrender his Tri-

Ergon patents; but that was a subject upon which W. F. had sworn a domestic vow. He says:

"My friend Greenfield, in his negotiations for the sale of my voting shares, at all times included the Tri-Ergon patents in the deal. Greenfield took the position that he had been informed again and again that these patents were valueless, and so I might just as well throw them in. There was a time during these sessions that, rather than go on any further, tired as I was, I was ready to surrender these patents. But Mrs. Fox took the position that that could not be; it was these patents that had gotten me into the difficulty; they were the one thing the Telephone Company wanted, and the one thing the Telephone Company was not going to get. She told Greenfield of the humble way in which we had started; our first year in the $11 a month apartment had been the happiest year of her life, and she was willing to go back to such an apartment, if she could take those patents with her.

"Greenfield frankly said that he could not be an impartial friend and advisor in this matter. The securities company, of which he was chairman, was my creditor for $10,000,000, which was almost half the capital of the company, and he had to think about that money. So throughout all this difficulty, Greenfield, who had constant access to my home, was urging that the thing to do was to sell these voting shares and give the Tri-Ergon patents with them. I recall one day when he and Harry Sundheim were at my home, and Greenfield was persisting that the transaction be closed, and that the Tri-Ergon patents be surrendered. Mrs. Fox was in the doorway, with only a curtain between us, listening to this conversation of Greenfield's. She came into the room, and went into a rage of a kind I would never like to see her or anyone in again; it resulted in a terrific expression of frenzy, and she finally dropped to the floor and passed out. For a while I thought she was dead; it took us half an hour to bring her to again. It was then that Greenfield realized that he must never again mention the Tri-Ergon patents, and that if there were ever to be a sale, it would have to be done without those patents."

Picture now Greenfield and Alvin Untermyer and W. F. in Clarke's office, arguing with Clarke and his lawyers over the terms of the sale. W. F. is to receive a certified check for $15,000,000, and he is demanding a 20 per cent participation in the new financing; which means not merely that he will make some extra money, but will be privileged to sit in at the conferences of the great bankers, whom he respects for their dignity and power, even while they have been holding him up. He has the fond idea that he is going to be able to make useful suggestions to them, and help them in running these companies, which he knows so well and which they know hardly at all.

Yes, he really thinks they are going to run the companies, and not merely run them into the ground. Accordingly, he requires that he be a director for five years; and that they agree to establish an advisory board, and make him chairman of this board, to give them the best knowledge he has. In the effort to make the bankers appreciate his knowledge—since they only appreciate what costs a lot of money—he makes them pay him a salary of $500,000 a year for five years. He agrees to give Fox Film a license for the free use of the Tri-Ergon and Grandeur patents; but not the patents themselves—no, for W. F. has to go home to his wife!

In the course of this bargaining came a curious development:

"We had gone into this conference at 10 o'clock Saturday morning, and were still drawing these papers at about 1 o'clock Sunday morning. I said to Clarke: 'When the bankers sent me a letter stating that they no longer objected to my selling my voting shares, they extracted from me a promise that the purchaser of my shares, if he did any financing, would have to do it through them; they would have to be in the syndicate, and at least three-fourths of the financing would be handled by them.' But Clarke insisted that the Chase Bank and Halsey, Stuart intended selling the securities necessary to give him the money; and for the greater portion of the evening I stood firm that Bancamerica-Blair, Lehman Brothers, and Dillon, Read receive no less than 75 per cent of the financing. In fact, for a while it looked as though the deal would fall through; but I had made this promise, and I was going to see that it was carried out.

"At about 1:45 in the morning, Clarke said: 'Some people haven't any sense. Here you have battled for three hours to give your bankers protection. Would you like to have me prove

to you that you have no bankers?' I said, 'Yes, I would like to
have proof of that.' He said, 'All right. Do you know Ned
Tinker?' I said no. (Tinker was then president of the Chase
Securities Corporation, and chairman of the Chase Bank.) Clarke
said: 'You ask him whether or not he made an arrangement in
behalf of Halsey, Stuart and the Chase Bank, that your group
of bankers were to have 50 per cent, and ask him whether or
not they didn't have that arrangement on last Monday.' Monday,
you understand, was the day of that meeting with the bankers,
which I called the 'Japanese meeting,' because they all behaved
that way. Here, you see, it was being revealed to me that
already, before I went to that meeting, my bankers had got
together with my enemies and made a deal to sell me out!

"Clarke got Tinker on the 'phone, and I said: 'Mr. Tinker,
Clarke tells me that last Monday you had met my banking group,
and that you reached an agreement with them that they would
be willing to take 50 per cent of the financing. Is that correct,
and with whom did you have that understanding?' He said:
'I have had that understanding with your group, and particularly
with Walker.' I thanked him, and called Walker at his home.
I said, 'I am selling out. I have been arguing here for three
hours to get for you 75 per cent of the financing as I promised.
I just talked to your friend Tinker, and he tells me you made
an agreement with him Monday whereby you agreed that you
would accept 50 per cent of the financing.' He said that was
correct—but urged me to hold out for 75 per cent anyway! I
said all right, and hung up the receiver, and dipped my pen in
the ink and immediately wrote in the 50 per cent basis."

The contract was drawn without the provision for 20 per cent
participation by W. F. Clarke was making a desperate effort to
talk him out of that idea. "Here," said Clarke, "your bankers
have 50 per cent, and our bankers have 50 per cent, and where
are you going to get your 20 per cent?" But the tough and
tenacious Fox meant to have this "gravy," bankers or no bankers,
and for that reason he did not mean to sign the contract as it
stood. He sought for a pretext.

"I insisted that the contract be read to Samuel Untermyer.
We called him on long distance telephone, and his son proceeded
to read the contract to him, line for line. There was a discussion

between his son and himself. He was asking for many correc-
tions and additions to be made. It was clear to me that Samuel
Untermyer was not satisfied with the contract, was not satisfied
that it had all that it should have. I felt that this was not the
proper manner of closing a transaction of this magnitude, with
the terms of the agreement being discussed over the telephone.
I announced to Clarke that Untermyer asked for the privilege of
reading the contract; he would be in New York early in the
afternoon, and would promptly start reading it.

"Clarke thought there was no occasion for the old man reading this contract. His son had drawn it, he had read it to his
father, the contract contained all of the things we had expressed
during the night, and the contract must now be signed. I can
visualize the scene of that room just as though it were here now.
We were all seated with Clarke having his back to the door, his
face to these lawyers who had listened all night and who were
now getting his ultimatum. He said: 'I knew darn well we were
wasting this night. I knew darn well you never intended to sell
these shares. I have conceded you every request you made during
the night. I felt I was giving you all the rope you wanted with
which to hang yourselves, and now that you refuse to sign the
contract, the deal is off'—and out he darted through the door.

"He left the entire meeting flabbergasted: Alvin Untermyer
who was so anxious to consummate this transaction, for he had
remembered the Japanese meeting, and was urging that I sell
out; and Albert Greenfield, who was there all night, and who
had seen the return of his $10,000,000 to the Bankers' Securities
Corporation. Greenfield had stayed in this room twenty-four
hours, so as to consummate the deal, and now he saw Clarke
dart out, and you can well imagine his attitude. I remembered
then clearly the words of my daughter of nine: 'What's the use
of having a head if you lose it just when you need it the most?'
I said: 'Let's fold up our papers and go home. I am perfectly
satisfied now that the deal has fallen through.'

"Samuel Untermyer was presently informed that the deal
was off, and he called up Mrs. Fox, apologizing profusely. He
hoped he had not been the cause of the breaking off of the deal
that had been worked out in the twenty-four hours; he had
insisted that the contract be held for his reading as a matter of

precaution to me. Mrs. Fox up to this time hadn't known the deal had been called off. I had 'phoned her every hour during the night, telling her of the progress, but I had not 'phoned her when the contract came to an end. I thought I could best explain it to her when I arrived home. But when we got there she knew all about it. Samuel Untermyer had just told her.

"I said: 'What did you say to him? What reply did you make?' She said: 'I told him not to worry about it. Mr. Fox didn't want to sign it. If he had wanted to sign it, there is nothing that Mr. Untermyer could have done to prevent him. He must have had another reason, other than the fact that Mr. Untermyer wanted to read it.' I said: 'How did you know—how did you guess that?' She said: 'Well, didn't you have another reason?' I said: 'Yes. During the night Clarke talked me out of my 20 per cent participation. There was no way of my getting back to it in this conference. That meeting had to break up and a new one held to secure this participation, which I hope will net me a substantial profit.'

"I went to bed. Greenfield went to bed. Alvin Untermyer went home. I told Greenfield that if he were awake, I would be glad to see him at my home at three in the afternoon. I knew the Twentieth Century train left New York at 2:45. I had a man down at the Grand Central station to see if Clarke would keep his promise to go back to Chicago on that train. The hour came, and my man 'phoned and said Clarke had not taken the train. At 3 o'clock Greenfield returned. I said: 'That fellow Clarke didn't go back to Chicago. He didn't call the deal off. He is right across the street.' I live at 270 Park Avenue, and Clarke at 277 Park Avenue.

"I hadn't told Greenfield during the night that Clarke had talked me out of my 20 per cent participation. When I told Greenfield about it, he said: 'Of course you were right. He hasn't any right to charge you with breaking up this deal. He broke it up. I will go right across the street and see him.' He found Clarke home, and came back in an hour, and Clarke said: 'All right, if you will sign the contract, I will give you a letter giving you the 20 per cent participation.'

"We waited until Samuel Untermyer arrived late that afternoon to read the contract. I said to Untermyer: 'Now before we sign the contract, be sure that you have a perfect arrangement, whereby these companies are going to pay you the million dollars that I had arranged with you.' Untermyer went over to Clarke's home with Greenfield and there discussed his million dollar fee, with Clarke agreeing to pay it. I insisted that that be done. I felt that Untermyer had earned his fee that I had arranged with him. He had carried out his part of the bargain, and prevented these corporations from going into the hands of the receivers.

"Of course the contract contained a paragraph that Clarke assumed the payment of all my lawyers' fees, regardless of the number that I had. That all became necessary in this picture, because of the conspiracy of Clarke and the Telephone Company; none of it became necessary because of any act of mine.

"We returned to Untermyer's home later that night. Untermyer insisted that the contract could not be signed until after the stroke of 12. This was Sunday, and no contract would be legal until at least one minute past 12 o'clock. It would have to be Monday morning. He made this announcement around 11 o'clock. We all waited for the clock to point to 12. I suggested that in view of the importance of the deal we wait until ten or fifteen minutes past 12—perhaps the watch we were going by was not keeping accurate time. So sometime between five and ten minutes past 12, this contract was finally signed."

REEL TWENTY-FIVE

CAPTAIN KIDD

AT last the enemies of our Fox have accomplished their purpose; they have got his voting shares away from him, and are the masters of his companies. Six months of desperate struggle, with every kind of pretense and chicanery that highly trained experts can invent, and they have won. Now we shall see just what their purpose was, and how sincere were their fine professions of altruism and dignity.

The companies now have a new head, and that is Harley L. Clarke of Chicago. We have already met the gentleman, but inasmuch as he has become so very important, let us go back, and remind ourselves that he first came to W. F. with a letter of introduction from Harry Stuart, which Stuart afterwards told W. F. he didn't really mean. Said Stuart: "If I know that bird, he will want more than that before long." And sure enough, the "bird" did want more, and persuaded W. F. to go in 50-50 on Fox Grandeur.

W. F. tells me of a German friend who came to this country, and was to meet Clarke, and was asked to form a judgment of Clarke's character, and reported: "Er ist ein Actienhaendler;" he is a share-dealer. A rather short man, stockily built, with a round sort of moon-face. Says W. F.: "When he talks to you, he rarely looks at you. He has a habit of indicating to you how clever he is; and also he has a peculiar habit of snorting. I don't think there is anything wrong with his nostrils or lungs, it is a nervous habit, and usually comes after he has made a point. He is the type of fellow it is easy to like. He has made himself popular. He is not the type of man that you can offend. He will take anything. He knows that I don't like him, but he has never given any indication of resenting it."

Six years back, according to the word of his lawyer, Harley

Clarke had been "broke." In six years he had acquired huge utility companies at home and abroad. Wiggin, his partner, and a chain of bond-houses—Pynchon, Hammons, West—had made huge fortunes out of his deals, and expected to make more. Clarke was president of the Utilities Power & Light Corporation, and had Insull for a partner. It was a $500,000,000 company, controlled in the most extraordinary way, by three shares of voting stock, the total market value of which was $9.

You can judge from this that Clarke has no conscientious scruples against voting shares. We have heard the high-priced lawyers denouncing the wickedness of the Fox for controlling his companies with voting shares representing only 5 per cent of the outstanding stock—perhaps $2,000,000 of market value controlling $40,000,000. But here is Clarke with $9 controlling half a billion! Also Clarke has his General Theatres Equipment Corporation, controlled by three shares of stock, a trusteeship with Clarke and two of his men.

This last named concern has grown out of Clarke's manufacture of projection machines. He has taken his International Projector Company, and merged it into a huge concern called National Theatres Supply, and in turn he has merged this into a still bigger concern, General Theatres Equipment, which controls everything in the field. 1,800,000 shares of this concern were issued; their high point was $66 a share, a total of $120,-000,000. 1,400,000 shares were kept for Clarke himself. Says W. F.:

"General Theatres Equipment was nothing more nor less than a bag of wind; the real intrinsic value of those shares, in accordance with the assets of the companies, was not more than $1 a share. It was Clarke's idea in buying the Fox companies to give a real substance and foundation to General Theatres Equipment. It was this concern, and not Clarke personally, which bought my voting shares, and it was in the name of this concern that the new financing was done."

Of course the news of the deal was in the papers at once, and very soon Harley Clarke announced his plans for financing. In so doing he revealed what he had been after all through those six months, while he had been sending A. C. Blumenthal and Will H. Hays and other eminent negotiators to the Fox. Then he and his bankers and his lawyers had made pretenses, but now they told, in plain figures. Money talks!

We are about to enter the top-most realms of high finance. I wish I could make it simple and easy but there is no way to do so, for the reason that those who contrive these financial laby-rinths deliberately make them difficult of understanding. About all I can say is that there is no need for you to follow all these twistings and windings, and unless you are a specialist in finan-cial tricks, you can run your eye over the pages to get the main point, which is the amount of profits which Clarke and his crowd took from the Fox stockholders and investing public.

You will remember that Fox Theatres had purchased a total of 660,900 shares of the Loew company, paying them $75,000,000. W. F. has been accused both in the newspapers and in court of having committed an act of absurd extravagance, because the block of 400,000 shares purchased from the Loew estate cost far more than the market price at the time. The critics overlooked or concealed the fact that this block carried control of the com-pany, and you cannot buy control at the market price; the moment you start to buy control, you force the price up to the skies.

Clarke has now decided that Fox Film is to purchase the Loew shares from Fox Theatres, paying the full cost price. The latter concern had borrowed $17,000,000 from the former for the making of the original purchase, and that sum is now to be wiped out. In addition, Fox Film will pay Fox Theatres $10,000,000 in cash and $48,000,000 in the form of 1,600,000 shares of Fox Film A stock at $30 per share. Clarke will then purchase these 1,600,000 shares from Fox Theatres, paying $48,000,000 in cash, and with this amount Fox Theatres will pay off its obligations: $15,000,000 plus interest to the Telephone Company; $12,000,000 plus interest to Halsey, Stuart; $10,000,000 plus interest to Greenfield's Philadelphia company; and the balance to various bankers.

That is all very pleasant and friendly; everybody gets his money and is happy. But why that sleight-of-hand of having Fox Film take the Loew stock, in exchange for its shares issued to Fox Theatres? If it is desired to have Fox Film own the Loew stock, why not sell Fox Film stock to the public, and use the money thus obtained to buy the Loew shares? The answer to that tells you what this whole fight has been about. The great financier from Chicago and his partner, the great Wiggin of Chase Bank, have a trick in mind, whereby they will take unto themselves the prosperity of the Fox companies, and make the investing public pay them two and a half times the price they are paying W. F. for his voting shares.

Yes, they are ousting the man who has had the bad habit of sharing his profits with his stockholders. There is to be a new deal now, and prosperity is to be for the bankers. In October, 1929, the shares of Fox Film were costing over $100 in the market, and by six months of lawsuits and injunctions and similar actions, plus slanders and scandals, they have been beaten down to a low price of $16 on January 3, 1930. But the bankers know perfectly well the true value of those shares, as represented by the assets; they know that the shares have a book value of not less than $75. They know that as soon as word goes out that the great Chase Bank of New York and the great utilities magnate of Chicago have taken charge of the Fox companies, the shares will start to rise. There is no gamble whatever about it. Within three weeks after the ousting of Fox, Fox Film has gone to $57. And who is going to get the benefit of this? Are the stockholders and the investing public going to get it? The answer is, not on the life of Harley L. Clarke and Albert H. Wiggin!

Under the terms of the Fox Film stock issues, the shareholders had what is called a pre-emptory right to new issues: that is to say, whenever it was proposed to increase the capital of the company, the stockholders had the first chance to take the new shares at the price of offering. There was no way to get around that—at least, there wasn't supposed to be, but what are Wall Street lawyers for? The idea of letting the stockholders purchase for $30 shares which were going to sell for $57 in three weeks—such an idea is absolutely intolerable to the Clarkes and the Wiggins of Wall Street.

So they invented the shrewd little trick above mentioned. Fox Film did not offer the shares for sale; no, it turned them over to Fox Theatres, as part of the price of the Loew shares, and Fox Theatres then sold them to Harley L. Clarke and his financiers! Just as simple as that! What it meant was that Clarke and the rest of the financiers had a profit of $27 per share, or more than $43,000,000 on the transaction. Of this they paid a total of $18,000,000 to the Fox, and the rest was a clean net profit of $25,000,000 on the whole deal. And that was what they had been after for six months! That was what the high-priced lawyers had been arguing for, and being so very dignified and pious about!

At least that was part of it; we shall see in just a moment what else. First let us hear the story of W. F.'s share in that particular bit of financiering magic:

"My 20 per cent participation had now become a sort of important document. I had a letter from Clarke providing that I participate in any financing done by either of the Fox companies. Twenty per cent of 1,600,000 shares of stock gave me a right to purchase 320,000 of these shares, at $30 a share, or $9,600,000. Nor was there any stipulation in this letter that after I had purchased them, I wouldn't have the right to sell them; I wasn't restricted. 320,000 shares at $57 per share is $18,240,000. After Fox delivered his check for $9,600,000, he would get shares which, if the market held up, he could sell for $18,240,000. It was well worth not signing the contract that Sunday morning at 10 o'clock, but making a new arrangement Sunday afternoon and evening, and signing the contract on Monday!

"Of course, we demanded our 320,000 shares of stock; but Clarke said we weren't entitled to that much. He said: 'I didn't give you a letter in which you had a 20 per cent participation. The letter I gave you was that you would have a 10 per cent participation, and that I, Clarke, would do everything in my power to get you 10 per cent more.' That was right. That's how the letter read. But he didn't have to exert much power to give me the other 10 per cent. He was in control of the situation, and therefore I had construed the letter to mean that I was entitled to 320,000 shares of stock. Clarke had told me that of the 1,600,000 shares of stock required, 540,000 were distributed among all the bankers. Clarke's company really had retained only 1,160,000 shares, and so he said I was entitled to 10 per cent of 1,160,000.

"I decided I would get legal advice, and have someone construe this letter. Samuel Untermyer contended that the maximum shares I was entitled to was 20 per cent of 1,160,000; that

if Clarke had to give 540,000 shares away, I, being associated
with Clarke in this enterprise, would have to give my shares
along with it. Reass contended that I was entitled to 320,000
shares of stock. We got other legal opinions. A firm in Philadelphia thought we were entitled to about 260,000 shares of
stock. I visited George Wharton Pepper, one of the outstanding
lawyers in Philadelphia, described this thing to him, and he
thought I was entitled to 320,000 shares. While this talk was
going on, the stock was fluctuating between $50 and $57. We
had advised Clarke we were making a tender of $9,600,000 and
we wanted 320,000 shares of stock. This controversy was continued until August 13, and finally settled by General Theatres
Equipment paying me $3,000,000 for the claim that Clarke had
given me."

In order to get part of the $48,000,000 it was paying in cash
to Fox Theatres, General Theatres Equipment sold $30,000,000
of its own bonds. This issue was underwritten by the Chase
Bank and by Hammons & Company of Boston, a great investment house. The commission on this deal was three points, or
$900,000. W. F. does not know exactly what was the relation-
ship of the Chase Bank to this deal; he only knows that the certified check for $15,000,000 which he got from Clarke was a
check on the Chase Bank; and a year later, when the bank had
quarreled with Clarke, Clarke told him that Wiggin had been his
full partner, and that the two of them had been using the funds
of the Chase Bank for the Fox deal.

The second form of financing was that General Theatres
Equipment sold 433,000 shares of its common stock at $48.50
per share. This issue was underwritten by two great investment
firms, Pynchon & Company of New York, and West & Company
of Philadelphia, with the Chase Bank again holding the bag, as
they call it. The commission of the selling group on this deal
was $3 per share, or $1,300,000. As the selling group managers
were also members of the syndicate which purchased these shares,
it is to be supposed that another large profit was made. You see
how these financiers buy something with their right hand and
sell it to their left, and thus they make two profits, and the first
is not disclosed.

These two financial jobs netted General Theatres Equipment

the $48,000,000 paid to Fox Theatres for the 1,600,000 shares of Fox Film stock. A total of 440,000 of these shares went to the syndicate which underwrote the deal. G. T. E. got 1,160,000 shares. And when they came to list the shares with the New York Exchange, as required by the rules, they listed only 1,000,-000 shares. The "application to list" states that the full price was paid for 1,000,000 shares of Fox Film; and the rest were gone—slipped into somebody's pocket!

Nor is that all. The condensed balance sheet of General Theatres Equipment, issued at the end of 1929, shows 1,955,000 shares of stock in the hands of the public. The "pro forma" balance sheet, which covers the acquisition of the Fox companies, states that there are now 2,847,000 shares issued. That means an increase of 892,000 shares. But only 433,000 new shares were accounted for by the Fox deal; so it appears that 459,000 shares were issued without being accounted for. To be sure, there were $6,000,000 in bonds retired, and these may have been converted into stock. That might account for 150,000 or 200,000 shares. But there is left somewhere between 220,000 and 270,000 shares, a matter of $10,000,000 or $15,000,000, which, so W. F. declares, disappeared without trace.

The generous bankers were determined to supply the Fox companies with great quantities of money; the public was in a buying mood, the bankers in a selling mood, and Harley Clarke would know what to do with the money. So the Fox Film Corporation proceeded to issue $55,000,000 worth of one-year notes. This time Halsey, Stuart and the Chase Bank did not call in any outsiders to share in the financing. They had some kind of fight with the Lehman group—W. F. does not know the inside story, but only the results, that each of the group, Lehman Brothers, Bancamerica-Blair, and Dillon, Read & Company, received $1,600,000 in cash without performing any further service. The $55,000,000 worth of notes were underwritten and offered by Halsey, Stuart and the Chase Bank, for a commission of $680,000. In addition to that, according to the "application list," the bankers got a bonus in the form of warrants to purchase 300,000 shares of Fox Film at $35 at any time during the next three years. If they exercised this right three weeks after the deal was made, they had a profit at the market price of $22 per share, or $6,600,-

000. Of course if they waited for further rises, they lost out. I am informed that the Telephone Company had to take $8,000,-000 worth of these notes, and that they lost out.

The best way of telling this story will be to follow these financial deals through to the end, even though it involves skipping over other important matters. All these financiers, operating in the spring of 1930, were certain that prosperity was coming back, and that they were going to have another grand and glorious "bull market." Instead, they had more panics, slumps, and a seemingly permanent depression. The Fox had got away with at least a part of his skin—$15,000,000 in actual cash, $3,000,000 in notes from Clarke, and the promise of a check from Fox Film to the amount of $41,666.66⅔ per month for five years. But the men who had hung him up and skinned him—well, let him tell the tale, and why he has such an abiding faith in a God Almighty who looks out for the punishing of his enemies!

First, the great firm of Hammons & Co. of Boston, which joined the Chase Bank in underwriting $30,000,000 worth of General Theatre Equipment bonds. Says W. F.: "There evidently was not a ready market for these bonds. There may have been a resentment by the investors against the attitude of Halsey, Stuart, Clarke, and the Chase Bank as against Fox. The result was that the syndicate met with reverses, and a large percentage of these bonds were never purchased by the public. The syndicate had the bonds hypothecated with their banks, and when these bonds declined in value, they were asked to put up more margin, and when Hammons & Co. could furnish no more margin, they were obliged to declare themselves bankrupt. It has been told to me that the Chase Bank now owns more than one-half of those bonds. The members of the great firm of Hammons & Co. of Boston were pauperized by that deal."

And second, the deal for the marketing of 433,000 shares of General Theatres Equipment stock at $48.50 a share: the Chase Bank "held the bag" for this also, and two great firms were wrecked by it. One was West & Co. of Philadelphia, one of the oldest banking-houses in the country, having been organized one year after the signing of the Declaration of Independence. The other was Pynchon & Co. of New York. This firm had twenty-eight partners, all of them men of wealth and most of them men of family. The firm had $20,000,000 capital, and at the opening of 1930 found itself with $20,000,000 of surplus which was divided among the partners. But then came this deal in General Theatres Equipment stock, and it was a terrible trap.

"General Theatres Equipment had already outstanding some 2,000,000 shares of stock, which was pegged at 48¾ a share; and if 433,000 additional shares were to be distributed to the public, the market would have to be maintained at all hazards. General Theatres Equipment, Harley Clarke, Chase Bank, Pynchon & Co., West & Co. were the syndicate that did the stock-market manipulating. As the general market kept declining, the job of pegging grew harder. A meeting of the Pynchon firm was called and each of the partners was asked to repay the $20,000,-000 that had been divided among them. They did put it back. I learned from fairly reliable sources that Pynchon, the head of this firm, had many years before presented his daughter with an elegant home on Long Island. When this difficulty came he requested her to permit him to raise a $300,000 mortgage against this home, which he did. When the final blow came, the $20,000,-000 of capital, the $20,000,000 of surplus, the money secured by the mortgage on this property, all was wiped out, and there was a liability over and above assets of thirty or forty million dollars.

"I am told that the day it was announced that Pynchon & Co. had been stricken from the membership of the New York Stock Exchange and their dealings no longer could pass, this incident occurred: One of Pynchon's partners, by the merest chance, had made a provision for an annuity, by which he was to receive $20,000 a year; and now Pynchon put his hand in his pocket, drew out of it a five-dollar bill and two singles, and calling this man by his first name, said: 'This is all I have left in the world. From now on it will be your responsibility to support me.' That's how thoroughly Clarke had done this job and ruined these men. All were heavy borrowers of the Chase Bank, and the Chase Bank took it on the chin."

And now for the greatest bank in the world, and its greatest chairman, Albert H. Wiggin, who had gone in with his partner, Harley L. Clarke, to take over the Fox companies. There were, you recall, $55,000,000 worth of one-year gold notes, issued by

Fox Film and underwritten by Chase Bank and Halsey, Stuart
& Co. In the course of that year, Harry Stuart observed how
Harley Clarke was running the companies, and he had time to
realize that this was the same Harley Clarke against whom he
had once warned the Fox. He didn't like the way things were
going, and he backed out.

"Long before the first year had expired there was a complete disagreement between Stuart and Clarke, and Stuart
announced to the Chase Bank that unless Clarke was removed
from control of these companies, the firm of Halsey, Stuart
would not renew the $55,000,000 worth of notes. The Chase
Securities Corporation defended Clarke, because Albert Wiggin
always was a partner of Clarke. The result was that when the
year rolled around, and it rolled around pretty fast, the Chase
Securities Corporation undertook to do the refinancing of the
$55,000,000 without the aid of Halsey, Stuart. The Chase Bank
then was obliged to refinance this money, and Fox Film in April,
1931, sold $35,000,000 worth of two or three-year bonds. The
West Coast Theatres Company in California hypothecated their
stock, and the Chase Bank loaned against it $15,000,000; another
$10,000,000 was raised in some other way; the total was about
$60,000,000. Subtracting from it the cost of the financing, this
netted the company enough to repay the $55,000,000 of notes sold
a year previously.

"The activities of Halsey, Stuart in driving Fox out of the
picture, putting Clarke in his stead, and then deserting Clarke,
resulted in all the bonds previously sold by Halsey, Stuart for the
subsidiaries of Fox Theatres being destroyed. Here are $40,-
000 worth of bonds, which were worth a full $40,000,000 in
November, 1929, and the market value of these bonds today is
probably less than $5,000,000. Of course, that doesn't hurt Hal-
sey, Stuart any, because it was not their money that was invested,
it was the money of their clients. It cost the clients of Halsey,
Stuart about $35,000,000 to give Stuart the pleasure of knowing
he had driven Fox out of business.

"With the retirement of Halsey, Stuart out of the financing
of the Fox enterprise, the duty and obligation to keep these companies in funds fell entirely upon the shoulders of the Chase
Securities Corporation. This concern was affiliated to the Chase

Bank, and the say as to how it should be conducted and run, to whom it should loan its money, what companies it should finance, was practically in the hands of one man, Albert Wiggin. This resulted in Chase Securities and Chase Bank having almost $100,-000,000 of their capital tied up in these Fox companies. When Fox controlled the companies, it gave the Chase Bank much worry to have $400,000 tied up in such enterprises. But now that Fox was no longer a part of these companies, it was a pleasure for Chase Bank and Chase Securities to have $100,000,000 tied up. More than one-third of the total capital of the largest bank in America tied up in one enterprise, owned and controlled by three shares of stock, the market value of which is a little more than a dollar, owned by Albert Wiggin's partner and buddy, Harley Clarke of Chicago—that is a perfectly proper piece of business!

"When the Fox was captured by Wiggin and Clarke, the 7,200,000 shares of stock of the Chase Bank had a market value of upwards of a billion dollars. The shares were more than $150 a share. But the hunt for Fox and his capture was not kept a secret. Everybody in New York knew about it. It didn't take long for everyone throughout the nation to know that $100,000,-000 worth of capital belonging to the Chase Bank and Chase Securities was tied up in this enterprise, and that the enterprise was being mismanaged and destroyed. It didn't take the people of New York long to know that with the crash of Hammons, West, and Pynchon, the Chase Bank was materially affected. No one talked about it loudly, for Wiggin was almighty; but it became a whispering campaign. What does the Chase Bank want with these Fox enterprises? What was this all about? And soon these Chase Bank shares began to decline, and people began to withdraw their deposits.

"In April, 1930, the deposits, capital and surplus of Chase Bank had reached more than $2,000,000,000. No longer were the great English banks to be the largest in the world—America had taken their place with the Chase Bank. But today we find that six or seven hundred million dollars have been withdrawn, and we find the shares of stock which had market value in 1930 of well over a billion dollars, today are worth about $175,000,000. Eight or nine hundred million dollars is the depreciation of those shares!

When we look at the Chase Bank's capital and surplus and undivided profits in 1930, and compare them with the figures now, we find that forty or fifty million dollars have been taken from the surplus, and these adventures of Albert Wiggin were being paid for not only by Wiggin, but by the stockholders of the Chase Bank.

"You will recall how my friend, Colonel Huston, had his Christmas dinner in 1929 with Wiggin at his home, and next day Wiggin sent word to Huston that he resented the interference by the administration in behalf of Fox. Wiggin was mightier than the President of the United States on that Christmas day. Chairman of the board of the largest bank in America, knowing that he must depend upon favors by the administration, knowing that the administration could be, and probably was, its largest depository, knowing that his bank was a member of the Federal Reserve system, he yet had the audacity to send word to the Chief Executive of the United States: 'I resent your interference in behalf of Fox—mind your own business!' It takes a lot of courage to do that. Yes, he must have felt his power as the Kaiser did before the war!"

This was spoken by William Fox in the spring of 1932. In January of 1933, as this book is going to the printer, the great Albert Wiggin retires from the Chase Bank, and young Rockefeller's brother-in-law, Winthrop W. Aldrich, is in control.

REEL TWENTY-SIX

THE BUSINESS OF LOOT

WE HAVE followed the fortunes of the Fox financiers. Let us now return to the date of the purchase, and follow the inside story of a motion picture enterprise under the management of a public utilities magnate.

Clarke and Wiggin, controlling the B shares of Fox Film and Fox Theatres, turned out most of the old directors. They kept Sheehan; also they kept the Fox, because that was written in the bargain. W. F. only attended one directors' meeting, and could never get word when another was to be held. They put in three stock market operators, and made Harley Clarke president of both Fox Film and Fox Theatres.

W. F. explains to me again and again that he did not take a petty attitude towards this new regime. The companies still bore his name, and he had promised the old stockholders that he would do everything he could for them. He thought he was going to be chairman of an advisory board, and was really going to have something to say. He was so sure of it that he bought a lot of Fox stock, and got stuck, along with everybody else.

He began his duties at once. He called upon Clarke, and impressed upon him the great importance of one problem in the activities of his companies—the contracts made with exhibitors for the use of film. That was the one source of income of Fox Film in the United States, and if that was impaired, everything was gone. Says W. F.:

"From the creation of Fox Film until the time I had my accident in July, 1929, it was not possible for any motion picture owner in America to use the pictures made by Fox Film without the contract that gave him that right being submitted to me. For if the contracts entered into were not properly scrutinized, passed on, and approved, it would be a perfectly simple

315

matter for those who were in charge of creating the relationship between theatre owner and Fox Film to enrich themselves.

"These relationships had been created at the beginning of Fox Film. Salesmen were engaged and dismissed, film exchange managers were hired and fired, but all of that made no difference to me. I knew by practical experience what each exhibitor throughout the United States could afford to pay for the use of our pictures, and it was my job to see that an equitable contract was made by Fox Film with its exhibitor customers.

"I told Clarke of the importance of this work; I explained to him that unless an experienced person handled that department of supervising the contractual relationship, there would result serious difficulties for the company. I told him how I guarded that spot in our business—the heart of our corporation. I offered to assist in the passing on these contracts, as an additional duty not called for in the contract between Fox Film and myself. I described to Clarke how simple it would be for salesmen and exchange managers to make private deals with exhibitors, and that such deals would be made if the sales organization realized that the person who had safeguarded the company against such danger was no longer with the company. I was willing to protect the company without further compensation, although the task would take at least one-third of a person's time.

"There is no system at present known by which you can measure what the fair charge should be for the use of pictures made by any film company to its exhibitors. It is different from any other manufacturing line I know of; in any other line there is a standardized price, but in the leasing of motion pictures to a theatre there is no such price. Every possible and conceivable condition must be taken into account in establishing this relationship; the number of seats a theatre has, the price of admission, the competition that it has, and your own competition. There are so many ramifications that it really takes almost a life study to enable a person to arrange these contracts so that they will be equitable both to the theatre owner and the film leasing company."

And how did the utilities magnate from Chicago receive these suggestions? He answered that he understood the matter very

well, the importance of these contracts; he was going to pass
upon them himself. W. F. remarks sarcastically: "Of course
he must have thought this was about the same kind of job as
reading a gas meter, or one for water or light." W. F. is
extremely contemptuous on the subject of readers of gas, water
and light meters presuming to enter the business of manufacturing motion pictures and managing theatres. He thinks they
are quite different businesses, and every time he finds a gas,
water or light man making a mess of a moving picture concern,
he exhausts his vocabulary of scorn. He tells me how Clarke
had an elaborate study made of the two Fox companies, and all
the results were embodied in a set of huge volumes; but this
information stayed in the volumes, and never got into the head
of any executive.

In the days when W. F. was in charge, "it was the law that
not a dozen packages of pins be purchased without a competitive
bid." Also it was the law that no commission was paid to anyone, in the purchases of $30,000,000 worth of merchandise. Says
W. F.: "Up to the end of my regime, no manager of one of
these theatres had power to buy 10 cents worth of merchandise.
It was all purchased at the home office by what we called the
meanest man in the world. He would argue longer about a
tenth of 1 per cent additional discount on the balance if you
paid it promptly than any other human could argue. He is the
type of man the newspapers have to check up the reporters'
expense accounts."

But now all this was changed over night. The Fox companies were no longer going to be run to save money for the
Fox and the Fox stockholders; they were going to be run to
provide income for National Theatres Supply, a wholly owned
subsidiary of General Theatres Equipment, controlled by the
voting shares of Clarke and Wiggin. Fox Film had been supplied with $55,000,000 worth of spending money, and the orders
now were to spend it freely for the benefit of the other Clarke
companies. Says W. F.:

"One of the new executives installed by Clarke, a man who
was proficient in reading gas, water and light meters, called
together the managers of Fox Theatres in New York and
announced to them: 'Gentlemen, the company has $15,000,000

in cash in the bank.' This man, formerly a utility man and now an official of the Fox company, said: 'The system of buying everything through a purchasing agent is at an end. Every man is responsible for his own theatre. No more checking at the home office. We have $15,000,000 in the bank—go to it. You boys go and replenish your theatres, and place your orders through the National Theatres Supply.'

"One theatre manager came to me and said: 'I was at that meeting, but my building was in such fine shape I couldn't spend a dollar to improve it. I was sent for. "Didn't you hear the instructions? You haven't spent anything." I said: "But I have nothing to spend it for—I have no occasion." The answer was: "We don't want the buildings in fine shape as under the Fox regime. We want them superfine, as under the Clarke regime. You go on and do something." I realized I would lose my job if I didn't. Only six months before this there had been laid in my theatre the finest carpet in New York. I notified them I needed new carpet, so they took up my carpet and laid down another at cost plus 15 per cent.' "

All the way down the line, stories like that kept coming to W. F. Out in California there was a theatre manager who ordered a marquee, one of those things like a canopy which make a cover for the sidewalk. He ordered it independently, making a good bargain; but a few days later the New York office got wind of the matter and forced him to cancel his order. It should have been placed through National Theatres Supply. So he placed it that way, and the marquee was billed to him at the price which he had formerly arranged, plus 15 per cent commission for National Theatres Supply.

And then there was Franklin, manager of West Coast Theatres, now transformed to "Wesco." Franklin was running something over 500 theatres in eleven states west of the Rocky mountains, and he was sent for by Harley Clarke and they had a row. Says W. F.:

"That I am sure is a fact, because I met Franklin as he came out of Clarke's office. I met him in the corridor, and Franklin told me he had just had a conference with Clarke, a terrific controversy with him. He did not tell me what the controversy was about. Later I learned what it was by rumors, and yesterday the story was told to me again, and it is for that reason I am telling it now. In this meeting between Clarke and Franklin, Clarke informed him that he wanted this group of theatres on the West Coast to be promptly reconditioned, and Clarke estimated that Franklin would be obliged to spend between four and five million dollars. Franklin protested, and said the expenditure was wholly unnecessary; that these theatres had been kept spick and span and up-to-date, and he protested particularly that the charge of four or five million dollars would destroy the profit that Wesco would make, and therefore he would suffer to the extent of the 10 per cent of which his contract called for of the profits made by Wesco. I am told that Clarke became very angry and said, 'I will order it done without you,' and Franklin reminded him that he, Franklin, was the president of Wesco, and that he would not sign a single requisition. Clarke insisted that Franklin do this job, and order these new furnishings and equipment from the National Theatres Supply.

"Franklin finally took this position: 'If you want it done, I will do it, but on one condition: that it be not subtracted from the profits of the company, so that it doesn't affect me personally. You have a right to do it if you will, because you are in control of the present company. If you want to affect its profits, that's your business.' On that very day Franklin's contract was abrogated by mutual consent, in consideration of which Franklin received $500,000 of the company's money. The fact of the abrogation I heard from both Franklin and Clarke; and as to the amount paid for the abrogation, Franklin told me he had received approximately $500,000, perhaps a little more or a little less.

"It is fair to assume that after Franklin stepped out, these theatres were reconditioned, and the work was done by National Theatres Supply; that is, the work was done by the regular merchants, but instead of the contract being made between those merchants and Wesco it was now made between those merchants and National Theatres Supply, and National Theatres Supply made its contract with Wesco."

I have told you of Clarke's statement to W. F., that he would not trust those executives of the companies who had turned against W. F. I have told how he put a padlock on the door of

22

Saul E. Rogers. One by one he got rid of the others. Sheehan went away for two years for his health, and has only just come back. The two Leos, brothers-in-law of W. F., were retained for a short while; then Clarke paid them for a year without giving them anything to do, and finally settled in cash for the remainder of their contracts. Says W. F.:

"There are now more executives—more vice-presidents, more officials, more wholly inexperienced, incompetent people in charge of performing duties that they never understood and never could understand. In numbers there are five to one; there were eight under my regime, and they have at least forty now."

Under such a regime the surplus funds of course were quickly got rid of. The operating expenses of Fox Film jumped more than $12,000,000 in 1930. Rumors of trouble began to come to W. F., and he couldn't see why that advisory board, of which he was to be chairman, was never appointed, and never held any meetings. He kept writing and urging, but it wasn't until October that the board came into existence. It consisted of W. F., Clarke, and Clarke's attorney, Otto Koegel, who meantime had been taken into the firm of Hughes, Schurman & Dwight. As a reward for their services in turning Fox Films and Fox Theatres over to Clarke, the Hughes firm had become counsel for both companies, an important job; and Koegel was taken into this firm as a part of the deal.

Clarke and Koegel were supposed to meet with W. F. and give him a chance to advise them. On October 11, 1930, W. F. wrote as follows:

"My dear Harley: Now that I have been elected chairman of the advisory committee of the Fox Film Corporation in conformity with the contract dated April 5, 1930, between myself and General Theatres Equipment Corporation, I have been considering the various problems of the company, and the most effective way in which I can give to you and to Fox Film Corporation the benefit of my knowledge and experience.

"Each production is a sure key to all of the business mysteries of the art. To the trained eye, the picture reveals with extraordinary precision every dollar that went into it. An examination of the usual itemization of its cost accompanying the delivery of each production will, conversely, clearly indicate leakages, over-expenditures, and other forms of needless extravagance. In a word, the major operations of the production department can be even more closely checked by an inspection of the film produced and the cost itemization than by a final audit of the department. The relation which cost bears to income and profit need not be emphasized to you.

"I am not certain that this comes within the sphere of my duties as they may be defined. If it does, I feel that I can give you an unerring check on the business of the company, which I am certain will prove of inestimable benefit to you and the company.

"My suggestion is that immediately upon the arrival of each production, it be sent to me at Woodmere with an itemization of its cost. I have a private projection room where I can give the picture appropriate study and analyze it with reference to its cost.

"If you entertain any lingering doubt as to the efficacy of this method, try it. You will get results that will prove amazing to you, as it has proven to others who have made similar tests.

"I am glad to know that the suggestion recently given to you and Mr. Koegel is now in process of adoption.

"Please understand that I am at all times ready to give you the benefit of any aid or assistance that you might require in your problems. You may regard this as an invitation to you to call upon me at any time to serve both you and the company in fostering the business of the Film Corporation. You will always find me available either at my Woodmere home or at my New York residence."

To this came a courteous answer on October 20:

"My dear Bill: I have your kind offer of the 11th inst., and shall soon avail myself of it. Just at present I am completing my studies of production, embracing all pictures of four companies for the past four years. The results are most interesting and have pointed the way to many economies already in force and many to come.

"Again let me say, I appreciate your friendly spirit of co-operation and remain,

"Sincerely yours,

Harley."

On December 4, W. F. wrote again; and so it went on until May 8, 1931. I quote a letter from W. F. bearing that date:

"My dear Harley: I have repeatedly written to you requesting meetings of the advisory board to meet some of the very vitally important problems which confronted the company from time to time (see my letters dated October 11, 1930, November 27, 1930, December 4, 1930 and April 28, 1931) and I have otherwise urged the necessity of permitting me to advise with you in the handling of matters that I deemed of vital concern to the Fox companies and their stockholders.

"It is not difficult for me to understand why I have been carefully excluded from all participation in these activities and why there was carefully concealed from me the execution of important matters that are now coming to light.

"As you know, I have in addition to my contract, a very substantial stock interest in the affairs of the company and its welfare is a matter of great importance to me in common with that of other stockholders.

"The fact is that both as a director and as chairman of an advisory board, I have been carefully barred from any knowledge of the inside operations of the company.

"I advised against a contract which, in my opinion, subjected the company to a needless loss of over $1,000,000 per year.

"The making of a license contract with the Western Electric for fifteen years, in view of the fact that Fox Film acquired the right to use the Tri-Ergon patents, was and is in my opinion a reckless waste of company money, wholly without any benefit. This was done over my vigorous protest.

"I warned you last October that production costs in my opinion were grossly excessive and I suggested a simple method by which I could check them. No attention whatsoever was paid to that, although as I anticipated, the failure to do it involves the company in an enormous loss which you had a ready means to avoid.

"Your well known policy of keeping efficient and experienced men who are under high salaried contracts in idleness while the work they are being paid to do is left in the hands of others, is an unnecessary duplication of expenditure that cannot escape criticism.

"There are other matters of equal importance, to which my attention has been recently called, that must be remedied.

"I repeat, it is not difficult for me to understand why I have been entirely excluded from activities of the business. Information is being brought to me daily of huge and meaningless expenditures and methods of operation that are seriously prejudicing the interest of stockholders.

"I am not now in the humor of politely asking for a meeting of the advisory committee. I am now demanding that such meeting be had at once. The fact is that you and Mr. Koegel are the other two members of the committee and without you, I cannot hold the meeting, else I would have held one long ago.

"I expect an immediate response."

The soft answer turneth away wrath, we are told; and we have been told by W. F. that Clarke is a man not easy to offend. We find him on May 9 making a soft answer to his "dear Bill." He is "somewhat grieved and not a little surprised" at the attitude shown by his friend. He tells his "dear Bill" that he has made repeated attempts to get him on the telephone. "On many occasions I have tried to reach you." From the 14th to the 25th of April, he called every day, twice a day, from New York or Chicago. W. F. says there is something suspicious about a business man who calls another man so often on the telephone, and never takes the trouble to write him a letter or send him a telegram, to have a record of the procedure. W. F. says that he never had any word from his employes that Clarke was trying to get him.

Clarke proceeded to make an appointment for a meeting of the advisory board during that week. Two meetings were held, but W. F. could get none of his plans adopted. On June 15, I find W. F. writing to Wiggin and Aldrich of the Chase National Bank, telling them that he has learned from the newspapers that he has not been re-elected as a member of the board of directors of Fox Film, and as they now control the voting shares, he reminds them that when he sold these shares, it was stipulated as a condition of the sale that the purchaser would procure the election and re-election of W. F. as a director for a period of five years from May 1, 1930. Said W. F. to the Chase Bank:

"It is said that the Class B stock of Fox Film Corporation

has now passed into the possession and control of your institution as part of an approximately $100,000,000 financing of Clarke enterprises. If that is true, accountability for the non-observance of the conditions of the sale and transfer of the Class B stock rests with you.

"In reliance upon the observation of these conditions I have acquired a very substantial block of Class A stock of Fox Film Corporation which I thought I was in a position to protect. My attitude with respect to that is reflected in the annexed correspondence which I recently had with Mr. Clarke and of which you are doubtless not informed."

W. F. asked for an appointment to discuss this matter, but he did not get it. I asked him why he did not take legal steps to enforce his rights; to which he answered: "What good would it have done? I had no power to prevent the things they were doing, and I could only have sat there and been unhappy at the spectacle."

You will note in the correspondence with Harley Clarke the reference to the Tri-Ergon patents. Fox Film was paying Western Electric, which was the Telephone Company and our old friends Otterson and Gifford, a million dollars a year for a license. But now, W. F. had granted to Fox Film a license under the Tri-Ergon patents, and W. F. was taking the position that the payments to the Telephone Company were unnecessary. Do you remember that scene in court, when Pratt, the counsel for Otterson, insisted that the Telephone Company was not satisfied to get back its $15,000,000 plus interest from the Fox companies, but also wanted an opportunity to run the Fox companies, in order to make certain that these companies would carry out satisfactorily a fifteen-year contract with the Telephone Company, which Pratt incorrectly stated had been signed. Now you see how the Telephone Company has accomplished its purpose; it has ousted the Fox, and put in Harley Clarke, and Clarke has signed this contract and is carrying it out. Winthrop W. Aldrich, of the Chase Bank, is a director of the Telephone Company.

There were several other suggestions made by W. F. which were wholly unsatisfactory to a utility magnate in charge of moving picture making. For example, W. F. called attention to the fact that there exists a Foxthal Company, in which Fox Theatres has a 50 per cent ownership. The other half is owned by A. C. Blumenthal, and Blumenthal owes the Foxthal Company close to $3,000,000, of which Fox Theatres should have half. W. F. makes the suggestion that Fox Theatres should collect that money, but he learns that Fox Theatres is not interested to collect it; on the contrary, it has paid an extra $500,000 to Blumy. This, of course, was part of the deal which was made with Blumy, for helping in the ousting of W. F. There was supposed to be an advisory committee of Fox Theatres, as well as of Fox Film, but this committee was never named, and W. F. was never invited to a session.

Of course this collapse of Fox Theatres was in the midst of a general collapse of business, and can't all be attributed to Wiggin and Clarke and Stuart and Otterson! But W. F. thinks he would have known how to deal with this period of recession. He points out the record which Fox Film made through the panic years of 1920 and 1921, doing the largest business in its history. The recent spell would have been a test of his mettle, and one thing that grieves him is that he was deprived of the chance to show what he could do to keep his ship afloat through the hurricane. How much more he would have enjoyed that than the melancholy satisfaction of pointing out the blunders of Harley Clarke!

REEL TWENTY-SEVEN

EMPTY SHELLS

WE have witnessed in detail the process of looting two prosperous business concerns. Let us now survey the results of this wrecking enterprise, clearly revealed in the financial statements issued by Harley L. Clarke and his successors in control. These statements have been carefully prepared by experts, and are meant to hide as much as possible; but our Fox takes them and strips away the verbiage and the trickeries. He says:

"Please bear in mind that the raiding party which looted the Fox companies never claimed that the liabilities of these companies were more than $91,000,000. That $91,000,000 liability was naturally reduced at least by the last quarter's earnings of 1929, which were more than $5,000,000; and was likewise reduced by the amount received for the First National stock from Warner Brothers which, after deducting the commissions, was $9,500,000. Subtracting these two items, almost $15,000,000, from $91,000,000 they advertised I owed, would leave the net liabilities of the companies $76,000,000. For the first quarter of 1930—and this was before I sold my voting shares—the Fox Film Corporation earned $4,700,000; subtract that from the $76,000,000, left the net debt a fraction over $70,000,000.

"You have a perfect right to inquire, therefore, what happened to the $103,000,000 of new capital that went into the Fox companies. There seems to have been borrowed $33,000,000 more than was required to pay the debts of these companies. Under the Clarke regime, it was reported that they earned during 1930 a fraction over $8,000,000, or almost sufficient to pay the full dividend paid that year. So the amount of debts owed and the new capital raised still leaves $33,000,000 of cash on hand. How did these funds find their way out of the treasury of the company? Why have the companies any debts now? In the last

326

published statement the certified accountant declares that the losses of Fox Film for 1931 were $4,250,000. There weren't any dividends paid in 1931. Subtracting the $4,250,000 from $33,000,000, there should still be $29,000,000 on hand and no debts.

"And yet when you examine the 1931 statement, you find the cash is nearly gone, and the company is heavily in debt. I am sure that on the reading of the statements you will be unable to see or imagine what happened to this thirty millions of money that was obtained by this company over and above its total liabilities."

W. F. analyzes the financial reports of his companies after he lost control, and shows how they have been manipulated. I am going to quote all these statements, because they are essential to the proof of his contentions; but I explain in advance that the matters are technical, and there is no way to make them simple. Those who do not understand financial terms may skip the rest of this "reel." Says W. F.:

"I have before me a statement of Fox Film as of December 27, 1930, from which it would appear that the company should have plenty of money. There is made a comparison between the year ending December 28, 1929, under the Fox regime, and the year ending December 27, 1930, most of it under the Harley Clarge regime. By manipulation and only by manipulation they were able to reduce the profits of the 1929 Fox regime to $9,469,-051, when the fact of the matter is that the profits that I left with that company, earned in 1929, were upwards of $13,500,000, plus the non-recurrent profit for the sale of First National shares to the Warner Company, which, after deducting what these shares had cost the company, gave a net profit of $8,500,000. These two items combined, the Fox Film Corporation earned in 1929 approximately $22,000,000. But here on their statement that I have before me, figures they prepared after I sold out, they show a profit of $9,469,051, and have shifted the difference to the profit made in 1930.

"Please bear in mind that in the first three months of 1930, before I sold out, we had actually earned $4,700,000; they show the net profit for the year to be $10,251,827. They show a net profit for the two years of a fraction under $20,000,000, when the fact of the matter is Fox Film Corporation earned in 1929, under my regime, $22,000,000. Is it not clear that in correcting these books they have simply taken the profits made in 1929 and deferred them on the statement of 1930? The profits earned in 1929 are greater than the profits shown here earned in both years. It would appear from this that Fox Film Corporation earned no profits in 1930, and that the statement that it earned $10,251,000 is an error.

"They are fine accountants. Here is an item of interest which shows how intelligent they are and how well they know how to keep books. In the year ending December 28, 1929, there is an item provisioned for Federal taxes of $1,266,000   Profit earned shown that year $9,469,051. They had a much more prosperous year in 1930, so their statement reads; they show that the net profit in 1930 was $10,251,827; but the provision for Federal taxes has shrunk from $1,266,000 in 1929 to $248,254 in 1930! Of course it is clear what they have done; this tax item gives it away. They paid only one-fifth as much Federal taxes in 1930, because they had made only one-fifth as much profits in 1930. The profits had been made in 1929, and then carefully spread over two years in the reports. It is interesting to know that the operating expense in 1929 was $42,739,000, and in 1930 it was $54,563,000."

W. F. naturally makes a great deal out of the fact that in the Fox Film report of December 27, 1930, they stopped their statement of income from film rentals with the record he had made.

"They give the activities here for sixteen years, a summary of the costs and rentals. Evidently in 1929 the gross rentals were at the peak, so they stopped at 1929. The cost of negatives of 1929 evidently is much less by millions than the cost of negatives of 1930. Therefore, they stop at 1929. But when you look at the opposite page, they give you a summary of the activities of the theatre holdings of Fox Film. During my regime, I had increased the number of theatres owned and controlled about as follows: 2 in 1927; 249 in 1928; 455 in 1929; and before I had sold out in 1930 it was 532. They gave the 1930 figures there, and they give it to you because with a greater number of theatres, the gross receipts are greater than in 1929. The cost of the negatives of 1930 was greater than the negatives of 1929, the last year of my regime; so they are silent, and give no figures on that point. The picture cost in 1930 amounted to $26,203,623.01, as against the highest cost that the company ever had in the history of its career, $22,743,665.29 for 1929.

"There is an explanation to be made of this item. The last year during which I was in my full physical strength to carry on the affairs of my company through the entire year was the year 1928, and during that year the cost was $16,185,102.75. But in July of 1929 I was disabled, and unable to carry on the conduct of the business, and it was then in the hands of the great executives who signed the round-robin letter. Just as soon as they found me lying on my back, it appears that they took full charge, and promptly mounted the cost of the production by more than $6,000,000. It is the cost of 1928 that I assume responsibility for, $16,185,102.75. The cost in 1930 had mounted to $26,203,-623.01, an increase of $10,000,000 under the Harley Clarke regime"

Later on in our talks, W. F. took up the consolidated balance sheets of Fox Film. He said:

"On August 26, 1930, Harley Clarke sent to the stockholders of Fox Film Corporation a letter; part of this letter is a balance sheet of Fox Film Corporation as of June 28, 1930. This letter and balance sheet is of great interest to this story, because it is the first balance sheet issued by the company after the new financing had been done.

"In connection with this letter, and the many other communications sent by Clarke to the stockholders, and the many items that appeared in the newspapers from time to time, and on the Jones ticker, each indicating how well the company was doing, and how everything was improving, how the expenses were being reduced and the income was being increased—all this reminds me of an old story of Joe Miller. It was about a man whose wife was at the hospital, dangerously ill. Each day when the husband called to see her, he would be told that visitors would not be allowed, but that his wife was improving. Shortly thereafter, when he called again, his wife was dead, and he was perplexed, and asked the physician this question: 'Doctor, is it fair for me to presume that my wife died of improvements?'

"In this letter of Clarke's to his stockholders of August 26, 1930, may I call your attention to the second paragraph in which he states: 'You will note that the current assets are two and one-half times the current liabilities. You will also note that the net worth of the company is $104,407,845.49, or approximately $40 per share on both classes of stock outstanding.' I call your attention to the fact that this $40 per share was just about one-half the value per share of the 900,000 and some odd shares that were outstanding previous to my selling my voting shares. Look at the balance sheet prepared by Touche, Niven & Company, dated December 28, 1929, where it appears that the value of the shares, plus the earned surplus of $22,400,000, was $73,063,000. That divided by 900,000 shares places the actual book value of these shares at $80 per share.

"The value of these shares had naturally shrunk when Clarke had 1,600,000 additional shares sold to himself at $30 a share. In doing that he had got for himself this terrific bargain, making, as I have shown you, a clear profit of $25,000,000 for himself and his associates. The owners of the other 900,000 shares of stock naturally found the values destroyed by this act; this issuance of 1,600,000 shares at $30 a share, for which the stockholders were deprived of their rights to subscribe. Their pre-emptory rights were taken from them by this manipulation.

"It was because of this that on August 26, 1930, Clarke boastfully told them that all of their shares were worth $40 a share, and that the net worth of the company as of that day was $104,407,805.49   What has happened to this net worth since then? This letter was written less than one year and nine months ago. What happened to the value? It wasn't lost during the year of 1930, because over Clarke's own signature there appears the statement in the annual report to the stockholders of December 27, 1930, that the profits for the year of 1930 were more than $10,000,000. If that is correct, then how was the net worth of $104,407,805.49 affected? In the statement issued as of December, 1931, there is a frank admission that there was no profit in the year 1930, but a loss of four million and some odd dollars. The $10,000,000 of 1930 earnings were not used to pay dividends—there were no dividends in 1931. The net worth at this writing ought to be $100,000,000. The consolidated balance sheet of December 26, 1931, shows the net worth at $50,644,298. It is exactly half of the net worth as indicated in the balance sheets of the previous year. In that report Tinker writes the shares down to $5 each, or $12,500,000 for the two and one-half million of them. But even that is too much. The net worth as the stock market now quotes the stock of Fox Film is two and one-half million times $1. What happened to the other $97,500,000?"

Before long we shall see William A. Gray, attorney for the United States Senate investigating Wall Street stock deals, taking up this matter of the Harley Clarke management of Fox Film and Fox Theatres. In his statement before the Senate, June 17, 1932, Gray supports the contentions of W. F , declaring that after the Clarke group took control, "at three different periods of time statements were given out with respect to the financial position of Fox Film at the end of December, 1929, and they varied with respect to the statement of the reserve and the surplus to the extent, in one case, of at least $6,000,000. In other words, they gave out a statement—it did not suit their purpose, and they gave out another. That did not suit their purpose, and they gave out another one."

Gray goes on to tell the experiences of John W. Pope, "one of the ablest statisticians in the New York district." Pope sent a wire to the members of the brokerage house with which he was connected, and to his customers and clientele, telling them to sell their Fox stock, "that he did not like the looks of the picture, and that their statements did not represent the true condition. For that, charges were brought against him before the New York Stock Exchange. . . . He went before the Stock Exchange and proved his case and was exonerated. All that shows the frenzied financing, and apparent financing, and the information that is given to the public about it, and when you get all through with it, you come to the conclusion that the public never knows anything about what is going on."

Now let us turn to Fox Theatres. Says W. F.:

"In analyzing the 1929 balance sheet of the Fox Theatres Company, you recall that the Loew shares were sold, and the Fox Theatres Corporation received for them the full amount they paid for them, $75,000,000. At that time there stood against Fox

Theatres the following debts: to the Telephone Company, $15,-000,000; to the bankers and brokers who held as collateral the Loew shares, $26,000,000; to Fox Film approximately $18,000,-000; a single bank liability, only one, for a note for $400,000, given in connection with the purchase of a piece of property in Boston that the sellers were unable to deliver, because the title was bad. The sum of $400,000 that appears on this balance sheet is on deposit in the bank that loaned it to the company; otherwise not a single dollar of debt to a bank. The only other liability item you will find is $1,400,000 due Herbert Lubin, payable over a period of four years in installments. This was in connection with the purchase of the Roxy Theatre. Therefore, the total liabilities that will appear on the December balance sheet of the Fox Theatres Company will be a total of $60,800,000. Therefore the company should have $14,000,000 cash on hand. In its operation of 1930 it earned a profit, and in 1931 it incurred a loss; the loss of one year and profit of another year about balancing. Where is the $14,000,000?

"This company paid no dividend last year. Not only has it not got it, but it is heavily indebted. It is unable to pay the rent of the theatres on lease; has defaulted in the interest on all its mortgages; and is now in receivership, bankrupt. Where is the $14,000,000? Who got that? How did it find its way out of the treasury of that company? Into whose pocket did it flow? What part of the $14,000,000 found its way out of that company into the treasury of General Theatres Equipment or of its subsidiary, National Theatres Supply? That's an inquiry that any stockholder of those companies is entitled to make."

And here are the balance sheets:

"According to a statement issued, dated October 26, 1930, and certified to by F. W. LaFrance & Co., who are the accountants for Harley L. Clarke and General Theatres Equipment Corporation, it appears that the net worth of Fox Theatres is $51,375,116.26. This statement shows that in the fiscal year ending October, 1930, the company lost in operation $2,484,824.07 and this amount has been subtracted, and the net worth is still $51,375,116.26. I now read from the balance sheet issued by Touche, Niven & Co. marked 'Revised to December 26, 1929,' which is the consolidated balance sheet of December 28, 1929.

This was the date of the last fiscal year that this company was under my management. On this balance sheet we find the net worth of the company $63,650,000; so there has been a loss of $12,000,000 from one October to another October. In the statement issued by the Clarke regime, dated October 26, 1930, they show a deficit in operation in that year of $2,013,133; so that leaves $10,000,000 difference, which perhaps can be located with a magnifying glass, but not with my naked eyes."

This Harley Clarke regime lasted for eighteen months. Then the Chase Bank, which was doing all the financing, couldn't stand it any more, and they gave Harley Clarke a dose of the same medicine which he and his friends had administered to the Fox; they took away his control of the voting shares, and kicked him upstairs, making him chairman of the board, and putting in as president Edward Tinker, formerly chairman of Chase Bank and Chase Securities. You will remember Tinker as the gentleman who made the deal for Chase Bank with the Lehman group of bankers, to divide the profits of the Fox financing, the deal which brought about the Japanese meeting. You will remember how W. F. called him on the telephone and he confirmed Clarke's statement about this deal. Now Tinker was put in charge of the Fox companies, to show how a real banker would run the moving picture business. W. F. went to see Tinker.

"We had two lengthy conferences which were arranged by a mutual friend. I indicated to him that even at this time it wasn't too late to save these companies, and that I was anxious and desirous of doing so. In these two conferences Tinker was very friendly. He said he wouldn't pretend that he knew anything about the running of a moving picture company; that he was elected as the only man that all the parties were willing to agree upon. I tried to find out what he meant by all the parties. He said the various groups that were now interested in that enterprise. He said: 'Why it was wished on me, I don't know. I didn't seek it. I practically told them I didn't understand it; but they said they all had confidence in me, and could agree on me in common as the man to run these companies.' He said he knew he couldn't run them, but what he was going to try to do was find a new staff of executives. If he could find the right men, they might work out their problems. He inquired from me about the still remaining Fox executives that Clarke had inherited, and I tried my best to give him a very accurate description of each one—his origin and his ability. He was certain that the present executives had proved themselves wholly incompetent, and that a new set would have to be provided. If that wasn't so, there would be no need of him being president of the company; Clarke could have remained.

"Our talks were of a kind that were intended to be frank with each other, and not conceal anything, or say one thing and mean another. I emphatically declared that he and all the executives that he would dream of hiring couldn't save this situation; that I had a definite plan in my mind which would result in the reconstruction of these companies; that I didn't want to be either a director or an officer of the companies. I wanted to be an outside man to do a job, and if I did a satisfactory job, I wanted to be paid; and if I didn't, I wanted nothing. I informed him that I had wanted $15,000,000 to get out, and I wanted $25,000,000 to come back. If I was engaged to do this job, I could rescue the Chase Bank's $100,000,000.

"I frankly told him that my doing of this work was wholly objected to by Mrs Fox; that although I told her that the price I was fixing for my return was $25,000,000, she had been urging me to have nothing to do with it. Her position was that the present stockholders of Fox Film were not the stockholders of the days when I controlled those companies; the Chase Bank and its gang of raiders in their manipulations had wiped out the original stockholders, and that even though I was to get $25,000,000, I ought never raise a finger to enable the Chase Bank to get out of this jam. I told him that in spite of her contention, I would like to do this job, complete it successfully, and thus write the closing chapters of my story."

Tinker thought over this proposition from the Fox, but he did not accept it. Very probably he did not have the power to accept it. He went on to run the companies, and they gave him a "rather high-class" board of directors, including Winthrop W. Aldrich, the new head of the Chase Bank, and General Cornelius Vanderbilt. W. F. is amused to note that the day the Vanderbilt name was announced, the price of Fox Film on the market dropped $10 a share!

He takes up the financial statements showing what this new regime was able to do; beginning with the annual report of December 26, 1931.

"You will recall an open charge that the directors under the Fox regime were rubber stamps for William Fox; his directors were supposed to be wholly incompetent. Sheehan, who was one of the directors during the 1929 period, complained in the affidavits he signed against Fox that at no time was he ever consulted with reference to the finances of the Fox enterprises. He appears on the list of directors of the fifty-two week period ending December 26, 1931, and he now finds himself in much better company than he did in the 1929 period. It is fair to assume that, having complained that he was kept in ignorance of the finances of 1929, he safeguarded against a recurrence of it, and insisted and demanded that he be kept informed as to the finances of the corporation during the period of 1931.

"My rubber stamp dummy directors of 1929, dumb as they were and as automatic as they were obliged to be, being only rubber stamps, were directors of a corporation that made a profit of $13,500,000, and a non-recurring profit on the sale of the First National shares to Warner Brothers of $8,500,000. The combined amounts were more than $22,000,000. And now let us see the record of the high-class directorate listed in the statement of December 26, 1931   Edward R. Tinker signs this statement and makes a long explanatory statement to the stockholders, in the most beautiful language, but it is all confusion to me. In spite of the fact that I founded this company, and operated it for fifteen years, his figures are wholly confusing to my trained eye—except for one fact, which is clear to me, and most likely was clear to all of the stockholders of the company: that there was shown a net loss after taxes of $4,263,557.56 for the year 1931, as compared with the $20,000,000 profit earned the last year that the company was under my control and management.

"The other most startling thing in this statement is the fact that on the balance sheet of the assets and liabilities there has been a change made in the method of bookkeeping. Amongst the current assets there now appears an item of inventory, and in bracketing, unamortized cost of $17,136,300.27. This item, under my regime, was never among current assets. On careful exam-

23

ination, I am wondering why the change was made; but on closer examination, it becomes evident why. If this amount had not been lifted from where I originally had it into current assets, the current assets that now appear as $23,402,481.05 would be less by the sum of $17,136,300.27; or, in other words, the current assets would be a little over $6,000,000.

"And then, on looking at the liabilities, I find the current liabilities of $16,637,895.78. If the inventories had not been lifted from where they were, and put into the current assets, the current liabilities would be two and one-half times as great as the current assets, and that wouldn't look good on any balance sheet; particularly in view of the previous notes, in which I called attention to the fact that the Fox companies had actually received, directly after I had sold out, new funds amounting to $103,000,000 with which to liquidate their maximum liabilities. The liabilities had been well advertised—by cable, by telegram, by radio, by newspapers, by mail, by whispering and loudly speaking scandal-mongers, as $91,000,000. In fact they knew that the liability was not that great, but assuming that it was $91,000,000, there was a balance left over of the difference between $91,000,-000 and $103,000,000, which would leave $12,000,000 of cash on hand. I have shown you the last quarter's earnings, plus the non-recurring profit earned on the sale of the First National shares, and the other items, which make it clear that $30,000,000 should be the cash on hand. But instead we find that there is a liability of $16,637,895.78. This has to be reduced by the current assets of $6,000,000, which leaves $10,000,000 more to be accounted for —a total of $40,000,000 that have disappeared!"

And now as to Fox Theatres, and what the Tinker regime has done to it.

"In looking over the record of the Fox Theatres Corporation, I find that it is now free of the entire group that had acquired my voting shares; it has been stripped of its directors, and nothing but employes remain. Whether it is the purpose now to push the responsibility of the wreck onto the shoulders of wage earners of this company or not, I don't know. I was amazed to read that Fox Theatres, which had occupied from its very inception the same building as Fox Film, was ordered out of the building. The Chase Bank wants nothing more to do with Fox

Theatres. They practically dispossess it. Now that the $75,000,-
000 that Fox Theatres received from the sale of the Loew shares
is disposed of, and the strong-box of the company has been
looted, and every asset the company has is hypothecated, the
wreckers are now ordering the junk loaded onto trucks and
dumped at some other place."

There is an interesting way to follow the fortunes of the Fox
companies, by noting the price of their stocks throughout the
long series of developments here set forth. We are now in position to appreciate such figures. In October, 1929, just before
the panic, Fox Film A stock stood at 101. During the panic, it
dropped to a low of 40. Then it came back, and on November
9, ten days after the panic, it stood at 71. But now came the
campaign to oust the Fox, with market raids, scandals and lawsuits, and during January, 1930, the price varied from 32 down
to 16. In February, with the Lehman financing plan, it rose to
34. On March 4th, the day before the stockholders' meeting, it
was 36, and at the end of March, after Judge Coleman was disqualified, it was 26. In April, after W. F. sold out and the
Harley Clarke regime came in, with new financing and wonderful
promises, it climbed to 57. From May to September it varied
from 40 to 50; and then began the long slide. In January of
1931 Fox Film high was 32, in July, 22, in October, 10, in
December, 5, and in July, 1932, $1. Then Wall Street got up
a little boom, to try to re-elect Hoover, and Fox Film rose to $5.
Now, as the book goes to press, it hangs around $2. Thus, in
three years, it has lost 98 per cent of its value.

24

REEL TWENTY-EIGHT

SUMMING UP

WE are now in position to sum up what happened to the Fox companies. The banking group which saw them, coveted them, conspired to get possession of them, and succeeded in its conspiracy—that group plundered them of considerably more than $100,000,000, and left them as empty shells. We have seen $40,000,000 missing from Fox Film, and $43,000,000 lost by the stockholders of that company when they were deprived of their rights to the stock at $30 a share. We have seen $14,000,000 missing from Fox Theatres, and more than that paid as commissions to the various bankers on the various financings and refinancings of both companies.

Of course, a part of these sums were paper profits. The financiers took 1,600,000 shares of Fox Film stock, and when the shares rose to $57, they figured they had $91,200,000. If they held on too long, that was hard luck which they shared with the rest of the upperclass gambling world; but it does not affect the conclusions to be drawn from this story. They meant to make the profits, and legally speaking they had the profits, regardless of subsequent depreciations.

You will recall that on March 5, 1930, Judge Aaron J. Levy of the Supreme Court of New York State rendered a decision upon the moral character of our Fox. This decision was taken up and quoted by Halsey, Stuart in so many affidavits and circulars to their customers and to the Fox stockholders, that one who studies the case as I have, comes to know it by heart. I did not stop to discuss it at the time, because we did not then have the figures. But now we have them, and can deal with Judge Levy. Said he:

"Here we have a little $1,600 acorn which grew into a sturdy $300,000,000 oak. Why was not well enough left alone? The

338

very Fox chopped down this healthy thriving tree with his own hatchet. The world knows much about avarice and cupidity, and I wonder if this is not another illustration. May he now be heard to complain? Has he placed himself in that position which justifies his assault upon the character of men? I think not."

Well, the world knew much about avarice and cupidity on March 5, 1930, but I have failed in my purpose in this book if the world does not know still more about avarice and cupidity now. Speaking as a Socialist, I indict the whole capitalist world for avarice and cupidity; I say that these qualities are the foundation-stone upon which the system is built. Its defenders glory in that fact, and proclaim the profit motive and self-interest as the necessary basis, the only possible basis of an economic order. Their college professors and newspaper editors invent high-sounding names with which to dress these qualities; transforming avarice and cupidity into individual initiative, enterprise, foresight, daring, industry.

Was that the point of view of Judge Levy? Was he speaking as a social revolutionist indicting our system of wage slavery and exploitation? I think not! Judge Levy himself would be the first to spring forward and deny such evil intentions.

The learned justice was called upon to decide one question: whether at the stockholders' meeting of March 5, 1930, William Fox should vote the B shares of these two companies himself, or whether they should be voted by the trusteeship controlled by Stuart and Otterson. Therefore the only meaning of any moral judgment was to compare Stuart and Otterson with Fox, and to say that the former were more to be trusted than the latter. That this was the actual effect of the judgment was proved by the use which Stuart and Otterson made of the decision, before the stockholders that same day, before other courts in future days, and in a pamphlet, of which they printed and circulated tens of thousands of copies.

Which shall we say displayed the greater amount of avarice and cupidity—William Fox, or those who dispossessed him and took over his companies? William Fox planted the little $1,600 acorn, and he watered and tended it until it had grown into a $300,000,000 oak. He had begun with some Fox Film common stock which had no par value, and in fact no value whatever; it was given as a bonus to those who purchased the preferred stock and thus made the enterprise possible. Every year he paid $4 per share dividends on that common stock, and so it acquired value, until in 1928 it reached $119 a share. The net earnings of the company grew from half a million dollars in 1915 to more than $13,000,000 in 1929. It had begun in 1914 by making four pictures a year, and in the end was making one every week; the rentals of these pictures rose from $272,000 in 1914 to more than $30,000,000 in 1929.

Judge Levy found fault because W. F. controlled these companies while owning only 5 per cent of their shares. He took those figures from Stuart and Otterson's affidavit, and they happened to be untrue; they were based upon the B shares only, whereas W. F. tells me that in addition to the B shares, he owned approximately 5 per cent of Film A stock and approximately 10 per cent of Theatres A stock. But what difference did that make to the stockholders?

How much the 5 per cent ownership really had to do with the case was proved by the outcome. When Fox Film and Fox Theatres were made subsidiaries of General Theatres Equipment Corporation, the control of both companies was vested in three voting trustees, each owning a single share of stock, the market value of which at the time W. F. told me this story, was 37½ cents a share. It sounds incredible, but so it is; $1.12½ managed and destroyed a corporation whose stock in 1929 was over $100,000,000. When Clarke added the Fox companies to his string he trebled the amount controlled by the voting shares, but he did not thereby save the concerns from bankruptcy.

It is interesting to note the situation as to stock ownership of Fox Film under the Clarke regime. How much confidence did the officers and directors have in themselves? On March 31, 1931, Harley Clarke, president, owned one share of A stock; W C. Michel, vice-president and treasurer, owned one; M. C. Brush, C. W. Higley, and W. F. Ingold, directors, one share each; J. R. Grainger, vice-president, none.

W. F. has shown you how, in less than two years, more than $100,000,000 disappeared from the treasury of his companies. Some of it was paper profits, but the greater part was real money, and somebody got it. It is evident that somebody meant to get it from the beginning. A campaign was planned and ruthlessly carried through, the outcome of which was the wreckage of two prosperous concerns, and the reducing to beggary of many thousands of persons, some of them deserving. I appeal the judgment of the Supreme Court of New York to the Supreme Court of Public Opinion, and ask again which side displayed the greater amount of avarice and cupidity.

As my farewell to Judge Levy, I think it apropos to quote a remark made to me twenty-five years ago by James B. Dill, at that time one of the five justices of the highest court of the State of New Jersey. This remark had nothing to do with Levy, who was an obscure young lawyer then, but it has to do with Judge Levy's court, which has not changed very much in twenty-five years. Bear in mind that Dill was not merely a judge on the other side of the Hudson River, but was the highest-paid corporation lawyer in Wall Street, and had been actively dealing with its big financiers and corporation magnates all his professional life. He said: "Sinclair, there are twenty-two judges of the Supreme Court of New York State, and all but three of them are owned. I can say to each of the nineteen, 'I know whose man you are, and exactly what you got for it,' and not one of the nineteen would dare to contradict me."

There are a number of other persons to whom we have to pay our adieus, and a number of loose ends of the story to be knitted together. For example, those eloquent and high-priced lawyers who did such a beautiful job of turning over the Fox companies to the wrecking crew. So many eloquent appeals they made in court, so many learned briefs they prepared—and always and everywhere they were so dignified, high-minded, and imposing. But when they got through, it was the wrecking crew who paid them—and with the money of the stockholders! W. F. got the facts somehow out of the files of the Fox companies. Hughes, Schurman & Dwight got a total of $520,000; the Berenson brothers of Boston got a quarter of a million; Isador J. Kresel got $50,000—all paid by the Fox companies for the wrecking of the Fox companies.

As I said before, this is one of the oddest developments I ever heard of in big business affairs. I know of only one thing to equal it, and that is when our great water and gas and light and power and telephone trusts go into what they call "educational" activities; buying newspapers and college professors and other lecturers, and compelling the consumers of water and gas and light and power and telephones to pay the cost of the poisoning of their own minds.

In May of 1932 the Irving Trust Company was appointed receiver for the Fox Metropolitan Playhouses, Inc., the principal subsidiary of Fox Theatres, operating its 175 theatres in and about New York. The same fate befell Fox Brooklyn, Fox Detroit, and Fox St. Louis. On June 22, 1932, Fox Theatres itself went into the hands of an equity receiver, upon a petition filed by the Chicago Title & Trust Company, a creditor claiming $410,190. The usual claim is made, that the assets of the concern exceed its liabilities; the stockholders will know in due course whether that is true. I note the significant item that "investments in subsidiary companies in the hands of receivers or trustees and in real estate on which mortgage defaults have been made, are listed at $21,360,000." Oddly enough, the petition for an equity receiver, agreed to by Fox Theatres, was prompted by the fear that an "unnamed creditor" might file a judgment, and this person was rumored to be our old friend Blumy, demanding $355,000 as part of his price for putting over the Loew stock deal in 1929.

Also W. F. thinks I should say a few words about the Roxy Theatre, which was owned by Fox Theatres. "Roxy" was a radio announcer who became popular and had a wide audience. He used that pull to raise money for the building of what was to be the biggest and grandest motion picture theatre in the world. Thirteen thousand people, mostly workers, took Roxy's word for it, and bought stock in the enterprise. The time came when the Radio Corporation of America and the Rockefeller interests decided upon the enterprise known as Rockefeller Center; a part of it was to be the biggest and grandest motion picture theatre in the world, located only four or five hundred feet away from the Roxy Theatre. The Rockefellers wanted Roxy to manage it, so they bought him away from his own enterprise, and now the Roxy Theatre concern is bankrupt, and the 13,000 investors will see their holdings wiped out.

Here is a table of the bonds of Fox Theatres subsidiaries, showing the prices at which they were sold to the public, and the prices at which they now stand. These are the $36,000,000 worth of bonds, which Halsey, Stuart unloaded upon their clients. Of course, the panic was the principal cause of the decline; but I think the ousting of Fox had some part in it also.

Bonds	Sold at	Now
Fox Los Angeles Studio...........	100	50
Fox Detroit Bldg........	97½	7
Fox St. Louis Bldg...............	100	8
New Eng. Poli Circuit.	100	10
Fox Metropolitan, N. Y.....	99	7
Roxy Theatre................. ...	99½	8

As to Fox Film, Harley Clarke has been ousted entirely, and Tinker moved up to the post of chairman of the board; a new president has been put in, Sidney R. Kent, an oldtimer, formerly production manager of Paramount. The value of Paramount stock, $2 per share, hardly seems to promise much for Fox Film. Kent is a forceful man, at least as a speaker, and devotes his oratory to convincing the moving picture world that it must prepare for drastic salary cuts. The newspapers out here give glowing accounts of the prospects of Fox Film, based on the fact that Kent has taken charge, and that Winfield R. Sheehan, having had his liver cured, has resumed his duties as production manager. Kent has said nothing regarding his attitude toward the question of a cut in that contract of Sheehan which provides that this year he is to receive $350,000; in 1933 $400,000; and in 1934 $500,000.

The Loew shares have been turned over to a separate organization, known as Film Securities Corporation, controlled by three trustees appointed by the Federal court. Thus the Department of Justice is satisfied that the anti-trust laws are being respected.

The British Gaumont shares were lost, and Fox Film is now suing Ostrer in London to recover £4,000,000 invested in that deal.

General Theatres Equipment is in the hands of a receiver. It is a corporation formed under the laws of the State of Delaware, which permit you to do anything. Now there has been filed with the Court of Chancery of the State of Delaware in and

for Newcastle County, a complaint of the bondholders' committee, through their attorney, Harold L. Fierman, asking that the
court instruct the receiver to bring suit against the Chase National
Bank and the Chase Securities Corporation to recover the sum
of $14,000,000, representing damages which General Theatres
Equipment sustained through wrongful actions of the Chase
concerns.

The long affidavit recites the story of the Fox financing, and
it appears that the banking group who were plundering the Fox
companies were also plundering General Theatres Equipment.
You will recall that General Theatres Equipment got 1,160,000
shares of Fox Film stock, and the banking crowd got 440,000
shares. General Theatres Equipment was not permitted to sell
its stock, but held it to enable the bankers to get rid of theirs
at a generous profit. Instead of selling its stock, General Theatres Equipment borrowed $10,000,000 from the Chase National
Bank, and put up the stock as collateral, and more and more
stock was called for, until the bank now has most of the assets
of the company. This process could be carried out because of
the fact "that at the time this transaction took place, a majority
of the directors of the corporation were under the control and
domination of the Chase National Bank, by reason of the fact
that the Chase National Bank held assignments of the participation agreements of the various companies, in which a majority
of the directors were substantially or vitally interested." Later
on the Chase Bank practically admitted its responsibility, by sur-
rendering its claims to this collateral, and taking the same shares
as the bondholders are getting in the reorganization plan.

Harley L. Clarke of Chicago is supposed to be ruined. But
W. F., who knows him well, has his doubts on the point; he
thinks Clarke surely has money put away. He thinks that Clarke's
losses, advertised at $100,000,000, were purely paper losses. (We
have arrived at a peculiar stage of culture, where a man's social
position is established by the amount of money he can boast of
having lost.) W. F. tells of several conversations with Clarke
on the subject of General Theatres Equipment stock. "He told
me one day that the value of the shares which he had lost was
$37,000,000. Some time later he evidently forgot what he had
told me, and this time he said his loss was $27,000,000. A third

time he told me it was $17,000,000. Some of those who were close to him told me they didn't believe that he lost one real dollar in the enterprise; he merely lost the market value of shares which had cost him nothing."

W. F. still continues business relations with his "dear Harley"; because Harley had agreed to pay him $3,000,000 as a substitute for his participation in Fox Film financing, and the payment was made in the form of ten one-year notes for $300,000 each, and long before the year was out, "dear Harley" was at the end of his rope. W. F. had given one of these notes to his friend Greenfield as a commission on the deal, and Greenfield was so lucky as to sell it without recourse. Says W. F.: "I tried to sell mine, but couldn't. I tried the Chase Bank where the notes were payable, but they wouldn't buy them. Wherever I offered to sell these notes, they would call up the Chase Bank and inquire whether they would be paid when due. The Chase Bank was unable to give the information."

This entanglement with Clarke was the means or getting W. F. a lot of information about Chicago financial methods, also Los Angeles and Hollywood financial methods. But that is a long story, and it would seem that Wall Street is enough for one book. In bidding farewell to Harley L. Clarke of Chicago, I quote W. F.'s final sentence: "He is now rather a pathetic figure, because he recognizes that he has been ousted."

Also there is a story for me to tell about W. F.'s friend, Albert M. Greenfield, president of the Bankers' Securities Corporation of Philadelphia. You will recall that Greenfield's concern loaned W. F. $10,000,000, and waited for the money, refusing to bring any suit; also Greenfield was W. F.'s "contact man," and was tireless in trying to help him out of his difficulties. He was the agent for the sale of the First National shares to Warner Brothers, and at the end for the sale of the voting shares to Harley Clarke. Greenfield was acting as a friend, but when he discovered that Blumenthal had had a contract in his pocket for $600,000, if and when W. F. sold his voting shares to Clarke, Greenfield went to Clarke and told him that this was unfair, and that if there was to be a commission, Greenfield should have half, and the result was that Blumenthal was forced to give Greenfield $250,000.

When this was all over, W. F. warned Greenfield to watch his step, the banking ring would certainly punish him; and sure enough, they did it that very summer. Greenfield was organizer of the Bankers Trust Company, which had some $18,000,000 of deposits. Another Philadelphia bank was in trouble, and the ring persuaded Greenfield to merge this bank, with its thirteen branches. Soon thereafter came rumors that the Bankers Trust was in trouble, and people began withdrawing their funds, not only from that bank, but from all the thirteen branches of the merged bank. As W. F. says, "Money goes fast when there are thirteen men handing it out."

W. F. went to Philadelphia one Thursday to try to help his friend, and told me a long story of his labors Friday, Saturday and Sunday. He addressed a meeting of the ruling bankers, at which he pleaded for his friend, pointing out to them what it would mean to the state's banking system if these two banks went to the wall. It was on Sunday night, in the board room of the largest bank in Philadelphia, controlled by Drexel & Company, the partners of Morgan—"right in the center of the old spider's web!" says W. F.

"At about 3 o'clock in the morning, I realized as clearly as it was possible that the destruction of Greenfield had to occur, and I made up my mind to test it to see whether I was right. I arose and made the most eloquent address of my life in behalf of Greenfield and the 125,000 poor depositors in the city of Philadelphia I said that if they permitted this bank to close its doors tomorrow, they would start a fire in the town. 'You will have 125,000 depositors who are going to be upset. You will find your newspapers printing nothing else. You will find a run on every bank in Philadelphia. You might think you are out of range of this thing; I tell you that that is not so. I am not here merely because I want to help Greenfield; I am here in behalf of the men, women and children who have their money not only in this bank, but in every other bank in Philadelphia.'

"I pointed out what a terrible condition had arisen in New York when the Chase Bank and others decided the Bank of the United States must be closed; every bank in New York was affected. This would not only start a run in Philadelphia, but it would be a story for the whole state of Pennsylvania. and would start other runs. I made the following proposal: 'Gentlemen, you claim all this while that Greenfield has $4,000,000 worth of bad debts on his books. I think you are wrong; I think a careful survey will show you that he probably has more. It will probably run to $5,000,000.' They were sure that it was only $4,000,000— that was more than sufficient to take care of those debts. I said I would loan $1,000,000 of my personal money. I said: 'I have just talked to Greenfield, and he says that when you liquidate his bank, if at that time there is any loss incurred by you, he personally will give you a guarantee for $1,500,000, and will collateralize that guarantee at this time. I have requested Greenfield to do that, to show his willingness to help the situation. After you have used up his one million and a half, you will have my million dollars, which you can have in cash or collateral.'

"While I was making this address, which I thought most eloquent, I noticed the president of the second largest bank in Philadelphia take his handkerchief out of his pocket, presumably wiping his face, and place it to the right hand side of his mouth, and then grin and laugh and smile at the head of the largest bank, the Drexel Bank."

W. F. was sure that these bankers were going to wreck Greenfield, and he decided to make an appeal to Herbert Hoover:

"I waited until about 8 o'clock the next morning, when I thought the President would be at his breakfast table. I called him on the 'phone; his secretary said he had instructions not to disturb him. I requested that the secretary give him my name at the breakfast table, and let the President say whether or not he wanted to be disturbed. A few minutes later the President came to the 'phone. I had in a brief way told him what was occurring to Greenfield. Since I had known of this since Thursday, he now severely criticized me for not coming to him promptly. By this time it was 8:15 and the Bankers' Trust never opened. I learned later that President Hoover had made a strenuous effort to locate those who might be of help before 9 o'clock, but that the time was too short."

Of course, it may have been pure coincidence that it was a friend of William Fox who was in the center of that crash; just as it may have been pure coincidence that the only two bankers in New York who showed sympathy for our Fox, Edward Rothschild of the Chelsea Bank, and Bernard Marcus of the Bank of the United States—were driven out of the banking business, and Marcus landed in jail. The result of that crash in Philadelphia was that there was a run on every bank in the city and in the surrounding towns, and something like a dozen banks were compelled to close their doors; but of course not Drexel & Company, the partners of the Morgans. The Morgans banks will be the last in the United States to close their doors—and yet it is my belief that some day they will close their doors!

REEL TWENTY-NINE

AFTERMATH

IT is proving a difficult matter to finish this book, because it keeps on happening. Fate. the busy spider, spins out new threads faster than I can put them into the web.

While W. F. was telling his story in my home, a committee of the United States Senate began an investigation of stock-market operations—particularly short selling—and put on the stand various independent operators, including Percy Rockefeller and Matthew C. Brush. W. F. brought a copy of the morning paper to my home and said that this "Matt" Brush had led raids on Fox Film stock during the worst of W. F.'s troubles. He said that he would like to know whether such gentlemen as Harry Stuart, Harley Clarke and Albert Wiggin had been in the "pools" which had been raiding his securities. I thought that this might be a proper question for the committee to investigate, and offered to telegraph the suggestion. W. F. approved my idea, and a telegram was sent to Senator Couzens, who wrote me that the matter would be taken up.

Soon after W. F.'s return to New York, he received a request from William A. Gray, counsel for the Senate committee, to come to Gray's office for questioning. He went on June 8, 1932, and I have before me a transcript of his examination. It appears that Mr. Gray, a criminal lawyer of Philadelphia, has very little interest in the doings of the great and powerful concerns which wrecked the Fox companies, but is interested in getting after William Fox, and trying to prove that Fox himself was responsible for the wrecking of his companies. It appears that W. F. has a great number of brokers' accounts, and that he has bought and sold large quantities of Fox securities, and Mr. Gray wants to know all about it, and goes after the information in the fashion of criminal lawyers. He asks great numbers of questions about stock deals which have taken place three years previously, and seems indignant that W. F. hasn't at his finger-tips the figures of some thirty brokers accounts of his own and his relatives. W. F. had to explain to him: "I was deprived of my records, the company was captured and I had no control and have no control of the records now.

"Q. Personal records?

"A. Everything I had is in their hands.

"Q. Whose hands?

"A. In the hands of my enemies

"Q. Who got your personal records?

"A. My personal files are intermingled with the company's files, and they are lying there now, and we must beg and plead to go through the files for an individual letter. If you had known all I had gone through from the day I met with that accident until I sold out, you will recognize l have no way of answering many questions you asked. I have no way and it is humanly impossible."

I will let W F. tell you in his own words about these hearings, beginning with his first visit to Gray. Writing to me, he says:

"I told Mr. Gray I was delighted that he had sent for me, and that I had a story to tell the American people. I asked whether he knew you had written to Senator Couzens. His reply to that question made it clear what his attitude would be to me. He resented my mentioning either your name or Couzens' name. He said that that matter he would take up later; he was the lawyer for the Senate committee, and he would carry on the investigation in his own way.

"I am wondering now, is it possible that Hughes, Schurman & Dwight had called on Mr. Gray and supplied him with a list of questions that should be asked of Fox about matters wholly irrelevant to short selling on the New York Stock Exchange. For every claim subsequently made in the complaints of Fox Theatres and Fox Film against William Fox was at the finger-tips of Mr. Gray, the attorney for the Senate investigation committee. Up to this time, you understand, I had not been sued either by Fox Theatres or by Fox Film. It was only after Gray had interrogated me for about three hours with heaps and heaps of questions, that I received a summons of the Fox Theatres Corporation.

"Many of the questions that Gray asked were such that I would have to refresh my memory and examine my books so that I could answer them correctly. At the conclusion of this first examination Mr. Gray was kind enough to give me a subpoena to appear in Washington. Attached was a complete list of all the records he would like to have me bring along. Everything he asked for was what Fox Theatres and Fox Film required in their lawsuits. Here was going to be a great haul. And please bear in mind that when you sit in the chair at one of these Senate investigations you have no right to representation. Hughes, Schurman & Dwight were going to try their case before the Senate committee, without my having a right to defend myself; my counsel was not to be heard. That is a fine trap to be caught in; a fine trick for the United States Government to lend itself to. The octopus, of course, knew all about this.

"Under my subpoena I was due to go before the Senate the following Wednesday. But Reass told me that Gray had not gone to Washington, and would like to see me again in New York. So I went to Gray, with the answers to most of the questions asked of me at the previous meeting. During the first meeting a stenographer had taken our minutes and Mr. Gray was kind enough to say that I could have a copy. During the second meeting, after he had proceeded for about one hour, I recalled that we had failed to ask whether we could have a copy of these minutes. We asked him. He promptly told me no; that we were to meet in Washington tomorrow, and the stenographer did not have time, and she was not physically able to transcribe her notes in time to give us a copy. I asked that proceedings be halted so that we could get somebody who would make for us a copy of these proceedings.

"You will bear in mind that I was under no obligation to call on Gray or to talk to Gray. The only rights he had were to serve me with a subpoena to appear before the Senate committee in Washington and there ask his questions. I made both these calls because you had written your letter to Senator Couzens asking for the privilege of my being heard. When the second stenographer came, Gray began bombarding me again with many, things that had entirely passed out of my mind, and then it became clear to me that he was not investigating short selling on the New York Stock Exchange, but that the information brought out would enable Hughes, Schurman & Dwight and Max D. Steuer to draw their complaints properly.

"There were matters involving many millions of dollars in these suits against me; but even so, I decided that I was going to Washington to appear before the Senate committee; you had issued a challenge and I was going to back you up. You must bear in mind I was no longer under any subpoena; my subpoena had expired on Wednesday, and Gray had not given me a new one. But I was going to Washington without any subpoena, voluntarily, as I had on the two occasions appeared before Gray.

"I left New York by auto at 6 o'clock in the evening and arrived in Washington at 3 o'clock in the morning. I was foolish to do that. It rained all the way. It would have been better to go by train. By the time I came to Washington I was ill. I looked for a doctor that morning at 3:30. I inquired from the clerk at the desk of the hotel and asked for the house doctor. He came at 9 o'clock, and found me suffering with pains in gall bladder and appendix, and called it biliousness and gave me a dose of calomel. Gray did not believe I was ill, so he sent two of his own physicians to examine me. They concurred in the opinion of the hotel doctor that I was ill. The next day the hotel doctor sent for a diabetic specialist, took my blood test, and found I had a blood sugar content of .250. The doctor wanted to know whether I was his patient. I told him I was. 'If you are my patient,' he said, 'I prohibit you from going anywhere where you will have a mental disturbance.'

"I was anxious to go before the Senate committee, particularly after I had read the proceedings of the two days. But my doctors told me they forbid me to leave my room; they told me I might develop into a permanent diabetic, and worse still I might go into a coma; that if I was his permanent patient or a relative of his, he would prevent me from going before the Senate committee. It is a customary matter during any of these investigations to permit any one who is in poor health and cannot appear, to file a written report either confirming or denying the charges made. But in reading over the proceedings in one of Gray's closing addresses, I discover him making the request that the committee should not grant me the privilege of filing a report. I am sure the Senate will not grant his request, but that I will have the privilege of filing my report, which I hope to do in the form of your book."

At the hearings before the Senate committee, Gray produced the evidence gathered from W. F.'s brokerage accounts. It appeared that he had been a member of various pools which had traded in the stocks of Fox Film and Fox Theatres, and also of Loew's, Inc. One of these pools had included, among others, John J. Raskob, Walter P. Chrysler, and Nicholas F. Brady. This pool had made a profit of $1,937,000. I quote from the Associated Press dispatch of June 17:

"Mr. Fox had freely admitted to him, Mr. Gray said, that he manipulated Fox stocks to maintain a public market; that he believed short selling a rotten practice, but that he would continue it as long as the New York Stock Exchange permitted it, and that he would do it again."

The effort was made by Gray to show that this had been in effect a "bear" operation. I quote from the account in "Time," June 27, 1932:

"Manager Ellsworth patiently explained that this pool had been formed to market Fox stock to finance Fox expansion. Holding an option on 500,000 shares from Cineman Fox, the pool sold 466,000 shares 'technically' short against the option, the balance covered in the open market. Manager Ellsworth said that the additional short interest had been built up to enable the pool to support the market, if necessary, not to depress it. He pointed out that the pool could have covered from the option at all times. On the total operation the pool cleared $1,937,000.

"Manager Ellsworth admitted having spent $24,000 for publicity, advising the public that 'they could buy for $30 a share of stock which we thought would sell at $60.' When Senator Couzens asked why the pool itself did not wait for the profit, Witness Ellsworth snapped: 'My business isn't to wait—it's to sell!'

"Frustrated in its attempt to prove that Cineman Fox's market manipulations had destroyed his companies, or that he had been a bad Bear, the Committee pounced on alleged income tax evasions. Counsel Gray said that Cineman Fox deducted market losses from his personal returns which had been paid by Fox Film."

This is a question with which I am not going to attempt to deal; I gave up my efforts to understand the income tax regulations some time ago, when I discovered that the Treasury Department considers that when an author has written a book and receives royalties upon it from his publishers, those royalties are "unearned income"!

What interests me about this senatorial investigation is the fact that the committee apparently has no interest in the large scale operations of the great financial powers, such as Chase National Bank and Chase Securities Company, but is only interested in the speculations of the small independents. Of course it is worthwhile to know how Harry Warner and his brothers made $9,000,000 selling their own stocks short, and how they got rid of their stocks and took instead the debentures of their concern, so that they are not involved in its depression. But how much more important it would be to know how the House of Morgan and the Chase Bank and the big investment houses, such as Halsey, Stuart, and Dillon, Read, and Goldman, Sachs, and Hayden, Stone have unloaded tens of billions of dollars of worthless stocks, both foreign and domestic, upon the small country banks and the small investors, and used their vast resources to manipulate these stocks on the market!

With regard to the suits of Fox Film and Fox Theatres against William Fox, it must be explained that in the purchase of the San Francisco Theatre, and of the Roxy Theatre in New York, W. F. had personally endorsed the notes, and therefore was liable for the results of the mismanagement of these theatres. The owner is now Fox Theatres, and the owner of Fox Theatres is General Theatres Equipment, now being reorganized in the interest of the bondholders. W. F. charged deliberate mismanagement of the two theatres and therefore refused to "go along" with the reorganization plans, so far as concerned the note for $2,300,000 which he had left over from his debts with Harley Clarke. W. F. informed Mr. Breed, the lawyer representing the bondholders, that he intended to sell at public auction the collateral which he held, consisting of Fox Film shares, and Clarke's half interest in the Grandeur Company.

"I likewise informed him that from April 7, 1930, up to this present day my lips had been sealed, but that I no longer intended to keep quiet; that it was my purpose to instruct my attorney to immediately begin suit against all the original directors of the Fox Theatres Corporation, Fox Film Corporation, General Theatres Equipment Co., Chase Securities Co., Chase Bank, and any one else who had anything to do with the management of these enterprises; that I was the owner of 100,000 shares of Fox Theatres, 50,000 shares of Fox Film, 40,000 shares of General Theatres Equipment and 20,000 shares of Loew, and I was going to begin such an action as would hold these men liable for the mismanagement of these companies; and that I would expect to be reimbursed for the losses I sustained by their idiotic mismanagement, and for their manipulation of the funds of these corporations in stock-market operations.

"Mr. Breed took a memorandum of all the shares I owned, what prices I told him they cost me, and was very much disturbed about the whole matter. He had been the lawyer for the Chase Bank in many other transactions, and he, it is fair to assume, apprised them of my belligerent attitude. A few days thereafter the collateral was sold at public auction. There was no bidder, other than a company in which I am interested, which bid $150,000 for the 108,000 shares of stock and $300,000 for the half interest of the Grandeur Company, the total being $450,000, which amount we credited on the $2,300,000 due on the note, less the cost of conducting the sale.

"The reply to all that I had said to Breed was to come to the auction room with a process-server, accompanying one of the lawyers from the office of Hughes, Schurman & Dwight, and serve me with a summons in a suit that is brought by the Fox Theatres against William Fox. Two days thereafter they permitted the company to consent to a receiver being appointed. It will now be the duty of the receivers to continue this action.

"About a week thereafter I received a most cordial letter from Sidney R. Kent, president of Fox Film Corporation, asking me to arrange for a meeting, and as a result of this Mr. Reass and I went to the office of the Fox Corporation. Ned Tinker received me; he is now, you will recall, Chairman of the Board

25

of Fox Film. He discussed a wholly unimportant matter at first, and we then withdrew into the adjoining room, where there were half a dozen or more men, all ex-employes of William Fox, all now lined up against him; men to whom I had given their posts and their bread and butter for years, and who were now sitting in this room for the purpose of cross-examining William Fox. They asked several questions which I hardly understood, and then requested that I sign a letter. This was the important corporation business that my dear friend Sidney Kent had referred to in his letter. Finally I said: 'If you will give me the papers, so that I can take them home and become familiar with the subject matter, then if I deem it advisable to give you any signed letter I will do so, but at this time I am unwilling to sign any letter unless I know what it is all about.'

"One of the gentlemen then said, 'Excuse me, just a minute,' and stepped out of the room and came back with another summons—this time the Fox Film Corporation versus William Fox. Also they sent me a letter telling me that I have been dismissed, and I am no longer to receive the payment of $500,000 a year. The conspiracy is beginning all over again. The story that I thought was closed is being reopened."

It is interesting to note that one of the things they ask for in their suits is the turning over of Grandeur and Tri-Ergon to them. They are not satisfied to have the free use of the patents; they want the whole thing. Says W. F., answering my question:

"You are right; they deny that I had any right to carry on a private business while I was president of the Fox Film Corporation, even though this private business was being carried on during a period when I was not receiving any salary from either of these two companies; even though I was devoting my time to these companies and was receiving no compensation; even though both of the enterprises were highly speculative and were entirely out of the scope of the Theatres Company and the Film Company, and even though when completed, and after I had spent a huge fortune in the development of these two enterprises, I consented to give to the two companies a free license under both of these patents, so that the Film Company and the Theatres Company were to receive great benefits without a single dollar of investment and without a single dollar of risk."

Another curious affair develops while I am completing this work. To make it clear, I have to take you back over the story, and follow through another thread in the many colored pattern.

You recall W. F.'s automobile accident in July, 1929. Three or four weeks after that accident he received a visit at his home from Harry Stuart, and afterwards there developed a sharp difference in the recollections of these two as to what happened at that conference. Six months later we find Stuart asserting in an affidavit, and also in a pamphlet distributed to the Fox stockholders, that at this interview and in subsequent ones he offered to take up the refinancing of the Fox obligations, but was refused consent to have the customary examination of the Fox books by certified accountants. W. F., on the other hand, denies emphatically that any such request was made, or that he ever at any time gave such a refusal. He declares that Stuart's visit was a social one, and that the principal subject of conversation was the securities company or investment trust which he was urging Halsey, Stuart & Company to create. He denies that there was any quarrel or dispute whatever, but that on the contrary he and Stuart parted the best of friends, and continued in such relationship until after the panic at the end of October.

In support of this contention, W. F. places in my hands the original of a letter received from E. W. Niver, manager of the New York office of Halsey, Stuart & Company. This letter bears the date of October 17, 1929, and is marked "Confidential." In it Niver informs W. F. that a letter of great importance is on the way from Chicago, and that Niver wishes to make sure he receives it promptly. He tells W. F. of a new investment trust formed by Halsey, Stuart & Company and the Insulls.

"Letters will be sent out tonight from Chicago to a few of our very good friends including yourself, inviting participation in a stock offering. There will be no public offering of the units described in the enclosure."

The concern is known as "The Corporation Securities Company of Chicago." The chairman is Samuel Insull and the president Harry Stuart; the vice-presidents are Martin J. Insull, Samuel Insull, jr., and Charles Stuart. There are to be 2,700,000 shares outstanding, and of these Halsey, Stuart and the Insulls are to take 2,000,000, and put them into a voting trust controlled by Samuel Insull, his son, and Harry Stuart   The "very good friends" of Halsey, Stuart are to have an opportunity to buy 700,000 shares of preferred stock and to get 700,000 shares of common stock as a bonus, the subscription price being $75 a share.

You will see, therefore, that the "very good friends" of Halsey, Stuart & Company contributed the sum of $52,500,000, and to this large sum the Insulls and the Stuarts added $30,000,- 000 worth of their inflated securities. The procedure was to issue to themselves 2,000,000 shares of the common stock at $15 per share; in addition, on chance that the venture might be successful for a while, they reserved to themselves an option to purchase another 500,000 shares of common stock at $25 per share. With the $82,500,000 in hand at the outset, this new concern purchased the securities of the Insull companies and put them away in its vaults, and never told any more about the matter than was absolutely necessary. Says the letter: "The corporation will not publish any lists of its holdings except as may be required by any stock exchange upon which its shares of stock may be listed." That was the way they did business back in the good old days of October, 1929.

I am giving these details, not merely to show that on October 17, 1929, W. F. was listed among "one of the few" of Halsey, Stuart's "very good friends"; but also because of the dramatic outcome of this huge financial venture. The Insull companies all drifted onto the rocks, and it was discovered that their network of securities had lost their value. In June of 1932 we find the Corporation Securities Company appearing in court before a Federal judge in Chicago, along with another concern, the Insull Utility Investment Company. These two owe large sums to the New York banks, and the banks are holding as collateral stocks which are now worth $10,000,000. The bankers come into court demanding their legal right to sell these securities at auction and get their money; but Judge Walter C. Lindley is pleading with them not to do it, because at the present prices of the securities, investors in the companies would lose everything they have through the sale. The judge had issued an injunction, restraining the banks from selling the securities, and their lawyers argue that this is the fourth time the banks have postponed a sale, and they stand to lose heavily if the securities decline further. The judge states as follows:

"I do not imply there is a 'Shylock' in this case, but it does appear to me that this is a matter of greater importance to the public than to the bankers. . . . We must not rock the boat in such trying economic times as these. Let's mark time a while and see what's going to happen."

There is something strangely familiar in this situation; you find yourself back in New York, listening to Judge Coleman arguing with Morton G. Bogue, attorney for Halsey, Stuart & Company, who is trying to have Fox Film and Fox Theatres thrown into receivership. Just as Judge Coleman was trying to protect the stockholders and the general public, so now Judge Lindley is doing; and the bankers who are making the demand are the very same New York bankers. There is only one difference in the situation; the whirligig of time has brought its revenges, and Halsey, Stuart & Company are now on the other side of the fence. Halsey, Stuart & Company are pleading for mercy—and, needless to say, they are not presenting any affidavits alleging prejudice on the part of Judge Lindley! Says W. F.:

"I wonder whether Harry L. Stuart now remembers his activities in removing Judge Coleman, who had tried his best to keep my companies intact; whether he is able to lay his head on the pillow at night and shut his eyes in calm sleep, or whether he sees before him a devil, dancing on his bed with a lunging pitchfork, laughing and jeering at him, as he laughed and jeered at William Fox and Judge Coleman."

You recall how Colonel Hartfield told W. F. of Harry Stuart's advice that W. F. should go abroad for at least six months, because he would not be able to stand the humiliations which the Stuart-Otterson trusteeship was going to inflict upon him. What an odd turn of events—it is Samuel Insull, the greatest of all utility magnates, who has gone abroad! And Harold Leonard Stuart, he of the carnation in his button-hole, has had the humiliation of being indicted by a Federal grand jury in Wisconsin, for using the mails to defraud. It has to do with his circulars offering the Wardman securities—those companies in Washington, D. C., concerning which we heard the indignant speech of Senator Blaine.

EPILOGUE

DURING the time that W. F. was telling me this story, I carefully avoided all questions as to what it meant to him, and what he thought ought to be done about it. I did not want to interrupt the narrative with arguments about politics and economics; especially I did not want to worry him by thrusting forward my own views. But after he had told the last fact, I started to ask about his ideas, so as to get a complete picture of his mind.

Our first topic was Herbert Hoover, who was so very cordial and friendly to W. F Says he:

"I am an admirer of Hoover. I would cheerfully contribute for his re-election. He proved himself a sympathetic person during my trials and tribulations. I often wondered, could he have done more to help me than he did. I have debated that in my mind again and again. I have sort of reached the conclusion that he did everything that was in his power. I have in mind Wiggin telling Huston that he resented the interference of the White House in the affairs of his bank and securities company. When I found myself in the most serious part of my difficulties, I did find a perfect willingness of the White House to give me every assistance. I found the President perfectly willing to have Henry Ford call him on the telephone, and to say: 'I would consider it a favor to the administration if you would help prevent these huge concerns going into receivership.'"

I asked if W. F. admired Hoover's policies as much as he admired Hoover's personality, and the answer was:

"I would never criticize Hoover's policies, for no one appreciated more than I his helplessness, that was made possible by the stupid voters of the United States, who elected him President and then gave him a bolshevik Senate and a bolshevik House. I am certain that if Hoover had had the power during these peace times that Woodrow Wilson had during war times, if he had had

360

the support of Congress and the Senate, we would have avoided at least 50 per cent of our present difficulties. I think most of our difficulties came through the fact that the Chief Executive of the United States had to express his thoughts to a Congress and Senate who by no means had the trained mind that he had, and therefore didn't understand the language he was speaking, and rather than help him do the things he wanted done, opposed them. When they finally did pass the constructive measures that he had conceived to prevent a further destruction of the nation, it was just a little bit too late. The damage had already been done. Many of the fine pieces of legislation recently passed to prevent a further depression were in the mind of Hoover at least two years or longer before they were passed; but he was never able to get his Senate and Congress to see his point of view, and therefore must not be charged with the responsibility."

In answer to that I pointed out very gently that if Herbert Hoover had been anxious to have some action to meet the depression, he had had it in his power to call a special session of Congress. Instead of so doing, he had chosen to wait from March until December, 1931, for the assembling of the new Congress. It had been perfectly well known in Washington that the thing which Hoover desired least of all in the world was to have that new Congress on his hands. On this, as on other occasions, I was pleased to observe that W. F. would recognize a fact when it was presented to him.

I asked what concrete remedies he had to suggest for the evils which he reveals in this book. He answered that he did not feel competent to make suggestions, but thought the readers of the book would prefer to draw their own conclusions. I urged the opposite point of view, saying that anyone who had become interested in his story would wish to know what he himself had learned from it. What did these bitter experiences mean to him?

So W. F. set forth two concrete remedies: First, he would like to see a law passed abolishing short selling: "a law that will make it illegal to sell shares of stock that the seller doesn't actually own and possess. The question of short selling should not remain a regulation by the New York Stock Exchange, or by the executives of any other stock exchange throughout the nation, but the United States Senate and Congress should enact such a law as will prohibit the selling short of any shares of stock listed on any stock exchange in this country. Any other remedy that may be supplied here will be wholly insufficient, and will result only in a whitewash of our present difficulties."

The second measure would be one forbidding national banks to have affiliates and securities companies, for the doing of those things which under the law the national banks are themselves forbidden to do. Says W. F.:

"When I was but a young man and borrowed that first $1,000 that I told you about, I remember what the functions of a banker were. The banker of a brief thirty years ago felt that his duty and purpose in life was to create an institution where people would be free to deposit their money, and he would create an executive staff and directorate to take this money, invest it, and loan it in such a way as to be perfectly safe, and he was willing to earn the difference between the amount he paid his depositor and the amount he was able to earn from his borrower. I believe that that was the purpose of banks throughout the whole of the United States, until this nation found itself after the war, or during the war, in what they called a 'new era.'

"Bankers then changed, and had a different purpose in life. They were not contented with earning the normal profits that a bank could earn on its capital and surplus. There sprang up what I consider the greatest evil in the financial world, and one of the causes of this great depression, even more than short selling. In these banks, which were supervised by the banking department, and whose accounts were carefully audited, there was found a subterfuge that would permit them to do things for which their charter was never intended; there came the fashion of creating an affiliate to the bank, called a securities company. This, in my opinion, is nothing more than a gambling scheme to use the funds belonging to the depositors for speculation.

"A bank's function is carefully limited by the charter granted from either the State or Federal Government; whereas the function of a securities company is limited only to what the directors of the bank wish to incorporate in their certificate of incorporation. Usually that is so broad that it permits a securities company to do anything, and surely all the things that were never intended when the charter to the bank was granted. One need not go farther than to read the charter of the Chase Bank, which was issued seventy-five years ago, to see what the wise fathers intended that bank to do; and then see what the Chase Securities Company can do now! But I don't intend this criticism for the Chase people only; a majority of the banks of the United States now have an affiliate; this is true of both large and small banks. The honest banker of thirty years ago has become a stock manipulator, using the funds of his bank to participate in various syndicates as they are offered to him.

"Attached to the certificate of stock of the Chase Bank today are your rights in the Chase Securities Company. The stockholder knows definitely that his bank is not only a bank, but it has a securities company, and a securities company has unrestricted powers. If that were not so, Wiggin could not have been the planner with Clarke to capture my companies, nor could he make personal gains in his personal relationships with Clarke. Do you suppose Clarke wants Wiggin with him just because he is Wiggin? Or is it because he is chairman of the board of the Chase Bank, and can manipulate $350,000,000 belonging to stockholders and $1,650,000,000 belonging to his depositors? I don't believe Clarke would be willing to be associated with the head of the Chase Bank or the head of any other bank, who had only the privileges granted to him by the charter of the State or Federal Government.

"Of course, the National City Bank also has a large securities company and many affiliates. The thing that destroyed the Bank of the United States was its affiliates. This is the most damnable practice that the banking world of this country has ever known, and the most necessary legislation I know of, by this Congress or any other Congress since the history of our Government, is a law compelling the dissolution of these affiliates and securities companies. The surest way to make a banker be a banker and have the respect of the community he had before this began is to stop him from becoming a speculator. We now find the Chase Bank not only running the Fox companies, but the American Woolen Company. Prior to the control of the American Woolen Company, and before the death of the president, that company was one of the most prosperous corporations America had. Now look at it! Since the Chase Securities Company has had it in hand, I don't think it has made a dollar, and that was about ten years ago. How many other businesses they took, I don't know.

"It was never intended that a bank should become a competitor of industry. A depositor or borrower from a bank always felt free to go to the president of his bank and tell him of his tribulations, and of his prosperity. You don't dare do that now or they will take your company away from you."

It appears that national bank examiners have not under the present laws the right to examine affiliates of banks. As regards New York State, an amendment to the law was passed, giving examiners this right; but our Federal legislators have not yet seen fit to follow suit, and that is one reason for the tremendous loss in bank stocks, and why banks have been failing throughout the country. Under the charter a bank may only buy what they call "legal securities"; but a securities company is under no such restraint. Therefore the banks have been speculating in real estate and other enterprises, and in the end they will control every business in the nation.

I asked W. F. what more fundamental plans he might have for the solution of our problems, and in reply he gave me quite a discourse. In reading it, bear in mind that this was spoken before the fad of Technocracy hit the country.

"About forty-one years ago, when I found my first job with a clothing firm, the day's work consisted of eleven hours a day for six days a week and a half day on Sunday. The total number of hours was seventy-one hours for the six days and Sunday. To the best of my recollection that was considered a week's work, not only in that line of business, but in all lines of business. This was, of course, prior to the modern machine age. It was necessary for the laboring man to work this number of hours to make, build and grow that which was necessary to sustain the population of this country.

"I distinctly remember six or eight years after I found my first job, when the laboring man complained bitterly at the number of hours necessary to work, and when conflicts occurred between capital and labor to where the week's hours were reduced to sixty. I distinctly remember capital claiming that labor was destroying the nation by its attempt to reduce the number of hours, and that capital charged labor was interfering with the prosperity of the nation. After the new schedule of hours was in effect for six months or more, instead of it ruining the country, it was discovered to be of material help to the nation.

"I distinctly recall some years later when unions were formed in many of the trades and industries of America, which contended that the number of hours were entirely too many, and the hours were reduced to fifty-four hours per week. I remember the cry of manufacturers of this nation that labor was the ruination of all things; that this reduction of hours would tend to destroy this country. But the reverse was found to be the fact. Manufacturers soon learned that not only was it practical to reduce the hours over a period of years from seventy-one to fifty-four, or approximately one-fourth less working hours per week, but that there was a constant increase in the amount of wages that could be paid per week, so that the laboring man was receiving more for fifty-four hours a week than he did under the period when he was working seventy-one hours a week.

"So I recall vividly the change that was constantly being introduced. When we found ourselves at the beginning of the war in Europe, and we realized that all nations were going to turn to America for supplies, a new schedule of hours was put into effect; five days a week at eight hours a day, and four hours on Saturday—forty-four hours. In fact, many trades insisted upon a five-day week, as for example the painters' and decorators' and paper-hangers' unions in New York. They refused to work more than five days a week, eight hours a day—forty hours. . The general unionized trades, however, had a schedule of forty-four hours.

"It was during the forty-four-hour regime that wages rose from $4 a day for a mechanic at the beginning of 1914 to $15 a day in 1929. It was during the shorter hour period that this country enjoyed its greatest prosperity. It is clear in my mind that the proper method to be employed by this Republican Government is a system whereby each year a careful survey should be made of the new modern machinery that has been inaugurated during the previous year, and then discover what is the number of hours that the 40,000,000 people who work for wages in America should work so as to supply all that the nation requires—not to overproduce and not to underproduce. It is underproduction that creates false values, and it is overproduction that brings on depressions.

"In my opinion, this depression is not only caused by bear raiding and reckless spending of money by the states and municipalities of this nation, or by the manipulation of bankers, but is mainly caused by a condition brought about during the World War. America, entering the war some time in 1917, shortly thereafter had an army of 4,000,000 men. These 4,000,000 men were the flower of the youth of the country, and they were now to devote their time not to build, but to destroy. I am told that not only did we have 4,000,000 men in the army, but that it required 4,000,000 more men who remained home to manufacture that which the 4,000,000 in the army were wearing, eating and destroying; so that some time in 1917, 8,000,000 of the most able men this nation had were devoting themselves not to upbuilding, but to the destruction of other nations and people.

"Men of ability and brain, realizing that 8,000,000 men had been removed, devoted their energy and time to inventing new machinery; so that when the war came to an end, there were 8,000,000 men that this nation very pleasantly got along without, and were it not for the fact that from the beginning of the World War in 1914 until long after the armistice was signed, there had been no program of building in these United States—were it not for that fact, we would have been in the depression immediately after the war. But there was accumulated between 1914 and 1919 five years of the usual annual building program that is customary in a country as big and as rich as this.

"I distinctly remember that as late as 1920 there existed in this nation a housing shortage, so that it was impractical for young folks to marry, because there was no place where they could live. I remember Samuel Untermyer appearing before the Legislature of New York some time during the year of 1920 and asking the Legislature to pass a law to compel the life insurance companies to loan $100,000,000 with which to build homes so that the housing shortage could be relieved. Not only did this condition exist in New York, but it existed in every city in the United States.

"Therefore, it can readily be seen that these 8,000,000 men who came back found employment at increased wages only because of this terrific shortage that existed, due to the neglect during the war. Perhaps in about 1927 all of the shortage had been overcome. We were in a momentum of building, however, and recklessly continued it until the summer of 1929. The overproduction that then occurred emphasized and is now emphasizing the depression that we are going through.

"I am informed that there are 40,000,000 wage-earners in America. The present number of hours now commonly given to labor are eight hours a day for five days, and four hours on Saturday—forty-four hours a week. If it is correct that we have 40,000,000 wage-earners, and if the report is correct that there are 8,000,000 unemployed in America, then it becomes a pure mathematical problem how to overcome this depression. If there still is employment for 32,000,000 people at forty-four hours a week, the mathematical problem shows that we have each week 1,408,000,000 working hours; the 32,000,000 people still employed, working forty-fours hours a week, work 1,408,000,000 hours. Knowing that 1,408,000,000 hours are sufficient to make that which the nation requires, all that is necessary is to divide 1,408,000,000 by 40,000,000 wage-earners.

"If that is done, you will discover that thirty-five hours per week is sufficient—that with thirty-five hours a week 40,000,000 people could be employed to do that which 32,000,000 people are doing now; and if my theory is correct, the number of hours that labor should be employed is the number of hours that it takes to give every soul in America peace and comfort and to supply him with everything he requires—which, of course, should be the system of this great Republic. Then the solution of our depression is a simple one, and is not one for union organizations to solve; let our Federal Government investigate and prove these figures, and if the same conclusion is reached by them, let Congress enact a law that the legal week's labor shall be reduced to thirty-five hours and no more, and within a week after that bill is passed and signed by the President, our depression is at an end.

"The strangest thing about all this is the fact that as the number of hours decreased from the time I got my first job, the wages increased, and the highest wage known in the history of America occurred in the years of 1927, 1928 and 1929, and the lowest number of hours that labor ever worked in the history of America occurred during those same years. It was during those years and for the first time that the United States Steel Corporation was able to make up its mind that six days constituted a week; and that Sunday was the Lord's day and a day of rest; it was during that time that the Steel Corporation changed its method of hours—made a man's work from seven days a week to six days a week, the thing it was afraid to do during the previous twenty-five years of its existence. Not only did it reduce their hours, but raised the wage, and the strangest thing of all is that during this period it made the largest profit in the history of its career, other than one of the war years.

"Of course, it becomes clear that if the American wage-earner is put on a basis where he is to spend a life of ease and luxury, as a reward for his labor during the hours that he works, he will have been raised above the laboring man of any other nation in the world, and he must be protected against the laboring man of other nations of the world which are unwilling to recognize the rights of labor as we are willing, and should. We will have to build a tariff wall so high and so wide as to shut out everything that is made in any other part of the world, until such time as their hours of labor are put on a par with ours, and until such time as their wages are similar to ours.

"All this is not new with me today. I have been talking this, and have had plenty of time to talk it, being out of business for the last two years, with everyone who would listen to me. On my last visit with President Hoover, in talking about the depression, he informed me that the Commerce Department had prepared figures showing that 93 per cent of all things we produce in this country is consumed here, and that only 7 per cent of what we produce in this country has been shipped abroad. It seemed to him a perfectly simple matter to slow down our energies to where, instead of producing 100 per cent, we should produce 93 per cent, the amount consumed here in this country. Slowing down can only come by the reduction of the working hours per week. You can't slow down by telling one manufacturer to make less, for no matter what you tell him, he will not make less. You can only do it by having a Federal law, setting the maximum number of laboring hours the man can work, and that maximum is a purely mathematical problem, with the facts as they are now known by our Government. What a beautiful country this will be to live in, when by Federal laws we find that the wage-earners' week will consist of working Monday and Tuesday, spending Wednesday with his family, working Thursday and Friday, and spending Saturday and Sunday with his family! If that is sufficient to produce all that we require, why work any more than that, and why not give the wage-earner this heaven on earth?

"My recital shows that the shorter the hours, the higher the wage and the greater the profits to the corporate interests. Simultaneously with the shorter hours, the article that the wage-earner buys must sell at a higher price. Let us say he is a shoemaker —we reduce his working hours, but permit him to earn as much as he has previously earned. As soon as that is done, the shoes previously costing $4 are $5. There is no harm in that, because all the wage-earner expects as a result of the labor he performs is to have a fine place to live in, with the modern conveniences that we have in this nation; to be well clothed, and have a dollar put away for a rainy day, and an education for his children. Once he has that, he feels he is in heaven. I say that of sheer necessity the price will be increased. The correct method is this, as I see it. It is right and necessary that if I am only going to work four days a week, and I am a shoemaker, that you, a tailor, will have to pay for the shoes I make a sum of money that will enable me to have the other three days of rest."

W. F. expressed the idea that I would "not be opposed to all of this," and he was correct. My only objection to it is that it cannot be carried out under the profit system of industry. When you reduce the hours of labor without altering wages, you are really increasing the wage per hour; and there are very sharp limits to the increasing of wages under the profit system. It can only be done in times of expansion and rising prices. The reason we all had high wages from 1927 to 1929 was because we were accepting one another's paper promises; we were living by taking in one another's washing. But now the water has been squeezed out of that washing.

Our friend W. F. sees that he cannot reduce the number of working hours and pay the same wages without bankrupting the manufacturer; so he proposes to let the manufacturer raise the price of the product.   But our friend neglects to follow that process through and ask what will be the effect of this upon the consumer.   As it happens, the consumer and the workingman are the same person.   When you raise a shoemaker's wage per hour, and at the same time raise the price of shoes, and continue that process all the way down the line, you have not really changed anybody's income: you have merely changed the terms in which it is expressed.   Men say that they are getting $5 a day instead of $4, and at the same time they pay $5 for their purchases instead of $4.   As the economists phrase it, nominal wages have been increased but real wages have remained untouched, and the purchasing power of the community has not been altered.   So W. F.'s idea that "within a week after that bill is passed and signed by the President, our depression is at an end"—this is merely one more dream of "prosperity just around the corner."

I explained to W. F. my own view, that this depression is due to the automatic process whereby great wealth has become concentrated in few hands, so that the masses of the people no longer have sufficient purchasing power to furnish profits on the swollen capital   Nearly thirty years ago, I wrote an open letter to Lincoln Steffens, pointing out how our mass of invested capital was increasing at compound interest, and saying that there must come a time when the amount had become too great for the consuming public to furnish profits upon.   In other words, capitalism was a self-eliminating phenomenon; the game of making profits must end with a crash when somebody or some group of bodies had won all the chips.

W. F. said he didn't understand that theory, and thought that the facts disproved it.   He pointed out, for example, how the United States Steel Corporation had started out with $500,000,000 worth of bonds, and then, "instead of adding to those bonds, as you picture the capital structure growing at compound interest, the facts are that $350,000,000 worth of these bonds are actually retired.   They have done exactly the opposite of what you think happens in the industrial world.   This makes it unnecessary to pay dividends, and they have passed the dividend, so that the common stock gets no dividend at all now.   Three hundred and fifty million dollars' worth of bonds only retired a couple of years ago, and the total value of 8,000,000 shares of common stock on which they have passed the dividend is $200,000,000, and it is a substitute for the retirement of $350,000,000 worth of bonds, on which there was an obligation to pay interest."

That picture is a tribute to the caution and good judgment of those who managed U. S Steel, but it does not counter my argument. In 1929 the capitalization of U. S Steel had swollen to over $2,000,000,000, and all that was demanding and receiving its toll from the consuming public; the paying of that toll was called "prosperity." But the time came when the public hadn't the money to buy all the product, and so the toll couldn't be paid. Now the steel mills are working at only 16 per cent of their capacity, and there are no dividends, and that is "hard times." Other concerns, which were less careful to change their bonds into stocks, are in the hands of receivers—and all for the same reason, because the capitalization had swollen beyond the point where the consumers could furnish the needed profits to pay the dividends and interest. Under our system, when there are no profits, there can be no production.

I have saved until the end the topic which I think lies nearest to the heart of W. F., and that is his Tri-Ergon patents and the use he is going to make of them. I told you how the "fly-wheel" patent, essential to all sound reproducing machines, had been granted by the United States Patent Office I have before me a copy of the complaint which was filed November 19, 1931, in the Federal Court, District of Delaware, United States Letters Patent No. 1713726; the American Tri-Ergon Company against Electrical Research Products, Inc.—our old friend Otterson, none other! How pleasant it will seem to the Fox when, after the due and necessary delays of the law, his petition is granted, that "the defendant, Electrical Research Products, Inc., its officers, directors, servants, agents, and all persons, firms and corporations associated with it or acting in its behalf, be perpetually enjoined and restrained by the decree of this court from directly or indirectly manufacturing or causing to be manufactured, using, directing the use of, or causing to be used, selling or causing to be sold, leasing or causing to be leased, all apparatus and/or methods embodying or employing the invention of said Letters Patent, and from infringing upon or contributing to the infringement of said Letters Patent in any manner whatsoever."

26

And even pleasanter when the court assents "that the defendant may be decreed to account for and pay over to plaintiffs all such gains, profits, and advantages as have accrued to or have been earned or received by said defendant, and all such gains, profits and advantages as would have accrued to or been earned by the plaintiffs or either of them but for the said infringement of said defendant, and also all damages the plaintiffs, or either of them, have sustained by said infringement."

This same suit is being brought against a number of other concerns which are in the talking picture business; but W. F. would be more than human if he did not take especial interest in the suit against the Telephone Company and its subsidiaries, which tried so hard to get these patents away from him, and led the fight to ruin him. In due course the Patent Office will be compelled to grant his claims to the photoelectric cell process, essential to all sound recording. I have told of the favorable decision of the Supreme Court of the District of Columbia, as sweeping as words can make it. When that patent is granted, and the suits won, Messrs. Otterson, Bloom, and Gifford will come to W. F to ask for a license to remain in the business of manufacturing sound recording and sound reproducing apparatus. W. F. has promised me that I may have the pleasure of being present at that conference. I have promised that I will be present, even though I have to come half way around the world!

He is still cherishing that dream of making educational pictures for schools, colleges, churches, and homes. In fact, he has already got the reproducing apparatus ready. He hopes to keep the price down by mass production, and to have a system of film rentals like a circulating library. He gives me a series of figures showing how many homes there are in America, and how many classrooms in American schools, and how many churches and synagogues and hospitals and other places where people would look at educational talking pictures. The figures are astronomical; but we Americans, who have seen the growth of radio in ten years, and of the "talkies" in five, should not find them incredible. I quote his statement:

"In 1927, when I first began negotiating with the Telephone Company concerning my Tri-Ergon patents, I drew for them this picture. First I contended that within five years every motion picture theatre in America would change from silent to talking motion pictures. There were 20,000 motion picture theatres in America; these 20,000 motion picture theatres would require equipment, and at this time the average cost to the theatre was a little over $20,000, so that the contract to equip the motion picture theatres of America would be 20,000 times $20,000. In the remainder of the world there were at least another 20,000 motion picture theatres, so in the theatre field alone there would be approximately $800,000,000 worth of equipment necessary.

"There were 250,000 churches in America, and at least that number in the balance of the world, and it was my opinion that when a cheaper equipment had been developed, and the equipment price could be brought down to approximately $5,000, there was an opportunity of equipping these 500,000 churches. The value of the equipment would be $2,500,000,000.

"There are 1,000,000 classrooms in America, and I argued that each of these classrooms would ultimately be equipped with talking motion picture reproducing units, and that a moderately priced equipment could be sold. I estimated a school equipment should be produced costing no more than $2,500 per equipment, making a total of $2,500,000,000. I went on to say that when American schools were fully equipped, perhaps a similar possibility could be developed in the remainder of the world.

"There are 15,000,000 radio sets in the homes of the people of America, and I argued that each home that had a radio was a prospective customer for home talking motion pictures. If an equipment could be developed at a cost of no more than $1,000 per equipment, there was a possibility of selling 15,000,000 of these equipments, a total of $15,000,000,000.

"In the latter figure the Telephone Company, of course, had no interest, because in an agreement made between the Telephone Company and the Radio Company, the former gave up all its rights to selling equipment to the home; this field was left entirely to the Radio Company. Since I sold my shares to Harley Clarke I have discussed the possibilities of the development of the home field with David Sarnoff of the Radio Company, and have indicated to him clearly that the home field can only be developed by the Tri-Ergon Company. In fact, since I sold my shares to Clarke, the Radio Company has, in writing, applied for a license from the American Tri-Ergon Company, which we up to this time have not granted. You will bear in mind that the Radio Company has a 50 per cent interest in all the patents claimed by the Telephone Company, and if the Radio Company thought they had patents governing talking motion pictures with sound on film, why did they apply for a license under the Tri-Ergon Company?

"I had stated that the motion picture theatres of America would be fully equipped in less than five years. I overestimated the time it would take, for in less than two and a half years the motion picture theatres of America were changed from silent to talking motion pictures. If the schools, churches, and homes of America have not as yet been equipped with this reproducing device, it is because incompetent men have had charge of this branch of the business, or because the Telephone Company and the Radio Company decided to go slow, knowing that the patents necessary to sell this equipment to schools, churches, and homes belong to the American Tri-Ergon Company.

"It is rather laughable to note the common term used by the Radio Company and by the Telephone Company with reference to equipments made by other manufacturers, of whom there are 100 or more; they are referred to as 'bootleg' equipment, when the fact of the matter is that every equipment now installed in America to reproduce talking motion pictures made with sound on film is a 'bootleg' equipment, including the equipment of the Telephone Company and the Radio Company.

"You asked me as to the possible royalties the American Tri-Ergon Company hopes to collect after it has gone through the delays that the Telephone Company is creating for it. These royalties are as follows: the charge now made by the Telephone Company to an exhibitor of motion pictures they call a service charge rather than a license charge, but in reality it is a license charge, because the employe of the theatre is perfectly capable of servicing this equipment himself. The amount they collect ranges between $25 and $40 per week. The 20,000 motion picture theatres in America pay well over $1,000 per year per theatre, or $20,000,000.

"The present producers of motion pictures who are under a license either by the Radio Company or by the Telephone Company, and who now pay royalties to either one of these two companies, manufacture about 600 feature pictures per year, each picture having approximately 6,000 feet, or 3,600 reels of feature pictures, and probably three times as many of the pictures not known as feature pictures, including comedies, educational films, newsreels, and other subjects used on the programs of the motion picture theatres, averaging about one reel each. That would be 7,200 reels at $500 per reel, or $3,600,000.

"In addition to this there are many millions spent by the studios for equipment for the recording of sound, and the field of manufacturing recording equipment will develop along with the other branches that I have mentioned. The million classrooms and the 250,000 churches in America, making a total of 1,250,000—a fair license charge to them would be $5 per week, or one-fifth of that which is now paid by the theatres. The prospective royalties from that field amount to 1,250,000 times $5 per week, or $325,000,000 in royalties from those two fields when fully developed.

"There are 15,000,000 homes in America. When they are equipped, a fair royalty charge per home would be $1 per week, which would net $780,000,000 a year. It is readily seen that the sums of money involved in the patents of the American Tri-Ergon Company would result in the largest sums ever collected in royalties for patents in the history of our Patent Office; the sums of money it will be possible for the American Tri-Ergon Company to collect are equal to the wealth of a nation. These latter two items amount to $1,105,000,000. If but 5 per cent of this plan could be realized, there would be a royalty collected of more than $55,000,000 a year.

"I don't think it is at all imaginary, or in the far distance, to hope that at least one out of every twenty homes in America will be equipped with talking motion pictures within the next five years, and I feel sure that when the time comes for those responsible for the education of America finally to adopt talking motion pictures, practically all of the classrooms will be equipped simultaneously. As to the possibilities of profit from the manufacturing of the subjects to be used in schools, churches, and in homes, that is so fabulous that I daren't venture to say what it would amount to per year. You will bear in mind that if the

American Tri-Ergon patents are sustained, no one can manufacture motion pictures with sound on film for the theatre, the home, the school, the church, or for any other use, unless a license is procured from the American Tri-Ergon Company.

"This is what was involved when the Octopus was carrying on his battle with the little Fox. Whether or not the Octopus really understood this picture as described now—whether he understands it any better now than when I first pictured it to him in 1927—that I don't know, but the fact is that I hope to live to see the day when the developments herein described will be fully accomplished.

"If we are successful, it is our purpose to take our rightful position and manufacture this equipment and lease it and do all the things that the Telephone Company is doing now, and do it properly, because we will be organized for that purpose, whereas the Telephone Company is not properly organized for that purpose.

"If ever I succeed in installing motion picture equipment in all the classrooms in America, I will accomplish that which is my ambition, to see the future children of America educated by talking motion pictures, uniformly educated, and we would teach them as much in three hours as they now learn in five. What royalty each classroom will pay is wholly immaterial to me. I am not so sure that I will want royalty; that part of the enterprise will not be for the purpose of making money. As to the figure of 1,000,000 classrooms at $5 per week, I would say that figure could be reduced to almost nothing as far as I am concerned. If the educators of the country should decide that these educational films should be manufactured by anyone else besides myself, I would be willing to authorize a company. My idea is that the texts would be selected by the Federal authorities, and the Government could well manufacture those pictures if they felt like it."

That brings my story to an end; and I have only to add what the story means to me and why I have taken the trouble to write it and to publish it.

In our country is a great machine of business and money which governs the lives of the plain people, and they do not often get a look into the insides of it. Here they have a chance, and they will be wise to make the most of it. The wholesale gambling and wrecking which you see here is going on, not merely with motion pictures, but with oil, steel, coal, power, food—and above all, money. It is going on, not merely in America, but in every great country in the world except Russia. The problem is a world problem; because of such things, hundreds of millions of people are homeless and jobless and starving, all over this earth. Can any thinking man or woman look at the picture and fail to realize that the great task of our day is the taking of industry and finance out of the hands of profiteers and speculators? Is it not obvious that the producing of the means of human life must be organized and ordered, and made into a social function?

During the World War I was publishing a monthly magazine, and in the issue of September, 1918, I addressed a statement to those whom I greeted as "Gentlemen of America: You of the older generation, statesmen, rulers and masters, who made the world in which we live, whose ideas and ideals had the shaping of it." The last two paragraphs of this statement will serve fifteen years later for the ending of this book:

"You have thrown us into a pit. Will you help us now to get out again? Rest assured, we mean to get out—that is the final resolve which this world-tragedy has taught to the common man. You who have the wealth, the leisure, the training in command, you have yet time to help us, if you will. If you can perform the supreme act of humility, of self-renunciation, if you can bring yourself to cancel your paper titles, to wipe from your hearts the ideals of private profit, and lend your skill and energy to the making of a free and happy world!

"Are we in America to have a Bolshevik revolution? Or can we contrive a new kind of revolution—a democratic revolution, in which men of all classes may unite in the abolishment of wage-slavery, with its curses of poverty, prostitution, crime and war? Rest assured of this one thing, gentlemen of America; with you or without, the work will be done; the world in which we live is going to be re-made, and never again will those who seek private advantage be masters either in politics or in industry."

Recent books by Upton Sinclair

THE WET PARADE

Kathleen Norris· "Upton Sinclair's 'The Wet Parade' is magnificent. Not in ten years have I read a novel so strong—so daring—and with so much thrill and humor and human weakness and strength on every page. He has painted the American scene as no other writer of our generation could."

Cloth $2.00

ROMAN HOLIDAY: A Novel

Gertrude Atherton writes: "An original and ingenious idea."

Cloth $1.50, paper $1.00

MOUNTAIN CITY: A Novel

Fulton Oursler· "A corking novel, always interesting and convincing . . . The narrative's interest magnetizes the reader as completely as anything you have ever done."

Cloth $1.50, paper $1.00

BOSTON: A Novel

An inside story of the Sacco-Vanzetti case, and the picture of a civilization. Floyd Dell writes· "To my mind, in spite of Tolstoi's 'War and Peace,' and some of Zola's things, there has never been any fiction quite like this of yours. The method really constitutes a great literary invention."

Two Volumes, $2.50

OIL!

A novel of Southern California. Sir Arthur Conan Doyle wrote: "I was amazed at the power of the book." Clarence Darrow writes. "Few novels have impressed me as much as 'Oil!'"

Cloth $1.50, paper $1.00

MONEY WRITES!

A Study of Present-Day American Literature. E. Haldeman-Julius: "All of 'Money Writes!' is great stuff! Congratulations! A hard job well done!"

$2.00

THE BRASS CHECK

A Study of American Journalism. John Haynes Holmes. "The book is tremendous. I have never read a more strongly consistent argument or one so formidably buttressed by facts You have proved your case to the handle. I again take satisfaction in saluting you not only as a great novelist, but as the ablest pamphleteer in America today I am already passing around the word in my church and taking orders for the book." Ninth edition, revised, with index.

Cloth $2.00, paper $1.00

PUBLISHED BY UPTON SINCLAIR, LOS ANGELES WEST BRANCH, CALIFORNIA

CPSIA information can be obtained
at www.ICGtesting.com
Printed in the USA
BVHW060004050222
627945BV00002B/23